BLOOD, DUST
AND SNOW

Diaries of a Panzer Commander
in Germany and on the Eastern Front
1938–1943

FRIEDRICH SANDER

Edited and translated by Robin Schäfer

Foreword by Roger Moorhouse

Greenhill Books

*Blood, Dust and Snow: Diaries of a Panzer Commander
in Germany and on the Eastern Front, 1938–1943*

Greenhill Books

First published by Greenhill Books, 2022
Greenhill Books, c/o Pen & Sword Books Ltd,
47 Church Street, Barnsley, S. Yorkshire, S70 2AS
For more information on our books, please visit
www.greenhillbooks.com, email contact@greenhillbooks.com
or write to us at the above address.

Image credits: Wehrkundearchiv Kwasny, Michael Schadewitz,
Paul Sander, Caraktère Presse et Edition

Map credit: Paul Hewitt, Battlefield-Design

CIP data records for this title are available from the British Library

ISBN 978-1-78438-830-0

Typeset by JCS Publishing Services Ltd
Typeset in 11.5/15pt Adobe Caslon Pro
Printed and bound in Great Britain by CPI Group (UK) Ltd, Croydon, CR0 4YY

Contents

Acknowledgements

The Editor would like to thank Dawn Monks, Joe Greenway, Oberstleutnant (ret.) Michael Schadewitz, Paul Sander, Jessica Aitken, and David Ulke for their invaluable help and assistance.

Foreword

What follows is a quite remarkable historical document. Its author, Lieutenant Friedrich Sander, was a tank commander in the Wehrmacht 11th Panzer Regiment, a unit that would fight in the Polish Campaign in 1939, in the invasion of France and the Low Countries the following year, and – as part of Army Group North – in the invasion of the Soviet Union in the summer of 1941. Seeing action both in the German advances on Leningrad and Moscow, that year it experienced some of the heaviest fighting that the new Eastern Front had to offer.

Lieutenant Sander, for his part, was in many ways rather unremarkable. Born during the First World War in what became the 'Polish Corridor', he moved west with his family during the post-war chaos and was brought up in the comparative comfort of Osnabrück. Perhaps because of those early experiences, he shared the nationalist zeitgeist, and was a member of various 'patriotic' organisations, before joining the Nazi Party and SS in 1934, during the first rush of enthusiasm for Hitler and the Third Reich. Conscripted in 1937, he was evidently sufficiently gifted at soldiering to be made an officer two years later, on the eve of war.

So far, so ominously familiar. Yet a couple of aspects of Sander's character set him apart: he was not only an acute observer of his surroundings – the situations in which he found himself and the people with whom he mixed – he was also a gifted writer, who set down his experiences with clarity and no little humour. It is these qualities, I suggest, that raise Sander's diary to the status of a document of genuine historical interest.

Apart from a short prelude in the camp at Sennelager, near Paderborn, most of Sander's diary is concerned with 'Operation Barbarossa', the German attack on Stalin's Soviet Union, which commenced on 22 June 1941. To a large extent, Barbarossa – named after the twelfth-century German king, Frederick Barbarossa – was the defining conflict of the Second World War in Europe, particularly when one recalls that fully four out of every five German soldiers who died in the Second World War were killed by Stalin's Red Army. Barbarossa certainly represented a step-up in scale from all that had gone before, dwarfing the French, Polish and Scandinavian campaigns in the number of men and machines engaged, with over 3 million Axis troops and 6,000 armoured vehicles advancing along a 1,500-mile frontier, which stretched from the Baltic to the Black Sea.

One of those armoured vehicles was the Panzer 35(t), commanded by Friedrich Sander. Built in pre-war Czechoslovakia by Skoda – Sander referred to his tank affectionately as a 'Skoda Super Sport' – the 35(t) was a light tank that shared some developmental DNA with the ubiquitous Vickers 6-ton tank of 1928. More than 200 35(t) tanks had been purloined by the Germans following their invasion of Bohemia and Moravia in the spring of 1939, and they had been pressed into service in Poland and in France, despite being obsolete.

That obsolescence was not unusual – Wehrmacht ranks in 1941 also featured numerous Panzer Is and IIs, which were similarly out of date – but it could be perilous for the men that crewed them. Not only did the 35(t)s of Sander's regiment suffer from higher attrition rates, due to frequent breakdowns and a lack of spare parts, they were also easily mistaken for the Vickers-derived Soviet T-26s. More seriously than that, the 35(t) was greviously undergunned when faced with the new generation of Soviet tanks, particularly the T-34. It was little surprise, perhaps, that Sander would complain – already in November 1941 – that his company did not possess a single operational tank; all of them had fallen foul of enemy action, mines and mechanical breakdowns. Thereafter, in the assault on Moscow, Sander and his men would be deployed as humble infantrymen; what one might call a *Panzer-Regiment zu Fuss*.

Just as Germany's military might was tested to destruction that year, so the ideological assumptions that travelled with its soldiers were increasingly tested too. It is often assumed – out of ignorance, or an extrapolation from the comparative civility of the French campaign – that the atrocities committed during the German–Soviet war were the result of some sort of cumulative barbarisation; a spiralling of tit-for-tat crimes. Yet, as Sander's diary demonstrates, many German soldiers were already fully formed in their Nazi 'world view' before they even set foot on Soviet soil. Sander himself is a good example of this. Whether he was observing the local peasantry or assessing the fighting resolve of his enemies, he saw the world unequivocally through the distorting lens of Nazi race theory. Even in his lighter moments, race intruded, such as when he saw a pretty girl and then chastised himself for 'falling in love with a Russian'.

This might appear trivial, but it shows the penetration of racialised thinking. Other, more sinister, examples abound. Red Army soldiers were routinely derided by Sander as primitive or uncivilised, criticised for their cowardice in 'playing dead' to attack from the rear, and earned only grudging respect for their tenacity under fire and their unwillingness to surrender lightly. And, one should remember, such underhand tactics – feigning death or pretending to surrender – often served the Germans as the justification for massacres of enemy prisoners, spurred by a moral and racial righteousness.

His ideological bolster notwithstanding, Sander was soon harbouring doubts about the offensive. Already in the winter of 1941, he was dismayed by the scale of German losses and by the chaos of the withdrawal from the gates of Moscow. Later, in the autumn of 1942, when his unit was engaged in trying the break the Soviet ring around Stalingrad, he was scathing about Germany's Romanian allies: 'swineherds,' he wrote, who lacked any military discipline and deserted with alarming ease. At the end of that year, he sounded an ominous note: 'The Russians are wearing us down,' he wrote. 'We are hopelessly outnumbered and, in many respects, technically inferior.' Soon after writing those words, Sander was injured and was sent home to begin a long hospitalisation.

To some extent, Sander's experiences mirrored those of countless soldiers in modern warfare: the boredom, the gallows humour, the indifferent food, the failing equipment, the resigned acceptance of your fate. And yet, this is nonetheless a remarkable book. For one thing, it is exceptionally well observed and well written. In another life, one could almost imagine Sander as a journalist or novelist, such is the acuity with which he observes the world around him.

Yet, more than that, Sander's diary is remarkable for who its author was. There are a few memoirs available by more senior German commanders – such as Hans von Luck or Heinz Guderian – but the viewpoint of a Lieutenant and a tank commander is a radically different one; the peril Sander experienced was much more immediate, the rations infinitely worse, the grim realities of soldiering all the more brutally real.

Sander experienced the visceral thrill, and the horror, of armoured combat; he reminded us constantly in his diary of the men that he lost, men whom he had known personally, men who had fought alongside him, who had slept in the same ditches, who had shared those same petty privations. In that respect, Sander's diary provides us with a something that is, perhaps surprisingly, rather rare: an erudite, well-written, thoughtful account of the harsh realities of combat for an ordinary soldier on the Eastern Front in the Second World War. For that, it is very well worth our attention.

Roger Moorhouse,
Tring, August 2022.

Introduction

In addition it has been noticed that diaries have been taken from captured German soldiers, which sometimes included entries which should have been kept secret. Such records pose a severe danger should they fall into enemy hands.

Soldiers who take letters and diaries into the furthermost lines can make themselves guilty of negligent treason and will, where required, be brought to justice after the end of the war.

Oberkommando des Heeres, 8 December 1939

It was the number which first caught my eye, just a simple five-digit number written in blue indelible pencil on the cover of a notebook at the top of a small pile of worn and frayed notebooks. It was a *Feldpostnummer*, a code the German military used as identification for its military mail service. Closer inspection showed that there were eleven books, and an accumulation of loose pages unceremoniously held together by a rusty paperclip. Flipping through the pages and looking more closely at the neat handwriting, I knew that I was looking at the wartime diaries of a German officer, Leutnant Friedrich Wilhelm Sander of Panzer-Regiment 11. A brief negotiation with the militaria dealer followed, and a few days later the diaries were safely on my office table.

Closer inspection showed that the diaries were special; not only was the diarist a keen, even obsessive, observer and talented writer, he also thought little of the rules that any campaigning diarist was bound to follow. Today, there is a persistent rumour that in the German army the keeping of a diary was strictly prohibited. That is untrue; in fact it was a popular pastime for Germans, an activity that peaked in the twentieth century and the period of the world wars. During moments of abrupt change, in personal crises, or under the influence of sudden revolutionary events or brutal wars, the keeping of a diary or journal offered a special and very personal form of coping and served as an antidote to loneliness and despair. It is more the case that in Germany, writing in war – be it in the form of letters or diaries – had a long tradition. From the end of the First World War, countless diaries were published, which were then replaced in the 1940s by a plethora of *völkisch* national war diaries celebrating the war and German feats of arms. 'Journaling' was not only strongly supported by the National Socialists, but was also increasingly used for propaganda purposes. Even front-line reports of the propaganda formations were often written in the form of diaries, and at the beginning of the war German soldiers were encouraged to keep personal journals. For example, in 1941 the Gauverlag der NSDAP published a pre-fabricated *Kriegstagebuch* which, according to the advertisement, contained 'room for photos, a printed war chronicle and a calendar for your own entries. 60 free pages of the best paper and forms for the home addresses of comrades.'

The National Socialist appeal to contribute to a heroic historiography of the Second World War through personal autobiographical memories prompted thousands of German soldiers, who themselves had grown up reading the martial diaries, autobiographies and letters of their fathers and grandfathers, to keep personal journals on campaign. Nevertheless, there were certain rules – written and unwritten – to adhere to, in particular if the diarist was a front-line soldier. It was strictly prohibited to take a diary, or any other personal correspondence, to the front lines, where they could potentially fall into enemy hands. It was prohibited to mention names, locations, to write in detail about military matters, to criticise the regime or the military. All this, however, was clearly nothing Friedrich Wilhelm Sander was concerned about. Being a *Panzermann* (a tank man), he could usually be found in the front line and often far beyond it, deep in enemy-held territory. This position did not stop him from recording his experiences and thoughts in his journal whenever there was time; almost daily, during periods of rest, in quieter moments and even in the turret of his tank during the advance and very close to the fighting. And neither did he hold back from criticising his comrades, his direct superiors, the general conduct of the war or from making critical political commentary. This is even more interesting, because Sander was a National Socialist and a willing tool and crusader for the regime.

Friedrich Sander was born in Graudenz in German West Prussia on the shores of the Vistula River in 1916. When the regulations of the Treaty of Versailles became effective on 23 January 1920, and the city was reincorporated under its Polish name Grudziądz into the reborn Polish state, the Sander family, like most of the city's German population, chose to leave their home and resettled in Osnabrück in the province of Hanover (today Lower Saxony). Sander attended the city's famous Carolinum, Germany's oldest grammar school, founded by Charlemagne, King of the Franks, in 804 CE. Most likely forced by his family's financial situation – which was not unusual during this time – he left the Carolinum early and was apprenticed to a merchant in Osnabrück. As a boy, Sander was a member of the *völkisch* national Bündische Jugend, and later – before or after its prohibition and dissolution is unclear – joined the Hitlerjugend. Shortly after his eighteenth birthday Sander joined the Allgemeine-SS and with it the National Socialist Party. After service in the Reichsarbeitsdienst (RAD – Reich Labour Service), he was drafted for compulsory military service on 1 October 1937 and about a month later trained as a radio operator in the newly raised Panzer-Regiment 11 in Paderborn. After further training as tank driver and later tank gunner, Sander was promoted to Gefreiter and set firmly on the path to become a reserve officer in the Wehrmacht, a goal which he achieved in 1939. He took part in the annexation of Sudetenland in October 1938, but not in the German attack on Poland in 1939, at which time – much to Sander's dismay – he served in the regimental replacement battalion. Nor did Sander see action in Germany's campaign in the west, in the Low Countries and France in 1940, when he remained garrisoned in Germany.

Eleven of Sander's diaries survive and it is clear that there was once at least one more, written during his time as an instructor in the Kampfschule (combat school) in Nisch, in Serbia, in 1944, of which a few loose pages survive. It seems, however, that he reserved his writing and observational skills for those periods during which he was on campaign, starting with the German invasion of the Soviet Union in June 1941. During quiet periods, when on leave at home or during longer 'peaceful' spells in occupied France – for instance during Panzer-Regiment 11's rehabilitation period in France in the spring of 1942 – Sander's voice falls silent. Sander tells us that he is writing for a purpose, and the boredom of everyday life, no matter if private or military, seemingly was not part of that purpose. The *Panzermann* documented the great events that played out before him and his own role within them, but apparently for no audience other than himself. When, at Tretjakova on 14 January 1942 after receiving 'a hammering' by the Red Army, he wonders whether he should continue to 'preserve the whole drama' in his diary 'for posterity', as a kind of documentary for some future reader, it is clearly just rhetoric. Sander's diaries are not only awash with critical remarks about his fellow officers, his superiors, on German strategy and tactics, even Adolf Hitler and 'Jupp' Goebbels, they also include vivid descriptions of the violence and suffering experienced by both sides during the campaign, the multitude of German casualties and atrocities conducted by the German army against Russian prisoners of war and the civilian population. Of course, Sander knew that he could never present his writings to a wider audience and his goal was not the documentation of Germany's struggle against Bolshevism.

Only once, in a new diary which he opens on 15 November 1942, while on a train taking him from rural France back to the harsh reality of war on the Eastern Front, does he begin to write with the intention of some day sharing a 'description of the sights we see … of the fighting we experience and of the tribulations we face' with his newly-wed wife Ruth. He does, however, quickly revert to his usual way of writing and continues to do so only for himself and for the cathartic experience of putting pen to paper. 'Finding the words to describe what I have experienced during that time – is that even possible? I don't know, but I will try – even if it's just to give myself some clarity and to unburden my mind,' he writes on 28 December 1942. In stark contrast to the vast majority of German soldiers' memoirs, autobiographies and diaries published after the end of war, Sander's diaries are not agenda driven, they were not written or edited to fit a political and social zeitgeist or to appeal to the tastes of a certain kind of audience. Sander's diaries offer a totally genuine and honest glimpse into the mind and world of a highly politicised young officer of the German Panzerwaffe during the first half of the Second World War and as such they are totally unique.

During the war Friedrich Wilhelm Sander was decorated with the Panzer Assault Badge, the Tank Destruction Badge (for the single-handed destruction of an enemy tank with hand-held explosives), both classes of the Iron Cross and, on 23 February 1943, with the German Cross in Gold. We do not know much about Friedrich Wilhelm Sander's experiences after the dissolution of the Kampfschule in Nisch, or even about his time there. He was probably again deployed in combat and we know that he was taken prisoner by the US Army in 1945. He survived the war. After his death, the diaries were probably acquired by a member of the veterans' association of Panzer-Regiment 11. Extracts were published in 1987 by the regimental historian Oberstleutnant Michael Schadewitz who had been given access to a set of photocopies of some of the diaries, and to whose kind assistance we owe some of the more important photos, including those showing Sander himself, used in this publication.

In my translation of the diaries, I have retained Sander's use of German names for places, though I have made changes to his sometimes erratic spelling to make things consistent. For authenticity I have also retained his use of language that would nowadays be offensive. I have provided the footnotes to give some brief explanations of terms or phrases that may be unfamiliar.

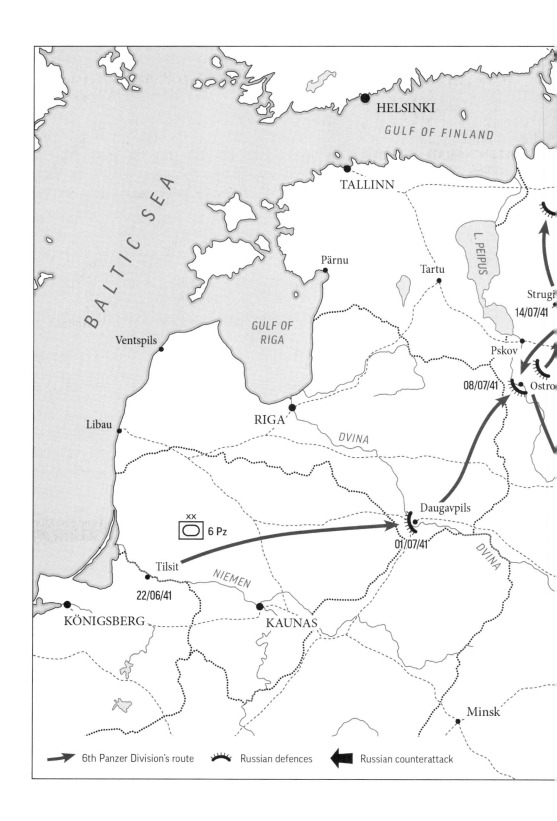

HELSINKI

GULF OF FINLAND

BALTIC SEA

TALLINN

Pärnu

Tartu

L. PEIPUS

Strugi
14/07/41

Pskov

GULF OF
RIGA

08/07/41

Ostro

Ventspils

RIGA

DVINA

Libau

Daugavpils

XX
◯ 6 Pz

01/07/41

DVINA

Tilsit

NIEMEN

22/06/41

KÖNIGSBERG

KAUNAS

Minsk

➤ 6th Panzer Division's route   〰️ Russian defences   ◀ Russian counterattack

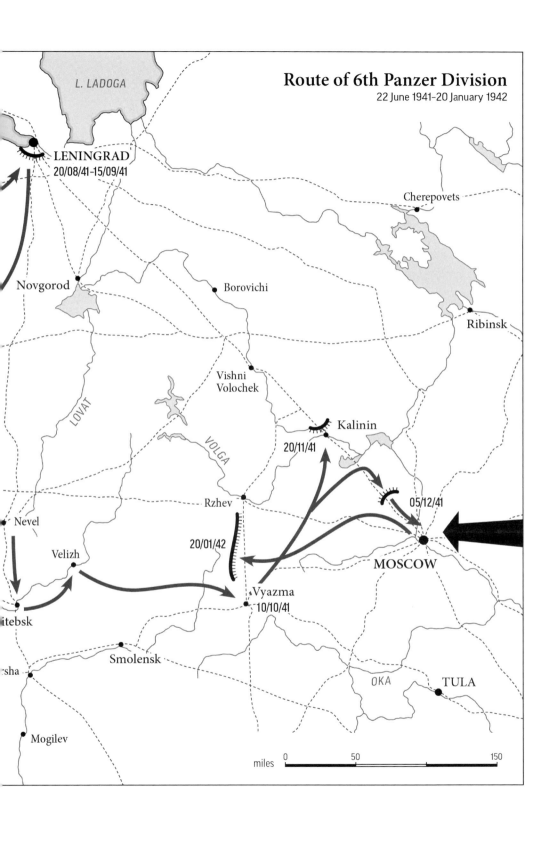

Route of 6th Panzer Division
22 June 1941–20 January 1942

L. LADOGA

LENINGRAD
20/08/41-15/09/41

Cherepovets

Novgorod

Borovichi

Ribinsk

Vishni
Volochek

LOVAT

VOLGA

Kalinin
20/11/41

Nevel

Rzhev

05/12/41

20/01/42

Velizh

MOSCOW

Vyazma
10/10/41

itebsk

sha

Smolensk

OKA

TULA

Mogilev

miles   0   50   150

1

21 April 1938–24 January 1939

On 12 October 1937, Panzer-Regiment 11 was raised in Sennelager under its commander Oberstleutnant Dipl.Ing. Philipps as part of the army build-up. This was the first time since the occupation of the Rhineland by German troops that a tank regiment was stationed in Westphalia. Due to the regulations of the Four Year Plan and the temporarily prevailing shortage of raw materials, the regiment's new barracks in Paderborn had not yet been completed. Thus, the regiment had to move to the Sennelager training area, which was not very suitable for the accommodation of a tank regiment due to its original design as a training area for mounted troops. Soldiers from the various regions of Germany had been transferred to Sennelager, where they formed the core of the new regiment. In Hanover, on 27 October, the Reich Minister of War, Field Marshal Werner von Blomberg, presented the young regiment with its standards, which were then ceremonially brought into Sennelager. Four weeks later, the first recruits, Friedrich Wilhelm Sander among them, arrived to complete their two-year period of service. The focus of the upcoming training was to familiarise the young recruits with their weapon, the tank. At the beginning, however, there was a shortage of almost everything, vehicles and materials were scarce and the accommodation was inadequate, making the training of the recruits more than difficult.

For the recruits, the average day began at 5.30 a.m. with early morning sports. This was followed by time for bodily hygiene (with cold water) and breakfast. At 7 a.m. the theory lessons began, given by the officers of the regiment: the soldier's oath, duties of the soldier, command and obedience, cartography, structure of the army, counter-espionage, discipline and disciplinary rules and similar topics were covered. Then followed NCO lessons on a variety of topics such as: behaviour towards superiors, saluting, rank insignia, weaponry, dress code, shooting practice, equipment, first technical instructions and the like. A short break was followed by drill, without and with carbine 98, weapons drill, shooting practice, general infantry service, marching and cross-country exercises. This duty on the parade ground and in the camp area was only interrupted by a ninety-minute lunch break and usually ended between 4 and 5 p.m. This was followed in the barracks by weapon cleaning, cleaning and mending sessions and repeated room, uniform and locker inspections which ended between 6 and 8 p.m.

After the first five weeks, there was training on the tank, as a driver, gunner or radio operator. This hard period of basic training ended in March 1938 with the final recruit inspection. From then on, the unloved formal service and the daily harassment were replaced by regular service as *Panzermänner*, the training in group and platoon formations as gunners, radio operators or drivers, as signalmen, medics, supply men or in the workshop company. Those destined to become NCOs or officer candidates received additional marksmanship lessons, tactical instruction and general schooling in a variety of subjects. Tactical instruction was conducted by the company commanders or one of the company officers and consisted of, among others things, cartography, preparation of reports and sketches, firing from the tank on the training ground, firing on the move, fighting methods of the armoured combat vehicles, combined arms tactics, sandbox exercises, command techniques and additional terrain training. In addition, the NCO candidates received general instruction in politics, history, party affairs, racial politics and other subjects and every week there was a fifteen-minute special lecture to train and consolidate personal conduct in front of comrades and superiors.

In early April 1938 the regiment started to move into its new garrison in Paderborn, even though some of the construction work was still not completed, and much of the interior furnishings were not in place. At first there was no running water, no electricity and no heating. As the weather at that time of year was still cold, especially at night, steam *Lokomobiles* were used to power the heating in the accommodation blocks. The roads were unpaved, the vehicle hangars still missing roofs and, because the kitchens were not yet operational, food had to be prepared in the field kitchens in the open. It would take until the beginning of 1939 for the construction work to be completed.

In Paderborn technical training increased and driving lessons were given to as many men as possible. At the time, German military driving training was among the best and most thorough in the world and included intensive technical and mechanical training, during which each driver learned how to repair his vehicle with the available onboard resources and without the assistance of the maintenance platoon. These were skills which would prove vital during the German army's lightning advances in the first years of the war. Physical exercise was also increased – there were daily sessions of football, handball, athletics and swimming, while the first major field exercises and manoeuvres were conducted in the region and beyond.

The first of the surviving diaries opens on 21 April 1938.

* * *

21 April 1938, Sennelager

Five minutes ago Unteroffizier Behle told me that we are supposed to stay here in our barracks in the 'Neues Waldlager' until June. Since our arrival, we have already been here for over six months and I guess that an additional one won't do much harm either. There is a positive side to it, 10 Pfennig more pay per day! That's the desert bonus! No – joking aside, the camp is really nice and I like it here. In the middle of the forest and the awakening nature, the roads and streets are all kept in good order. Our new barracks, however, are not completely finished yet, not everywhere has running water and food can only be drawn from the field kitchens. I'd rather stay here in Sennelager for another month.

There is not a lot to do now, so shortly after the Easter holidays. Probably because the men who are regularly based here are still on leave and many of the recruits are being employed in the Wehrmacht Motor Racing Championship. This morning, when three of us were sent to the coal depot, we watched the proceedings for a while. Quite interesting.

In the evening we were tasked to rearrange the rooms in the Leutnants' barracks and while we were there, we could see the motorbikes and cars racing around the corner at the hospital building. They were all completely spattered with dirt and mud – including the drivers. Sadly the three vehicles of our regiment could not participate in this particular race as our men knew the area too well, which would have given them an advantage during the orientation drive. We all felt very sorry for them, particularly for our Feldwebel John who, a few weeks ago, had won a silver medal. His start number, painted on white fabric, now adorns the wall of our maintenance workshop.

Now, while I am writing this, I am sitting in our mess marvelling at the enormous amount of beer consumed by the grunts of IR64. That – at least in my opinion – is the nice thing about our service branch, there is a lot less boozing. We always have to have a clear head, drivers, the crews and wireless operators. All comrades act accordingly and only rarely does one run riot. If that happens, well – then they are probably trying to drown the same feeling which I had when I had to leave Osnabrück a couple of days ago. Even though I did drink a lot of coffee, I was still thirsty. Yes, coffee! First at home and then – after my old father had gone back to Hamburg – in the Cafe Laer, where I waited for Ruth. Ruth, with whom I would have loved to talk without being disturbed. I found a table in a corner, well separated from everyone else and I guess that is why she did not find me when she came in. I spent half an hour waiting for her and then, after leaving, ran into her on the way to the station, when there was just enough time for some empty words and the expression of disappointment at having missed one another in the café. Maybe the relationship is a waste of time after all, but I guess I have to wait and see. If there is one thing one learns in the army, it is patience.

22 April 1938

Today we had a cushy number again. In the morning Wahlberg, the little Rhinelander, and I 'worked' in the cellars. In the evening I had to hand over two rooms in Officer Barrack 11 to a Leutnant of IR109 (Ettlingen). Later in the evening three of us helped the two pay-mongrels* of our Abteilung to move. One of them, Zahlmeister Mohle, is also from Osnabrück and used

---

* *Zahlmeister.*

to be a student at our grammar school. He is a nice guy and while packing the boxes we talked about our time in Osnabrück.

Sennelager forms the final stage of the German Army Motor Racing Championships and it is very interesting to watch the proceedings at the start and at the finish. There are contestants from all three service branches and it was fascinating to see all the motorbikes, cars and lorries being started at 19.00. A lot of people had assembled there. Several important people from the Bosch company were shuffling around between the motorbikes with boxes of spark plugs and to assist where they could. Some of them were wearing wide trench-coats and, God, these light things just looked incredible, just right to swagger around in. Some comrades informed me that these men were directors of Bosch! I didn't care about that – the best thing today were those coats. I need to get one of those one day.

There is sheer excitement among some of the radio operators in our room, the ones chosen to work with race control and the two Panzerbefehlswagen. Excitement not only about the race as such, but also about the journalists and *Wochenschau* reporters who flocked around the black uniforms, the two tanks and the Fug* sets in great numbers. Unavoidable really that everyone was filmed and comrade Erich Lammers's voice was recorded on a wax record. He had to say a few words through his throat microphone, technical terms used in our trade, and the whole recording was later played by the Reichssender Cologne. Wiese was properly envious. He had been boasting about the fact that he had been photographed several times, but I guess Lammers does not begrudge him that small honour.

Some news is making the rounds. According to this, all men of the signals platoon in their second year of service are supposed to be transferred to a new regiment which is being raised in Harburg! To Harburg! That would be the ideal patch for me. But for now we are supposed to stay here in this drill ground until June. I am on leave between 3 and 8 June on Pentecost and then four weeks off to Jüterborg for live firing exercises. Whatever happens – if I stay here or go to Harburg, both options will be good.

---

* *Funkgerät* – radio/wireless.

26 April 1938

Yesterday evening our two Gefreite have returned from their paternal leave. Moser, with his big mouth, right in front as usual. Good Lord, the things he claims to have pulled off there! Hähnlein, from Schweinfurt, immediately started to give us one of his monotonous songs. When I expressed my sadness at the fact that he hadn't unlearned any of his singing skills during his leave, he became angry, told me to shut up and pointed out that the number of freckles in my face had increased and that I reminded him of a crumb cake.

At the moment my eyelids are so dark that it looks as if I have makeup on, just like one of those dames working on the funfair. All due to the dust we stirred up yesterday night while shovelling coals. When we finally arrived here with our diesel and 200 kilos of coal on the back we looked like negroes. But in general there is just nothing to do – even less than on the construction site where I worked when I was in the RAD.

On Saturday, with five men of the staff, we had to act as orderlies in the officers' mess, where a comradeship evening was staged for the participants of the races and several invited guests, about 650 people in total. I didn't get any tables to serve, but instead someone hung a small vendor's tray filled with cigarettes and cigars around my neck and then I was shoved out to sell my wares in the halls of the mess. At 1 a.m. I did the till: 5.50 Reichsmarks in tips! But for that I had to keep my eyes open like a hawk. Several comrades had to pay losses from their own private purse after some officers had made off without paying. I enjoyed the evening. I wasn't on service and as such I drank everything I could get my hands on: wine, beer, schnapps, champagne, liqueur, apple juice and lemonade. It was good that the kitchen missy had supplied me with a generous dinner, otherwise I might have got into trouble that night. We only arrived back at our room after 3 a.m. When we came in, we were greeted by the sight of Wiese's naked, white arse glinting in the moonlight. He was deep asleep, and we three roared with laughter, so loud that the whole floor was woken up. At 03.30 we went to sleep and after only ninety minutes, badly hungover, we had to get up again for firing practice. Yes indeed, firing practice on a Sunday. That's how it's done here in the regiment while the races are taking place during the week. The results were predictable. Nothing to write home about.

But back to the comradeship evening. The whole show started at 6 p.m. and the guest list included ten army Generals, one of the Luftwaffe, a few Admirals and countless other high-ranking officers. Our regimental band in black uniforms played some swell marches. The highlight being the fanfare marches at 11 p.m. Our fanfare blowers and drummers did an amazing job and got lots of applause. There were so many big cheeses there, not only from the military, but also from the Party, civilians in top industry positions, that we could more or less ignore the junior officers – a Leutnant counts for very little in that kind of company. The Bosch directors I had seen earlier were there as well. The members of the Kriegsmarine left a superb impression, snappy and in superb uniforms. A stark contrast to the wild bunch of the Luftwaffe officers there. I could not help noticing that even the highest Luftwaffe officers were quite young and not as bent by age as some in the army. Both the mariners and the flyers sang lots of cracking songs and when our band had played a particularly good tune, the boys of the Kriegsmarine started a perfectly timed rocket which even included whistling. The mariners are great chaps and they also won several of the races.

5 May 1938, Paderborn

Today I finally have the time to make another entry into this book. I am lying in bed, watching two of our boys sweeping the room while the Volksempfänger standing on Moser's locker is thundering the beats of the Italian national anthem into the empty corridors outside. Yes, now it is May, Hitler is on a state visit to Italy and for the last few days our broken Volksempfänger has supplied us with all kinds of reports and music from that beautiful land across the Alps – all via German radio channels, of course. And every evening and up until deep into the night – after the Unteroffizier on duty has made his final round – we are listening to dance music. All the proper hits which are sung and whistled by each and every one of us during and after service. Our current favourite is 'Im Mai, da sind die Frauen nicht treu', the lyrics of which are something like: 'In May the women are not faithful, then their heart often loves two or even three. Yes! One man to go out with and another one to take home! But please, that is the custom in the month of May!'

Radio exercises! Yes, of those we have eight or ten each week and they are fantastic because they take us out into the surroundings of Paderborn. Our superiors are the best and it is not rare for us to find ourselves doing absolutely nothing except for enjoying the sunshine and often we come back to barracks way too late. But our superiors always brief us properly: 'We exercised at cow-shit village and then had an unexpected engine breakdown. Understood?' – and in truth we were just joyriding around in the 50-kilometre zone. Old Feldwebel Metzen, Unteroffizier Schulze, known as 'Little Muck', and Unteroffizier Reimer are superiors of a kind one doesn't find on every corner. One Tuesday Uffz. Behle and us drove down to Nieder- and Obermarsberg, where he visited his 'girlfriend' Hilde. Behle is a proper adulterer! Thomas had to wear his engagement ring, on the right hand of course. How we laughed. In Obermarsberg we raced through the streets in a manner which made the locals' hair stand on end. The whole place is gloriously situated on a mountaintop. The mountain itself is riddled with tunnels of an ancient copper mine. We walked into one of these tunnels but didn't get very far. Behle, currently without proper employment, by the way, would love to join our platoon. And he gets on well with all of us, especially with the Little Muck. Later that evening, while we were having a break, the two had started fooling around and in the course of the 'fighting' the Little Muck had thrown a full thermos flask of coffee into Behle's back – so hard that it had nearly knocked him over. After that, Behle's attempts to catch Little Muck were spoiled when his sciatica suddenly flared up. That made him even more angry.

6 May 1938

We have been out and about again for the entire day. In the morning we were in Weine, behind Büren to visit RAD-Abteilung 5/161 'Wewelsburg', and we also came past the actual Wewelsburg. The drive to Weine took us through difficult terrain and I had to navigate by map, which wasn't exactly easy to do. Metzen was driving me mad with his constant bickering. When we reached that shithole Niederntudorf I asked our driver to make a brief stop to give me the time to orient myself. That was a mistake, as now everyone started to make fun of me: 'Did they really teach you nothing in the SS?' – I replied that at least I had learned to read a map. At Weine we started our work. First local installations with tree hooks, followed by some more work underground. I had to carry the heavy carrying frame on my back. That was a slog, running after the Kübel for 4 kilometres. Along the roads I had to cover the cables up with turf slabs and in the curves I had to tie it all up. When I finally reached the terminal station I was soaked with sweat. And all of that work had been good for nothing. Neither was anyone interested – Metzen and the Little Muck had already driven away to do some shopping – to make sure that none of us would starve.

On the way back we drove past a female RAD camp which is situated close to Büren, right on the top of a mountain from where one has an excellent view. Metzen ordered us to stop and then started chatting up some of the RAD girls. As we had driven in with roaring engines, all the barrack windows were soon lined with girls who had heard the commotion we had caused. After a short while, in which Metzen realised that he wouldn't be able to score there, our Wild Hunt continued. We learned that the girls hardly got out of the camp as they only had arrived there in April. They could have visitors on Sundays only. That they had only arrived a month ago was well visible as none of them had turned chubby from all the good food yet.

After a difficult drive we arrived late for lunch, but that didn't matter too much. A couple of hours later we were out again, this time driving to Bad Driburg. The Unteroffiziere Langer, Marx and Little Muck, as well as Feldwebel Metzen, were surprised at the number of pretty girls in the town. We drove to the water tower at the Kreuzberg, pulled off a number of hair-raising stunts with our vehicles and then, with howling engines, thundered down a very steep and narrow, winding path leading down the Kreuzberg before cutting through a quarry. At the other end there were scores of spa guests who shook their heads in disapproval. Then we drove up the Rosenberg, through the spa facilities there to the RAD camp, where I spent an hour and a half talking to old comrades. Weissert was still there, while

Bohn and Schwarze, both now squad leaders, had returned from school where they had sat their final exams. Jörgens, who had recently become an uncle, was lying on his bed – lazy and disrespectful. They introduced me to the infantry reserve officer candidate who temporarily, but regularly, pleased Lisbeth Bulling last winter. A nice guy, I do hope that he enjoyed the experience. Weissert told me that the first review had gone completely awry. The ancient General responsible for training, this old man who had chalk trickling from his trouser legs,* had told them that they hadn't trained their men correctly and as a punishment there was now a curfew of four weeks. When we raced back through the streets of Driburg, I nearly soiled my pants in terror when Little Muck decided to show off his driving skills. We then stopped at a farmhouse to buy eggs. The farmer packed them all in a box, except for two which would not fit. And I was also the one who had to carry these two eggs when we arrived back at the barracks. One can expect the hooting, cheering and remarks which erupted when I climbed out of the Kübel holding the two eggs in my hands.

10 May 1938

I have been transferred to the regimental staff as a wireless operator. Yesterday I had to report to Leutnant Ehrenberg. I am not sure if I like it here, it was certainly more cushy on the staff of II. Abteilung. Last Saturday I went on leave for the weekend. What a disappointing waste of time that was. Especially so in regards to a certain young lady. When I called her, she told me that she had to go to church on Sunday. After that we met to go on a stroll where we talked about meaningless things and mostly at cross-purposes. Damn, I should really listen to my mother – now that I am in the army I should stop trying to live such a solid life as if I was striving to become an Orthodox priest. It is absolute nonsense: 'Pull yourself together and behave,' I say to myself. 'Don't behave like other comrades and the Unteroffiziere' – I have a girlfriend at home and I owe this to her!

---

* A play on the German saying that someone has a calcified brain. This General's brain is so calcified that there is chalk trickling from his trouser legs.

Girlfriend? More like an acquaintance really. I can have the same kind of conversation with any other educated girl. And the worst thing is that she doesn't share my political Weltanschauung and there is no compromise in that regard.

13 May 1938

There is little sense in me being a wireless operator as I am always getting travel-sick. Now in the regimental staff, to avoid losing a well-trained wireless operator, they have put me in a Kfz.17 in which one is supposed not to get travel-sick so easily because of the good suspension. But then they take roads which can't be described as such any more and I nearly puked on my wireless set. Boy, oh boy! What a race that was today. The performance of the eight-cylinder Horch is superb. When comrade Hörsting failed to drive it properly, Leutnant Wilts took the wheel himself. Very quickly after that, I felt so miserable that I had to switch places with Hörsting so that I could at least look out in the direction we were travelling. The wireless work as such, however, went very well. Uffz. Pohle was first operator and responsible for the telegraph key while I, as second operator, had to write, encrypt and decipher the messages. I also worked with the *Zielvier Tafel*.* I had been rather nervous about all this, but it all went pretty well. Even though I felt absolutely awful.

16 May 1938

'Today at 20.00 you will report to your Korporalschaftsführer with a washed field cap' – that was what Jonny Meyer just said to me. Jonny is the golden-blond Spiess of the regimental staff and today is a Monday. A Monday typical for a little Landser like me. It started with uniform inspection and alcohol-evaporation-hour and ended with another review of all the uniform parts the Spiess objected to. Yesterday I had been on leave at home, and this

---

* Celluloid map template.

morning my bacon-like, greasy lid drew the attention of the Spiess. I have just come back from presenting the now-clean cap to Unteroffizier Pohle. It passed inspection and I was allowed to walk free.

There is a different wind blowing in the regimental staff. Gone are the days of: 'Comrades, please make sure your uniforms are clean and in order, I will have to conduct an inspection soon!' – The Spiess here just kicks the door open and then it's: 'Korporal, take this down!'

Today we have been on tank exercise 'auf der Lieth'* and it didn't go particularly well or at least not how Uffz. Pohle would have wanted us to perform. But who cares what … Gefreiter Rübsam has just been here and literally forbade me to write any more in my diary. Secrecy of service-related matters and so on. I'd better stop now.

18 May 1938

Today is Wednesday and service ended at 16.00. I am now sitting here waiting, until someone in this lazy mob starts making coffee. We have some of the worst blighters here in the staff – the worst being Hörsting, Beyhoff and Michaelis, and all of them are in our room. In the evening there was sporting exercise. A handball match: team of the signals platoon vs. team of the light platoon. Our lot lost big time. Last week it was we who won the game. Later we played dodgeball, which is always lots of fun. Some of the comrades haven't played that before. I took a 3-kilo medicine ball in the face – thrown by Beyhoff with maximum force. That was a nice feeling.

Today we filed our applications for leave on Whitsun. It all has to be done according to the book. They have pinned a sample application to the board and we have to copy that to the letter. Later Leutnant Ehrenberg told me that non-swimmers will not be allowed to take leave. This seems to me an acute problem. Yesterday evening there was an extra swimming lesson in the indoor pool, but hardly anyone went in. All afraid of the cold water. At midnight there was an alarm and we were thrown out of bed. Following that we drove around in the Kfz.17 until 04.00, when we had

---

* A training area near Paderborn.

to send a number of messages. All went well and at 04.15 we assembled at Benhausen for debriefing.

21 May 1938

Saturday today, much running around yesterday and today: cleaning the rooms, locker and room inspection. It is great fun – the whole company is tackling the stairs and hallways and then starts cleaning while everyone is singing or whistling. Often we clean to the tunes of the Badonviller March or to the song 'Schön ist's bei den Soldaten'. And to be honest, cleaning in this manner is great fun. Would make a nice scene in a movie when six whistling men in a line are rhythmically brushing the cleaning water over the floor. Now everything is clean and shiny. The kind of military cleanliness I always envisaged before I joined up. The chairs are brilliantly white, as white as the flowers on the many apple trees which are growing around the barrack buildings. Not a single grain of dust remained. The floor is just as clean as the polished surface of our table. And the lockers! A dream! Gefreiter Rübsam has decorated his handkerchiefs and laundry with colourful silk bands. Fitzer copied him and did the same in his locker. Even Beyhoff and Hörsting were working on their lockers! As if the Leutnant himself would do the inspection!

We stood in front of our lockers for about thirty minutes before the Spiess and five Unteroffiziere came in. At that moment there were only three of us in the room. Rübsam was with the Oberst, Makowsky was with Oberleutnant Thölke and Michaelis with Egon – all of them as batmen. As I am the new guy in the staff company, the Spiess took extra time to inspect my locker and a lot depended on the outcome of this inspection. I was happy when the Spiess nodded at his Unteroffiziere and said: 'Good!' Then he took a look at my trousers, the tunics and coat, but again couldn't find anything to complain about. Then he inspected Hörsting's locker. There were no major problems with it, but there were enough small details to catch the eye of an Oberfeldwebel like Meyer, who thundered: 'Damn you, man! This is nothing to brag about – needs to be done again', before he and his entourage left the room without a further word.

1 June 1938

I am on guard duty for the first time since joining up. Block guard at the regimental staff. At least that gives me time to write. Tomorrow we are going on leave! I already have my ticket and I hope I am getting out of here early enough. Leave ends on the 8th and we have already received our subsistence allowance. That's always nice. At the staff of II. Battalion we only got 4.95 RM. Now they want me to pay 15 RM for a pair of headphones which were stolen from me while I was serving with them in the 'Altes Waldlager'. Either this or I have to organise a new pair from the regimental staff. 15 Reichsmark and upcoming leave, damn it, I will have to 'organise' a replacement.

This morning we did a forest run, 5 km – Garrison competition. A cycle squadron of the 15. Reiter-Regiment has won the whole thing. Second place, 7th Company, Panzer-Regiment 11. I had to take part in the Staff II team. I was always in the leading group. Even though I had promised myself not to put any effort into the whole thing. But after the start signal it somehow felt stupid to crawl forward at the rear, so I started to work my way towards the front. The route was quite a nice one, always shaded by trees, past the enormous fishponds at Neuhaus – start and finish at the Schützenhaus, where there is dancing every Sunday. Maidservants' ball, of particular interest to us soldiers. And in the immediate vicinity lots of forest, with paths and benches. Loads of benches. 'Most practical,' says Wollberg. But that aside, the Schützenhaus is really quite nice. And why should one spend every Sunday in the cinema, when one can be out there in beautiful nature.

In the previous days we did a lot of outdoor exercises. On Friday we were out all day and at the end, having worn the headphones for hours, I had the worst of headaches. I acted as the second wireless operator in Egon's Kfz.17. Egon had been in a terrible mood and we raced through the countryside like devils. The speedometer mostly showed 80, often between 95 and 100 km/h. And that even though he had in the past ordered Hörsting and Michaelis not to drive faster than 55 km/h after the signals squadron had wrecked their Kfz.15/1 during a wild race. There is not a single working radio vehicle in the regimental staff any more. They have all been wrecked, so they have to do lots of work on foot, hauling 3 kilometres of heavy telephone cable down to Benhausen, then installing the line, running through their exercises before packing up and arriving back in barracks completely exhausted. One has to give it to them, they have learned to march long distances! And we could see that during today's forest run.

On Monday we were out of bed by 4 a.m. Company exercises, cooperation between the light platoon and signals platoon and messenger platoon. That was quite interesting. I was in the Kfz.17 of the messenger platoon. The exercise area stretched from Dahl, Dringenberg, Schmechten to Gut Danhausen near Bad Driburg. Wild driving back and forth. Our platoon was acting as 'armoured enemy' and the signal men had to engage in combat with their carbines and smoke bombs. We also had some gas in a bottle. With all the shooting we really enjoyed the day. At the end we all assembled at Löhr's farm near Danhausen. I helped with the harvest on that farm while I was in the RAD in 1937! Herr Löhr and his wife were very happy when I greeted them and Frau Löhr at once supplied me with one of her giant ham sandwiches, which I shared with Uffz. Reuter of the motorcycle squadron. The Löhrs also gave me a huge bunch of lilac to decorate our rooms with. The sandwich tasted heavenly, but then everyone in the camp knew of Frau Löhr and her cooking skills.

As we drove through Driburg I peered through the windows of the car to see whether I could spot some old acquaintances, but there was no one I knew around. Unteroffizier Pohle promised us that we'd come back to Bad Driburg after Pentecost. I hope we do.

Yes, tomorrow I am going on leave. More of the usual, I guess – a wave of worries and concerns which only the civilian has and then, after a few days of boredom, one can't wait to get back into the army. One should really get a woman and get married – that way there would at least be someone who is truly happy when one comes home on leave. And at least then there would be someone to pass the time with easily, otherwise that all depends on luck and the amount of cash in one's pocket. I don't like the idea of running around with a whole bunch of girls on each arm like some of the comrades do, or like that tango-boy Vigier. He, by the way, I met in front of the Wiemuth on Saturday night, talking to Eisenhofen and Gläser. The whole lot of them, including Furlkröger and Arntz, had been inside and had not behaved very well. That had resulted in a threat by an Unteroffizier of the 15. Reiter-Regiment who had told them to get lost immediately. Vigier was boiling with anger that it had come to this. This is his one positive side, he hardly drinks anything and so never loses control and misbehaves.

To come back to the looming days of leave, I am wondering if I will be seeing my 'true love', the one who keeps doing my head in, or if I will somehow find another little lady to attach myself to. Maybe I will run into an old acquaintance – but I already know that this period of leave will pan out just like all the others did. A young soldier like me should be out having a fling with somebody! The comrades with whom I share a room already think I am an old buffer. Well, maybe I am just that, just like Chico in the American film *Seventh Heaven*. That, by the way, was a really good film, even though most of the guys in our room didn't understand it properly.

Damnation! There are several bleeding cockchafer beetles and some fat moths which are distracting me from writing. Earlier on I collected the cockchafers and placed them on Schwegmann's face. But even when three of the beasts crawled around on his mug it did not wake him up! Schwegmann is on guard duty with me and is snoring on one of the beds here in the guardroom. As is Tiggemann, who is occupying the second bed and is snoring so loud that the walls are shaking. I should ram one of those beetles down his throat, that would stop his snoring. Well, if he isn't of a similar disposition to Jürgen Rothert, the guy who eats cockchafers if you buy him a glass of beer. One has to have iron nerves to cope with all this, cockchafers, moths, snoring comrades.

2 June 1938

Three-quarters of our training period are now over and I am on the way to become just as stupid and stubborn as Petermann. Petermann's real name is Peter Schürmann and he has been transferred here from Nachrichten-Abteilung 16. They say his parents must have conceived him while they were drunk. But good grief, that guy even looks stupid! Sticky-out ears, a huge snout under a narrow brow, little eyes like a pig, a hint of a hump on his back and unnaturally long arms. And that imbecile is now serving as a radio operator and is driving everyone insane with his complete lack of orthography. Just one example: he spells the nice name of Bad Driburg as 'Batterienburg'!

[*page torn out*]

I might not have been happy when my leave came to an end, but I surely wasn't very sad either. After the first exercise it was as if I had never left. On Saturday after Pentecost I went to Bad Driburg in my black uniform. The thermal baths there are really nice. Will go there more often. On the following Sunday the regiment formally marched into Paderborn. Quite a show that was, seemingly the entire population was out on the streets to see our parade. I marched on foot, all the vehicles were crewed by officers and NCOs. Then in the evening, a regimental ball in the Schützenhaus. Many girls there too, but none were quite right for me. I sat with a group of former grammar school friends, Jupp Wellinghoff, Fritz Burg and Leutnant Adolf von Knoblauch of RR15.

All the men were supposed to be back in the barracks by 3 a.m., but 162 men failed to do so and came much later. Wasn't punished severely. Service on Monday wasn't too bad. Schuhknecht and I worked <u>inside</u> the 2-cm tank. On Thursday I went to Bad Driburg again where, for the first time since I left the RAD, I met the two spring-mermaids Paula and Liesbeth again. The spa guests made big eyes when they saw how cheerfully Liesbeth greeted me! In the evening I met the sisters Elli and Thea Thöne, with whom I used to go walking in Kreuzberg. I had intended to have lunch with the Abteilung, but I was too late for that and went into Cafe Börger instead. In the evening, after having spent my last Pfennig, I ran into Elli and Thea again, who were going dancing in Cafe Stute. They really wanted me to go with them, so in the end I did accept their invitation and we had a nice chat with one another until at 10 p.m. it was time for me to go back to Paderborn. Liesbeth accompanied me to the Stellberg and then I raced back on my bicycle which I had brought with me from leave. I also brought my blue bathrobe. Both will come in handy. Last Sunday I was in Osnabrück. Same proceedings as always. Herbert had gone to Bielefeld to attend some SS-event, so I decided to go swimming. I only needed to catch the train at 9:16 p.m., so I had the evening for myself.

On Monday the whole unit drove to the Sauerland for a large manoeuvre exercise. I was astounded when I saw the large number of radio vehicles in the individual units assembled there down to and around the Möhnesee Lake. It all went well, even with several small defects in our Kfz.17 and not only that, the team Sander–Ernsting received special praise when it was all over. It all ended with a terrain exercise near Vellinghausen. I had been there before, staying in the local youth hostel during the 900-year anniversary of the town and a certain young lady stayed there too, during her time in grammar school. She had met a young soldier there, and she spoke about him very often. Maybe time to write a card to Ruth?

In the Pollmannskrug it was too expensive and I could only afford two glasses of milk. In the evening we drove to the beautiful Möhnesee and then back, through the Sauerland, to Paderborn, where we arrived at 9 p.m. And how nice when we saw the service schedule for the following day – technical service in the morning and then to Bad Lippspringe for a swim! How nice a soldier's life can be, even if not every day.

15 July 1938, Paderborn

God damn it! My fountain pen is broken and I can't buy a new one. I am constantly broke, it's been like that for weeks. I already had to borrow 2 Marks from Michaelis to be able to get my bicycle repaired – the frame had broken and needed to be welded.

I am still not sure how long I should stay in the army. Time is passing too quickly and suddenly one has turned old without noticing it. Last Sunday I was at home and everything was unchanged. Mother has hardly enough to live on, so there isn't enough for me to eat, not even thinking about taking a food parcel with me when I leave. Father is living quite well in Hamburg, has a car and every day he smokes cigarettes worth at least 1 Mark. And I can't even go on holiday properly. Herbert intends to visit the old man in Hamburg, so yesterday I sent him my suitcase. His suitcase is broken and I hope he brings my leather case from Hamburg, it will be quite useful here.

At the moment we are in driving school where we are learning to drive a lorry. Second week already and it is great fun. We six students are being taught by Feldwebel Flachsbarth, the maintenance sergeant. We are all making good progress – Hürtgen, who already has a driving licence for tanks, in particular. Then there are Unteroffizier Morawsky, Klusner, Schwegmann and Grauler of the motorcycle squadron – the latter three have big mouths, but are all incredibly stupid! I am performing best, however, as I have already driven a car before I joined the military and I also already have the tank driving licence.

With the driving school we get around a lot. On one morning, in heavy rain, we drove to Horn where we had a coffee in a small guesthouse. In the nice hotel next to it there was a pretty blonde girl standing in a window and she joked around with us a little. When we drove away, I noticed that she kept waving after us for a long time. I should really make an effort to get back to Horn to get to know her better, or get to know her at all. I really liked her a lot.

31 October 1938, Paderborn

Yes, since 15 July a lot of water has gone down the Rhine. Between passing my driving test and our mobilisation alarm, Rübsamen didn't allow me to get my diary out and it ended up in my home storage, where it remained until now. Rübsamen, the vile swine, is now an Unteroffizier and I am still a lowly Panzer gunner. When he walks past I have to snap my heels together, but that isn't happening often any more. Since the Sudeten campaign I have been transferred back to the staff of II. Abteilung.

Today I am manning the regimental switchboard in the garrison. I have often done so in the field, in the Sudetenland and all the exercises and on manoeuvre, but this is the first time I am doing it on a stationary set. It is a bit more complicated outside, where one has to operate in barns and old sheds, but the amount of work here is much higher. There is a literal wire entanglement spanning across the two boxes in front of my face. But now, at 21.00, it is getting quieter, which gives me time to write. Wrote a card to Mother to tell her why I didn't come to visit on Sunday and sent another letter to Herbert. Maybe another to Kurt Schwarz? I could tell him that I might be able to see him in Schweinfurt in a week or so. But that is still not certain, so it is better to save the paper. Could write to a certain young lady in Osnabrück – but she can wait. She left me waiting until she finally sent me a more or less proper photograph of her and now I can wait until my next period of leave until I get another one from her as a kind of souvenir. It has to be said that she now has at least half a dozen photographs of me. But that doesn't matter.

More importantly, I might soon be a reserve officer candidate – that will be important for my future. What my chances are I don't know. Today is the date on which the Abteilung will pass the names of the candidates on. Whether I have been picked, I don't know. On 3 November the promotions will be made public and from a semi-official side someone has already drawn a chevron on my sleeve with a finger.

A comrade just walked by singing the song we have composed:

> Dream of the Sudeten, of Czechoslovakia;
> Dream of Mr Benesch, and his bunch of criminals;
> Dream of beers in Pilsen, and of beautiful women in Prague;
> With you I want to dream of the Moldau tonight.
>
> The engine hums its unchanging tune,
> The tanks are rolling into Czechoslovakia:
>
> When Hitler's colours fly above this Gau,
> A tank gunner returns to his little Frau.
>
> The engine hums its unchanging tune,
> The tanks are rolling into Czechoslovakia:

We composed several songs like this when we were in Czechoslovakia, including a particularly good and juicy one about the driver of an old Krupp tank.

1 November 1938

Will we finally get promoted or won't we? The answer to this question is keeping us all awake. I was transferred into the recruit instructors' course yesterday. That's at least something, but I still wonder when I will know more about reserve officer Sander. In the army one needs to be patient and have nerves like a rocking horse. This will probably be the last time that I will be sitting at the switchboard. It is interesting to see that now, after office hours, all the cheap soldiers' brides are calling; from Lippspringe, Geseke, Senne, from all parts of the world, and of course from Paderborn in particular.

A little calculation just for the sake of it. The citizens of Paderborn are no great friends of us soldiers. But what would the miserable gits say if the army moved out of Paderborn and no one paid the citizen tax any more? An Unteroffizier in his third year of service (first year as Unteroffizier) pays a monthly amount of 2.50 RM as citizen tax. A total of 30 RM per year. We have eight companies and three staff with twenty Unteroffiziere in each. At the lowest count that adds up to 6,600 RM in tax and that doesn't include all the officials, employees and workers. Officers are paying a lot more than that. The people in Paderborn would do better to shut up!

Mother has sent me a parcel today. Included my laundry, half a loaf of white and half a loaf of black bread. The white I have already eaten. No money. No other choice now but to pay for the required pair of dress trousers myself. Can only do so in instalments – I have already paid 10 RM and it is supposed to cost 42 RM. And I still need to pay for my dancing lessons – I won't be getting anywhere in life that way.

7 November 1938

So much for my training course. I am so sick of all the drills in the second year of service. But anyway, I am now a reserve officer candidate and will have to tolerate all this for a few more days. I was really lucky, I am a reserve officer candidate and recruit instructor. The promotion to Gefreiter should come through in a few days and with it the pay backdated to 1 October. Money will probably be here on Thursday, the day on which our course will be inspected.

On the 10th the 'Studious' is supposed to do an inspection and Oberleutnant Streger, our course commander, has promised us a few days of leave, but that still needs to be confirmed by the commander. I hope it works out.

I hope to get back to Osnabrück soon. Damn, since I saw Ruth again a few weeks ago I can't get her out of my head. To be frank I am a real idiot for not being able to finish with her. I have known her for five years now and nothing has changed since then. Far too long. But now an end to these thoughts – in the next two or three years I will have to look at girls only from a distance, and I also need to learn to dance first. The relatively quiet winter half-year here in Paderborn would have been ideal for that – if I hadn't been turned into a recruit instructor.

Funny, only a week ago I was so unhappy I could have died because without an Abitur there seemed to be no chance to become a reserve officer. And now that the whole thing has been sorted and I have passed all the questions, I couldn't care less.

10 November 1938

Today is Thursday. A very busy one. Today we have received our promotions and I am now a Gefreiter and recruit instructor. I guess there will be a bit of waiting required before the official appointment to officer candidate comes through. Today our instructors' course was inspected by Herr Major Koll. The inspection went well, as expected, and in return we did receive a few days of leave. I am allowed to go home tomorrow and I only need to return on Wednesday before the arrival of the new recruits. A huge surprise.

In addition all reserve officer candidates had to present themselves to the regimental commander Dipl.Ing. Oberst Phillips today. We were presented by our Fähnrichsvater Leutnant Schmidt. Let me characterise him quickly: a pair of spotless boots, a pair of eighty-horsepower trousers, but a remarkable pair of 'romance novel legs' (meaning that at first it looks as if they will not get together, but then they get together in the end, like in a romance novel). He has a wasp waist and shoulders like Max Schmeling. A huge mouth! He roared at us like a bull, told us that we couldn't even dress ourselves properly, he called us wimps, wimps who didn't know how to behave. But when the Oberst came to review us he became as meek as a kitten. All this reviewing is quite tiring, but then the only reason – as we all know – is to find out if the worker's scent is still clinging to us, or if we have been born for a higher purpose.

After the inspection, my essay about education was handed back to me. Leutnant Engelhardt of 5th Company had already talked all the essays through with us during the previous lesson and had made a point of saying that mine was the only useful one. Not bad for someone without Abitur. Today I have polished the floors of my room. I want to make a good first impression when the new recruits arrive on Wednesday and Thursday. From the halls outside I can hear the laughter of all the former Panzer gunners who are now Gefreite. They suddenly all feel powerful. I am not with them because Germuth, the new Unteroffizier, or 'Guggi' as we call him, had come up the stairs and in the dark I had failed to recognise and greet him. But let him, I'll soon be an Unteroffizier myself.

24 November 1938

Fourteen days have passed and they have been quite memorable. Last week I was at home from Friday evening to Wednesday morning. Spent most of the time in bed with a terrible cold, stomach pain, headache, fever. Wasn't nice. But there wasn't anything for me to do anyway. I have to learn how to dance, otherwise I really don't know what to do with my spare time instead of going to the cinema, and most films I have already seen in Paderborn.

My recruits arrived on Thursday evening. Four young flowers, two men from Cologne on the Rhine, one from Wuppertal and one man from Halle in Westphalia. One has to know how to approach these Rhinelanders to make something useful out of them. I am far too serious for their club. And I already received the first rollicking for my four recruits. The gits had gone on exercise without their neck stocks and in addition two of them hadn't shaved properly. And only because I had been unable to keep my eyes on them because I had been Gefreiter on duty. As a result I am now not allowed to ask for leave on Sunday. We are really getting it from all sides. Damn, how have they drilled us in the first days. Everything we did was wrong. They let us stand in the rain and cold for hours in full view of our recruits, who see us in that unimpressive state. No wonder when one is freezing to death, not much we could have done. At least the lunch tastes a lot better after such torture.

I am also proud to announce that Ruth Wiemann has finally supplied me with a proper photograph of her. I have met her several times, that is all I can say about this matter. I have also met with Anneliese and her sister – Annie has grown massively in width and is determined to marry a guy who serves in the Oldenburg RAD. I wish her all the best.

My four men are doing quite well really and their demeanour towards me is acceptable. While I was away yesterday, Guggi snowed in to inspect the lockers of two of my men. He found faults in both of them. I have personally inspected each locker on a daily basis, so it can't have been that bad – but I know what Guggi is like, I have my own experiences with him. Well anyway, my men don't worry too much about it, least of all Reiss, the fat footballer from Wuppertal. They are all making an effort and are pulling their weight, so I will not discipline them any further.

25 November 1938

Today we got a rollicking during drill exercises. First time the recruits were wearing steel helmets. With that iron pot on their heads they found it hard to sing properly. Resulted in a few extra hours of drill. I am feeling a bit sorry for the chaps – and in all honesty, there are some who were drilled and pushed much harder than that, men like Goldhorn and Arntz, for example, and they have turned into bad soldiers anyway. Yesterday I showed my four heroes what a proper locker inspection in the army looks like. In fact only Reiss's locker wasn't entirely in order, the others were looking quite tidy. But then, just to make sure they'll put even more effort in the next time around, I whirled the contents of all of the lockers around and threw half of it on the floor.

To be honest, I am not enjoying my new role at all. In the past the days just flew past and now one is standing on the parade ground shouting at the men while at the same time one is being shouted at by one's superiors. Time hardly passes that way. All the joy I felt only a year ago after joining the army has been blown away. Damn, and when I look at the photo of Ruth, I can't help thinking that this is over already. If only I had a woman on my side, someone who could give me some stability. Otherwise I only have Mother and Herbert, and I don't care too much about either of them. I have no idea yet what to do later, who I will work for and what to do. I have – to say it bluntly – no goal in life. And that is a nasty attitude. I used to make a great effort to become an officer candidate and during my time in the RAD did everything to become a troop leader. But here at home, or privately, I have no motivation and even the prospect of becoming a Feldwebel doesn't do it any more since I realised the number of disadvantages connected to that role. Later I am supposed to take over my father's shop, but I can't be bothered about that. Yes, what am I to do?

At the moment I am clinging to the thought that my recruits will soon be ready to be left to their own devices without constant supervision. That will allow me to go into town again whenever I want, and how difficult can it be to find a fairly attractive girlfriend? But, on the other hand, I have no real interest in that either, I can't explain it – change of subject!

A few weeks ago I ordered a pair of dress trousers from a tailor. But damn, when I collected them recently, they didn't fit properly. Lots of creases around the zip at the front and not fitting properly at the side of the legs. God, I am angry! Used my meagre pay to buy these trousers and then they don't fit! The fabric is rubbish as well. A lesson for the future! Not the first time I have experienced what it means if one has clothing made by a cheap tailor – in the end it's never worth it and fabric and cut will never look classy. That will the last time I fall into that trap.

Have been 'listening in' in the lecture hall today. A catastrophe! All the craftsmen and labourers who can't even write properly in normal circumstances were breaking their fingers during the speed-writing exercises.

8 December 1938

St Niklas is over and I have received neither a parcel nor a letter from Mother. Well, never mind. On Tuesday I went to the marksmen's club house to attend an event organised by the SS. The local theatre group performed a play with the title 'The Last Farmer', and it was well received by everyone. A travelling engineer then drove me back to the barracks after 23.00! An impeccable man. Damn, I am tired and my handwriting is looking abysmal, I am off to bed!

9 December 1938

Tomorrow is payday. I am getting my 7.50 RM plus 8.80 RM subsistence allowance. I will invest that in a new briefcase. While I am training the recruits my skiing holiday won't be happening anyway, so better to invest in something practical. I hardly get by with my pay, mainly because I am always hungry like a starving bear. The small portions one gets here just don't do it. Today I received mail from Mother. She is still in Hamburg. She tells me that we'll now be moving to Hamburg in July. She is enthralled by the big city. As far as I am concerned they could move earlier. I can hardly go anywhere anyway during my leave.

The mornings consists of a one-hour lesson followed by two and a half hours of exercise. Then there is lunch from 11.00 to 13.35, followed by more exercise between 14.00 and 16.00. Alternatively there is shooting practice. Then one hour of Morse tapping and one hour of rifle cleaning. Then coffee and dinner in one sitting followed by cleaning and tidying from 19.00 to 23.00. Every day the same: 'Danz, open your bloody mouth when you are singing!', 'Danz! Tighten the grip on that rifle, you are a soldier, not a bleeding hunter!', 'Pull your belly in, fatso!', 'Arms straight, you dunce!', 'What? You don't want to sing any more? Sing and swing your crutches, you lame ducks!', 'Come on! Faster, you wet towels!', 'Hold your rifle upright! Are you too stupid to walk, Danz?', 'That is a rifle, not a crutch, Addau! Stop leaning on it!', 'Danz! One-two, one-two, half-turn, halt! Present!' – 'What? Who allowed you to move, Förster!', 'The whole platoon, to the right, *marsch, marsch*! – a dozen rounds around the square! You can thank Förster for that!', 'Sonnenschein! You wretch! What do you think you are doing?', 'Into line *marsch, marsch*!', 'Linning! It is a miracle that you can walk at all with your enormous feet!', 'This way, gentlemen! This way! Try to walk in the same direction! It is not difficult, straight forward, just like the bull pisses! Deiss, pull your stomach in! Schmitz, straight back! Push your arse back, man! We know you like doing that! Look at how Schmacht is standing there! Like a freshly fucked squirrel! Gralla, shut your gob, you are letting a draught in!' – This is how it usually starts and it then goes on for about two and a quarter hours. Schmaldt, Panzer gunner, approached me to register an invention: he wants to mount loudspeakers onto a car which could then drive up and down the parade square playing records with insults and aggressive shouting. That way we Unteroffiziere and Gefreite would not have to shout ourselves hoarse any more. In addition he recommends putting a parrot with a microphone on top of the sports hall. That way the parrot could constantly repeat the most common phrases and orders: 'About turn, you wet towels, about turn, *marsch, marsch!*'

But then, some of the guys are indeed lazy dogs. And when I try to bring a bit of change into the system and let my gentlemen do anything else but running – something to build their arm muscles, for example, then I get barked at by the Feldwebel! I ordered Danz to do some press-ups – and that got me a mighty rollicking for gross ill-treatment! And that's not the only instance where that happened. I ordered the recruits into an infantry gallop holding their rifles with outstretched arms – they threatened me with incarceration for that! And, last but not least, I had ordered Weiss to pick up a rifle cartridge from the ground with his teeth. I did that because the wretch had carelessly dropped it on the ground and pretended not to have noticed. The amount of trouble which that got me into is hard to believe. From now on Gefreiter Sander won't make an effort any more.

11 December 1938

Still the old tune with me and the women. And even though it is looking better in monetary terms I still don't know how to dance. 'Dear boy, it is a sin that someone of your build doesn't know how to dance!' – I would have enlisted myself for dance lessons, but due to my whippersnappers there is no chance for that. Yesterday I inspected rifles and lockers until 23.00!

15 December 1938

On Monday Herbert sent me a wristwatch. It is supposed to be my Christmas present. It will come in very handy when I want to be reminded of how long this boredom will go on for.

24 December 1938

Today is Christmas Eve and I would have liked to go on Sunday leave. But our goat would have liked to have a long tail and got a short one instead. When you are in the army you must never expect something to happen. You will be disappointed. I am now hoping to get out on New Year's Eve. I am sitting at the switchboard together with Obergefreiter Otto Schulz. As it is Christmas we have each received six beer vouchers and a plate with a bar of chocolate, six Atikah Green cigarettes, a pack of figs, two apples, nuts and some gingerbread. Later we staged a small Christmas celebration with the few men of II. Abteilung's staff who are still present here. We started by drinking beer and singing two Christmas carols. Wasn't very uplifting. The boss held a brief speech. Wasn't very uplifting either. And then Backenecker took the stage and improvised a little show in which he fired out jokes and funny anecdotes. With such talent it comes as no surprise that he also played the role of Servant Rupert and as such distributed the 'special presents'. Leutnant Glässgen, commanding officer of the staff, received a bottle of Trypsin to combat his receding hairline. Charlie Zangenmeister got a celluloid monocle which he could wear in his left eye. Feldwebel Middelmann got a telephone for use in his office, he didn't have one before. Our armourer Streck was given a tiny tin cap gun with 100 caps. By that stage we had reached the point of 'getting utterly drunk', one which I had intended to avoid and so I decided to go to bed. Just in time as the jokes were getting rather filthy at this point.

25 December 1938

The first day of Christmas and a letter from Ruth arrived which contained a small photo of her. That made me very happy. Yesterday night a man on watch shot himself in the thigh. He must have been in terrible pain, he was screaming so loudly that at first we thought he had shot himself in the scrotal sac. If that had happened I would have felt sorry for him, even though he is quite obviously an idiot. But a shot to the thigh is nothing to worry about. Certainly not as bad as what happened to Robert Gläser the previous summer. He was standing on top of the 2-cm tank and busy removing the KWK-30, which had jammed, from the turret. While he was doing that a blank 2-cm shell which had been lodged in the breech went off and the splinters of the wooden projectile were driven into his body. The little finger on his left hand and several sinews were gone and his thighs had been lacerated by the little wooden splinters. But, even worse for a man, not only his thighs. But he was lucky as they managed to stitch him back together again. The unlucky man who shot himself last night was taken into surgery immediately and they removed the pistol round from his knee. Can only wish him 'Merry Christmas'.

Our second little Christmas party was a bit better than the last one. Even though Zera had already drowned his sorrows in the canteen earlier while Hornke and the others followed his example with mulled wine later on. We ate potato salad and sausages. Each of us got a packet of 'North State' or 'Overstolz' and a small marzipan cake. Then the recruits had to serve us mulled wine and after I'd had about 2½ litres of that stuff I played a game of morris with Unteroffizier Ebener and then buggered off to bed. The wine has coloured my teeth dark red, nearly black. Have to polish them up before I go on leave, they are all broken anyway.

24 January 1939

Gefreiter on duty: Gefreiter Sander – a nice change that! Even though one can't sleep for a night, it offers time to write letters and to add a few lines into this silly book. A lot has happened since my last entry.

The driver of this Skoda 35(t) is proudly posing in front of his vehicle, which is decorated with flowers shortly before departure from Freystadt. The double-x insignia on the left side shows that the vehicle belongs to 6. Panzer-Division.

The population of Freystadt lining the streets to bid farewell to Panzer-Regiment 11.

The author, Leutnant Wilhelm Sander, just before the beginning of the war against Soviet Russia.

Before the storm. Unteroffizier Wassmuth reads Hitler's order of the day for 21 June 1941 in front of the men of 5th Company, Panzer-Regiment 11.

At the divisional command post of 6. Panzer-Division on 21 June 1941.

21 June 1941: Even though weighing only 10.5 tons, Gefreiter Tamschick's Panzer 35(t) was too heavy for this wooden bridge.

The Skoda of Oberleutnant Theodor Langenbruch crossing a shallow stream.

Oberfeldwebel Erich Oswald with mounted infantry of 129. Infanterie-Division during the attack on Gaure on 21 June 1941. Oswald did not survive the war; he was killed on 19 February 1945.

21 June 1941 at 4 a.m. in front of the Russian border fortifications.

14 September 1941, the last day in front of Leningrad. From left to right: Müller, Wiegand, Sander, Graw, Goßler, Albert and Oberholz.

A German heavy 15-cm howitzer destroyed during the battle of Raseiniai is being inspected by Major Löwe (of Panzer-Abteilung 65) and Hauptmann Stern. Erich Löwe was killed in action in December 1943 in command of Schwere Panzer-Abteilung 501. Hans Stern, then in command of 3./Panzer-Regiment 11, transferred to the Waffen-SS in 1943. In 1945 he took command of the SS-Panzer-Brigade 'Westfalen'.

The Panzer 35(t) of Leutnant Vielbaum during the battle of Raseiniai.

Unteroffizier Theo Sander, as driver of Leutnant Friedrich Wilhelm Sander, during the early stage of the war in Russia. Theo Sander, who was not related to the author of the diaries, was a highly experienced Panzermann who had already steered a Panzer 35(t) through Poland and France.

Engaging heavy Russian tanks north of Raseiniai.

During the battle of Raseiniai, the tank of Feldwebel Aures was hit in the track. Exiting their tank under heavy enemy fire, the crew repaired the damage and returned to the fighting. Tank 731 is the vehicle of Leutnant Vielbaum.

The 8.8-cm Flak gun commanded by Leutnant Loede.

Destroyed German anti-tank gun and vehicles near Raseiniai, crushed and overturned by heavy Russian tanks.

The effect of German Nebelwerfer rockets at the Dubysa bridge.

Burned-out Russian vehicles after a Nebelwerfer strike.

An immobilised and abandoned Russian KV-1 near the Dubysa crossing.

A destroyed flamethrower-armed Russian T-26 tank.

The advance continues, further and further east.

A Soviet KV-2 heavy assault tank, repurposed as a road sign.

Technical revision of 5th Company's Skodas at Samoschje.

A pioneer bridge across the Düna [Daugava] near Livani.

The aftermath of the ambush on the Russian transport column on 4 July 1941.

Near Pskov on 14 July 1941.

A small German cemetery at an unidentified location.

Inspecting a downed Russian Tupolev SB-2 bomber.

A card game on 22 July 1941 – Leutnant Sander is in the background.

Inspecting an abandoned and
captured Russian KV-2 tank.

A tired-looking Leutnant Sander has spent the night in a Russian dugout, some time in August 1941.

The recovery of the body of Gefreiter Mashäuser; his wrecked tank can be seen in the background.

'Skoda Super Sport', Sander's Panzer 35(t) (523) at Lake Peipus. From left to right:
Obergefreiter Szepanski, Leutnant Sander, Obergefreiter Müller, Obergefreiter Tutasz.

On the morning of 9 September
1941. Leutnant Sander, Leutnant
Lope and Unterarzt Dr Niessen.

A destroyed Panzer III near Sabino in September 1941.

Resting after the fighting at Muratowo.

At Muratowo railway line.

A self-propelled Flak gun of 6. Panzer-Division.

Aftermath of the minefield encounter of 2 October.

The graves of Feldwebel Goßler and Unteroffizier Wiegand, killed in the minefield on 2 October 1941.

Volokolamsk, 30 November 1941. 'There they had hanged eight partisans, two of them women, on a gallows. A big sign announced that these people had taken up arms against the German military. Eight people on one gallows, that's a sight one doesn't see often.'

Gzhatsk, November 1941: Sander and his hosts Tamara and Natascha.

'Panzer Division on foot', December 1941.

Oberleutnant Sander during the German retreat, Klin, 14 December 1941.

2

17 June 1941–1 October 1941

On 22 June 1941, Panzer-Regiment 11, as part of 6. Panzer-Division, having reached its assembly areas, crossed the border near Tilsit. It formed part of Panzergruppe 4, led by General Erich Hoepner, who had held command of 1. Leichte-Division before the German attack on Poland. The armoured core of the division consisted of 47 Panzer IIs, 155 Panzer 35(t)s, 20 Panzer IVs, 8 Befehlspanzer 35(t)s and six additional Befehlspanzer – it was the only division to deploy the small, Czech-made Panzer 35(t).

The Panzer 35(t), known to the crews in Panzer-Regiment 11 and Panzer-Abteilung 65 as the 'Skoda Super Sport', or 'old bucket', was already completely obsolete in 1940. The Skoda works in Pilsen, Czechoslovakia's biggest arms manufacturer, had started building the light tank Model 35 in 1936 and had successfully exported it to a number of countries prior to the German annexation in April 1939. After Czechoslovakia was incorporated into the German Reich, the Model 35 was incorporated into the German arsenal as Panzerkampfwagen 35(t), where, because of its very similar armament, it was deployed in the same role as the Panzer III, but it was far less suited for it, mainly because of its weaker armour protection and less powerful main gun. The Czech tanks were fitted with German radios, which made it possible for the different vehicle types to communicate with each other and to be led by a superior staff. To enable communication inside the vehicle, an intercom system was installed. Holders for the German gas masks were added inside the vehicle. The original alternator, magneto and starter were replaced with Bosch equipment. The performance of the 37-mm gun and the good durability of the tracks were considered advantageous over the German Panzer I and Panzer II, but the riveted armour was criticised. The most important alteration was the adaptation, in line with the Wehrmacht's operational concepts, for a fourth crew member acting as loader for the main gun and as gunner at the turret machine gun. To make room for this man, six rounds of the main gun and 900 rounds of machine-gun ammunition were dispensed with. However, only men shorter than 1.70 m could be used in this capacity, as the turret height was limited.

The German plan in the northern sector of the front was to annihilate enemy forces in the Baltic states, to seize the Baltic ports, thereupon capturing the cities of Kronstadt and, more importantly, Leningrad. As soon as German forces crossed the Soviet border, they ran into heavy resistance, but all objectives were taken in the second half of the day. On 24/25 June, Kampfgruppe von Seckendorff, of 6. Panzer-Division found itself at the receiving end of a counter-attack by the 2nd Soviet Tank Division, which was equipped with heavy KV-1 and KV-2 tanks whose armour was virtually immune to German anti-tank fire. Near the village of Raseiniai the seemingly invulnerable Soviet tanks rolled over the German infantry and entered the artillery positions. In the ensuing battle, the timely deployment of some 88-mm anti-aircraft guns turned the tables and after losing several tanks to their fire the Soviets retreated.

Not far away, Kampfgruppe Raus, the second battle group of 6. Panzer-Division, engaged with a single KV tank which had shot up two German transport columns and had effectively cut the Kampfgruppe's supply and evacuation line. The story of the ensuing battle against the lonely Russian tank has entered the realm of legend and has been told more often than many other similar and more important engagements. With speed and aggression, 6. Panzer-Division continued to overrun every enemy position in its path, broke the Stalin Line and crossed the Düna and advanced on the Luga River. In only three weeks it had churned through 800 kilometres (497 miles) of enemy territory, over sun-baked roads, across swamps and forest, and had opened the gateway to Leningrad, the attack on which began on 8 August 1941 and which immediately ran into heavy and determined resistance. As the division fought its way through a series of strong field fortifications, Duderhof Hill, south-west of Leningrad, was taken on 9 September 1941, opening up the view to the city's harbour and the buildings of the city itself. Yet already on 6 September, a decision of far-reaching importance for the further course of the campaign had been made. After it had been realised that the exhausted, ill-supplied and heavily depleted German troops of Army Group North were no longer capable of capturing Leningrad, the decision was made not to attack, but to invest the city instead. Having put aside his interest in Leningrad, Hitler declared the northern sector a secondary theatre of war. By doing so he yielded to the urging of the General Staff and ordered preparations to be made for the attack on Moscow, shifting all expendable forces from Army Group North to Army Group Centre by 15 September.

6. Panzer-Division was transferred to the central front to join the offensive against Moscow.

* * *

17 June 1941

In the morning at 09.30 the company stood assembled on the parking square, ready to leave. Behind the fence of the school yard on which the vehicles have been standing for the last three months a dense crowd of people has assembled. Many schoolchildren among them have been given a day off just to see us go, and a few *Arbeitsmaiden** had postponed their potato-peeling duties in the camp to bid us farewell. The Spiess makes his report and then the boss arrives, not too early like he usually is on exercises – and I report to Oberleutnant Bethke. The boss then briefly addresses the company, whereupon we are dismissed and mount our vehicles. And then, our trusty old LT Skoda 35(t)s are rolling again. The old buckets perform admirably.

My driver is my old comrade Theo Sander. I already got on well with him in Paderborn, where we had been in different companies. Now that we are sitting in the same vehicle, it will only be a matter of time before we become even better attuned to one another. My wireless operator is Häring,

---

* 'Working maidens', members of the female labour service.

a member of the 'Five of the Fifth', the wonderful singers of our company. Like Theo Sander, he has seen action in France while Theo has already driven the boss in Poland. He had also received the Iron Cross there. Only Erdweg and I, assistant gunner and commander, have not been on campaign so far. Time will tell how this is going to pan out. There is a bottle of champagne in my luggage which I will crack open to commemorate the first attack.

The mood in the tank is excellent. Erdweg is playing the harmonica, Häring is also sitting on the turret and is reading a funny book, a collection of jokes, drawings, caricatures and humorous anecdotes. Whenever he reads a particularly juicy story he laughs loudly while we glance at the contents over his shoulder. But that aside, I also have to keep an eye on my gang while having a look at our surroundings. The summer landscape with all its lakes is quite nice and the towns and villages make a tidy impression. After dusk, during a clear night, there is a technical stop – it is so cold that Erdweg and Häring are putting on their coats; then, when the journey continues, they make themselves comfortable to catch some sleep. Little Erdweg rolls himself up in the fighting compartment amid ammunition boxes, luggage bags and fuel canisters, sleeping the sleep of the just right below the gun. Häring stretches out next to the fuel canisters on top of one of the hatches above the engine. A wonderful fan-driven warmth radiates from the other, open hatch, sending my wireless operator into a blissful sleep. Red-eyed and tired, only Theo and I keep staring into the night. One can see the sway of the light dots of the distance control lights of those in front, while looking back there is the long, long line of lights of vehicles following behind us. At all the crossroads and passage points there are beams of light of hand-held torches carried by the marshalling sentries who seem to appear out of the dust and haze like ghosts, before quickly disappearing behind us.

18 June 1941, Rastraum I – Forest, 7 kilometres east of Preussisch Eylau

I am sitting in a meadow in Rastraum I, in the hope I will be safe here from the huge swarms of mosquitoes. Down at the forest where the tanks are, it is just unbearable. We spent the rest of the night sleeping next to the tank after having taken great care to camouflage everything. Now we have finally stowed everything away properly, we are fuelled up and have conducted a last technical check.

In the evening the journey continues, further and further east. Just like yesterday, many aircraft passed over us. It is a nice and reassuring feeling to know that in the worst case we can always firmly count on 'help from above'. – In the morning the whole corps seemed to have met at the same water pump near a hunting lodge to wash. Charlie Zangenmeister needed a batman to hold his soap and mirror while he was shaving…

A tank of my platoon has broken down. Oberfeldwebel Oswald, gearbox damage. Tough luck! All the others made it. Because of the mosquitoes we have stuck neck scarfs under our caps in the style of the Foreign Legion. I suppose we'll resume the advance soon. In the meantime I have been ordered to give Russian-language lessons to some intelligent NCOs. The boss has gone to Königsberg, about 40 kilometres away. At 19.00 it continues. We drive across very dusty roads and have to put our goggles on. At 22.00 we arrive at a crossroads and have to halt to let another division pass. This grants us a few hours of sleep, so we all lie down in a roadside ditch. Too wet for my taste, so I had a kip on the engine deck of the tank. Wonderfully warm and a tremendous place to sleep.

24.00 – Start engines, mount! – *Marsch*! And so we continue through the night. In the evening we had been at Allenburg, marching through Wehlau through the night. A few kilometres before Insterburg we move into a forest and camouflage ourselves. Setting up a tent, we lie down to sleep. Except for Oswald's broken-down tank, my platoon is still together.

19 June 1941, Rastraum II – 10 kilometres east of Insterburg

In the evening in Rastraum II. A forest about 10 kilometres from Insterburg. Slept from 05.30 to 11.00. As soon as the sun is out it is getting way too hot inside the tent and one starts to sweat terribly. The mosquitoes, on the other hand, don't molest us that much. Only good that my blood isn't sweet. I hardly have any visible mosquito bites whereas some comrades have big, bulbous lumps where they have been bitten. A few moments ago I returned from the repair shop, where they are working feverishly. 'General Jack', head of repairs, sleeves rolled up, was standing at Oswald's tank, roistering away. I couldn't resist laughing. Feldwebel Wünsche, who was there with his tank as well, came over to us when he learned of our troubles getting a new gearbox. 'Jack is easy. You only have to praise the transport boxes he has designed for the Panzer IIs, if you do that he'll get you everything.' Wünsche, such a rascal. The road near the workshop is terribly busy. Military, military and more military – even the navy is present, probably naval Flak. The tank is supposed to be ready by 22.00.

20 June 1941

At the Groosten country estate. We spent one night here, unexpectedly we could do so in bed. Slept like groundhogs until 10.00. Seven of us had a wonderful breakfast of fresh black bread and eggs, followed – an hour later – by lunch with the Schattauer ladies, who have been great hosts. Who knows when we'll have a night like this again? The tanks are parked in a mosquito-infested forest which is part of the estate. We are very close to the border here. The Memel territory is only a stone's throw away. On the other side the quarters will be far worse than this one. We are sitting here with the youngest daughter of the house and I have to say that one can only marvel at the women and girls who run this place. She drives a tractor and a lorry and – when needed – acts as motorcar chauffeur of the estate. In command of a few prisoners of war of the 'Grande Nation' and a few old men, the ladies, mother and three daughters, run the 670 acres of the estate. When one thinks about the women at home, doing their duty in the Red Cross, in the Fluko* and in other positions – it is a joy to go to war for gals of that calibre. In the coming night we'll resume our advance, across the river,† towards our 'special duty'.

---

* Flugwachkommando – aerial observation command.
† The River Memel.

21 June 1941

In readiness in the deployment area. On our left, attached to a different infantry regiment, is Kleinjung and his platoon, tasked to attack along a forest aisle. Langenbruch is doing an extra turn attacking with the motorised parts of the infantry division across the right. We arrived at the final Rastraum. Severe rollicking from the boss because the marshalling of the tanks was conducted too slowly and with too much noise. We slept well in a mosquito-free and dry forest and then waited for further orders from the commander of the infantry. At the same moment at which the boss returned with the same, a dispatch rider brought the address of the Führer to the soldiers of the Eastern Front. It was read out by Unteroffizier Wassmuth, with his distinctive voice, standing in the Kübelwagen of the boss. The whole company was assembled around it, everyone was listening eagerly. Serious faces during the Führer's deliberations and while his final words were read out it was clear: the show would go ahead.

Off we went into our final deployment area 1½ kilometres in front of the border, passing artillery positions and huge storage dumps with fuel and oil. Everywhere we passed, soldiers of the infantry came running up to the road to see the tanks which would give them the support they needed to break the first resistance on the other side. Landsers of all ranks were avidly waving at us and, looking at them, I am sure that these are just the right men to 'do a turn with'. They are from a north German division, consisting of Oldenburgers, men from Bremen, Hamburg and Schleswig-Holstein. After a brief meeting with the commanders and our boss, we discuss some last details and then lie down at 22.30 to catch at least a few hours of sleep.

22 June 1941

Wake-up call at 02.30. It is arse-cold and we have been molested by midges. But never mind – it's a Sunday and today it's showtime. 02.50 fire up and forward march. Leutnant Schöner and his platoon in front, then the boss and the heavy platoon and myself – the new boy and his rabble – at the rear. From the Jura forest we advance against the Sakalyne position and the line at Burbiskio to the bridgehead of Gaure. As soon as we leave the forest, all hell breaks loose. I can't see anything at all, but I can hear some of our guys open up. Eventually I and my lot also reach the spot where nothing seems to be going forward any more, because a long anti-tank obstacle is halting the advance. A few bunkers are behind it, built from wood and sand, very solid work. The advancing infantry had been taken under fire from the bunkers. Several wounded and two or three killed were the result. The boss and a Panzer IV with Oberleutnant Leonhardt drove up to the wooden boxes and fired directly into the firing slits from a range of 5 metres and less. The fellows inside did not get out and kicked the bucket instead. They were Mongolians.

Once the pioneers had cleared a path, the company attacked this position and thus spared the infantry from an intense firefight. We assemble on the road behind the position. A few houses are burning, animals are running around in panic, a few Panje carts loaded with frightened children, bags and baggage stand around.* After a while we continue. I have fired on some bunkers, five shots in total, and a few single rounds from the machine gun into a trench. Got a rollicking from the boss as I had driven too far on the left, stayed too far behind and so on. No one is born a master, and I will get the hang of it soon. Oswald is in a foul mood as his wireless has stopped working. We now advanced on the positions at Gaure, but there we found several kilometre-long tank obstacles, consisting of dug-in wooden poles. Behind that several of those large bunkers made of wood and sand. They were taken under fire by our artillery, but didn't suffer a lot from it. So again the Panzer IVs went forward with Oberleutnant Leonhardt firing their shells at point-blank range into the bunkers' firing slits while the intensity of the artillery fire increased steadily. Whole salvoes of high-explosive shells crashed into forests, gardens and other places in which the Russian infantry sought to find cover.

Soon afterwards our infantry launched their attack and when they had reached the tank obstacle we started moving forward ahead of them. 1st Platoon on the right in a broad wedge, 3rd Platoon on the left in the same

---

* Panje became part of German soldier's lexicon from the First World War, when Polish and Russian civilians addressed them, adding 'panje' – master – to every sentence. German soldiers transferred the word to the speaker and panje became the German term for a Russian farmer or peasant.

manner and we, of the 2nd Platoon, in the gap behind them. The platoon of 6th Company gave covering fire, suppressing the bunkers from which a 7.6-cm gun and an anti-tank gun were firing. Then we raced forward to reach the infantry which was waiting for support in the area close to the bunkers. We could just drive through the tank obstacle by using the road. Russian stupidity. The brothers dig an anti-tank ditch and leave a bridge leading across it intact. They build a bunker line with a road cutting through the tank obstacle in front of it.

Once we had crossed we halted next to a trench. I was standing in the turret when suddenly there was a loud bang on the ground next to us. Our infantrymen threw themselves on the ground and chucked some hand grenades into the trench. I had ducked back into the turret and we advanced towards a homestead on a rise in front of us. I had the feeling that they might have their mortars up there. While doing so we traversed the turret to the rear, halted and fired a few rounds into the rear entrance of a bunker. The whole company had assembled at the homestead. The platoon commanders met with the boss and the infantry battalion commander to discuss how to conduct the advance on Gaure, our target of the day. Gaure was also the target of two other Kampfgruppen and we sought to make sure that we got there first. We were attached to another infantry battalion which was already advancing on Gaure. My platoon and an attached Panzer IV (613, Fw. Pfleghaar) were to support their attack. We caught up with the leading infantrymen in the forest, they mounted up and off we went.

First vehicle OFw. Oswald, followed by his group vehicle Uffz. Hünecker, behind which came the Panzer IV. I followed behind the Panzer IV and behind me came the second group with Fw. Giersig. When we came out of the forest we sent a few shells into the village to draw enemy return fire. With my gun I fired upon the small spire of the church, about 700 metres away. The first round hit, so I placed a second one a bit further down. One could see the shell detonating. There was a bunker marked down on our map of the defences, so we had to be careful when entering the village. When we got to the centre of the village the boss was already there. The infantry dismounted and looked for a crossing point.* There was a half-

---

*　Of the Sesuvis River.

finished bridge, with a ford next to it through which our vehicles could cross. Shallow entry, water about 30 centimetres deep, sandy ground.

At 14.10 our platoon secured the village exit. The infantry chaps were grateful for our support and joked and waved as they marched past our tanks. Then the members of my gang, together with the infantrymen who had ridden on our tank and Oswald's crew, finally cracked open the bottle of champagne in celebration of our first attack. To be honest, I expected a lot tougher going on that day, but then it was a lot harder for the infantry.

As we were standing in front of the furthermost position, we could witness an aerial combat above us. Eight bombers had flown in from the Red side towards Tilsit. The artillery observers who were sitting on the rear of my tank alerted me to the fact that something was 'brewing' above us. Three Messerschmitts then shot down four of the bombers. I saw how one Me engaged one of the heavy, modern bombers. Even through all the noise on the ground, one could hear the shooting above us. Flames erupted from the bomber's fuselage, the bird swayed to the side and then flipped over and fell towards the ground. A long trail of smoke still lingered in the air for a minute or so while on the ground there was a crashing sound. A thick, oily black cloud rose up and signalled the end of the Red bird. The advance continues towards the east.

23 June 1941 – written during a break in the fighting

I sit in the turret, a pair of binoculars hanging around my neck, headphones on and microphone at my throat. We marched from Stegvilai, a bridgehead across the Sesuvis, to Raseiniai. The dust is terrible. When we reach Kalnynai a messenger drives up to tell us that enemy armour has been reported from the right. We prepared for combat and turned our fronts to the right. I don't really believe there is anything coming. Ahead of us something is burning. It must be a bigger place, Raseiniai, I guess. The direction is about right. These giant pillars of smoke are the best signal to announce: we are here! Far better than any signal flare. They spring up wherever there is enemy resistance. If one fires his gun into one of those wooden Lithuanian shacks, those shanties catch fire immediately. Yesterday morning, during the attack on the first position at Sakalyne, we could clearly see the smoke rising up from Tauroggen and it was thick enough to block out the sun. Now, here on the road, I can see smoke rising up along the whole horizon. I wonder how long we'll have to stand here. Yesterday the phrase was 'Panzer forward!', today it seems to be 'Panzers out of the way!'

Günther Eggers has fallen. I have seen his grave. His Panzer II, number 601, stood on the roadside opposite, its right side holed like a sieve. 4.7-cm anti-tank gun. He got a shell through his back and was – and one can only thank God for this – killed immediately as the next shell had ripped off both of his hands. A short greeting, hands in salute to the cap, and our Panzer rolled on. Nearby was the grave of a dispatch rider. His steel helmet rested on the wooden cross, while on Günther's cross they had placed his field cap. How often had I put on this old battered cap with its scratched visor for fun in the casino. A year ago Günther and I had been at officers' school in Halle and with Günther I had driven to France to visit the regiment in the same year. I had lived together in Thorn and with him and Jochen Müllenberg I had celebrated New Year's Eve there. He was always with us young Leutnants when there were evenings 'of little actual importance' and we also sat together with him on our last officers' night at the casino at Freystadt and at 4 in the morning Oberleutnant Glässgen had forced him to make a speech on the 'behaviour of young Leutnants when facing a superior officer (especially Oberleutnants)'. Yes, Günther, a great friend of the Arbeitsmaiden, several of whom acted as waitresses on our company evening, has now fallen. His parents will receive a letter from the company commander, who is heartbroken just as we are. There will be a death notice in the local newspaper and his little, blonde sister will cry for him.

We, however, will march on, with him in our thoughts. He will fight at our side and his death will not remain unpunished!

At 11.00 we left Stegvilai and now it is 16.30. We are still standing along the road to Raseiniai waiting for enemy tanks which aren't willing to arrive. Some signals troops of the Luftwaffe have started laying an FF cable towards the front. They told us they did the same job in the forest behind us earlier. Just like peacetime work, not even wearing their steel helmets, they suddenly saw a column of fifteen Russians cross the road only a few metres ahead of them. A proper, little firefight developed. Casualties on either side: none! Two of the signals chaps, young Leutnants, have only just left after climbing up on my tank and asking all kinds of questions. Their interest dropped significantly after I had shown them the cramped inside of our fighting compartment, upon which they expressed the view that they wouldn't like to do our job after all. Still no sign of any Russians, but several of our bombers just flew past over our heads. One can easily recognise them all since they started carrying yellow markings.

24 June 1941

With our tanks we are standing a few hundred metres in front of Raseiniai waiting for our deployment. In the morning Russian tanks broke through and they had reached the southern exit of the village behind which we are now standing. A short while ago we were being shelled by Red artillery and had to fan out on the field to our right. The wind is carrying clouds of fine, white dust towards us which is thrown up by the vehicles of the baggage train driving down the road. By now we all look like flour millers, our black uniforms completely covered with dust. We wouldn't mind that, if we could only advance again! Our I. Abteilung suffered casualties. The 2nd Company was entirely surprised by much stronger Russian forces. Leutnant Bock, Leutnant Kasten dead; Hauptmann Burgstaller badly wounded. The CO of 1st Company, Oberleutnant Höher, was wounded and is expected to die.

The furthermost line is supposed to be about 4 kilometres in front of the village of Raseiniai. We lost a bridgehead across the Dubysa. The infantrymen here are not from northern Germany; it will have to be seen how they perform. The infantry with which we drove into our first attack were really good and attacked like 'Blücher playing with tin soldiers'. Heavy artillery is standing behind us and is sending one 15-cm shell after another towards the Russians. We can hear the heavy shells howling over our heads. Most of the Russians here are tough fighters, especially the Asians whom the Russians have thrown into the battle here. We saw that when we encountered the Mongols in the trench between the second bunker line and those who let themselves be killed by Leonhardt's 7.5-cm instead of surrendering. I witnessed another case at Stegvilai. For two hours our tanks had been standing there surrounded by our infantry. Nearby there were batteries of our artillery and the roads were full of our vehicles. Then suddenly, about 20 metres away from a Panzer II, a lone Russian soldier rises up from the tall grain and throws a hand grenade on the tank. When that bounces off the tank's side and detonates on the ground, the Russian takes aim with his rifle and fires on the tank's commander. The bullet went through his shirt collar and only grazed his skin …

'Whamm!' – for a moment there my pencil slipped when something exploded in the field behind us. But never mind. Five hundred metres behind, a heavy artillery battery keeps up a relentless fire. And among all the noise I can't help to notice that several small blue butterflies keep circling around my tank. Just like … [*continued in entry for 27 June*]

25/26 June 1941
[unbound fragment of text on loose pages, inserted here]

[…] find a way to get to grips with these big lumps.

During the night from 25 to 26 June, the Russian attempts to break through our positions on Hill 126. In the forest west of Bagno Ilgoszyly we tankers and the riflemen had him surrounded and now he tried to escape towards the north. But he didn't manage to achieve this and had to withdraw into the forest with heavy casualties. The many lorries they left behind on the roadside all went up in flames and thus, like torches, illuminated the path we would take during our counter-thrust which my men would have to launch at dawn.

A brief meeting of the leaders in front of the vanguard of riflemen and then the attack is rolling. Across Zvegiai, towards the village in front of it, through the forest behind it, towards Hill 141, where we are to link up with an element of 1. Panzer-Division.

[page missing]

The hull of the tank with the tracks is about 4 metres wide. Each track on its own is nearly 75 centimetres wide. The whole thing is camouflaged in green and up to the turret ring is over 2 metres high. At first sight it has quite a comical look about it, in stark contrast to all the thought which went into the design of our own tanks: all its armour is vertical and the entire tank is so awkwardly set up that it looks like a huge box on caterpillars – a 'shithouse on tracks' (mot.).

But we have learned that these boxes need to be taken very seriously as even 5-cm AT guns and 7.5-cm tank guns fail to have any effect on them. But one must just stay calm!

In front of the forest lots of hectic activity: '5-cm Pak to the front!' The commander of the lead tank climbs out of his vehicle and sprints towards the forest. At the same time I see how his Panzer IV is carefully rolling backwards. Damn! What is going on there? There is no shooting to be heard, but the entire advance has halted?! Via the radio I ask the commander of the lead tank, who has just returned, what is going on. 'There is a huge tank standing in a clearing!' is the reply. I tell him to take a fuel can to the enemy tank and to set it on fire, but he isn't keen to do that himself. I open the turret hatch and dismount, shove the pistol into one trouser pocket and a few egg-grenades into the other, and then sprint towards the clearing. There is an enormous Russian tank there and its 15-cm gun barrel is pointed menacingly on our small Skoda tanks, which look like dwarfs compared to that giant. My heart starts pounding against my chest – this is probably what a hunter feels like when he is suddenly facing an elephant.

It is standing about 30 metres away and up until now it has neither fired nor moved. It's just standing there. An eerie silence hangs over the clearing. A few riflemen make a jump towards the Russian tank, so I sprint towards it as well. In the corner of my eye I suddenly see a Russian infantryman rising from a foxhole, but before he can do anything he's hit by a burst from a machine pistol and collapses. One of the riflemen climbs onto the Russian tank, ignites a stick grenade and pushes it into the barrel of the 15-cm gun. There is the muffled sound of a detonation and fragments of the grenade fly out the front of the barrel. And suddenly there is movement inside the tank. I am standing so close to it that I can hear the voices of the crew inside and an odd clanking, metallic sound. I want to climb up the tank myself, but it is damned high to climb up from the rear, so one of the riflemen is helping me to get up. I am standing right behind the turret, when the crew suddenly starts to traverse it. They are taking aim on a Panzer IV. On the rear of the turret there are two holes from which two plugs are hanging from wire cables. I use my pistol and fire two shots into each of the holes before, as quick as I can, I climb in front of the turret, fish a grenade out of my pocket, ignite it and chuck it into the gun barrel. All that is happening in seconds. At the same moment I can hear the metallic clanking noise again. It must be the sound of someone opening and closing the gun breech.

The grenade fails to roll through, there needs to be some kind of blockage to cause a barrel burst, so I roll my second grenade down the barrel. Again there is a muffled detonation and there is smoke coming out of the two viewing mirrors on the turret front. Hurrah! That one must have hurt the crew! But there is still movement inside the turret. I think to myself that there must be another way to finish the brothers off, so I climb onto the turret using the two rungs welded to its side. In addition to the two protective covers for the optics, there is a flat turret hatch. But that is properly shut and doesn't move and while I am fiddling at the hatch, the crew suddenly traverse the turret.

For a second I can't help smiling – usually, if one wants to roll forward, one slowly accelerates a Panzer IV, but suddenly our good old 7.5-cm gun vehicle – seeing that the mighty 15-cm gun is taking aim at it – makes a jump forward, as if the driver had accelerated in fourth gear while being chased by the devil himself. And quite weirdly, while being traversed with the turret as if on a carousel, I have to think about my time as a recruit, when we were first introduced to the Panzer IV and all climbed onto the turret to be turned around on it. The little DKW engine did that very nicely. An odd thought in a situation like this, but it only lasts a second. I jump off the turret onto the hull. There is a cover on the top of the cylindrical mount of the gun and I ram another grenade into the gap between the two. Bang! The thing explodes and takes the metal cover with it. I take a look at it and realise that there is a slit there, probably to allow ventilation of the fighting compartment. A rifleman hands me a stick grenade, but that doesn't fit through the gap so I place it on top instead and pull the igniter before hurrying into cover behind the turret. With a bang it detonates and I suddenly notice that someone is pulling up the plugs on the metal wires with the intention of closing the holes through which I fired a moment ago.

I fire another round through a hole and the plugs fall down. But while I am doing so, I don't realise that my head is right in front of the other hole. One of the riflemen on the ground shouts, 'Careful! Watch out Herr Leutnant,' and while I am turning around there is an ear-deafening bank and a bullet whizzes past my ear. I am not hurt, what a tremendous amount of luck.

I jump off the tank and ask a Feldwebel of the riflemen for a few cartridges for my pistol. While I am loading my magazine, I see Feldwebel Oswald running across the clearing towards the mammoth tank with a fuel can in his hand. I shout over to him: 'That's how to do it,' and at the same moment he throws the opened can onto the tank's engine deck. The fuel runs into the grid protecting the air ventilation system and everyone waits until enough of it has run into the tank. Then Oswald throws a hand grenade on it. It bursts and a jet of flame shoots up! Hurrah! The tank is burning!

I have just started to look for my own tank, the good Skoda Super Sport, when all of a sudden the turret hatch of the giant tank lifts and a Red soldier starts climbing out. As he isn't lifting his hands and is showing no intentions to surrender, the riflemen shoot him dead. His body falls from the turret onto the earth below. Well, that has cost us more than enough time. I climb back into my tank. We start rolling and my radio operator signals that I can use the radio. I order my platoon to continue the advance and designate their next objective. Looking through my binoculars I have identified a Russian 3.7-cm Flak battery on the hill ahead and now we are charging it hell for leather. We are leaving our riflemen behind, they will have to catch up with us later. The Russian gun crews, however, have already made a run for it. The foxholes around the Flak guns are filled with equipment and weapons.

There are still some Russians in a house to the right, but before we can even get there some Kradschützen* come up and shoot two Reds with their pistols and then throw hand grenades through the windows. Everyone who is not already dead is burning to death now, as the wooden house with its straw roof is catching fire immediately. Via the radio I order my men not to fire on the Flak guns, they are worth a lot of money, and then the advance continues on the right side of the road past Tawtusze. But what is that!?

---

* Motorised, lightly armed and highly mobile infantry units of the army of the German Wehrmacht and the Waffen-SS which were usually integrated into the Schnelle Truppen or rapid troops.

'Driver halt!' – through the binoculars I can see a tank. Turret at 10 o'clock, 400 metres on the right of a cluster of houses; a Christie tank.

Turning the turret, I shout, 'armour-piercing shell!' and take aim through the optics. The loader shouts, 'Ready!' – and 'Wham', the shell leaves the barrel. With the binoculars I observe through the lowered turret hatch. Good, that one hit the turret. 'Another armour-piercing! – ready?' Erdmann, my loader, replies, 'Ready!' That one hits the hull at the rear, right into the engine and it starts burning. The advance continues, there is marshland on the right, so I warn the platoon via the radio. On the hill ahead I can see vehicles of 1. Panzer-Division. I fire a white signal flare, our Skodas are easily mistaken for Russian armour. I fire a second white signal flare and then we roll on to a hedgerow about 100 metres ahead. Theo Sander, my namesake, suddenly shouts: 'There is another of those heavy Russians over there!' And truly – just ahead there is a T-28, a giant tank with three turrets – it's easy to identify. 'Armour-piercing!' – 'Ready!' and 'Whamm!' right into the turret. Another into the rear of the hull and it starts smoking, and a third one for good measure. Faces blackened by powder fumes and uniforms coated with dust, we arrive on Hill 141. Lots of excitement and joy on both sides – the pincers have closed and the Russians are trapped.

I report our positions to the commander of the tanks of 1.Pz.Div. and then radio back to the company to make my report. There is time to survey the battlefield. On the right there is a Russian 15-cm artillery piece of the latest design and there is also a flamethrower tank which is burning brightly. A few deep gulps from our canteens – the Lithuanian heat makes the tongue stick to the palate. It has really been worth it. In the evening the boss treats each tank crew to a bottle of champagne.

03.00, 27 June 1941

My last sentence was supposed to continue 'just like the larks in the sky above us, whose song we can hear whenever the artillery is not firing'.

Now, in the cool morning air, the larks are singing again. I hope the cool temperature will help me to overcome my tiredness. We are standing on Hill 132 near Jagielaie while the whole of 6. Panzer-Division is rolling past us. It seems that after having formed the spearhead of the advance since Raseiniai, we are now being granted some rest. But even if that is badly needed, there is no one in the company who wouldn't rush to spearhead the advance through the whole of Russia, if our Oberst Koll asked us to do so.

Now that there is some time I will try to describe the fighting in the previous three days. I just didn't have the time to do so earlier. The last time I tried was when we were suddenly taken under fire by Russian artillery. In the afternoon we were shifted forward to the left of I. Abteilung, which was positioned on Hill 123 behind Raseiniai. Together with the 5th Company, we were to form a firing front to repel an ongoing enemy tank attack. Ready for battle! Quick radio check while moving off (working fine), and then full speed through the burning town. A petrol can falls off the tank in front of us and spills its contents into the street between the burning buildings. We were lucky that our tank didn't catch fire!

Rumbling crashes of explosions – it's kind of fun. Inside a tank one doesn't panic too quickly and we are used to those sounds. What exactly is happening is hard to judge during the approach. In a garden on the left side of the road a Leutnant of the artillery lies in the grass, his face covered with blood. His head turns towards us as we rumble past him, so he isn't dead yet. We continue to the reverse-slope position on the hill where the artillery is locked in heavy fighting with the enemy. On the right side of the hill in particular one salvo after another slams into the ground. One can't see where the fire is coming from. We platoon leaders are called to the boss, who explains that he wants our company to stop the ongoing enemy advance and to launch a counter-attack towards the Dubysa crossing. We move into a firing position on top of the hill and spot a tank which is slowly driving left to right along the forest edge at a distance of about 1,200 metres. Then it turns towards us. The artillery throws volley after volley towards the other side and now and then there is cheering and applause among us: bull's eye! That was right on target! Damn – missed it! The Russian tank, however, unfazed by the shells detonating around it, continues to advance slowly and calmly. Next to a barn on the edge of the forest we identified another large tank, which didn't move. Those things which the Russians have on the roll there seem to be quite enormous. The moving tank then suddenly turns and disappears into the forest on the horizon.

Then suddenly a shout over the wireless: 'Enemy tank from the left!' We take a look through the binoculars and identify yet another of those flat giants prowling through the terrain, heading towards the road on which Kampfgruppe Raus was supposed to arrive to assist us. The artillerymen throw their guns around. Sharpish work, one has to admire the speed with which they manhandle their heavy 10.5s – they order a few of our own tanks out of their line of fire and then open up. Again the shells fall very close to the target. The Landsers cheer after every near miss, but just like his comrade at the forest edge, the huge tank rolls on undeterred. Then it disappears behind a house about 1,500 metres away. Everyone is anxiously waiting for it to reappear. After about three minutes the beast rolls on and the 10.5s continue to fire. Major Zollenkopf is watching the show while standing next to my tank. I ask him if it wouldn't be better to let those things get a bit closer. And indeed the artillery is suddenly ordered to cease firing, but the Russian tank seems to have had enough and turns away towards the right. A few minutes later several Kübelwagen drive up the street towards us, the leaders of Kampfgruppe Raus – their vehicles following behind them.

And then finally we deployed to counter-attack. 'Bethke, forward march!' A long drive to the burning barn ahead, carrying the riflemen along with us. A few shots into the mammoth tank, which suddenly starts to burn. Then a few shots into an armoured target on our hard right, not visible to our driver and effects thus unobserved. The 7th Company is getting in our way. We drive around the edge of the forest to where the field kitchens are.* The infantry is only a few metres ahead of us when suddenly, on the left of our tank, a Russian stands up. The swine had pretended to be dead when our infantry came past him! That's an old classic, pretending to be dead and then firing from the rear. But that isn't a good idea when facing tank-men like us. Theo Sander! Floor the accelerator! Turn left and run over him! Problem solved. That man won't hurt anyone any more.

At that moment there were only machine-gun targets ahead of us, Russian infantry which crawled back into their trenches at our approach. The trenches zig-zag into the undergrowth of the woods. And again not a single one of them surrenders! Not a single Russian walks towards us with arms raised.

---

* Sander is referring to the Russian field kitchens.

Why is that? I even have learned how to say nicely: 'руки вверх!'* They have probably been scared by their commissars. But we can't debate with the soldiers of the Red Army. Instead we just gun them down. And then forward! Just forward! Our turret hatch is nearly fully closed, only leaving a small open gap, just to make sure that no one can throw a hand grenade inside. In a forest aisle to the right stand two enemy tanks which I have overlooked because I was in the lead and driving fast to aid the progress of the infantry. Oberfeldwebel Oswald and Unteroffizier Hünecker, however, fired on both, but drove on without waiting to observe the effect of their fire.

We were advancing, when suddenly there was a very hard, metallic and frightening bang. At the same moment I feel a sharp pain at the back of my head, for a moment my vision blacks out and then turns red. I try to find out what has happened to my skull. Above me a little bit of the edge of the turret hatch is missing, the observation mirror is smashed, the leather padding on the inside of the hatch torn and there is hole in the light signal apparatus in the turret. Tiny metal splinters cover the breech of the gun and the rest of the turret is strewn with fragments of leather and similar splinters. I ask Erdweg to tell me what's wrong with my head, which is hurting a lot. I feel the back of my skull and there is blood on my fingers. Everything seems to be all right, however, as otherwise there would be more blood. Erdweg confirms that there are only a few small scratches in the skin. Lucky me! One of my first thoughts after being hit is about making sure that we all stay in the tank. Stay calm! Is there a fire somewhere? If so, put it out with the extinguisher! But there is no fire and Theo is already driving on. Through the small gap under the turret hatch I search the surrounding area with my binoculars. And there! Enemy tank on the left! Turn the turret around! 'Erdweg – AP shell ready?' Erdweg has no clue what's going on but shouts a reply: 'Ja!' Theo needs to stop! It is loud, so I shout the order. Now I can take aim properly! My sting hits between the hull and turret. Visor 300, ready and fire! Then stand up quickly to observe the effect with the binoculars and down again. The shell has to be ejected manually and Erdweg is not ready yet. 'Erdweg! Faster, faster, faster!' Erdweg shouts 'Ready!' and with a 'bang' the shell leaves the

---

* 'Ruki werch!' – Hands up!

barrel and hits its target a bit further towards the rear where the engine sits. A flash on the other side, just a second long. I observe again through my binoculars and smoke is rising from the engine!

Next to the Russian tank, about 300 metres away, stands a German armoured half-track of the riflemen. It had withdrawn there to evade the Russian tanks. While I am still watching it goes up in flames too. I send a radio message to my platoon: 'Watch for friendly vehicles, only fire on enemy tanks and vehicles!' Then I receive the order: 'Hold fire! Stay in your position! Let the riflemen catch up!' In front of us something is going on, but I can't really see anything through the curtain of trees ahead. I open the hatch, which allows me to see the scale of damage on the outside. Two mirrors gone, the outside of the turret full of small scratches and scars, three petrol cans leaking and the fuel spurting out of the holes. There is a substantial hole in the engine hatch. The shot must have come from behind and from the same anti-tank gun which managed to damage the track of Oswald's tank. He radios in at the same moment to report that it was shot off by anti-tank gun fire from the left. He asks what he is supposed to do, but I have my own face smashed in, so what am I to tell him? 'Repair the damage if possible and drive on. If not, stay where you are.'

I then jumped off our tank to remove the shot-up petrol cans and to sort out the shredded tent squares and coats. After replacing the mirrors, we reversed the tank 50 metres and then took cover in a roadside ditch because the air was full of shells and projectiles fired blindly our way by the withdrawing enemy tanks. Together with some riflemen we take a look at our surroundings from the safety of our ditch. The Russians had done a lot of damage to the Kampfgruppe of I. Abteilung. In the rye field on our right there stand the remains of one of our 5-cm anti-tank guns. It has been crushed into the ground. Another one stands at the entrance of a homestead in front of our ditch. We can't see any German dead. The tank which we shot into flames earlier had now thoroughly started burning and suddenly its ammunition exploded. While I am taking cover I spot one of my old comrades of the staff, Unteroffizier Karl Buttler, whose Panzer II is parked nearby. We greet one another joyfully. I tell him how happy I am that I can finally participate in a war without being condemned to wither away on some other posting. 'Man! You are bleeding!' he said. 'Get a medic to put some dressings on that.' But I am not bothered by it. As long as my head isn't being cut off, it's all not too bad.

It continues. We mount up and overtake the advancing riflemen. No sign of the enemy tanks, which seem to have withdrawn behind a hill towards our front. Pedal to the floor, we are going after the Russkis. I drive on the right wing, the road on which the riflemen are advancing to my right. Along the road we come across the battered wrecks of the vehicles left behind by our Kradschützen. They had been among those elements of our troops who had formed the bridgehead across the Dubysa and which had been overrun by several of those mammoth tanks the Russians deployed. They had to flee as quickly as they could, there was nothing they could have done to stop these 'rolling shithouses'.

The riflemen rely on our tank company and if we don't stop during an attack by the Reds and if we don't sacrifice ourselves when necessary, then the riflemen and all the other people don't have an anchor and our line, our whole front, will collapse down to the rearward areas. Every Landser knows well what that would mean. And during this particular attack they can clearly see the effects of a panicked retreat. German vehicles everywhere, crushed motorbikes and Kübelwagen which had been run over by the giant Russian tanks which didn't even have to fire a shot. Crushed like old tins underfoot. Tanks of the 2nd Company stand around in the area. Abandoned by their crews to be captured by the Russians. Such a scene should never be repeated.

The attack rolls forward. My platoon is ahead of the lead elements of the 7th Company. One more quick stop to allow for a final quick look on the map which I carry in a leather satchel strapped to my chest next to my pistol. The Panje huts forward on the left – that must be Daugodai. The hill behind it must be opposite Point 121 and 2 kilometres further forward is the Dubysa! But what is that – a tank is standing on the hill to the left. We approach slowly, halt in front of a line of hedges and observe the enemy through it. Indeed! A Christie! 'Load armour-piercing', 'Ready', 'Fire!' and 'Bamm', right on target. Just to make sure it doesn't get to return fire, I fire a second round into it, which hits near the engine deck. By then several of our tanks have also spotted the Christie and take it under fire. Soon it is burning brightly.

I drive straight across the road, between the crushed remains of some armoured personnel carriers, to take a reverse slope position on the hill on the left. And behold! – in the distance, at 1 o'clock, 1,200 metres, the forest edge next to the barn frame. Enemy tank! I report this to my platoon, who immediately take it under fire. A few Panzer IVs engage the target as well. At this range they can do that with more chance of success than we can. We haven't got enough ammunition to keep up this firefight. Our remaining AP shells are soon spent. I soon cease firing, because even though every third or fourth shell we fire is on target, I can see them ricocheting into the sky. The Panzer IVs with their AP shells do not fare any better. Darn it! That must be a giant. 'Sander, Sander, Sander! – close up to 500 metres! For now, cease fire!' I transmit the same order to the rest of my platoon, as it doesn't make sense to engage those beasts at that range. From my turret I shout over to Werner Vielbaum of 7th Company (Tank 731), so he orders his men to cease fire as well.

We can't advance any further as we have to fuel up first. After driving cross-country the whole time, now is the time to stop. Damn! There are even more of the big brutes! And now the brothers are pulling back. If we can't catch up with them today we'll have to engage them again tomorrow, when they will be refuelled and resupplied with ammunition. Better to finish them now. But they are running. It is quite unbelievable, these super-modern chariots turn their tails from our Skoda Super Sports. Yesterday they just crushed our I. Abteilung under their tracks, and now they are running. It can't be clearer than that. It is not better weapons that decide victory. Again and again it is the all-conquering and never-tiring will of each and every member of our company.

Whether we like it or not, we have to form a hedgehog position, the company of riflemen between us. And then the lorries with fuel and ammunition have to be brought forward. In the meantime the Russian is disappearing. He did, however, pump a lot of fire towards us while we were doing so. Oberfeldwebel Oswald got a 7.6-cm shell through one of his mud-guards and one of his track-support rollers was ripped off. Leutnant Schöner has been wounded in the hip and in the hand. A Kübel drove him down to Raseiniai, from where an aeroplane will fly him back to the Reich. Through my partially closed turret hatch I can watch Obergefreiter Vossbein repairing the track of his tank. His crew had dismounted as well and were assisting him. They are doing that even though bullets keep swishing around. Vossbein and his commander Feldwebel Aures are not bothered. Soon they have fixed the track and now they are reversing the tank slightly. Ducked low, like an Indian on the warpath, Aures is marshalling his tank back to the road with hand signals. Soon the fire weakens.

The houses and barns 600 to 700 metres ahead of us have gone up in flames. Russian riflemen had taken position there and had opened a flanking fire on us from the half-right. The fires have chased them away. The flames of the burning Christie tank on our hill and the burning buildings on the other side form a wild picture. The Red artillery, probably self-propelled guns, are still firing upon us. An 8.8-cm Flak battery sets up its guns behind us and sends some well-aimed greetings across to the disappearing Soviet tanks. The chaps manning the 8.8s are held in high esteem among us. Leutnant Loede is one of the gun commanders. Numerous kills are marked as rings on its barrel.

The riflemen dig in, Leutnant Langenbruch and I secure the road while 7th Company takes up position on Hill 122. All remaining tanks have been withdrawn to make them invisible to those on the other side. The boss supplies me with a large cup of hot bean coffee and together with the riflemen I start organising the defence for a potential night attack. There is little sleep for me during the night. I don't believe that the Russians will come again. He didn't come, he retreated. At dawn, the Nebelwerfer-Abteilung which had been attached to us with revolver-barrelled launchers, fired a few salvoes of its rocket-propelled shells over to the Russians. The Landsers on our hill cheered them with astonished faces. Our Korps artillery also plastered the Dubysa crossing with 15-cm shells and our 7.5s joined the concert quite nicely. For us that was a nice and soothing feeling. To cover their withdrawal, the Russians fired on us as well. But that withdrawal could just as well be an assembly for another attack. As such I watched the proceedings like a hawk.

On the next morning (25 June) the Russians scored a few very nice hits with their artillery. The observation apparatus and the rangefinding platoon of the rocket-launcher battery snuffed it, as did some artillery observers. The commanders were nowhere to be seen. It was then that our boss and the leader of the riflemen on our hill decided to capture the Dubysa crossing themselves. If we really had to wait, then we could do it just as well in an all-round defensive position there. During the night the commander of the riflemen had sent two reconnaissance patrols down to the river and they had reported weak enemy resistance and the withdrawal of most Russian troops. The advance, which our two companies now conducted autonomously, led past the wrecks of armoured cars, lorries and guns. A hollow-way led to the river and the still entirely undamaged concrete bridge. On the other side a huge Russian tank had become stuck in a ditch. It had been abandoned and was entirely undamaged. We crossed without being challenged and deployed for all-round defence on the other side of the Dubysa. Then the 7th Company pulled past us and we were to lead them forward. I was so tired that I could easily have fallen out of the turret and it was difficult to keep one's eyes open anyway because of the terrible, ever-present dust. I […]

27 June 1941

In the all-round defensive position of 5th Company. Wake-up call at 02.30. At 03.00 drive to Hill 132 (Jagielaiei), where we wait for Abteilung Siebert. It doesn't arrive, as there have been some last-minute route changes. Instead we head down to the forest where 7th Company has been at home since Leutnant Vielbaum has been killed […] In the forest we then waited for the advance to continue. Theo Langenbruch and I want to visit Vielbaum's grave. He was killed as leading platoon commander in the woods behind Suypaiciai, west of Bagno Ilgoszyly. During an engagement with a Russian mammoth tank which was standing right on the main route of advance he was shot through the chest by a Russian sniper who had been sitting in a tree. His grave lies under a big wooden cross at a crossroads. I don't want to write a lot about Werner. He was a model reserve officer. Just how well liked he was is mirrored in the elaborate decoration of his grave. I always got on well with him. He was a pleasant comrade, not just a good one. Now that he lies here under the big cross, his bride in Soldin doesn't need to wait for him any more. Werner Vielbaum is the second officer of our Abteilung to be killed. I haven't asked any of his men of 731* about details yet. They are still tired from the battle. Together with 'Franz of the 7th' and Feldwebel Jordans, I took a look at the big Russian tank which had been blown up by our pioneers after the battle. It stood right in the middle of the road and blocked the advance of the 7th Company. A burned-out Christie and the wrecks of several other vehicles were lining the road.

In the evening we continued, I had washed myself before we set out again but after only fifteen minutes I was just as dirty as I had been before. It has been a terrible day.

Sunday, 28 June 1941

Drove all night and I am bone-tired. There is nothing to help one staying awake and there at several points I nearly fell out of the turret. Now we are the divisional reserve on the advance to Dünaburg and are standing in the forest behind Svedasai. Yesterday, thank God, the dust disappeared. It has been absolutely terrible up until a thunderstorm brought refreshing rain yesterday evening. We followed the route of 8. Panzer-Division and came across the traces of previous fighting. The crew of a Christie tank had apparently tried to run away; we found their dead bodies a few kilometres further on, in a cornfield where we had to halt to eat and drink. One gets used to the stench quite quickly, as terrible as it is. Far worse was what I found in an open building in which another light tank was standing. This had been blown up as well and parts of it had been scattered 500 metres into the landscape. That, however, also applied to the crew of the tank, whose burned bodies had been equally torn apart. There the stench of the flesh mixed with that of burning rubber, and I made sure we got away from that place as quickly as possible. We continued driving through the night.

The demands on the men – not only in battle, but also on the march – are enormous. Sometimes the medic issues a few pills which keep us awake and then it goes on, forward, ever forward, without light, eyes nearly glued shut with sweat and dust, thirsty, tired and unwashed. At 02.00 in the morning

---

* 731 is the tank number.

we came across a stream, the bridge across which was unable to take a load and where Oberleutnant Glässgen and his gentlemen were directing the traffic by screaming and shouting a lot. While they did so, the Adjutant and the commander with his dialect and all the company leaders butted on them. No need to describe the resulting chaos. On the other bank local Jews had been put to work by the locals. Serves those brothers right. Beards cut off, they can now repair the roads.

During the night we drove across an area where it hadn't rained. We were so tired that we failed to realise that, after a second thorough wash, we were now getting completely dirty again. At about 08.00 we stopped to refuel and have a small bite to eat. While doing so we realised that Oswald needed new rollers on the idler arms of his tank, but we drove on regardless. When we came through the area of Ymegala, we noticed that the Lithuanians were flying their old national colours from their houses: green–yellow–red. In the villages and smaller towns there were men in olive-green uniforms with swastika armbands in the Lithuanian colours. I asked one of those men, who to my surprise even greeted me with a 'Heil Hitler!', what kind of wild association he was a member of. With a radiant smile he explained that he was Lithuanian Partisan. A few of these weird forest Heinis even carried rifles and were guarding some scruffy Jews working on the streets.

The streets, by the way, deserve their own chapter. Unpaved, only covered with a layer of gravel and – in dry weather – a layer of fine, white flour-like dust. And even if there is only a little rainfall, then these roads – which are already marked red on our maps – turn into a mud bath of a kind no one in Germany could ever imagine. In the dust it's nearly impossible to breathe, while it takes a gust of wind to make the man ahead visible for a brief moment. Behind Svedasai, at about 18.00 we make a halt inside a pine forest. I have forgotten to mention that Theo Sander's vehicle broke down. Gearbox defect, the transmission shaft of second gear seems to be broken. As such I had no other choice but to pack up my things and then, accompanied by Feldwebel Funk, the commander of the maintenance platoon, drove over to the boss where I switched over to another vehicle. As Oswald's tank had broken down too, I had no vehicle with a transmitter any more. I hope Oswald's tank will be fixed soon as mine will take a while to repair. Fitting a new gearbox will take two to three days and when that is done, they will need to find us, which will take a few days as well. One tank, which had broken down two days before the first battle, was returned to us yesterday. It had taken Feldwebel Matussek and his driver Unteroffizier Esser a while to overtake all the vehicles ahead of them to catch up with us finally. The Russian, or rather Lithuanian or Latvian, roads are at least wide enough. There is enough room.

Every soldier on our side knows what the great objective of all this is. And not only that, they have all grasped the deeper sense of it. 'There, just look at it! All that rich soil and there are acres and acres of it. But it's all so badly cultivated! In this country we feel like the Goths and Vandals once did, when they migrated from their overcrowded lands and, weapon in hand, sought new soil for themselves! If these people here are incapable of cultivating the land, then they have no claim on it! Just look at the sheep and goats, so squalid and ill-bred. Bring German settlers here! They know about cultivation and animal breeding.' There are a lot of things to see here for the Landser, even though life is not the same as it was in France. It is, however, a great political education for them for they can learn about the wider plans of the Führer. They can witness the difference between German culture and the state of affairs in Lithuania. They can see the women here going to church in their dirty and grey gowns. Most walk barefoot. Some have wooden shoes, which they often carry in their hands even when going to church. Hats seem to be unknown. At best the womenfolk are wearing a white headscarf, but even this is usually dirty and grey. Scruffy cads, the lot of them, and many a Landser can't help comparing them to the French women whose acquaintance we made last year.

The children look equally squalid. Wild hair, unwashed and just as dirty as we are after three days on their terrible roads. With their tattered clothing they are lining the roads, with dirty fingers shoved up their noses in devotion, marvelling at us as we roll past them in our tanks. The men are also ragged and dirty. They all wear breeches even when they walk barefoot. Footwear seems to be more commonly worn by the men. Most men wear high boots made of soft leather, sometimes the shafts are made of felt. They wear sheepskin jackets or similarly tattered jackets and vests. The Russian rubashka is not often seen here. A clean-shaved man is rarely encountered – if one is spotted, he is probably coming from a funeral or a similarly important event.

1 July 1941

Today we receive money! Always a great day when you are in the army. But what are we supposed to spend it on here? Yesterday night we were in the process of going to sleep, but were still standing around for a while with a group of older Feldwebel. The boss joins us, and we chat about the heavy tanks we encountered, the fighting that lies ahead and what one could do with this beautiful country. All kinds of vehicles race past us down the dirty road and suddenly our 'war correspondent' pulls up on his motorbike and shouts: 'Prepare to move out! Commanders to HQ!' We didn't quite know if we should be delighted about the news or annoyed, because it had cost us a night of well-deserved sleep. In a jiff the tents were pulled down and packed up, our outfits prepped for the night march and vehicles made ready. Corporals and Feldwebel in the courtyard were in a boisterous mood. Amid all the jokes and inanities someone suddenly started to hum a tune. One man after another joined in and soon everyone was loudly singing the song of Marushka the Polish girl.* Then Krautwurst, Leutnant Schöner's driver, shoved a harmonica between his lips, upon which it went on full tilt!

The farmer who owned the farmstead we had moved into with our company was a Latvian who, during the World War, had been held prisoner for seven months in Limburg an der Lahn; he stood at the door with his wife and listened to the music. His eldest daughter, a squeaky-clean, intelligent girl of about 17 years whom I found exceptionally attractive, was standing with them. During the day I'd had ample opportunity to watch her at work. Even with all the heavy agricultural labour on the fields and in the stables, she kept herself well groomed, and some of the more inquisitive infantrymen even managed to watch the girl through their binoculars while she was bathing herself in a stream down in the valley. Now that beautiful girl, whom I had taken to my heart, suddenly approached me with a bunch of sweet-smelling wild roses. She said something in her own language which I didn't understand. I did, however, realise that it was something good and nice and I felt it too because she kept holding my hand with hers for quite a while in an affectionate manner. I have no idea why these people here

---

* The song is 'In einem Polenstädtchen'.

suddenly wish us a good journey and lots of luck. The man had of course learned a bit of German during his time as a prisoner.

Apart from that I have realised that the whole area on the Latvian side is a lot cleaner and more cultivated than on the Lithuanian side. The cattle in the fields are premium, brown breeding stock, which is quite a contrast to the small, ugly and unprofitable goats kept in Lithuania. The wooden houses are clean and not covered with rotten straw, but with proper shingles. In general the properties here are more spacious, cleaner and better looking. The farmer offered us fresh cow's milk as soon as we arrived and soon after brought out two finely cut glasses which he filled with home-brewed beer drawn from a pretty ceramic pot. In return he asked me for some cigarettes as he would love to smoke but could never get any tobacco. He was delighted when Unteroffizier Hagemann issued him with two large packets of Russian cigarettes. Franz, the tall football player, without saying anything, gave him a large pack of tobacco which had got damp. He didn't really understand what we said, but he kept lifting his cap while saying 'Danke sehr, Danke sehr!' while Frank for the briefest of moments lifted his cap to return the greeting. We then moved out, into the pouring rain, the white roses the girl had given me attached to the front of my tank.

A moment ago I had a swim in the Düna which, between Dünaburg and Jakobstadt, forms a respectable stretch of water, 300 to 350 metres wide and quite deep. The banks everywhere are nice, sandy and well suited for swimming. The current isn't too strong and doesn't carry a swimmer too far away. The western bank, from Dunava to here, is lined with old German positions from the World War. With our tanks within some of those trenches, we waited for the Russians in the morning, but none had shown up.

The whole thing last night was a joke. With two battlegroups we marched through the whole night, reaching the Düna at 04.00 in the morning and an hour later we were sent into a forest to 'deal' with 2,000 Russians. On a map printed in 1884 the forest looked enormous, but in reality it had already been thinned out quite a lot and was riddled with small settlements. Our 7th Company with II./Schützen-Regiment 114 advanced from one side and our company with I./Schützen-Regiment 114 from the other. The result: from 06.00 to 12.00 not a single Russian was found! My platoon had been left behind near a road as a reserve and thus I was able to take two Russians prisoner, who had been walking down the banks of the Düna. I sent three men of the recce platoon out to search the houses nearby and the only thing they could find was 3 pounds of butter. And for that result, sparked by the omnipresent fearfulness of the divisional staff, we had to sacrifice a night of much-needed sleep. Instead we raced through pouring rain, wasted hours waiting and burned a lot of much-needed fuel which we could have used elsewhere.

We are now standing at a Düna crossing and wait, wait, wait. It has only just stopped raining and everything is already covered in dust again. The company together with the boss is having a bath in the Düna. I have to stay with the vehicles in case there are any surprises 'from above'. From here I can see how some of them have swum across to the other side, where they have refloated an old boat. I can hear their shouting and cheering all the way up here. The crossing point must be nearby, there is Flak on all the heights watching for Red bombers. Now and then a few of them appear. On Sunday evening some flew over our farmstead. They were all shot down by a young Leutnant in a Messerschmitt. Just as the last one went down in flames, he himself was hit by a rear-gunner and had to force land his machine nearby. He was lightly wounded in the head. The three bombers had been his first victories.

We crossed the Düna today over a pioneer bridge near Livani before continuing our advance towards the east. Tomorrow we'll advance further with the Vorrausabteilung* of the marching group Oberst Koll. At this point long columns of riflemen, horse-drawn troop carriers and whole companies of infantry roll past the farmstead in which we have taken a defensive position. I can't help noticing that there are large numbers of captured Russian lorries in use. Wiehler, a Feldwebel on the ammunition lorry, is supposed to gain his assault badge with me. I am happy about that, the man is not bad. Tomorrow we will continue. Who knows if the Russians will stand and fight.

---

* Lit: 'advance detachment'.

Thursday, 3 July 1941

For once I had slept well. Up until 8.00 a.m. Szepanski, the driver, Tutasz, my assistant gunner, and Müller, W., the wireless operator and I, the commander of '523', slept like the night owls. Then the advance resumed over the little bridge, past the farmhouse, a few wounded Russians were treated by a few Latvians. Behind the farmhouse stood a Christie tank which Kleinjung, taking revenge for the fallen comrade Eggers, had destroyed during the night. We advanced along the road towards Rezekne, where groups of prisoners came towards us in groups of two and three at the sides of the road. For them the war was over. Such a rabble of regional soldiers is never reliable. The Russians knew this when they put the Latvians to work in the baggage trains without issuing them arms and ammunition. The Latvians and Lithuanians wear a different uniform from the Soviet Russians. Currently the latter are wearing the rubashka as their summer uniform, a canvas shirt of earthy brown – khaki colour. The Latvians and Lithuanians can be recognised by their long haircuts and the olive-green uniforms with yellow or red piping.

Having passed through Rogovka, we turned towards Karsava, where our Kampfgruppe was tasked to capture a supply train, but we were too late. The Luftwaffe had been quicker. There was still fighting in Karsava. Both our Panzer IVs were moved to the heights at the junction to Baltinava and started firing quite a few shells into the village. Would have loved to capture it to find some spoils. But that was impossible as the road of advance diverted just in front of the village and railway line. Only the 8. Panzer-Division would pass through Karsava. We would only touch its road of advance near Gauri, crossing it once, to continue our own advance towards the Latvian–Russian border. But even before reaching Gauri we were tasked to support Aufklärungs-Abteilung 6, which was employed as our Kampfgruppe's advance guard. We advanced and received instructions. Aufklärungs-Abteilung 6 had encountered enemy movement on its right flank on the main road from Karsava to Augspils (Suwalki to Petersburg). We were tasked to hit the flanks of the units retreating from Rezekne across Karsava. Again I was to advance on the right wing. This I did until we arrived at the main road, on which we rushed towards the retreating Russians. There was swampy ground on the right side of the road which forced me to keep behind the boss on the road itself, which was lined with the wrecks of lorries taken out by aerial bombing. We followed it for about 5 kilometres without encountering an enemy and then turned around. Some Landsers, following their unfailing instincts, had assembled around one of the lorries where, next to some bales of cloth, they had found a few boxes of pralines, biscuits and chocolate. Five prisoners have been rounded up and now sit in the trench next to the road. We hurry up and chuck all the boxes onto the tank before heading back to the crossroads, when – what the devil is this? While we are distributing the spoils, a Soviet armoured car races towards us across the road and not one prick is manning the guns. Aures's platoon was supposed to be keeping watch, but they apparently failed to do so. One does become cursedly neglectful out here. Then the armoured car is among us, something flashes up, there are shots and crashes, and the vehicle rams itself into a trench 50 metres ahead of me on the left side of the road. The turret hatch flies open and a man in a blue overall jumps out. I open fire on him with my pistol. A few shots and my magazine is empty. Funkmeister Moser hands me a new pistol and then off we charge towards him. But the fellow has escaped, just like our five prisoners, over the cornfield into the forest. What should we do with prisoners when the Russians run away at the next best opportunity? One learns over time.

Following that we were allocated our tasks for the night, as there was an expectation that we would be facing enemy forces pushed out of Karsava by the 8. Panzer-Division. Prisoners confirm that there are still several tanks and a battery in the forest around the area of the trig point. We might just be a company, without pioneers and artillery, but we are the 5th and we'll give the Soviets a warm welcome. My platoon is allocated to Leutnant Eggert. Together we'll form the lead element. My vehicle is the furthermost on the left side of the road, which descends slightly from Ladrinki towards Karsava. Giersig is on my right, Unteroffizier Schirmer behind me. He is to give us covering fire. One of his machine guns isn't working. On my left there are three more tanks, two of them of the Abteilung's light platoon. Then a group of pioneers is attached to us after all. With six K-rolls and a row of Rampenminen* they create a barrier which the Russians won't be able to pass.

---

* K-rolls, an abbreviation of Klaviersaitendraht-Rolle, were concertinas of plain wire. Rampenminen were improvised anti-tank ramp mines consisting of explosive

85

On the right of it is a marshy hollow, and next to that a large bomb crater. The left is covered with brushwood. Soon our tanks are well camouflaged. But it takes all my rollicking skills to get the stubborn assembly of Tutasz, Szepanski and Müller, W., to camouflage my tank well enough. That I did the right thing to focus so much on camouflage would become clear throughout the night and the next morning.

By the way, I have to point out that it was my assistant gunner Tutasz who destroyed the armoured car the other day. He was still in the vehicle and had quickly jumped into the turret to use the always loaded gun. The Russian had then fired on the tank of the boss, hitting the upper edge of the turret. The boss, standing next to the tank, got a splinter in his foot and some flying rivets lightly injured his head.

Anyway, now all the crews are inside their vehicles waiting with bated breath for the expected Russians. Now it is gradually getting dark. We are being kept on tenterhooks. I look at my watch: 23.45. And then suddenly, in front of us, a cloud of dust which, even though the road is littered with abandoned vehicles, is quickly coming closer. The fellows in their lorry come closer and closer. Now it will run unto a mine and – crash! – with a loud detonation the thing is blown sky high. I see how a man is thrown into the ditch, but he continues crawling on. We open fire on him. Then two more men jump off the remains of the vehicle. The buggers! Now out of the tank to catch the guys before they report our position. I search the area with Jürgensmeier, Feldwebel in the reconnaissance platoon, and in the darkness we manage to catch two of the Russians; one has managed to get away. Jürgensmeier escorts the two to the rear and I get back into the turret and wait. It is gradually getting lighter when a second cloud of dust approaches. We let it close in. The ramp mine barrier is gone and the pioneer group has gone back to fetch new mines. That means we have to shoot and open up with our machine guns. There is only one man on that lorry, who stops his vehicle right at the wreck of the previous one and then tries to crawl away. On the right of his vehicle is a large fuel barrel which has fallen off the other lorry and that suddenly ignites and the burning fuel

---

charges fitted with pressure fuses, laid under a sloping board or ramp at railroad crossings, bridge approaches and similar sites.

scorches the legs of the Russian, whose crawl ends right in front of our tank. The burning barrel then also sets fire to the second lorry, which is loaded with ammunition, tank ammunition, and now detonates about 75 metres in front of us. The explosion sparks a chain reaction, blowing up all the fuel canisters and barrels on the lorry which has been stopped by the mine. A tremendous spectacle; similar fireworks I had – at best – only ever seen at Hitler's birthday and during the Russian night attack on Hill 121 at Zvegiai.

Now it is Friday, 4 July 1941

02.00: We kept staring into the night. Maybe we would be able to finish some tanks off again. It clears up sufficiently for us to use the optical sight for aiming. And then the tension increases when there is movement in the far distance. Clouds of dust are closing in and it is good that the wrecked vehicles in front have ceased burning so I am not blinded by the flames any more. And now the dust clouds are coming closer. Through the binoculars and from my elevated position I have a clear and uninterrupted view for about 3 kilometres. The road is packed with vehicles; there seem to be no tanks. The vehicles are all camouflaged against aerial observation and it looks as if there is a whole forest rolling towards us. I wonder: if they will all dismount and launch an infantry attack! The boss radios in: 'Keep calm and let them come closer. Hold your fire.' And the Russians are coming closer and then halt their lorries 150 metres in front of me. I can hear cursing and shouting and then several of them walk right towards me. They have not spotted me yet, my camouflage is too good. Then they start pointing fingers at my position. I let them come closer, while at the same time I am listening to the boss on ultra-shortwave. The Russians are wearing wide coats and round peaked caps. Only a few carry rifles and steel helmets. Most of them look like officers. Now their group splits up and five walk towards the burned Russian, who is lying in a trench 75 metres ahead and is still alive. They look at the two scorched lorry wrecks and speak to the wounded man. Then they start shouting and look directly at my position. They appear to be high-ranking officers, among them a man in a black uniform, apparently a commissar. And while the brothers are still standing there, shouting and gesticulating, the firing starts.

A truly infernal concert! An MG 34 on my right fires first. It must be that of Oberleutnant Eggert. In the same second I too pull the trigger and keep firing, belt after belt. There are plenty of mass targets on the road. On my left the Panzer IIs of the light platoon of the staff company pour flanking cannon fire on the lorries more than 500 metres away. The Russians in front of my vehicle drop as if they have been mown down with a scythe. A bit further back the Russians try to get into cover in some bushes on the roadside. A few high-explosive shells for them. They now try to get from the bushes, across a field, into a forest about 400 metres away. On a sports field it takes about a minute to run 400 metres. Running for one minute through the stream of fire of the three MG 34s of the Panzer IIs will most likely be their end. And trying to cover the distance in a crawl is sheer madness. Not a single one of them makes it to the safety of the wood. Some turn around, seeking safety in a desperate infantry attack towards the right where the baggage train, Aufklärungs-Abteilung 6 and the two Panzer IVs of Oberleutnant Leonhardt are. The whole assembly is now welcoming the Russians, who are storming forward under shouts of 'Hurra'. When they are 100 metres away the two Panzer IVs start sending 7.5-cm high-explosive shells towards them. But the Russians continue coming. When the baggage train and Aufklärungs-Abteilung 6 are withdrawing due to 'lack of ammunition', the Panzer IVs pull back as well. Due to that a lot of Russians are able to work their way by foot into the great forests in the north to rejoin their own troops. The lorry column, however, is ours. The vehicles are mostly undamaged, some have been abandoned with engines running. Now some Russians try, at a respectful distance about 1,000 metres away from our elevated position, to turn some lorries around and drive away. But that is well in range of our machine guns, so I send a few belts into their direction. That is effective. As soon as someone rears his head in the roadside trenches, the meadows or the road itself – ratatatat – a few salvoes, and it's sorted. Some of the gunned-down Russians in front are still moving. Szepanski finishes them off with a rifle.

And then, quite suddenly, aircraft! We hear the bombs whooshing down, and for a moment all of us inside the tank are quiet. Where will they fall? We can still hear them whooshing down through the air and then – boom! – 150 metres away they come down – boom! – one – boom! – two – boom! and so it goes on until the sixth has exploded. Tutasz is panicking. He wants to get out of the tank, because the rascals up there could hit us. But inside the tank we are far safer than outside in the foxholes. Just as we have finished counting the impacts, another of those vultures approaches, dropping its eggs into the meadow on our left. They, however, will be more harmful to his comrades than to us 200 metres away. Then the spectacle is over and a few fighter planes turn up. A reconnaissance plane makes an appearance as well. I fire a white signal flare to mark our position. The sun is rising. A few men walk forward to look for anyone who might still be alive. Two Russian Lieutenants are. I ask the boss what to do with them and he sends an ambulance motorbike to pick them up. Leutnant Langenbruch takes my tank to drive forward to film the whole junkyard ahead of us. In the meantime I am enjoying a few of the captured biscuits and take a few swigs from my canteen. Gosh, I am thirsty! I have now taken a seat in the foxhole in front of my tank. That way I am less of a target for the more fanatical Soviet Russians in the area. The two wounded Russian officers have gone when Oberleutnant Bethke and everyone else who is staying up there in the farm of the German-speaking Latvian woman comes down to have a look at what has happened.

On the right there is a basket case who can't walk. A bit further on another one who hasn't gone stiff yet. Damn, the dog has just pretended to be dead! I kick him in his arse and then push him back to the rear, up to the farm, where a large number of prisoners are slowly gathering. While I am taking a closer look at a Russian who shot himself, a man wearing a square patch with a thick golden stripe, the boss and Leonhardt have discovered a still-breathing Russian in a waterhole ahead. We are trying to pull the poor bugger out. The boss is bending down and at the same moment the wretch pulls a gun, a revolver, out of the water and fires on the boss, staring at us with a hate-filled face, contorted into a satanic mask. Oberleutnant Bethke throws himself to the ground and the shot misses him. I pull out my pistol and send a bullet through the Russian's skull while at the same time he is slumping down under a burst of bullets from Unteroffizier Buttler's machine pistol. I am livid with anger! Such pigs! We are trying to help the wounded and they fire upon us! This is the price one pays for our damned humanity, because of which we are treating the scum in way too soft a manner. I take my pistol and fire a round through the head of another wounded guy. With a stertorous breath, the swine collapses. If I had the pretending Russian before me now, he could have saved himself the effort of walking to the collection point. I am such an idiot, having preached to my men again and again that we are the nation of culture and that we have to act gently. But here we get our comeuppance for being soft! And we are not alone – at the Dubysa bridgehead, after they had pushed us back with their super-heavy tanks, they had put bullets through the heads of our riflemen. And then the sadists carved the hammer and sickle into the chests of our fallen.

Nearby a bomber is shot down and goes down in flames. A man manages to bail out with the parachute. After the Russian has come down, and our Landsers are walking up to him to take him prisoner, he draws his pistol and fires on them, so he gets what he deserves. Another one, also coming down with a parachute, throws a hand grenade even before he has touched the ground. A second aircraft is shot down in flames, pulling a long trail of smoke behind it. During its fall, the air-gunner stays at his machine gun and keeps firing at a German column until the machine impacts on the ground. The brothers we are facing here are active troops of the best Leningrad regiments and they offer resistance to their last breath. It will take a long time for them to beat their commissars to death, as they did at Minsk, and maybe it won't happen at all. Anyway, the business with the wounded has been a lesson. From now on there won't be any humanitarian stupidity any more.

In the evening I lay, freshly shaven and washed, at the entrance to a potato cellar on the grass in the garden. I had fallen asleep while writing in my diary. Suddenly a crescendo of crashing and whooshing sounds around me. Branches splinter apart, little fountains of earth spurt up and then a pair of Ratas roars over our heads. The beasts have strafed us with their machine guns and, as if by a miracle, none of us was harmed. We keep resting for another hour before we again hear the roar of engines. Three bombers come over and drop their eggs close to the farm's garden. What a mess! Shortly afterwards two more fighter aircraft turn up, but this time our quad-Flak has deployed about 1,000 metres away, just at the spot where the two Ratas now turn around to attack a column of our vehicles. The first is shot down immediately, the other bumblebee falls a few kilometres further on. Seems that our Flak is able to do more than lay down curtain fire and finish off tanks and bunkers. I have now witnessed that several times. And after the recent scraps with those rolling shithouses of the Reds, we are all quite fond of our 8.8-cm Flak-Pak. A kind of moral backbone for our Landsers.

When in the late evening the endless columns of our division rolled down the road that is being secured by our company, we received a special mission. At Baltinava, about twenty Soviet tanks threatened our rearward lines and our divisional staff was feeling especially threatened again. As such we were relieved of our well-deserved sleep to roll out and look for them. On one hand, that was quite interesting as we were introduced to a new type of pioneer ordnance: rocket shells, which only have a minimal muzzle blast and which we could literally see flying through the air. The propellant charges at the rear of the huge coffers were spewing fire and in a steep arc they were falling into the forest in which the tanks and some infantry were supposed to be. An eerie crashing and bursting followed! Bits of wood, branches and earth were thrown up, spinning into the sky. These shells were incredibly powerful.

Back on the road, Hauptmann Saalbach came towards us in his Horch. At the side of the road stood two of the six buckets which Leutnant Loeck and his Flak hadn't finished off. He had destroyed thirteen of them with his Flak and with hand grenades during an armed patrol. Then we arrived in the area where the buckets had broken through. Visibility was low and I had to make an effort to see anything at all. In a trench ahead, however, I could make out a dark silhouette. That had to be a tank! I took a look through the binoculars and, yes, it was a tank and it had got stuck! I tried to take aim through the gunsight but could not see anything. Close in, have another look and try again – but again not able to see. A third try, get even closer, take a rough aim at the silhouette in the trench. Load armour-piercing shell. 'Ready! – Fire!' We don't have tracer ammunition so I can't see where our shot landed. It was clear that it had missed. A few more shots! Sod it! – none of them hits the target. On the left I then spot a Polski tank, one of the ones that the Russians had taken from the Poles – a few rounds on that too! My driver, the fidgety sock, is beginning to see enemy tanks left, right and centre, but observing and correcting the fall of our shot – that he can't do! I am fuming with anger – and even more so when Tutasz shouts over that we have run out of armour-piercing shells. There is nothing to be done with high-explosive. Theo Langenbruch is next to me and has more ammunition. But he also only manages to score two hits on the Polski tank.

Behind us an infernal fusillade has started. Our Panzer IV, having heard something about tanks on our left, spotted a dark shadow at the edge of the forest adjacent to us and started pumping shell after shell into the trees. Such an idiot! There is nothing there. Leonhardt is a nervous mess! Result: a Skoda tank behind him confuses Leonhardt's wild muzzle flashes with that of the enemy and fires! And he aims well! Right into a fuel canister, which bursts violently apart. At the same moment the Panzer IV fires again and the resulting muzzle flash ignites the fuel! The crew of the Panzer IV bail out – there is wild shouting and screaming. Silhouetted against the brightly burning flames I can see the crew members jumping off their vehicle. Quick-witted, one of them starts putting out the flames with the fire extinguisher. I drive further forward, call over to Theo that I am getting out and grab a few hand grenades. Theo Langenbruch doesn't want to join, he believes it all to be useless. But I then see how Leutnant Loeck is sprinting towards the tank on foot, so I get out too and join him. A few hand grenades next to and in front of the tank – just in case, should any of its crew be there. A turret hatch is standing open, a clear sign that the crew has buggered off. Then something shoots at us from the trench. One hand grenade and the bastard is quiet. I also tried to lob a grenade into the turret hatch, but the thing misses. Leutnant Loeck now tries and climbs up the tank to make sure it doesn't miss. What a shite day! It is getting cold and there is dust everywhere. I bid my farewell to Loeck, who himself is based at the railway embankment. And then we drive back, past the long column of riflemen and anti-tank guns, all of whom have no one to engage any more. We are going back to Ledinki, where we arrive at 01.00 in the morning – dead tired and unsuccessful.

5 July 1941

I am livid with anger! Yesterday the divisional command post alerted us that there were about twenty enemy tanks and masses of Russian infantry reported in the forest of Baltinava. We were now supposed to do some tidying up. After 40 kilometres on dusty roads we arrive there, only to find that Leutnant Loeck of 3./Flak 3 has already destroyed twelve of them with his gun and finished off another six with hand grenades during a combat patrol. Six tanks had escaped, and we were now supposed to take them out on the way back from our 'glorious special operation'. I was lucky enough to be in the lead position and, what happens? It is slowly getting dark and even though I can still see through the binoculars, I can't see anything through the optics, and most of the twenty shells I fired on two Russian tanks which had suddenly appeared ahead missed. One was a Polski tank, the other a funny machine-gun tank with two turrets. The crews had bailed out and fled, but I could not prove that any of my shots had hit. A very bad end to a day which had started in quite a promising manner with the destruction of some Russian lorries. But one thing at a time, as it all started with the march to Vilani.

In the morning at about 03.00, after waking up, the routes which would lead us deeper into Russia were announced by the boss. Via Livani on the Düna, the route led us towards Vilani. We had always wondered why the Russians never blew up any bridges when even a piss-filled ditch would have stalled us for hours. And now at Vilani, for the first time, the bridge had disappeared and our whole advance ground to a halt. On that morning I was not lead platoon, but arrived later, which meant that I could only follow what went on ahead via the radio. A group of motorcyclists of the regimental staff of Schützen 114 had driven right into a line of Russians and our lead tanks were now on the way to bail the lads out. When the Russians then retreated towards the left – towards the destroyed bridge – we had already resumed our advance in a west–east direction trying to get to Welonen in a roundabout way. I, Giersig, Schirmer and Wichler – who had only caught up with us later due to a technical breakdown – now formed the tip of our advance to Vilani. It was raining heavily. The rest of the marching group was only to follow us if the bridges at Ustrone and Veemurani were still intact. My platoon had been tasked to reconnoitre. To assist us, we had been assigned a pioneer Leutnant and a group of riflemen under Leutnant Jung. It all went okay until we arrived in front of Vilani, where suddenly there was firing going on. Again it was impossible to see who was firing upon whom. Giersig drove in front of me and the rain was pouring down. It was hardly possible to identify a target through the optics and even less so through the binoculars, which were immediately sprayed with rain.

A few Russians were making a run from a house ahead on our left when Giersig suddenly opened fire on the crossroads 400 metres in front of us. He had spotted an enemy anti-tank gun, which I would not have spotted with the best will in the world, even though I was right behind him. When the shooting in front died down a little, we drove forward and when we arrived at the crossroads the first elements of our march group arrived behind us. I shared Giersig's joy at his well-aimed shot, which had damaged the armoured shield and the sight of the anti-tank gun just at the moment when it had been moved into a position to engage us. Together with Oberleutnant Feige's riflemen, we drove further through the town before turning right into the advance road which would take 6. Panzer-Division to Dricani.

When exiting the town we halted to allow the rest of our Kampfgruppe to catch up, as ahead of us the Russians, with a strong motorised force, were withdrawing under the protection of some armoured reconnaissance cars. From where we stood at the town's exit, we could see one of them observing us from the reverse slope right where the road led into a forest. I would have liked to bag the fellow, so I spoke to the boss about it. Surely anything would be better than to keep waiting. So in the end it was decided to deploy two groups of riflemen and my two groups on the right and left side of the road against the one armoured car. I was to dismount to first ascertain the Russian's precise location. This I did and then started to wander around with the riflemen. Through the rain-soaked terrain I then worked my way up to the forest and then through it before reaching the road. While doing so, I could hear that down in Vilani the vanguard had started to move again, which resulted in an enormous amount of noise, which seemed to have frightened away the Russian on the road, who had long disappeared when we arrived there. We now stood there, soaking wet and left with nothing. The only little success the platoon could report was the anti-tank gun that had been destroyed by Feldwebel Giersig, that was all.

We had just mounted up again to rejoin our company when Feldwebel Wichler reported to me that there was something wrong with his vehicle. Again the gearbox had ceased to work. Admittedly our overloaded buckets had had to accomplish an awful lot in recent weeks. With his vehicle,

Schirmer pulled him to the road. After he had done so, he was to catch up with us. When the company rumbled past, we attached ourselves to it and then had to halt inside the forest. Suddenly, crashing and whistling sounds – but no way to tell from where the shooting was coming. Just next to me several branches were ripped off the trees. I quickly ducked back into the turret, as I believed that there were enemy riflemen around. In the meantime Unteroffizier Schirmer reported back. At that moment I did not know that the projectiles that were darting through the fir trees had fatally wounded the Feldwebel Wichler. It had happened just after Schirmer had left him to drive the few hundred metres through the forest to my position. Wichler had been standing in front of the tank, giving instructions or something like that when one of these projectiles, of all things, hit him. It pierced his body from the left to the right hip. The poor fellow! He had always been at the front with his ammunition carrier and now had been supposed to earn his assault badge with me and my lot. How unfortunate. He was a good soldier.

Through this forest we then advanced further towards the village at the top of the hill. Suddenly things ahead got hot. The riflemen dismounted and we overtook them and advanced on the village in which Leutnant Langenbruch was engaged in combat. Over the wireless we heard that there were several enemy vehicles ahead and how Langenbruch, with his calm voice, allocated targets to his platoon commanders. Four enemy tanks were standing there with an infantry gun further towards the entrance to the village. Suddenly, however, an anti-tank gun started firing on us from somewhere. The boss abruptly reversed, forcing me, standing right behind him to offer fire support, to do the same to avoid being rammed. We stopped behind a burning house, which was lucky for us, as the brothers manning what actually seemed to be another infantry gun could not see us behind it. Ahead of the riflemen we then advanced further along the right side of our road of advance. The fire on the right of us ceased. The enemy seemed to be retreating. In front of a railway line and a swamp we could look further down the road. On my side on the right I could only see forest, shrubs and a homestead in which I could see a few muzzle flashes. I opened fire on them and it became quiet. I also briefly fired upon some riflemen 1 kilometre ahead on my right, but other than that there were no targets for me and I generally don't open fire just to steady the nerves. I have already experienced running out of ammunition once at Davgedy, where the remaining high-explosive shells I had left failed to make any impression on the enemy tanks. Over the radio Feldwebel Wünsche continually passed on a stream of reports on enemy riflemen heading towards the bridge with explosive charges. It was also he who spotted and destroyed the Russian armoured car which had already been spotted and very much destroyed by Langenbruch. I don't like people like that.

A bit of machine-gun fire was exchanged after the Russians had withdrawn towards the farmhouse behind the road, but I only observed. We then returned to the cluster of houses and set up a defence there. The Russians had retreated and didn't molest us any more during the night. We slept, only disturbed by a few Russian bombers, in an old wooden barn. Usually we always sleep in the tents to avoid catching fleas and lice. One hardly ever encounters a Landser in the houses. These hovels, with two rooms at the most for a family of twelve are way too dirty for our taste.

Saturday, 5 July 1941 [*continuation*]

In the morning there was time for a sleep in. We slept until 10 a.m. People are working on the vehicles. Our uniforms are being cleaned and we wash ourselves. There is not much going on. It is now nearly evening. I am seriously angry about how the spoils have been distributed. Feldwebel like Wünsche, Bartneck, Oswald and other members of the consortium have captured whole bales of cloth and loaded them on the prize lorry. I don't want the men to be short-changed so I express my recommendation to the boss to split everything with everyone. He tells me that the Feldwebel don't agree. Such a thieving, ignoble riffraff, all serving their own interests. I am not having that again and the boss agrees, he is sick of it as well and orders all the spoils to be sent to Germany immediately.

I am writing when suddenly the company is ordered to assemble in battle dress. Quite ceremoniously. And then, once we are all standing there, 'Old woman Moser' – our commander Oberstleutnant* – makes a speech. About Raseiniai, a chapter is now closed and so on. Nice of the man, I think to

---

* Alfred Siebert.

In better days: a young Friedrich Sander as a scout camping on the banks of the Rhine at Zons in 1932.

Camping at the Weser River in 1932, the tent is marked with the logo and name of the 'Reichsschaft Deutscher Pfadfinder', a scout association which existed between 1932 and 1934 as the last interdenominational confederation of the *Bündische Jugend* before it was finally banned by the Reichsjugend leadership.

14-year old Sander in his scout uniform, 1932.

In the RAD camp at Driburg, April 1937 (Sander top right).

A festive evening with the RAD in Driburg.

Sentry duty in the Driburg RAD camp.

RAD camp, Bad Driburg

Group photo, Bad Driburg RAD camp.

The Bulgarian Tscholpanow company being trained by Sander and his men.

Training Bulgarian assault gun crews on a Panzer IV.

With Bulgarian soldiers and Serbian civilians.

After an exercise in January 1944 with Leutnant Albert and Oblt. Tscholpanow.

Oberst Zimmermann welcomes Buglarian generals.

Review of the Bulgarian Stug company.

With the Sturmgeschütz-Lehrkommando (FP.24469) in 1944.
From left to right: Lt. Albert, Bulgarian Ult. Milew, Oblt. Sander, Oblt. Tscholpanow,
Hauptmann Heimke, unknown.

Training Bulgarian troops in urban combat tactics, January 1944.

Nr. **11969** ✻ Grenzübertrittsausweis (Weiß-Grün) für Angehörige der deutschen Wehrmacht

Lasciapassare di frontiera (bianco-verde) per appartenenti alle forze armate tedesche
Granična propustnica (bielo-zelena) za pripadnike njemačke oružane sile
Legitimaţie de trecere a frontierei (alb-verde) pentru persoanele din cadrele armatei germane
Preukaz ku prestúpeniu hranic (bielo-zelený) pre príslušníkov nemeckej brannej moci
Határátlépési igazolvány (fehér-zöld) a német véderő tagjai számára
Разрешително за преминаване границата (бѣло-зелено) за чиноветѣ отъ германскитѣ
въоръжени сили

Der   Oberleutnant Friedrich Wilhelm S a n d e r , Feldpostnr, 24 469
II — D — Господинъ   (Dienstgrad, Vor- und Zuname sowie Dienststelle) — (Grado, nome e cognome, ufficio di appartenenza) — (Čin, ime i prezime, službeno mjesto) — (Gradul, prenumele şi numele de familie, autoritatea) — (Vojenská hodnost, krstné a rodinné meno a služobné miesto) — (Szolgálati rangfokozat, vezeték- és keresztnév, szolgálati hatóság) — (Чинъ, име и презиме, както и служба)

reist in der Zeit vom   16. Februar   194 4 bis   18. März   194 4
viaggia dal ..194. al ..194. — putuje za vrijeme od ..194. do ..194. — călătoreşte în intervalul dela ..194. până la ..194. — cestuje od ..194. do ..194. — utazik 194. ..tól, 194. ..ig terjedő időben — време на пжтуването отъ ..194. до ..194.

einmal — und zurück — wiederholt*)
una volta - e ritorno - ripetitamente*) — jedamput - i natrag - opetovano*) — dus - şi întors - de repetate ori*) — jednorázove - a zpät - opätovne*) — egyszer - és vissza - ismételten*) — единъ пжть - и обратно - повторно*)

von   S e r b i e n
da — iz — din — z — отъ   (Gebiet) — (Zona) — (Područje) — (Teritoriu) — (Üzemie) — (Terület) — (Страна)   ból

durch   Kroatien-Ungarn-Slowakei-Protektorat-Deutschland
attraversando — kroz — prin —   (Durchreisegebiete) — (Territori di transito) — (Područja proputovanja) — (Ţări de tranzit)   keresztül
cez — презъ   de tranzit) — (Üzemia, ktorými sa prechádzajú) — (Átutazó terület) — (Страна на преминаването)

über   je   nach Belangen
passando da — preko —   (Deutsche Grenzübergangsstelle) — (Posto di passaggio della frontiera tedesca) — (Njemačke granične prijelazne
peste — ces — презъ   stanice) — (Locul de frontieră german) — (Nemecká pasová kontrola) — (A német határátlépési kirendeltségen át) —
          (Германски граниченъ пропускателъ пунктъ)

nach   H a m b u r g / Deutschland
a — u — la — do — за   ba

im — Eisenbahnzug — Flugzeug — Kraftfahrzeug Nr.
in ferrovia - velivolo - automezzo N... — vlakom - zrakoplovom - samovozom br... — cu trenul - avionul - automobilul No... — železnicou - lietadlom - motorovým vozidlom č... — vonaton, repülőgépen, teherkocsin ...sz. — съ желѣзница - самолетъ - моторна кола №..

Die Fahrt darf in den Durchreisegebieten nicht ohne zwingenden Grund unterbrochen werden.
Il viaggio non può venire interrotto senza motivi di forza maggiore nei territori di transito. — Putovanje se bez nužnih razloga ne smije prekidati u područjima proputovanja. — Călătoria nu poate fi întreruptă în ţările de tranzit fără un motiv bine întemeiat. — Na územiach, cez ktoré sa prechádza, nesmie byť cesta bez nutných príčin prerušená. — Az utazás az átmenő területeken kényszerítő ok nélkül nem szakítható félbe. — Пжтуването не бива да бжде прекжсвано въ страната на преминаването безъ принудителни причини.

          Dienstreise erfolgt
          in Uniform

Eemerkungen:
Osservazioni — Opaske — Observaţiuni — Poznámky — Jegyzetek — Забележки

          Belgrad   den   16. Februar 194   4
          il — dne — dňa —
          194.. ..hó ..n

          Durchlassscheinstelle der Wehrmacht 95
          I. A.   *(signature)*

(signature)
(Eigenhändige Unterschrift des Ausweisinhabers)
(Firma autografa del titolare)   (Unterschrift, Dienstgrad) — (Firma e grado) — (Potpis, čin) —
(Vlastoruční potpis vlasnika iskaznice)   (Semnătura, gradul) — (Podpis, hodnosť) — (Aláírás rangfokozat) —
(Semnătura proprie a deţinătorului legitimaţiei)   (Подпись, служебенъ чинъ)
(Vlastnoručný podpis majiteľa preukazu)
(Az igazolvány tulajdonosának sajátkezű aláírása)   Hauptmann
(Собственоръченъ подпись на притежателя на личната карта)

*) Nichtzutreffendes streichen. — *) Cancellare ciò che non interessa. — *) Nevažeče precrtati. — *) A se şterge ceeace nu este valabil. — *) Čo sa nehodí, škrtnúť. — *) A meg nem felelő törlendő. — *) Излишното се зачерква.

Nur gültig in Verbindung mit — Soldbuch — Truppenausweis — Nr. 69 ... Soldbuch oder Truppenausweis ist nur deutschen Dienststellen vorzuzeigen. Dieser Sonderausweis ist nach Beendigung der Reise an die deutsche militärische Dienststelle, bei der sich der Ausweisinhaber zu melden hat, abzugeben.

          7535 43 2 B

A border-crossing permit allowing Friedrich Sander to travel from Serbia to Hamburg in Germany, issued in Belgrade in February 1944.

myself, that he wants to express his thanks to the soldiers. But then he starts rummaging around in his pocket. 'Leutnant Langenbruch!' – Theo walks over to him. Old Siebert rummages around in his trouser pocket again and then produces a small box: 'In the name of the Führer you have been awarded the Iron Cross 1st Class.' He hands the box over to Theo. And it continues with Oswald, with whom I finished off the tank, and Aures, who has been 'in the thick of it' since France. After a Feldwebel of 6th Company has been decorated with the EK1, he flips the paper he is holding over and reads: 'Leutnant Sander'. Then he rummages around in the other trouser pocket and pulls out a little paper bag. I am angry about all this! Even Father Christmas brings his presents in Mother's potato sack and not in his trouser pocket. And for this kind of benediction I have risked my life …

Anyway, now I have visible proof that I am not a coward. Even if Krautwig also has the Iron Cross, I at least know what I got mine for. And in the evening there wasn't even anything to drink. That was quite disappointing, but I guess we can catch up on that after the war. On the same day we had to march across Augspils towards the Russian border, where we parked our vehicles in a farmstead surrounded by an alder forest and set up our tents. In the evening a few bombers come over and drop their eggs on Augspils. One can hear it here and we can see the impacts. Flames are burning high, some wooden houses probably caught fire down there. We are going to sleep.

Sunday, 6 July 1941

At 10.00 someone outside the tent is shouting my name. That makes me quite angry, I don't want to get up that early. I try to ignore the calls, but then someone begins to dismantle the tent from the outside and we three occupants, Szepanski, Tutasz and I, suddenly find ourselves crawling out of the wreckage. Outside I find Theo Langenbruch, who is waving two letters in front of my nose. 'By the way, no human being sleeps that long on a Sunday!' That is right, it is a Sunday, and we have been at war for fourteen days. We carefully wash ourselves. The cool water is wonderful and there is plenty of it. No problem to use two bucketfuls. One for soaping up and washing the body. The other for the face and for shaving. My beard doesn't need shaving yet, so I have more water to waste. Grab a fresh shirt, hang the 'Knight's Cross of the Unknown' across my neck, put on a tie and jacket and then have a cup of coffee. After all it's a Sunday and that's why I allow myself to eat a few of the biscuits we captured from the lorries on the road. A lovely Sunday morning coffee, the only thing that's missing is a newspaper. And this arrives in Tutasz's mail. The *Rheinisch-Westfälische*! Not a lot of news in that rag. I am writing a few letters. Then the boss comes up and takes us with him to bathe. There is a small stream nearby, he says, in which it is possible to swim. When we get there they won't allow us to swim. A few Landsers are standing there and tell us that swimming is forbidden as the other side hasn't been cleared of the enemy. The small stream forms the border between Latvia and the old Soviet Union. No one knows what it's called, something unpronounceable. Ultimately we did take a bath in the stream between Latvia and the Union. Just like our soldiers bathed in the English Channel and were proud of it.

In the late evening we advance on the large main road towards the north and cross the old border where a large tank is standing in the stream next to several bunkers. The Russians had started to build a strong bunker line there, but didn't manage to finish the work. Behind the border the houses are uninhabited, there are huge marshes and forests growing on swampy ground. An injured horse and two cows are the only living beings we encounter in the first 10 kilometres. A few bombers fly over, are attacked by German fighters, and two of the six are shot down. We are approaching Ostrow, which lies on the Velikaya. The bridges have been captured in a surprise attack by 1. Panzer-Division. Both are now the target of Russian bombers. The whole town of Ostrow lies in ruins. Only the outer walls of a few stone buildings are still standing, as are the churches, but they are burning brightly. We are marching on.

Tuesday, 8 July 1941

On Monday we left the forest 3 kilometres north of Ostrow and drove to Prudy, where we arrived at 23.00. From there we advanced to Boldino, where the 7th Company was already engaged in a fight for the bridge on the main road. We are to repel a flanking attack by heavy Russian tanks. There is a strange mood. All is very quiet; someone should make a really obscene joke to conjure a smile onto the faces. Everyone has become very serious. Now the Russians are shooting at us. At first we were standing on Point 68 together with the boss and the Russians sent over some shells. We had to run to find cover between the tanks. One can always die a hero's death out here, but to be killed in that manner – that can be avoided.

My tank, 523, has broken down and I have to switch over into Giersig's tank. Unteroffizier Schirmer and Feldwebel Giersig drew lots to see who had to leave the crew. By then the fireworks had started behind us. Our own artillery had started hammering away. An infernal crescendo of sound. We draw lunch and coffee and I warn my men to be careful. I noticed a certain recklessness recently which I don't like. A tank drives up from the left. A man walks ahead of it, marshalling it across the terrain. It is driving very slowly. Men are gathering to see what's going on. The tank stops and the short guy who had been walking in front turns towards me: 'Where is the baggage train of the 7th Company?'

I don't know the answer to that, but I ask him what's going on. The man looks at me: 'We have the body of Leutnant Kleinjung on the bow of the tank.' That reply nearly knocks me over. Should I start to cry? Should I begin to swear and scream? I feel sick and walk over to the tank. And there lies Kleinjung, right under the machine gun. He was shot in the head after having left his vehicle. The poor fellow. He received his EK on the same day on which I got mine. There is still some life in his gurgling lungs. I will make the Russians pay for that. I walk over to the boss to inform him about it. Oberleutnant Leonhardt also came up to look at Kleinjung. I call for a medic and a Sanka.* Our medic Meyer places Kleinjung on a blanket and bandages his head, from which a thick mass, the brain, is oozing. There will be payback time soon.

A messenger comes running. Russians are expected to attack with several of their giant tanks. Feige with his 1st Company of the 114s is in front and he is asking for reinforcements. We have to leave immediately. Everyone is tense and in that moment the boss makes a silly remark and we all break

---

* An ambulance truck/car.

out into laughter. The mood immediately changes. We move out with Kübelwagen and motorbikes. About 500 metres in front of the stream which the Russians don't want us to cross, behind a hill, there is the command post of our marching group. Shells and bullets whistle overhead but it is relatively safe there. There is a shot-up Russian anti-tank gun – made by Rheinmetall! The artillery observers, the Adjutant's tank and several signals vehicles are standing around. We take a good look at the area and start marshalling the arriving vehicles into position. My platoon is held in reserve again. Ahead, 7th Company is still fighting. We are supposed to stop the Russian armour if they manage to break through our first line. 7th Company sends a report of its vehicle inventory: two vehicles lost to enemy fire, four lost due to terrain difficulties. They still have six working Skodas and two Panzer IVs. Willi Loope's tank got shot up too. He and his entire crew managed to bail out. No one knows what happened to them yet. The Sanka is called forward, there are casualties. Medics rush to the front. Message by radio: artillery is firing on withdrawing enemy tanks and infantry. Another radio message: one of our infantry platoons has managed to establish a bridgehead on the other side of the stream, but there are casualties and they require a medic. That's today's job done, I guess.

Gosh! Two Red fighters, Ratas, just flew over. They were about 1,000 metres up and everyone ignored the two. But only minutes later, out of the blue, they were back, racing towards us on a very low level. I am sitting in the shadow of my tank, writing my diary, when their machine guns start firing and the bullets are hammering into the road. Everyone who can pull a trigger is now firing at the two fighters, who manage to get away unharmed. The fire on the other side has become a lot weaker. It is now 18.30 and only single shots can be heard from several kilometres away and now and then a single mortar shell falls nearby. Work continues tomorrow. The 7th Company has been badly mauled. As well as Kleinjung, the second officer has been killed. Feldwebel Meyer, who had quickly married the sister of the landlady Frau Schilling in Freystadt before we left, was killed yesterday. The company's medical Unteroffizier was killed yesterday evening at the station in Prudy. The riflemen had a lot more casualties. The quad-Flak unit has had one man killed, several wounded. Several men of the artillery were killed too. Tough day, but our 5th Company has had worse.

Tomorrow we'll probably see action again. Ahead of us we appear to be facing the last stronger enemy forces in front of Petersburg. Yesterday evening an unusually large group of eighty prisoners marched past us. Mostly fresh recruits. 7th Company and the riflemen had caught them at the station in Prudy, where they had just arrived. Prudy was one big signal again. We are here! The flames of the burning Prudy could be seen from kilometres away. There was a church on a hill between the wooden houses which were going up in flames one by one. Then the flames sprang over to the church. Tragic, as the kolkhoz farmers always use the churches as grain stores. We can always use grain, as well as meat. Along one road there we counted over twenty dead cows. The farmers in the area had driven all their cattle away to make sure they wouldn't fall into our hands. We have enough to eat, so that doesn't matter too much.

Soviet Russians live damned miserable lives. Today I went inside a house of one of those collective farmers. There is no way to get rid of the stink one finds in these one-room shacks, not even with hours of ventilation. A few roofed stairs lead into the living quarter. The Panje lives in the 'bel-étage' while all his livestock lives in the 'souterrain'. The Botocudo and other jungle tribes live in the same way. The conditions in the 'one and true Fatherland of farmers and workers' are even more dirty and degenerate than those in Lithuania. The cattle serve as auxiliary heating in case the enormous oven doesn't suffice. The roosts for the members of the multi-headed family are usually behind that oven. We finally found all the cattle here near Boldino, which is how far the Panjes got. A Russian shell had exploded amid the herd, but none of the cattle had been harmed. The Russian shells are far less effective than ours, but their tanks are superior and they have good snipers.

Friday, 11 July 1941

When I had filled the last diary page on Hill 98 and then climbed into the tank for the attack I didn't know what experiences would lie ahead of me. It is probably a good thing that I can't look into the future as there must be no deviation. Forward, forward and again forward! Our destiny is forged by us, not the other way around.

[9/10 July] It was at about 17.00 our field kitchens brought hot bean soup just before the launch of the next attack. I spoon up a few mouthfuls and then climb into the tank. Ready for battle, radio check, and off we go. In a column of five vehicles we set off from the station at Karamyschewo. Feldwebel Opetz and Unteroffizier Riedel of the 4th Platoon had been transferred to me. My three wireless operators have disappeared. It's a bloody disgrace. Now we are to launch a joint attack with our riflemen and all three wireless operators of my old platoon have buggered off. I am foaming with rage! The brothers must have gone out 'foraging' and not a single prick has seen it necessary to give me notice of that. Now I have to leave without them. We are the reserve platoon and roll down the road from Karamyschewo. On the left and right of that road our 5th, 6th and 7th Company attacked earlier. Our reconnaissance had reported enemy entrenching activity on the hill near the village of Pikalikha and along the houses on the same level along the street. They are the same troops who had been kicked out of Karamyschewo earlier. I stood next to the foxholes they left in a hurry about two hours ago. When our riflemen approached, a whole lot of Russians had approached them, waving leaflets dropped by us in which the German government guaranteed to treat well all soldiers of the Red Army willing to surrender.

I had personally interrogated three of them as well as I could. They told me they were members of a rifle regiment. The Germans had done a lot of shooting which had caused their regiment to disperse. Their commander had run away. One of them, speaking a mixture of Russian and Yiddish, told me that they had had forty tanks to support them, but they had all 'loyfa weg'.* Tanks with wheels, not with tracks, he explained. I suppose we are going to run into those soon. Anyway, we are following up as reserve platoon. One of Leonhardt's Panzer IVs is standing in front of some bushes in which several Russians are hiding. Our riflemen spotted the danger first, but at that moment the wretches had already gunned two of them down. Feige is angry. He shouts and rages and orders his men to get off our tanks. Maybe he has finally understood that the terrain has always to be thoroughly searched. But what do Kelletat and all the other rifle brothers say? 'That isn't

_____

* 'Run away.'

their job!' Well, that's why they are now missing two of their riflemen. But who cares, the war goes on.

From there the attack continued from the village ahead of us along the road leading from Sskoff towards the west. Russian infantry tries to stop us. A few rounds of 7.5-cm and some machine-gun bursts and the brothers go running. But one has to be careful, very careful, as there is always the probability that they have hidden one of the AT guns somewhere. We work ourselves closer towards the road and the Russians have run away again. Yet some of them have hidden themselves in the bushes and tall grass, and when we turn to the right the brothers open fire on our Panzer IV, which is full – what a surprise – of riflemen who clambered on it as soon as they thought the fighting had ended. A few hand grenades silence these Russians.

Our objective of the day is Jamkino and I am trying to reach it at all costs. We are racing on and for a while there is nothing to see until I notice a large number of hoofprints on the road. Cavalry must have been here. What a shame, they would have made an excellent target for our machine guns. Shortly afterwards the leader of the advance detachment of riflemen, a few vehicles ahead of us, reports that there are about twenty Russians further ahead alongside the road. He tells us to switch our engines off so that the riflemen can lay an ambush for them. But no one is coming. The brothers must have escaped elsewhere. Along the road we drive past growing piles of Russian weapons, ammunition and uniforms. By then we are all infected with the fever of the hunt. Bethke radios in to tell me to hurry up, and the leader of the vanguard of the riflemen sends a messenger relaying the message that I should speed to 30 to 35 kilometres per hour. But that is out of the question; 20 kilometres per hour is just right. It allows us to see everything, the engine doesn't overheat from going too slow and it doesn't overstrain the steering brakes. We are making good progress and suddenly we run into German troops alongside the road. They are the vanguard of our Kradschützen who advanced on a path parallel to ours together with the recon detachment. They chased the Russian rearguard into the next village, but were too few to give chase. We, however, continue to chase the brothers. In the next village there is chaos. The Russians had to abandon all their artillery there because the road had turned into a terribly sandy path. There is no way that this 'road', which is marked red on the maps, could be made any worse. But we continue through the sand and dust. My eyes are burning and I can hardly see a thing. And then suddenly a German soldier ahead of us. Unteroffizier Willy Meyer of 1./ Kradschützen 6 is standing at the roadside and busies himself gathering loot from some abandoned vehicles. I immediately recognised him because of his glasses. I open the turret hatch and shout and wave to him – I don't know if he recognises me. I button up again. Soon after, there is a horse cart in front of me. A civilian, Panje Russki, who is also out to loot and to pick up some abandoned horses. A third horse is already tied to the back of his cart. I speed up to get closer and he suddenly turns his head, staring at me with frightened eyes. Probably didn't expect that the engine hammering behind him would be German.

We drive past modern cars, smeared with mud for camouflage, toppled-over carts and limbers, exhausted horses and abandoned guns. If only we could cash all that stuff in for prize money. And finally, in the distance, trails of dust rise up leading into the woods on the right. That is them! We are without our riflemen, but now that doesn't matter. I am just reporting the target to the boss when suddenly there is a flash in front and a shell swishes past us. One hundred metres in front I identify an anti-tank gun. I fire an explosive round, which flies apart on the outside of the gunshield with a 'bang'. I ignore the gun and open fire into the dust trails in front, from where it flashes up again and again. By now the Russians have disappeared into the woods. Another flash in front and I finally realise that they are all firing at me. I am standing about 500 metres in front of my platoon. Henn's Panzer IV hadn't advanced any further. Thus I reversed 100 metres and then ask the boss what's happening.

I am tasked to take my platoon closer to the forest and then to continue the advance once the riflemen have caught up. They arrive only moments later.

We are surrounded by about 200 small and large pigs which the Russians couldn't take with them any more. We come through several small villages and then into a swampy forest. One platoon of riflemen is far ahead when it is suddenly taken under fire. Tanks! At the side of a copse of trees near a farmstead there is a Soviet tank which is firing on us. We are ordered to halt our tanks and to switch off the engines. A 5-cm Pak is ordered forward to do the job. I sneak forward with it to observe closely what's happening. With eight men we manage to push the anti-tank gun to a position about 200 metres away from the tank, which we identify as a Christie. In the darkness this isn't easy to identify. It is standing there with its engine running and we can see the shadows of people running around it. I coordinate an attack plan with the commander of the AT gun. He will wait twenty minutes before he fires. During that time I will head back to assemble my tanks and the Panzer IV. As soon as the AT gun has fired the first shot we'll fire up the engines and will charge down the road. A few bursts of fire into the houses on the left and right and then we continue towards Yamkino, our objective, which – according to our commander Oberstleutnant von Seckendorff – lies only two more kilometres ahead of us. How wrong the judgement of a person suffering from 'Kreuzschmerzen'* and the urge to win a prestigious victory can be. It was more than twice the distance.

When the shot barks out, we charge forward at full speed across a road lined with burning houses. I am in third place. Opetz in his Skoda and the Panzer IV are ahead of me. At breakneck speed we race through the sparks and heat. Flames are rising high into the dark night sky and are illuminating the whole area. And that is lucky for us because suddenly, on the side of the road is an armoured car! I fire a round without optics, without stopping, and 'Bang!' – right on target! I am so close that some small splinters fly into my face. I have no time to think about it, however, as only seconds later the blood freezes in my veins. One hundred metres ahead there is an enormous Russian tank which is traversing its 7.6-cm gun towards me! Opetz has already raced past it. The Panzer IV drives by on its right side and fires a round into it. No effect. Now I fire on it too and suddenly I can see a blue light flashing up on the Russian tank. For a brief moment I think that my 3.7 went through, but then the flames die down and the buggers continue to traverse their gun towards me. I shout at Szepanski to take us off the road into the field on the left, but he fails to understand quickly enough. The steering brakes don't work that well either. I scream and I shout and finally Szepanski manages to pull the tank off the road, across a meadow towards some undergrowth ahead.

---

* Lit: 'cross pain', which usually translates as 'back pain', but was also a pun for those who tried to win a Knight's Cross at any cost.

There is movement there so I open fire on it and send a group of soldiers running. Thank God that the vehicles behind me have also pulled into the meadow and that the Russian giant is unable to see us in the dark.

My gun doesn't eject the shell casing, so I can't fire any more. Then I notice that the huge Russian tank is rolling backwards. It is in fact slowly rolling towards us, but has its turret traversed to the rear. 'Hand grenades!' Tutasz hands me the last three. I shove them into one trouser pocket and pistol into the other one before I exit the tank. Outside there are two Russians wearing steel helmets. The two approach me. I hasten towards one of them, rip the rifle out of his hands and wave my unloaded pistol under his nose. The other guy jumps away to the side and disappears behind a gun limber into the woods. I take the belt off my Russian and with a kick into his backside I push him towards the 'route of advance for prisoners of war'. With his hands raised he starts jogging down a roadside ditch.

The big Russian is now going backwards at full steam and will soon be where we are. We race to fetch a petrol can from our tank and remove its lid just in time to throw it on the 52-ton beast as it's rolling past. I try to keep up with it as it doesn't stop, but at this moment I don't give a shit about anything any more. There is an open petrol can on its engine deck and the contents are leaking out, but it's not emptying fast enough. Damn it to hell! I can't keep up running next to it. In front of me there are Russians. I wish I had an axe with me. Instead, I lob a hand grenade on its back, near to where the intake covers are. From our side they are now also firing on the tank. I throw myself into the dirt, the grenade bursts, but the petrol doesn't ignite. It must all have run into the engine. What bad luck! At this point I am foaming with anger. Opetz's Skoda tank is standing right on the road which the Russian is now approaching and, seconds later, with a loud crash, the giant slams into the little Skoda and, with a breaking and grating sound, pushes it off the road into a ditch. For about a minute the Russian keeps standing right next to the Skoda and flames start flickering through its engine deck. I am delighted that my petrol can seems to have worked after all. The tank is still standing and I am still prone in the dirt.

At this moment van Dyke is coming towards me, supporting the wounded Unteroffizier Schmidt, who asks me to call a Sanka, as without one he'd soon bleed to death. I am about to take a look at his wounds, when suddenly I hear the engine of the Russian tank blubbering to life. Van Dyke has to take care of his wounds, I can't help him now. Together with Masshense and Aures, we walk towards the tank, but it drives further down the road when we get near. It is too fast to keep up with, so we return to Schmidt, who has got a big hole in his chest. His right arm is hanging down limply and there is a deep wound in his right shoulder and a few shell splinters stick out the flesh next to it. He is still demanding that we get him the Sanka, but there is no way we can do so anytime soon. He was later picked up by one of von Esebeck's staff cars. Masshense and I fetch another petrol can and start walking. The Russian can't have got far. Leutnant Ritgen and a few of his men have joined us and are walking down the other side of the road. My own tank is still intact and my men in position so there is nothing stopping me walking off. The burning houses are still illuminating the area and there is a possibility that the Russian can spot our shadows against the flames. We continue approaching the colossus through the undergrowth. Just forward and never falter. In general the Russians are more afraid of us than we are of them – always forward.

By then it was past midnight and is now Thursday, 10 July 1941. On the horizon we can already see a thin red line of dawn. After Masshense and Aures, it is now my turn to carry the petrol can. To catch the tank from the side we walk through a field of rye. We walk and then we walk some more. We failed to catch the brother in front of the bridge leading over the swampy ditch. As such, we continue walking. Ritgen, Walther Leckenbusch and Obergefreiter Gustav Klein are walking on the other side of the road. And so we continue for about four more kilometres through fields of grain, gardens and across swampy meadows. A half-finished anti-tank ditch can't stop us. The fuel can is getting heavy. Feldwebel Jürgensmeier of the staff, who volunteered to join us, takes it off me. Whenever we catch sight of the tank, however, it drives further away from us. We are delighted when all of a sudden a half-track comes down the road. It is towing the 5-cm anti-tank gun which we had put to good use at the farmstead. The tank is standing about 250 metres further down the road, so the crew unlimber their gun and fire a Panzergranate 40 (AP shell with tungsten core) on the tank. The hit sends parts of its suspension system flying into the air, but it is still not finished. The crew place a few smoke grenades and the tank resumes its drive up the road. We limber up again and climb into the half-track. We have chased the giant through four villages and the sun is coming up. We have to give up and I have to return to my men and see how they are doing. At least Yamkino has been reached, which makes me feel slightly better about all that walking.

Finally my tank pulls up in Yamkino, I stop it and climb on board. I have to hurry to get into the turret as at this moment Russian artillery starts thundering into the village. A few houses have already caught fire and in front one of our tanks suddenly bursts into flames. Bang! Bang! Bang! The heavy coffers slam into the buildings. In less than half a minute more than half of them have started burning. We are manoeuvring our tank into cover in a garden behind a house when some of our Kradschützen come racing down the road towards our side. We inquire what's going on and are told that not far ahead three of those 15-cm-gun-armed 52-ton shithouses are raking the area with gunfire. Our tanks have pulled off into a field to the right and drive down there to get instructions from the boss. Oberleutnant Zangenmeister and two Panzer IVs are standing behind a barn. He looks completely worn out and has no clue what is going on. I spot Theo Langenbruch nearby and walk over to talk to him. I can see in his face that something nasty must have happened. He is looking very serious and the shooting alone would not shake Theo that much. And then he tells me that the boss has been wounded and taken to the rear. His loader Lange was wounded as well. One tank of our platoon had been destroyed, its commander was killed. Shells are crashing down all around. We decide to pull our tanks further forward towards a row of scrub and to camouflage them there before the sun comes up. I tell Tutasz to secure the area towards the road. Zangenmeister, however, is the most senior, and it should be him to take control here. But he is still standing next to his Panzer IV and is smoking one weed after the other. He seems to be thoroughly shaken. The men are standing cluelessly around him. A few guys from the Flak, also not the bravest specimens of their kind – which in general is really good – are with them. One of their guns, still on its limber, is burning behind them.

Slowly but surely we are learning more about the situation. The Oberstleutnants Siebert and von Seckendorff have arrived safely at the rear. There had been some super-heavy Russians in front of us who with their shooting had set fire to pretty much everything. Our 10.5-cm battery is unable to fire as it is under the most heavy fire itself. With my naked eyes I can see the wrecks of several of our vehicles in the area where we briefly halted earlier in the night. We were lucky indeed. Shells are coming now down left, right and centre. Range is about 1,500 metres so, as soon as one spots the muzzle flash, one has to hit the turf as the projectile will hit less than a second later. I can count three spots from which they are firing, so these must be the three howitzer-armed 52-ton tanks. Nasty feeling to lie opposite these beasts. The Adjutant makes a sudden appearance and hands leadership of the company to Langenbruch, while Böttcher and I stay in command of our platoons. We can be glad that Theo and not Böttcher has taken over. Böttcher is a proper firebrand and regularly gets on the bad side of his men. Just now someone has asked for him, but he is nowhere to be found. Has made himself scarce.

I go and look for my tank. We are all terribly thirsty. Between two of the barns there is a well. Our new Unterarzt and the Sanitätsfeldwebel* are using the huge wooden lever to pump up water, which they intend to filter with the tornister water filter. I shout at them to find another well as this one can be observed by the enemy. But they ignore me. I haven't walked 100 metres when there is a sharp detonation, I throw myself to the ground and at the same moment bits of barn roofing are raining down. A second later, I haven't even managed to stand up again, a second shell hits the other barn and sets it alight. With satisfaction I notice that the assembled medical ranks at the well have taken the hint and have hurried away from the scene.

It is about 03.00 when I see the two Panzer IVs of Oberleutnant Zangenmeister moving out of their firing positions where they had been placed to give fire support to our Skodas and a 2-cm Flak. I have never seen anything like it. We have to hold this position at all cost and Zangenmeister doesn't appear to feel responsible for that. Now the two Panzer IVs are standing behind another barn about 15 metres away. A heavy shell crashes through the roof and wall and the resulting explosion damages the suspension system of one of the Panzer IVs. At this moment Zangenmeister shouts over that he is pulling away to the rear. Theo gives a fitting reply of a kind I can't reproduce here. After all, I am younger than he is. Theo is angry and exclaims that he will never call him 'Oberleutnant' again and that from this point he will

---

* Unterarzt is a licenced surgeon of the highest NCO rank. The SanitätsFeldwebel is a medical sergeant.

just be 'Herr Zangenmeister'. The manner in which I am describing Charlie's behaviour here might sound funny and probably not half as bad as it actually was. But he was the oldest among us and according to Prussian custom he should have assumed leadership and responsibility for all our forces there. He would just have had to take any decision, even if had been a full withdrawal. I could have taken the responsibility for that, after all, enemy fire was heavy enough. But instead he moved his own vehicle out of the line of fire, after only two enemy shells, which hadn't even been fired directly at him. That is not what a Prussian, a German officer, does. He withdrew his remaining men and the one working tank he still had towards the edge of the rear of the village. We warned him that his movement would draw enemy fire on all of us, but he didn't listen and reversed about 200 metres to the rear.

We are still on our bellies in the dirt. Behind us is the tank of Oberleutnant Börger, his three men are lying in cover behind it. He himself was only visible for a few moments when the firing started and now he has disappeared without a trace. I stopped trying to find out where he had gone. Theo, however, in his direct manner, states that he must have run away. The Oberarzt* ducks down low and makes his way towards the tanks standing more towards the middle. To be honest, I wouldn't have thought the small fellow to be that courageous. That deserves respect and he'll be a useful guy to be with out here. I am so thirsty that it hurts, even though I have started licking the morning dew off the grass and plants nearby, but then I discover a bit of peppermint candy which has been hiding in my pocket. One of those little sticks the Latvians make. How wonderful. It is the edge of my thirst. I break it and hand half of it to Theo, who is by now the only one still lying next to me. In such moments little things like that are the greatest treasure.

The Russians are still spitting into the village. Even more so after Zangenmeister in his tank took to its heels. Sadly enough, its shells fall short and much too close to where we are lying. Another flash on the other side, 'Wham!' – the shell detonates nearby. Theo and I look at one another. 'Damned shit, that was way too close!' It is raining clumps of soil and dirt, half burying our arses. And just because of Charlie. Why the hell couldn't

---

* 'Senior physician', commissioned medical officer rank equal to Oberleutnant.

he have stayed in cover. And again, 'Bang! Wham!' A pillar of dirt rises up in front of us and iron splinters are howling over us. That was much closer still. And now comes a horrible minute as we both expect the next round to be on target. In such moments a human being learns to pray, even if it has never prayed before. What little worms we are, watched over from above. He has got us in his hand. And if it gets you, that is destiny. That is why one has to stay calm and fortune is with those who dare and who challenge destiny. 'Wham!' – the next one lands 50 metres behind us. We look at one another again and both can't help laughing. 'That would have been a nice funeral,' Theo says. It is now 06.00 and at 10.00 there is supposed to be a commander's briefing. And the Russians might have already attacked by then. Here it's only Theo and I and a Feldwebel and a handful of men from the 6th who are not scared of the big Russian shithouses. In the worst case we have to do it the old way, with petrol cans and hand grenades. The Russian infantry is not particularly good, we can deal with them. If! If they'll come! They did not, however.

At 08.30 the fire has died down and we receive the order to take our tanks over the open field ahead. So either we'd get badly roughed up by the Russians or we'd find that they had disappeared. And they had disappeared. We and the still living members of our company report back to Oberst Koll and I can't help grinning when I see the immaculately turned-out 'headmaster' behind his desk. We were standing there with mud-covered, soaked uniforms, dirty, unshaven faces, torn uniforms. In Theo's case with a triangular tear which offered an excellent view of his underpants. The immaculately turned-out General who had been in this case far enough in front to be able at least to hear the guns, is looking chastisingly over his thin spectacle frames as we dirty bastards rush in to disturb him during his briefing …

13 July 1941

Suddenly we were shaken out of our sleep. Without having time to beautify myself, I am being rushed to the Abteilung! Nobody knows what's going on. Theo, Wilhelm Lope and I use a motorcycle combination to drive into the village. In a relatively clean farmhouse, which has been thoroughly scrubbed by some Landsers, they have set up a table with maps and – for seating – placed several folding beds around it. There is also a single bench and I decide to sit on that instead, thus avoiding the risk of collapsing with one of the rattly bed frames.

In the meeting we were now informed that the 5th Company has been disbanded and is to join up with the 7th Company. That means all remaining vehicles will join the 5th, while everything that comes from repair in the future will be collected under Theo, who remains on 5th Company strength. I am ordered to transfer to a 7th Company with two platoons. I am shocked. Am I supposed to share the fates of Kleinjung, Möllenberg and Vielbaum? Never! And either way, even if they order me into the 7th Company, I will take the principles of the 5th with me. There will be no 'quick, quick' or a 'that will do'. We will not be hastened into an untimely but certain death by the gentlemen with 'hurting necks'* who then hold empty speeches after my demise. My corpse and those of my men are too valuable for that. I don't give a shit about all the other things they then talk about. I am furious! Bethke told me himself that he doesn't want any more officers of the 5th to transfer as cannon-fodder into the badly led 7th Company. But an order is an order, and there is nothing we can do about it. I dare to ask what will happen to Oberleutnant Böttcher, upon which the commander lets me know, leaving me no doubt about it, that I am not in a position to ask such questions and that Böttcher is at his disposal only. Incidentally Böttcher hasn't even been called to join the meeting. In addition we learn that Zangenmeister has been transferred to the rear. His nerves!

I head back to the forest, when I notice a few comrades of the regimental staff, so I head over to them to say hello. I then try to find Robert Gläser, who is sitting with Hauptmann Saalbach, whose shoulder I decide to cry on. I don't try to hide that I am livid with anger and he tries to sweeten it for me by explaining to me what an honourable task I have been given. After all, there'd be no one else who could effectively replace Oberleutnant Neuling if that was needed. I have enough of it anyway and thus I say

---

* *Halsschmerzen haben,* lit: 'to have neck pain' – i.e. 'aching' for a Knight's Cross, which was worn around the neck.

goodbye as quickly as I can. I then drown my anger by guzzling a whole bottle of cognac with Robert, who also supplies me with two additional bottles, one for each platoon condemned to leave tomorrow. I am really grateful to him. We always have a use for schnapps, it raises the low spirits a little. It is time to sleep.

14 July 1941

It starts at 07.00 in the morning. I report the arrival of me and the rest of the bunch to Neuling, who greets us with some kind words. When he is gone, I relay the best regards of the boss to the boys and share my thoughts about it all with them. Then we walk to our vehicles and the whole gang rolls down the road over which we just recently chased the Russians. Then we arrived at the big Pskov–Luga–Petersburg road and along it, towards the north, for a good while. On the way we pass long columns of refugees. After a while, in which our column is bombed several times by Red aircraft, we turn west towards Lake Peipus into the rest area of 36. Infanterie-Division. We roll on, way too far, however, as the guys there don't know where to marshal us to and thus we spend several hours rolling aimlessly through the landscape.

I am dog-tired. We are in one of those mosquito forests again and it is difficult to bear. These 'Stukas' are pestering us relentlessly and we are all suffering enormously. I cope with them a bit better than the others. Maybe I have sour blood, or I might be sweating less. I am sitting on the turret and enjoying the 'high altitude' air. Most of the little pests are in the grass. My eyes are falling shut. I had intended to go to bed at 22.30, but then got distracted checking on the platoon's sentry posts. When I finally lay down in the furrow in a field near the forest edge I could not find any sleep because of the hum of the mosquitoes. The beasts manage to squeeze through the smallest openings. Listening to the cursing and rants of the tormented men, I finally fall asleep. That was at about midnight. An hour later I am woken up by stabbing pains. Mosquitoes and fleas are covering uncovered patches of my skin. Big, chunky fleas. We are still in the area of Lake Peipus and the men again and again ask how far we'll keep going. Are we going from Leningrad to Moscow? When will we arrive in Petersburg? Everyone has got a fresh taste of the local road conditions. Log roads through swamp and log roads across sand. Three weeks of dust, dust and more dust. I can't stand it any more. Clean your weapons, drive a few kilometres and suddenly guns and rifles are so dusty they can't fire any more. Last Thursday I washed all my black uniform in petrol and I managed to clean it pretty well. It took only two hours on the following day and I again looked like a flour merchant.

Today's route took us mainly across roads west of the big Marijampole– Petersburg Rollbahn and they mostly led through sparsely inhabited wood- and marshland. We had to have a tank in front of each lorry; there would have been no way they could have traversed the more difficult parts by themselves. Without major breaks it took us thirteen and a half hours to cover a distance of 105 kilometres. The boss, who travelled by himself in his own car, arrived only three hours earlier. The remainder of 6. Panzer- Division travelled along the same marching route for a while. Just behind Osepo Yepnoe there was a minefield and several of our dispatch riders drove into it at the side of the road. It wasn't even possible to recover the maimed and scorched bodies of those boys. The Russians had used wooden mines which couldn't be found with our magnetic detectors. Every step into one of those irregularly laid minefields meant near-certain death.

15 July 1941

Initially the plan had been that we, together with the infantry, would form a vanguard in the advance on Leningrad. It's at most 150 kilometres until we reach our objective. I have no idea why they let us sleep until 06.00 in the morning. But then, sleep was desperately needed. There was a thunderstorm in the night and it poured with rain. I do feel sorry for those who didn't set up a tent. We have been surprised by such rain once, and since then we set up a tent whenever its possible. Tutasz and Szepanski scare out the mosquitoes by smoking some *papyrossis** or a cigar. After the rainfall, however, the masses of mosquitoes swarmed about. The beasts know how to find even the smallest patch of uncovered skin. 'Ssssss', they land and then

---

* Russian cigarettes.

one can hear the distinctive 'smack' of a hand often followed by some juicy curse. Now, however, we have reached an area where not only the mosquitoes bite. There are cleg-flies, gadflies from the corpses and fat horse-flies and all those are determined to stab you. It's not uncommon to see men with swollen hands, cheeks and eyes. The beasts are everywhere! I hope there are none in Leningrad.

Yes, Leningrad, every soldier is looking forward to this metropolis of Russian Europe and inwardly I do feel the same. I am looking forward to the end of this period of fighting here in the East. What's going to happen after that, nobody knows. But we'll have reached an important target and that makes me happy when I speak of Leningrad. The average Landser though is looking forward to more mundane things. Every Landser in my platoon has by now asked me: 'There will surely be schnapps factories in Leningrad, Herr Leutnant?', 'Are there fur shops in Leningrad?', 'Will there be mosquitoes in Leningrad too?', 'We'll finally get food other than pea soup and blood sausage!', 'The women here are all so dirty – will they be washed in the big city?' Yes, Leningrad is the objective of dreams of all comrades.

We are about 150 kilometres away from it and progress on the terribly bad advance roads is slow.

On the main road Soviet tanks launch a desperate counter-attack. It is the only place where they can do so as everywhere else there are wooded swamps and the bridges across the streams are too weak to carry them. But even on the Rollbahn the 52-tonners often need to bypass bridges. 1. Panzer-Division has turned left, west in front of Luga, and 269. Infanterie-Division halts the Russian attack – which according to the Ia of 36. Infanterie-Division is carried forward with strong forces – about 30 kilometres in front of Luga. While I am writing this, Wilhelm Lope has climbed up to me on the tank. He is in command of the heavy platoon which is attached to the 7th Company. The infantry chaps are mightily impressed by the three large tanks. Everywhere our tanks are being photographed. If only there'd been some PK men on the long stretch of sandy road yesterday. They could have shown the people at home that we are not only fighting the enemy over here. They should have a close-up in the newsreels which shows how the enemy 'Stukas' dive onto their victims, who would like nothing more than just a few moments of sleep after a twelve-hour drive through dust and heat. They should have filmed all the broken-down vehicles which buried themselves more than half a metre deep into the hot sand. Wherever something really interesting happens the brothers are not around. The little Kfz.70 (Krupp-Protze) with all-wheel steering which hops across rough swampy ground in such a way that the passengers get seasick, when all the steering causes the brakes of our tanks to smoke in narrow turns and when the faces of the tank commanders are caked so thickly with dust that they are incapable of closing their eyes any more – that they should make films of. Well, I should probably stop moaning now. I haven't taken many photographs myself recently, but then I only have reserve film left.

Wilhelm Lope and I talked about a few general things. The subject of Iron Cross awards is a pressing matter for all of us. I hope the 5th and 7th Company and the platoons of 6th Company who have contributed most to the success of the division won't be gypped too much when it rains medals the next time around. After all, Bethke managed to squeeze some out for our 5th Company. He also recommended me for the EK1, but if and when I will ever get it, with all those other candidates in the staff, is more than questionable. But I am already happy with Bethke's appreciation as he is a highly respected and much-revered leader, a man who can carry his men along with him. I am looking forward to seeing what Theo Langenbruch will do with the remains of our old lot. I surely don't enjoy serving here with Neuling. The whole mood here is very negative. He only ever looks on the bad side of things and is terribly soft and moody. With his facial expression of constant suffering he'd make a good 'tortured Jesus' in the Oberammergau Passion Play. Yesterday I apparently addressed him in a harsh tone when I asked him why exactly he chose to camp in a mosquito-ridden forest again and not at the nearby village which had a water supply. He was clearly miffed about that. The reason is that he is afraid of Russian bombers, which on the day before had dropped some bombs onto that village, which had resulted in a few dead infantrymen. In the evening he confronted me about that and I apologised. I hope this whole thing of having a mixed company attached to an infantry division is over once we reach Leningrad. I can't bear it much longer. And if that results in trouble, I do not care. I don't give a shit about it any more!

Yesterday the men have – crew by crew – received Russian shirts. Genuine rubashkas which are buttoned at the collar and only reach to the bum. A piece of rope around the belly or an old leather belt, trouser legs worn over the boots, ruffle up the hair and ready is the *mushik*.* Of course we immediately took a few photographs of ourselves in that dress. Now it is nearly 11.00 and we still have no idea what's happening today. We keep waiting stubbornly.

16.30

We are marching west towards Lake Peipus. What has happened now is what I never wanted, and what Bethke described as 'total madness': the infantry is requested by platoons, and Neuling deploys us in that manner! It is absolutely sickening. It's always the same old story: the platoon leader and his men find themselves in a tight squeeze; he doesn't know how to help himself with his few tanks and without the fire support of the company – and is getting shot up! But now there is no more going forward because ahead the Russians have blown up the bridge across the piss-filled ditch in front of Dubrova. The brothers finally seem to have discovered how they can stop a gang like ours. But never mind, pioneers have already rolled to the front, where they have to build a new bridge. The wooden frames they call bridges here are usually so badly built that they can hardly carry the weight of a Panzer IV anyway. Virtually all of them need reinforcing.

We were tasked to capture an airfield at Gdov. Now the bridge is broken, it is now 18.15 and we are still standing on the same spot. By now it has rained and after that I caught some sleep on the turret of 701, with which I am leading the remainder of the company. Here one learns to sleep in any position. We are in the middle of a forest of pines which are growing on the sandy soil. For days now we have been rolling through steppe-type terrain, sparsely populated by a few dirty Russians. Woods, swamps, bogs and always terrible roads. In the winter the men have been saying that they would rather be with Rommel in Tripoli. A pious hope, which was somehow understandable. By now, however, that tune has changed quite a

---

* Russian peasant farmer.

lot: 'In Africa Rommel doesn't have roads as bad as these', 'Then soldiers of Rommel in Africa at least get 5 litres of clean water each day and aren't forced to wait for the field kitchens with hot tea!' Without filtering we can't drink from streams and rivers here. After today's rain the thirst doesn't feel as bad and temperatures have also dropped a little. The sun is back but the roads are not as dusty at the moment. I am wondering what the roads at Lake Peipus towards the north look like. That's the advance route we'll be taking, which will then take us even further north to the Gulf of Finland between Kronstadt and Leningrad. There we'll block everyone who is still trying to get away towards central Russia and Leningrad from the direction of the Baltics and Reval. Now things ahead seem to be moving again. I'll write more later.

I am wondering how far we are going to go today and what our objective of the day is. We have now advanced twice, for about 500 metres each time. During the second halt Szepanski removed a link from the right track of my tank. In the meantime I have eaten something. Two sandwiches with cheese and one with blood sausage. And it's not even Sunday. Anything but blood sausage is usually reserved for Sundays. Otherwise the tinned stuff, the name of which our boys from Cologne can pronounce so well, is the pillar of our daily meals. Blood sausage in tins, liquified from the heat of the tank, is usually served in the mornings and evenings while lunch often consists of pea, lentil or bean soup. That in turn has the effect that the air in our tents during the nights is a lot warmer. And it also seems to aid the Landsers' digestion, woe to those who dare to go deeper than 15 metres into the woods alongside our routes of advance and get lost in a maze of paper and fly-covered little piles. One can easily find the advancing army. Just follow the smell.

We are now near the village of Gyloschki. The stream which is flowing here is called Pliossa. There are houses on our left and they have a surprisingly clean, well-kept and peaceful appearance. They are, however, all slightly wonky; that especially applies to the only non-combustible elements of them, the chimneys, which are all curved, bent and are slowly slipping out of position. We are now across the bridge. The Russians had set fire to it after dousing it with petrol. There wasn't much left of it. The bridgehead on the other side had been well reinforced, foxholes everywhere. A few houses are still burning. A lorry is standing at the roadside and is flying the breakdown flag, and two infantrymen are waving to us. We think they want us to tow them away, but when we drive over they just want to hand three bottles of vodka up to us. I am moved. We have gained a good reputation with them.

19.15, 17 July 1941

A shame that I didn't manage to take a swim in Lake Peipus. The wind is blowing from the north and it is quite cold. The water is freezing and one can be happy not to have been forced to swim through it involuntarily as the Russians were. Yes, together with 36.ID we have chased the Russians into the lake. Since yesterday some of them have been trying to get across on small boats. We had dispersed Russian forces in front of Gdov and had taken a large number of them prisoner when they were trying to flee on the road leading to Narva. Now I am sitting here while our tanks are being repaired. From the twenty-two tanks we had at Yamkino, five were still running this morning.

18 July 1941

We have withdrawn back to Gora, a village at the lake, which is also home to the staff of 36.ID. I am wondering why there are none of those 'little Stukas' here, but I guess that the cold north wind has chased our little friends away for the time being. But now I will write about what happened after we had crossed the destroyed bridges yesterday.

On 16 July we left the woods behind the lake at Alfonsovo at 02.00. Neuling buggered off and left me in command of the rabble. Poppelreuter was further ahead with the infantry vanguard. We had only put three vehicles on the road when suddenly everything halted and we had to wait until 05.00 until we slowly crept forward again. Another kilometre and the waiting started again. At 08.00, we are a few kilometres away from Tscheremschina, Neuling's Kradmelder arrives and calls forward to the front. There is shooting ahead and the artillery is firing as well. Poppelreuter's platoon is somewhere in the village which one can see ahead. We are sent to secure the reverse slope position on the left side of the road in front of the village. Further to the right is Matussek with two Panzer IVs. With me, I have three tanks myself, Feldwebel Ulrich with his three Skodas and Räuber's Panzer IV. We secure the road to the village towards the left where we perceive Russian activity. I have just positioned my vehicles when I see a thick pillar of smoke rising up on the right where Matussek has headed with his platoon. What has happened?

Then we see Matussek with his driver Esser walking back on foot. 'What are you doing here?' 'Well, that is our tank burning up there! They fired a few rounds right into it!' 'Damn! Has everyone managed to bail out?' 'Yes, only it's tragic, all our stuff is still in there!' I feel for him. Matussek had driven up the hill on the right side of the road, when suddenly he received machine-gun fire from a distance of about 1,000 metres. At that moment Matussek was outside, walking ahead of his tank to guide it over difficult terrain while another member of the crew was walking behind it. And just as Matussek turned around to see where the machine gun was firing from, the first anti-tank shell hits the ground nearby. He and his man jump into cover while Esser, still driving the tank, is continuing to roll forward. A second AT shell hits the track, enough of a threat to make the two men still inside the tank bail out and dive into the high grass. In the next seconds four more AT shells hit and the Skoda goes up in flames. As the Russian machine gun was still firing, the two had crawled back to the reverse slope. Two more pillars of smoke rise up from the edge of the village. Through my binoculars I can see nothing, but I soon learn that two tanks of our vanguard were too daring and had driven too far forward. Through my glasses I can see two more of our tanks in cover on our side of the village. Soon after I spot some of our men carrying a stretcher. On it lies a man with a black tank uniform. I have no idea what has happened.

For now we are called off the hill and are to advance to the next village together with the infantry. I am tasked to lead the assembly. Nine Skodas and three Panzer IVs, without the Poppelreuter platoon. I will be responsible for all this lot, while the 'company commander' stays at the regimental command post and 'will stay in radio contact with me'. Why he is not coming with us I don't know. Well, never mind. The advance stalls, tanks are called to the front. I am driving Ulrich's tank while he is driving in mine. Ulrich made a calm and very good impression on me. I don't quite understand why Neuling calls him 'anxious'. To evade a minefield we roll past between the houses of the village, avoiding the main road. In front everything stops. Because Neuling hasn't briefed me at all about the situation, I get out of the tank to take a look myself and ask the commander of the infantry who is lying among some of his men in a roadside ditch. He doesn't have time to talk to a lowly Leutnant, however, as just at that moment Russian projectiles whistle over our heads and we are also fired upon from the left and right side of the road. I am still not entirely sure what is happening and ask an older Landser, who tells me that the Russians are counter-attacking and that both German companies have now been fighting there for two days and have run out of ammunition. Our tanks were badly needed. On my stomach I crawl back to the tank and I am unable to avoid crawling over the torn-up Russian corpses while I am doing so. I shout to the loader to open the hatch, and carefully lift it upwards. A deep breath, and then – one, two, three – jump up, fold the long legs into the turret and let the body slide down behind them. Then I pull my head in just at the moment when a volley of small arms fire hails down on us. As long as there are no anti-tank guns around, however, everything should be fine.

Raging rifle fire ahead. In addition, Russian artillery is now plastering those 300 metres of the village between us and our infantry on the other side – exactly that stretch of ground which we now have to cover. But that's how it is, so 'Panzer, *marsch*! Vanguard half left through the rye field! Remainder fan out to the left of the line. Ready to fire, advancing Russian infantry ahead. Care when crossing through our infantry line! Panzer *marsch* and attack!' We cross through the thin line of our infantry who wave to us enthusiastically. I liaise with an infantry officer of 11./IR118 who tells me that the Russians had attacked in enormous numbers and that he had never seen anything like it. Now, however, their attack had stalled. In the end it only takes a few 7.5-cm shells and a few shots from our Skodas and the Russians start running. It's the usual scene. Some of our machine guns are hammering into those who try to run into the forest on the left, while our Panzer IVs are sending shell after shell into the undergrowth on the right, into which most of the brothers are trying to escape. It's utter chaos, bellowing cattle are running around and one by one the houses go up in flames. Wherever something moves, our tank machine gun is scything everything and everyone down. Nothing is staying alive. In that manner we stood there for quite a while.

By 12.00 it has become a bit more quiet and, with the means of communication available to me, I try to contact the Oberleutnant by radio, but not a single arse is answering. Wilhelm Lope can understand me well, so it can't be my radio. We try for more than ninety minutes, but no reply from Neuling. The only thing I can hear is the angry voice of Wilhelm emitting a stream of insults and obscenities. In the end I give up. The infantry has by then been supplied with ammunition. I intend to continue leading the men without being hindered by the incompetence of the boss.

At 16.00 our artillery opened fire on the edge of the village ahead of us to suppress enemy anti-tank guns. At the same time we followed the advance of our infantry, overtaking them before exiting the village. The artillery then shifted its fire further into the forest ahead. It all went smoothly in a textbook manner. In the forest we found a dead Russian Major and took a large amount of documents from his body, one being a fire plan of their artillery. We also pull a few prisoners from the undergrowth; they don't want to answer any questions so we send the scum off to the rear. On the way we surprised a few Russians who seemed to have tried to get to us armed with explosives, incendiaries and tar mixed with petrol. The black piping on their dead bodies indicates that they were engineers.

Behind the village is a road through the forest. I didn't want to cross that without pioneer support, so I lined my boys up in a line, drove 1 kilometre forward and stubbornly waited for a pioneer who could check the area ahead for mines. I will not risk losing any vehicles through mines: three shot-up and burned-out tanks are enough.

When we reached Lipjagi we turned left into an open field to help the infantry get past the still-burning village. They were very grateful to have our tanks to support them. The infantry then headed towards the railway line running alongside Lake Peipus and the Gdov–Narva road. We were right behind their lead elements when they suddenly stopped and called us further forward to take fleeing columns of Russian infantry under fire. There were several burning lorries and groups of Russian infantry running towards the lake. We had just crossed over the railway line, when we received a report that a transport train was heading towards us from Narva. This appeared soon afterwards, so we swing our turrets around and give them hell. Russian troops jump off the wagons while it rolls past, and we open up on them with cannon and machine guns. Wilhelm Lope is overjoyed. That's a proper feast for him. With his cannon he fires a few shells into the locomotive, steam shoots out of the boiler. Hurra! We finished that one off nicely! We are soon standing at Werschaljany. Lope and his tank and Bartneck with his three Skodas are with me. When we get further towards the lake the infantry continues to advance alone and takes possession of the airfield.

19 July 1941

12.18 – I have just been to the field kitchens and got myself two slices of bread and some coffee. That was necessary. I was so hungry that I very nearly fainted. I had been asleep for about two hours when I was suddenly woken up by wild shooting. First I fail to understand what is going on and it takes me a second to realise: the Russians are trying to break through! Just outside the tent! It's whistling and hissing over our heads and through the bushes and fruit trees. Where exactly the Russians are is hard to tell precisely. It's banging from all corners and sides. Just up quickly into the tank! The turret hatch doesn't open! Try the driver's hatch instead! I have to climb over Kuhlbörsch, who is already at the sticks because he has been sleeping in the tank. With one arm I pull myself up on the gun and *marsch, marsch*! Off we go. First we head straight towards the village road as only there will we have a field of fire and will be able to see what's going on. But we are not getting that far, because all of a sudden Kuhlbörsch takes our vehicle straight into the ditch opposite the road and it immediately sheds both of its tracks. In addition the floor hatch comes to rest on a big stone boulder. Now that wasn't very talented – we have to bail out.

I draw the pistol from my pocket and return to the garden which is home to the rest of the company. Some men are running around wildly while others just stand around with their hands in their pockets. The boss is nowhere to be found and no one knows where he is, so I have to organise a defence with that rabble. Jürgensmeier turns up and I give him a whole lot of men who are standing around. I then send the whole assembly to the edge of the village which I think is most threatened. I gather up some more men with which I intend to secure the north side, where all hell has broken loose. The vehicles of the baggage train, mingled with tanks and the self-propelled Flak, are clumped into one big pile, so I start to get order into that first. This motley crew makes me want to puke. Unteroffizier Vogel and his crew have their tent set up 200 metres away from their vehicle. He and his gang are still calmly asleep! I have woken that fellow up all right! Never in my life have I encountered someone that stupid! But he is not the only one to make a fool of himself. The shooting seems to be nearby one moment and far away the next. It seems that the Russians are coming from the north, trying to thrust through our open flank in an effort to help the Russian forces encircled at Gdov. Anyway, we have enough troops down here and if they are not asleep like the members of our gang, we'll beat the living daylights out of the Russians.

Soon all our lorries have disappeared from the open field and have taken camouflaged positions under trees and next to house walls. The crews are standing in readiness beside their tanks. Those tanks which are not roadworthy, I put in such places where they at least have an open field of fire to the north. The boss, Lope and Platoon Ulrich then head out on the road to Gdov, from where dense Russian columns are approaching with the intention to turn north and to break through to Narva. I have to stay behind with the remaining lot. Well, at least that way I can catch up on some sleep. The little bit of shooting doesn't concern us massively any more. I crawl beneath a tarpaulin on one of the maintenance lorries, which offers protection against the ice-cold wind from the north which started blowing yesterday. It is freezing cold. Under that tarpaulin I catch up on some much-needed sleep. In the last two nights we have only slept for about three hours in total.

At midday the whole business is over. A dispatch rider delivers a message which orders the remainder of the company to the crossroads at Wercholjani. There we are to fall in behind the heavy infantry platoon of IR118 and then march to Gdov. I tell my people to get ready and then head out, with all my stuff, ahead of the baggage. The scene at the crossroads is terrible. Dead Russians wherever one looks, the whole area is littered with them, dead horses between them and shot-up vehicles at the side of the road. Among them there are more and more Russian dead. In some places draught horses are still standing in harness in front of abandoned and destroyed field guns. There is quite a large number of those on the road and a heavy Flak battery too. Never before have I seen so many dead, shredded corpses – they lie on the road, in the ditches and in the fields. At Ledinki there was a whole pile of corpses in front of our vehicles, but not nearly as many as here. The few kilometres from the crossroads to Gdov are full of carts, gun carriages, limbers, cars, cannon, lorries and all kinds of other equipment. Then we roll into town. Through the haze we can see Lake Peipus on our right. A few boats are visible too. Apparently they are Russian, evacuating fleeing troops to the north into still-unoccupied territory. We park our vehicles alongside an old town wall and give the men time until 15.50 to equip themselves with anything they might be lacking. There is not much for them to organise here. Many houses have burned out, the others are bustling with Landsers.

The Russians have been given hell here. I decide not to stay with the vehicles, but walk down to a square open space alongside the lake where the prisoners are being kept. Under the trees there are large numbers of wounded who are being treated by women dressed in riding boots and trousers. A Russian surgeon, who looks more like a butcher, is standing between them with his hands in his pockets, doing absolutely nothing. We don't have enough dressing material for all the wounded here. The Russians themselves carry nothing of the sort with them. A woman in a civilian coat, under which the uniform of the Russian women's battalions is visible, approaches. She wants to have a passport proving that she have been discharged here and asks to be allowed to stay with the wounded. She is sent to find and fetch white linen which can be used as dressing material. The Flak has taken the duty of guarding the prisoners.

One of the Flak soldiers is calling for a Leutnant Sander. In the first moment I hesitate, trying to place the man and wondering where he knows me from. But no, I have never seen him. I then go to see their commander, a Leutnant of the Flak, who introduces himself to me as 'Sander' and then looks at me with big eyes when, for a laugh, I say 'Sander!' in return. Then laughter on both sides. He tells me that his ancestors were farmers and fishermen in Hanover and Mecklenburg. But that's only as a side note.

Sander then gives me permission to take a close look at the prisoners. There are 1,500 of them. Alongside a fence, separated from the others, there are about twenty more. They are Volga Germans who had been forced to serve in the Russian army. Admittedly the creatures are not very confidence inspiring. But anyhow, they have at least some German blood in their veins and thus they have been separated from the Mongols, Caucasians and Russians. They only speak broken German, strongly mixed with Russian, and they find it difficult to understand our High German. After all, their ancestors were Swabians who had come to the Volga as settlers. For me they are Bolsheviks just like the others. They too have taken up arms against us and have fought in the ranks of the Red Army. But then, the Party knows best what to do with such people. The other Red Army men are a savage-looking lot. A few civilians are among them, Communists in civilian clothing, caught carrying weapons. Two more men in civilian dress are brought up, they had tried to set fire to a captured petrol storage and in the process had fired on our men. Flak-Leutnant Sander's question about what to do with the pigs is met with a short reply by an Adjutant on the General's staff: 'Shoot them!' The two are led behind a house, a few minutes later a few pistol shots can be heard. Done – sorted, a couple fewer fanatical Bolsheviks.

More and more prisoners arrive. The space is filling up quickly and there will be enormous numbers of that riff-raff out there, hiding in the scrub along our advance route. They will only surrender after days, when the wretches get hungry and thirsty. Two whole regiments are still out there somewhere in the woods at Gdov. They try to escape towards the south-west of the lake, where there are none of our troops yet. They should be hamstrung pretty soon. Nearby two Generals and their staff are assigning defensive sections to the regiments. Near the Generals stands another prisoner, a Lieutenant Colonel of the Reds, who doesn't look as animalised as the dead officers we have seen so far. The Captain who shot himself at Sedinki and the dead Major at the village of Lipjagi, whose documents we had been able to capture, matched the image of the Bolshevist upstart far better than this man, who made a very good and calm impression on me. I ask the Sonderführer translator if I am allowed to talk to the man to find out his age and about his family. The officer then tells me that he is 39 years old. His father had been a *kolleschski sovetnik* under the old tsarist regime. The Sonderführer explains to me that this was a kind of a higher-ranked state chamberlain. The Russian had heard us talk about the commissars, and then remarked of his own accord that there were commissars in every unit from company level upwards. From 1940, however, their power had been much reduced by Timoschenko and only the officers had the power to command. The commissars were left with political supervision.

The two Generals, the commanders of 36. Infanterie-Division, 56. Infanterie-Division and some Korps commander (two stars) had ended their briefing. The latter, a friendly and corpulent man, then took the Russian officer away in his car. I took a few photographs of the prisoners and then returned to my company at the town wall where we awaited new orders from Neuling.

20 July 1941

Our subordination to 36. Infanterie-Division ended yesterday. We have caught up with our old lot in the 6. Panzer-Division. There have been some big changes. Theo Langenbruch, together with all men he still had with him, have been transferred to 1st Company. Hille has become company commander. Oberleutnant Glässgen is leading our lot with the usual self-aggrandisement and has conducted himself towards me in quite a nasty manner. Well, let's see what's coming next. Up until then I will keep my composure, that way so far has brought me greatest success. Neuling has gone to the regiment to report the return of the company. After that he will have spoken to Hille about vehicle replacements. I wonder what news he is going to bring. And I hope he'll bring some mail too. It is now 17.00 in the evening, I have had a bit of a kip from 2 to 4.30 p.m. In the mornings we get up at 05.00 to be able to get to work from 06.00. They are now already working on my tank, however, so that doesn't need to be done in the morning. Our four vehicles are with the 7th Company again. Yesterday evening Krautwurst, Schöner's former driver, arrived here. Then there is my vehicle, which I had to take from Feldwebel Bartneck, including Bartneck's driver and Gunner Rink. Obergefreiter Tamschick is the radio operator. Bartneck is a nasty customer. He had hoarded a tremendous amount of stuff, which he spent hours packing up when I took over from him. The fact that he took one of the two tins of ration sausage for himself, and several additional tins of meat as well, was totally excessive and shows what kind of a character that man is. But he is known for that kind of behaviour among the men of the company.

I am sitting here in a Russian farm cottage. Our tank is parked alongside the wall outside. This afternoon Unteroffizier Cossenjans the medic and the driver of his motorcycle combination Gefreiter Hoyers have cooked and fried a chicken and potatoes here. It's been ages since I last had such an appetising smell in my nostrils. Gefreiter Hoyers is from Hamburg, and due to his dialect is commonly known as 'Hein'. He is a good-natured, stocky fellow, who reaches up to my chin. A racing driver, driving instructor and mechanic by trade. Previously seven years of service in the Reichspost and then maintenance sergeant in the OT. He is a masterful organiser. For the 7th Company he has organised a small Ford lorry and also a captured Russian one. Thus they had allowed the two to continue to drive around in their own motorcycle combination, although they would have preferred a little car instead. Hein is married and has four children. He is a reservist, 28 years old and a very good soul. He is also 'on the ball' like no other soldier. The two ate their chicken, but they forced me to have a bit as well, and from the fried potatoes too. I have made sure that everything when the two couldn't eat any more went straight to Panzer mechanic Hoppmann of the 5th Company who today, a Sunday, has been slaving away like mad. That boy and his mates are constantly at work, without having the time to enjoy any of the few comforts we soldiers are able to get hold of out here. When we called him into our cottage, Hoppmann was wondering what else he was supposed to do for us, but then he made big eyes when the nice, fat potatoes were offered to him. Hoppmann has been in charge of repairs since Feldwebel Spieler was hospitalised with jaundice.

We have organised two stools and a sturdy table for our place and now we can sit comfortably for eating and especially writing. With my little notebook, I am usually sitting up on the tank where I write whenever we have to wait for our advance. It has become oddly cold in the past days and one has to keep one's fingers in the coat pockets. One is really freezing in the cold north wind. One has to put a pullover on at night. Now it is 22.00 and I am taking our four tanks, the maintenance platoon and the petrol lorry back to our old lot. They are further up towards the front and will probably be among the first to be deployed. After all, we are not too far away from Petersburg any more. Today we received mail, a lot of very nice mail. That put me into a proper Sunday mood. Soon we'll be back with our I. Abteilung.

21.00, Monday, 21 July 1941

I will make an attempt to put a few lines on paper amid the enormous number of mosquitoes.

It was absolutely impossible! There were thousands of mosquitoes, undeterred by the smoke of a multitude of fires. So I have now installed myself in a cottage in which NCOs and men of the old 5th Company are playing cards. They have cleaned the hovel nicely and made sure it is free of any vermin. I have to admit that the houses up here in the area of the Gulf of Finland are all quite clean and I was surprised that one can find so many images of the saints in them. I have taken one of them. Its lines are rather unique and remind me of our ancient religious depictions of bishops and saints. I have also taken a look at the chapel here in the village. To our eyes it all appears to be a bit tacky with the many gilded paintings. The Black Madonna of Tschenstochau, the painting heavily varnished and, except for the uncovered parts of the body like hands and face, over and over covered with gold and silver. The painted areas, unprotected from the air, darken over time and contrast strongly with the bright silver, giving the impression that there is a Jewish or Asian woman looking at the observer.

In general it is surprising that the Bolsheviks allow the Orthodox farmers up here to follow their old religious customs. They are using the *Kolkhoz Farmer* newspaper as wallpaper, on which they then hang the old painting of the saints made in the days of the tsars. Incidentally we have found many old banknotes of the tsarist period in the houses, some quite valuable 1,000-ruble notes.

The farmer's house is packed full. In the window our company radio is playing the news. 'In the East everything is progressing as planned!' Soon, at 22.30 there will be a bit more space, when the sentries take their posts. We have put quite a lot of them out, as it is not particularly nice to be surprised and slaughtered in one's sleep by a Red Army attack at 03.00 in the morning, 13.00 or 23.00. There is a lot of action in this area. Even though we are resting we only do so with a pistol in the trouser pocket. The Russians often and unexpectedly break through in places and then we have to recapture the ground they have gained. I wonder if the Russians will be making another appearance here again. In a village not far from here larger formations have been identified and taken under fire by our artillery.

Now Hille is leading the company. Theo has the 1st Platoon, Karl Bongardt the 2nd, Feldwebel Wünsche the 3rd and I have the 4th, which now consists of four vehicles and my own. I wonder if we will be attached to the 65ers. I wouldn't really like that. Hauptmann Stern, who was decorated with the Knight's Cross for his actions in Rasenaiei, is said to be very good and calm. But now lights out, aircraft are coming.

14.00, afternoon, Tuesday, 22 July 1941

We have put our chairs and table underneath the barn door. Tamschick the radio operator is digging a foxhole and Rink has to help clean one of the farmer's houses. Tonight we can then write our letters in there. One can dare to enter the houses here, as they are generally all quite clean. In the evenings one can then find some protection from the mosquitoes in them while writing letters and other things. There'll be card players again too. As the group members don't know what else to do with their money, some Landsers have started gambling for quite large sums. Thankfully that has now been forbidden by Stern. The chaps call it twenty-one and it's often about pots of 100 Marks and more. This is really not my thing. If they at least played skat instead, where one doesn't have to rely on individual luck.

At midday there are significantly smaller numbers of mosquitoes airborne. In the evenings it is literally unbearable. I just realised that I could do with a few minutes of sleep. More later.

* * *

Now then, I have slept enough. There weren't mosquitoes even inside the tent. Probably too hot for the nasty buggers. By the way, if it's too hot for the mosquitoes they are usually replaced by fat horse-flies. Anyway, one day there will be an end to it.

This morning I was with the baggage, which is not far away. The tailor and the shoemaker were also at work there, so I took the opportunity to have my trousers repaired which were quite spectacularly torn. I also accessed my suitcase, depositing several maps of our advance route in it. The key I keep in the document case which is stored on Oberfeldwebel Oswald's lorry, together with the captured material, but I managed to open it by trying a few other keys. I wonder when I will ever be wearing the clothing inside it again.

Here in the village everyone is keenly looking for additional supplies. The crews of the 65ers closer towards the road have discovered a pile of potatoes in the cellar of one of the houses there. Rink, my assistant gunner, has found a large piece of honeycomb. Rink and Tamschick have liquified it over a petrol fire. I have just seen that Feldwebel Goßler and crew have caught three chickens further up in the village. Oberholz is now scrubbing the washing bucket in which the cleanly plucked and gutted beasts will soon be boiled over the Primus cooker. Tonight the four men will have a great dinner. A few more supplies never do any harm.

Yesterday I was up on the roof with the aerial observer of the Luftwaffe signals platoon. The view from up there is quite spectacular. The land around here is really very beautiful. The village here is up on a hill which is surrounded by and overlooks a dense area of woodland. Behind that there are swamps. The air up here is really nice. The many mosquitoes seem to come from the land below. At the edge of the hill, in a ravine, there is a crystal-clear spring with drinkable water. Next to that there are two wells from which the local field kitchens draw their water. Well, at least they used to, until some damned idiots made one of them unusable when they washed themselves there and polluted the water with soap. What a mess! The water supply is a difficult matter out here. Each unit should be equipped with tornister filter apparatuses. It is odd that equipment like that is only ever found in the staff headquarters, isn't it? In that of II. Abteilung, Glässgen, Ritgen and Möscher the physician have one of them in their quarters. It is a disgrace when officers receive special rations or supplies of any kind. A common thing, especially in the unit staffs. The gentlemen sit together in the evening, talking about all the commodities they'd like to have and then they send one of their men out: 'Hey you! Listen up! What don't you go and fetch us …' or 'Isn't this and that available here anywhere?'

Ah well, I should not complain. If one's crew is on the ball, they can indeed organise all kinds of things. Just need to look at Henselke, no idea how he has managed to find us that chicken. And how Rink, who is a rather slow-paced character, found that honey, only God knows. Right now the air is filled with an enormous booming, humming sound. Twenty-five German bombers are returning home from a mission. They are coming from Leningrad, which is only 120 kilometres away from here. And now the fighter escort is returning as well. They are racing back to their airfield and our best wishes accompany them. Since the start of the campaign in the East our Landsers have learned to respect the Luftwaffe. All along the Rollbahn we have seen what even a single bomber can do to a marching column. One fighter after another is now returning. The yellow band around their fuselages and the yellow wingtips are glowing in the sunlight. Everyone is delighted to see them.

I have looked at the map and we are indeed only 120 kilometres from Leningrad. Yesterday our 58 Infanterie-Division stood only 5 kilometres from the Narva. It is also possible that the bombers were deployed there, to make sure that Woroschilow's withdrawing troops are being kept on their toes. The railway line along the Narva is also being bombed relentlessly. The Russians are still attacking, but their men are very clearly exhausted. If even the Russians are folding like that now, how must the French have felt when they experienced the same last year!

Today, at about 19.00, Hille arrived with the news that Theo Langenbruch will be transferred away to the leadership reserve of the staff on II. Abteilung. That's the right thing to do. Langenbruch has done much more than his fair share of the fighting. A bit later today we'll all sit down together for a nice chat. At the moment everyone is still sitting outside playing cards. Tomorrow I will take charge of 1st Platoon, now equipped with vehicles from our old 5th Company. Here in the house some of the men are brewing coffee and preparing dinner. There is always sufficient food here, all well prepared by Enz, our head chef and Unteroffizier. The coffee supply situation, however, is worse. The grain coffee doesn't taste very nice, but it's good enough when one is thirsty and one can still sleep after having had a few cups. The boss has got himself a samovar and is using it to make tea and coffee.

15.00, Wednesday, 23 July 1941

A lot has happened today. Several Russian bombers came over and scored a few direct hits on the artillery column of the 1. Infanterie-Division. Nasty, very nasty for the artillerymen. Seven of them dead, fifteen more or less severely wounded soldiers, twelve horses killed and Tamschick, my radio operator, wounded when a bomb splinter hit his calf. That's the result of an attack by five Russian SB-2 bombers and of some clowns shouting: 'They are Germans! They are Germans!' without having clearly identified them. Tamschick was in great pain and couldn't put any weight on his right leg with the splinter in it. The boy made a brave face, however, and tried not to show how much it hurt him. Langenbruch and Neuling have driven him to the hospital in Walovo now. I had sent Tamschick out to fetch oil for our tank from the vehicle baggage train. At that moment the artillery column of 1.ID was just passing the crossroads and one of its sections turned off the road to have a break here in Likowska. Then five Red bombers appeared and flew over the main road without anyone identifying them as Russian. Only when they began to fire their machine guns into the column 200 metres to our right were they identified correctly. At that point they had also released their bombs and Tamschick, who had seen what was going on, had thrown himself into the roadside ditch for cover. The bombs slammed right into the two still undamaged houses which are being used as a staff HQ and a field dressing station, while others fell among the densely packed carts and vehicles of the artillery section. Not normal high-explosive bombs, but particularly nasty splinter bombs which had a tremendous effect on the large, unprotected targets. Seven men dead instantly and another two died while they were being prepared for transport to hospital. Eighteen more wounded in addition.

Just as bad is the loss of twelve horses; the beasts are irreplaceable out here in the East. Some ammunition carts were also heavily damaged. After the dust had settled, Tamschick had started tending the wounded. After he had bandaged a man who had lost an arm and also had a large bomb splinter sticking in his thigh, he suddenly noticed the pain in his own leg. He then tried to walk over to the Kübel of the boss, but only managed to walk a few steps before the pain made him collapse. Before Theo and Tamschick left we shook hands with them, wished them all the best and 'break a leg' and then they drove away.

In the morning at 8 a.m., Theo said farewell to his company, which he had taken to his heart. We also took a few photographs. Yesterday night I had brought half a litre of schnapps, good Russian stuff, and I poured the contents into the samovar. I don't think I ever drank a better cup of tea. At 10 p.m. we had to put out the lights because of the Russian flyers, but we still sat together in the darkness for a long time after that. Later Enz came over and whispered into Theo's ear that he still had some food left for us in the field kitchen. Theo, Oswald and I went there and were given the most excellent beef liver with new potatoes. God, they tasted nice. All washed down with a big cup of bean coffee. After all the coffee and tea it wasn't surprising that I couldn't find any sleep. The tent isn't entirely sealed either; there are a few rips and tears which he tried to cover up with a mixture of German and Russian tent squares, but even those didn't do the trick. All through the night, ssss, one, ssss, two, the damned mosquitoes came in. At the moment it is 23.00 and I am sitting with Feldwebel Rehberg and a few men of the 65th in a Russian hovel. An oil lamp is flickering. I am writing, Rehberg is reading a novel while the other boys are playing cards. A paper sketchpad is used to keep the tally. After the war the sums will be added up and paid out. They are not playing for money here. Only for entertainment. Yesterday I had to laugh when Leutnant Karl Bongardt, with a stern face, said to Oswald and Wünsche: 'Gentlemen, you still owe me money!' I wondered how enormous that sum must be if someone wants to have it back while there is a war going on. Wünsche asked: 'How much was it again, Herr Leutnant?' and Bongardt replied: 'Oswald needs to give me 6 Pfennings and 14 Pfennigs from you!' And then he did indeed collect the debt!

Now then, the tanks of the Neuling company which I have been waiting for here have just arrived. Outside one can still hear the hum of Russian bombers and as such I want to get the guys away from the crossroads as quickly as possible. All through the nights the Russians are circling above and they have already dropped some bombs on Wolovo.

Thursday, 24 July 1941

We are still resting in Likowska today. Yesterday another platoon of the old 5th Company arrived here. II. Abteilung is only raising the platoons now and is then transferring them to I. Abteilung and Abteilung 65. Wilhelm Lope also ended up in Abteilung 65. I saw him yesterday evening with the platoon of heavy tanks which is going to go to 3./65. Simon is also going there. Just a moment ago Jungkamp skidded round the corner in his Praga, next to him Knust, who by now has also been promoted to Leutnant. They are also going into the leadership reserve. They have both done their share at the front. That they are sending Wilhelm Lope, a married man, to the front again, though, that I can't quite understand. Well, at least old foxes like him and me know that we have been through every single day of this campaign right at the front. One day there will be a blessing from above for us two as well. One can't share the single EK1 that the II Abteilung has received so far. And that had gone to the senior physician. I hope our lot won't be entirely fucked over when the next batch of medals is due. That is of great concern at the moment.

21.00, Friday, 25 July 1941, Likowska

Seems we'll stay here until Monday. There is no way the infantry and heavy weapons will have deployed before that. The Reds are now clearly showing signs of deterioration. It is quite telling that they fill their infantry up with alcohol before an attack. It's pretty bad for them; 2,300 dead Russians are lying here in front of the lines of our bridgehead. Today I. Abteilung had an officers' briefing led by Hauptmann Stern. He always leaves a very calm and sensible impression on us men of the old 5th after our previous experience with Bethke. There are several officers in I. Abteilung that I don't particularly like. Everts, Niemann and Böhme, all three have been with me when we were still reserve officer candidates under Christian Schmidt. They are all good men. But then there is Herbert, the regiment's fattest Leutnant, whose whole bearing doesn't fit in at all. During the party of the 7th Company in Freystadt he behaved particularly badly. Leutnant Herz is a particularly nasty tango lad. The dandy looks just like a Jewish boy. Today he was wearing sunglasses again and bragged and lied in a disgusting manner. When one shakes his hand it feels as if one holds a cold, damp, feeble piece of meat – he is unable to reciprocate with a firm, manly grasp. He'd be proper Berlin-Kudamm* material. Then there is Marse, the chap who ruined the chance of promotion of the good Werner Handschuh, but who is now an Oberleutnant in I. Abteilung. And Oberleutnant Haffmeyer, the former Adjutant of the big boss, who once forced me to do a handstand in front of Major Stephan. He even brought his fleabag rough-haired dachshund with him on campaign! Something Dr Menke, our surgeon, is mutinous about. The Adjutant Himmesbach is quite all right, I think. He is quite friendly, but that leaves not much of an impression on me. Such men as Oblt. Bethke and Theo Langenbruch, Rudi Schöner and Kleinjung, Möllenberg, Vielbaum and Eggert – such men are missing here.

We received mail today. Father has sent me four films, so I can start taking photographs again! It's always great to receive mail. I am sitting in the mosquito-free schoolhouse. There is a window on the western side, through which, in the fading light, I have a great view across the swamp towards the dense birch forest of the kind so common here in this region of Russia. I can also see the clouds of dust thrown up by the columns of the main road of advance. They mix with the evening fog to form a dense, white haze which announces the position of valuable targets to Russian bombers far and wide. I have just lit a candle as I have lent my oil lamp to Hille and Bongardt, who are playing cards in the other room. The racket the guys make for a game worth 8 Pfennings is enough to make one's eardrums burst. The sun is now setting, but the light of the candle is still good enough to write some more. Right next to me, Kübelborsch is falling asleep. He has

---

* i.e. nightlife.

been promoted to Gefreiter today, together with all the other men with one year of service. For bravery in the face of the enemy. They really deserve it. Have all greatly distinguished themselves in virtually every battle out here in the East. Masshense, the chap who ran after my tank at Jamkino, in particular. Van Dyck, who cradled the wounded Unteroffizier Schmidt in his arms, as well. Henschke and Ashauer, who fought at my side at Gdov when the Russians attacked during the night. They all deserve it.

Last night a lot of Russian bombers were out and about. It is a nasty feeling to know that these Red Heinis are circling above. One feels like a little worm; there is nothing one can do for protection. No Flak is firing and none of our fighters can be seen. Then the bumble bees fly on and start pounding the advance routes. And just when one has fallen asleep, the next batch comes along in the dark. I suppose they are looking for the nearby airfield and I hope they'll never find it. Now it's lights out and off to the tent. May God protect us from the mosquitoes.

15.00, Saturday, 26 July 1941, Likowska

Listening to some amazing music on the radio. I have had a cup of coffee with sugar and dunked some biscuits into it. Then I closed my eyes and imagined that I was sitting in the Alster Pavilion where a great band, of the kind I listened to last winter, was playing. But I must yearn for home. When in the future one sits together with the old comrades, then we'll wish to be back here, in these days were we experience unique events, even with a lot of cursing and complaining. After dinner I quickly gave my clothing a wash. That was more than necessary. The collar of my shirt was already getting greasy. I don't really want the men to wash my clothing, my undershirt, the socks and the black shirts. In wartime it's best if everyone takes care of his own things. At least I think that way and I act accordingly.

We are stubbornly waiting for the next deployment. Leningrad has to fall and we will capture it! I am wondering how stiff the Russian resistance will be. They are crumbling slowly but steadily by now. We have already smashed their best divisions in Lithuania. Anything that will be facing us here has to be driven back with the greatest force. It is said that Woroschilow has ordered that his troops are not only to halt us, but to defeat us fully. I can't quite see how they are supposed to achieve that. We have to be patient and must not complain. There will be plenty of opportunities to prove that one is not afraid. We wait, and when we decide to offer ourselves for combat, then we'll have to hit our opponent with all available force and without quarter. And when that is done one must not become reckless just because one was fortunate enough to survive. Never must one tempt fate.

Here we are in Likowska, where we are not directly confronted with an enemy who harasses us now and then with his Martin bombers and Ratas; one should at all costs avoid taking a walk in a bright white shirt. Those wild wasps can appear out of nowhere. Whenever something like this happens I order my men into their tanks or into other available cover. And they will get a bollocking should they fail to comply quickly. Down at Lake Peipus I have done the same to some men of the 7th Company who had left their tanks during the fighting to search some dead Russians for their pistols. Tank crews, commanders and gunners should be inside their vehicles and not in hospital or, in the worst case, in a cheap mass grave. As long as the infantry is shooting, that is where they need to be.

I just learned that Tamschick did have a lot of luck too. When the bomb exploded, he was standing next to the full oil canister. This was completely shredded by splinters, but had stopped some which would otherwise have hit Tamschick. Just one into the calf – that was bad enough. We have furnished our tank with a sunroof, which we fashioned from a Russian tent square. That way I can now sit on the turret to write. A good place and way to kill time. And comfortable too. In a moment I will go down to the spring on the other side of the village to wash myself thoroughly. After all, it is Saturday today.

Sunday, 27 July 1941

Just back from a company briefing. Woke up at 07.00, briefing at 08.00, food at 11.00 and at 12.00 we'll drive down to the bridgehead to relieve the guys of the 65th. We have acquainted ourselves with the terrain and studied the map. Oberst Hille was already down there personally to take a look at the proceedings. According to him this is the toughest position our division has had to defend so far. Over 4,000 dead Russians are lying around up there. The Reds have firmly entrenched themselves all around the bridgehead and because of that there are no plans to enlarge it further. When we assemble for the great attack we'll have to capture their positions anyway, so why go to the effort now. There'll be more heavily entrenched Reds a few kilometres ahead anyway. In the morning Hille issued all kinds of rules of engagement – well, I am wondering what we'll encounter there. They have already finished off seven of the big buckets down there and at least three more have recently been observed. Maybe it'll be us who finish those last three off. But I don't want to fantasise. Better to look at the facts. I also don't like to designate any crew members to take the job of 'assault detachment on foot'. I'd rather do that myself, that way I won't have any comrades on my conscience if something happens to them. And something is bound to happen. What use is it if I give that task to Laurenzi, my new radio operator, and he lacks the drive when the moment arrives in which he is needed? Aures will get out without orders if he's needed, there will be no need to ask him. I am taut with excitement about what the next days will bring.

So today is Sunday, the sixth!! which we have spent on the ground of the Soviet Union. We all wish that the preparations are finished soon and that we can attack again. But we have to live from one day to the next and must never think too far ahead. Better to catch a lot of sleep and then attack with steady nerves.

For the third time yesterday, while I was sitting on the thunderbox, a mosquito bit me in my most delicate parts. How bad is that! The mosquito plague here is just crazy. At home no one can imagine what it is like here, where you automatically swat your hands at all the buzzy beasts, just like horses and cattle do with their tails. And then the dust and the heat! Even though it's not 72°C in the sun, the inside of our iron coffins easily reaches that temperature. And it's not rare that one spends twenty hours, from 03.00 in the morning until the night, inside our buckets. When one needs to relieve himself outside, another man has to take his position at the guns. We have all experienced something like that. And if one has saved a little swig of coffee, that is often shared with the crew or some poor, thirsty infantryman. Those poor buggers are getting even less than we are. Supposedly we can soon enjoy the 'roads' of the Soviet paradise again. Never in my life will I be able to forget the dust. It makes one look like a flour miller, someone wearing flour sacks and not a black uniform. But anyway, all is well if we only capture Leningrad! We must take possession of Leningrad!

In the area of the new bridgehead the water is supposed to be better as well. This is very important, as so far we have washed with something that resembles liquid manure, or in the best case old and stale rainwater. Yesterday evening Rink and I were down at the well to fetch some water. Some resourceful chaps had dug a deep hole right next to the outlet and then drew the clear water from it with a pump. Being hosed down with clear and fresh water was delightfully refreshing. Just now my Unteroffizier Albert, my current driver, and Unteroffizier Förster, who joined up with me and is now in command of a tank, received the EK2. Gradually the awards are coming in.

We are now at the bridgehead. This little bit of ground has already soaked up a lot of blood. Everywhere there are crosses. About 300 German soldiers are said to have fallen here in the bridgehead. On the other side, though, there are 4,000 dead Russians.

21.00 – It is getting dark. Thank God, the mosquito density here is much lower than it is in the forests in which we have been based previously. Our troops are spread out, up to and including Zagorje, where I have just been to visit Leutnant von Huis of the staff of Schützen-Regiment 114 and to organise some heavy field telephone cable. Sadly that is nowhere to be had as we are now in the 3-kilometre zone in front of the enemy and only double-circuit lines are allowed here. Well, then we will have to do without a telephone. But while I was down there I took a look at one of the bunkers and I did really like it. I'll make sure we'll build one of those here as well, because rumour has it that we'll be here for about fourteen days. Such rumours travel from high command to the officers, from them to the old Feldwebel, from there the young Unteroffiziere, who then spread the information to their own crews. Latrine rumours like that spread like wildfire. Always exciting to find out what is actually true.

As long as we are not taken under all too heavy fire by the Russian artillery it should be quite bearable here for a while. Right next to us in the valley, down a 6-metre steep sandbank, there is a little river which invites us to bathe. We'll make use of it tomorrow. Today my platoon is on standby. Several times now Russian reconnaissance patrols have probed across the river and have come right up to this area. The infantry on our side isn't deployed very densely. Unteroffizier Dahlmann has just been down there to establish communication with the infantry. They have one platoon per 300 metres of ground, which isn't very much in that heavily wooded terrain. On the other hand the heavy Russian tanks won't find it particularly easy to traverse the swampy woodland either. After the great casualties the Russians have suffered here, they are now switching to a defensive posture, digging themselves in on the other side. In front of Petersburg they are supposed to have raised three new armoured corps! Whether that is true, I don't know. The Russian is an opponent who has been clearly underestimated by our politicians! Anyway, from today I am awaiting the outcome of the next few days with even greater excitement. I hope the air tonight won't be filled with too much iron.

Monday, 28 July 1941

At the bridgehead, 14.00. Last night an infernal concert started. At precisely 00.00 the Russians attacked us along our eastern line. Our tracer rounds looked like fireworks on the Kaiser's birthday! Our company has not intervened, only the heavy howitzer 200 metres on our right did. And when one of those 15-cm barrels is sent flying it makes quite a racket! Several impacts on the meadow next to the river, about 100 metres from here. I don't know why there haven't been any impacts in our company sector yet. The 65th wasn't hit either, only one single shell came down here at that time. I haven't slept much. At midnight the concert started, the Russians pounded our eastern line and a lot of stuff came down in the river here. At 01.00 the whole conjuration suddenly ended. At 02.00 I finally fell asleep but an hour later the Russians opened up again with all calibres; so heavy was the fire that it made the earth tremble.

* * *

21.00: All formations are ordered to prepare to leave at 22.00. Our unit will be the last armoured formation to leave the bridgehead. The infantry is now taking over fully. Our own riflemen have already moved out. Seems I have built my nice dugout in vain. I had brought two large loads of picket fencing from the village, so much of it that I nearly collapsed under the weight. All that digging, all those calluses and blisters on our hands, all in vain! Our foxholes had become really quite comfortable – well, in the coming hours we will have to leave them. At least there is some comfort in the knowledge that we only had a one-night performance of the drama here. Now the infantry corps are to catch up with us and then the advance on Leningrad is to continue. The Russians here always fire at the same time – so it's basically harassing fire. In the mornings between 03.00 and 04.00, then from 08.00 to 09.00, when the field kitchens are crossing the bridge. And now during the early night they are plastering us again.

Oh, by the way, together with Unteroffizier Grawe I went down to the church, where the grave of Leutnant Leppelmann is situated. Leppelmann had fallen at the crossroads ahead; from there we wanted to go down to the dam where one of the 'heavy tanks' which had steamrollered through Company Marquardt is standing. From the church I took photographs of the dam and the power station. The Russians must have seen me and sent a few salvoes of machine-gun fire in our direction. The bullets scythed through the grass just where Grawe and I were standing. Because it was so foggy, I decided to take a photo with a longer exposure time. But just when I had raised my head over the wall of the churchyard to line up my shot – ratatatat – another burst of bullets smacked into the grass next to me. I had to make do with a quick snapshot before I went back. We dropped the plan to go to the dam. After our return we ran into Paul te Heesen and Edu Brüggemann, who had taken a motorcycle combination to get to the bridgehead, just to find out what was going on. All together we then headed down to the company's assembly area, where everyone greeted the old comrades.

Now it is getting dark, I have to finish for today.

The remaining photographs in this book have been taken from the album of a member of one of the heavy companies of Panzer-Regiment 11. Two of them show a captured Russian T-28 tank, pressed into German service as a *Beutepanzer*. It is known that the T-28 was deployed by 4th Company, which is the unit in which the few identifiable men in the photos also served.

None of the photographs has ever been captioned or dated, but it is clear that they were taken during the first months of 'Operation Barbarossa', in summer and autumn 1941. While it might be possible to tie some of the photos to certain events and dates, I have decided not to furnish the photographs with captions (which would in many cases just be stating the obvious) and to continue to allow them to speak for themselves. Many of them are of exceptional quality; often photographed through the vision slit or from the turret of a Panzer IV, they offer a superb visual back-up to the diaries of Wilhelm Sander and a fascinating view of the campaign from the perspective of a Panzermann in Panzer-Regiment 11.

Tuesday, 29 July 1941

12.00, Likowska: This morning at 08.30 the company moved out of the bridgehead. The infantry had taken over the positions of our riflemen yesterday evening and had immediately started to throw their fireworks on the Russians. When our last vehicles exited the woods to get on the road, the Russian artillery began firing. That we are not facing an easy opponent here can be seen by the graves of the fallen comrades which line the road in great numbers, especially closer towards the bridgehead. There are mass graves full of Russians too. The trees here are mostly splintered, and the many water-filled shell and bomb craters lend it quite a spooky look. But anyway, the Russians are crumbling, the prisoner interrogation reports make that quite clear. Even if we have to wait a while longer until we attack again. The main thing is: we'll roll forward again! We have advanced closest to Leningrad now and are happy about that success. When we are rolling towards the bridgehead again, the infantry will have closed up, and together with the 'Queen of All Arms' we'll then finish off the Red divisions. Up until then: 'Panzer *heil*!' and 'Batten down the hatch!'

Wednesday, 30 July 1941

Likowska: Today is Oberleutnant Hille's birthday. For this festive event I organised all that was necessary for a small birthday surprise for the boss. Early in the morning the sentries had picked a bunch of flowers in the meadows and gardens which Fahnenjunker Lappe would present to Hille. Then, early in the morning before the wake-up call, the whole company assembled around Hille's tent and then started singing 'Alte Kameraden' for the birthday boy. When we sneaked up to his tent, Hille was still deep asleep. But when the first notes had been sung, there was movement inside. When we had finished singing, a completely surprised Oberleutnant came out of the tent and we pressed the bunch of wild flowers into his hands. Hille then held a little speech and expressed his gratitude to the company. All in all a commendable celebratory effort, considering the situation we are in. The Spiess donated a bottle of cognac for the boss, which was then emptied by us 'administrative authorities', with a side dish of a packet of biscuits and a good cup of coffee from the samovar. We are all sitting on the stairs of the Red school. Who says that one can't have a few comfortable moments in the field? Between cognac and coffee I had to write evaluation reports from the Fahnenjunker, who had already prepared everything for their journey to Paderborn. They'll be joining the Waffenschule in Wünsdorf.

The brothers had been quite a burden. Rink and Ashauer had not initially been chosen by the regiment, and from then it had been my job to get the two up to scratch. Rink had been lucky and had received a last-minute permission via the telephone, only Ashauer was supposed to stay here. As he had really done his best while he was in our company, I had personally spoken to Wilts, Bauer, Hagemeister and finally to the Oberst himself to make sure that the unlucky fellow would get his posting, and he did agree as well in the end. The boy was incredibly happy when I brought him the news that he could go as well. In addition to Ashauer, Rink my gunner, Lappe and Henschke, Kuhlbörsch – one of the drivers – were also leaving to become reserve officer candidates.

20.00: Led by Hille, we have now arrived in Samoschje. This is now the place where our reinforced company will be for a while. The village seems to be home to enormous swarms of mosquitoes, but never mind, we are now getting used to them. In addition to our lot of the 5th, there is also Oberleutnant Eggert with three Panzer IVs and Leutnant Spiekermann with his pioneers. His men have just conducted a search for men over 14 years of age. Result: one man, a one-eyed hydrocephalic of about 30 years of age, and five old Rasputins, one of them on crutches. All of them have long beards and scruffy hair. Hardly anyone has any teeth left in his mouth. They all assemble in the village square where our tanks are, none of them having any idea what was going on. I tell the old codgers to sit down. They laugh at my attempts to speak Russian and immediately relax a little. Then I ask them where the partisans are and suddenly they are all excited again. I guess they misunderstood what I had said. They'd be far too old, they explained, while pointing at their toothless jaws. Waterhead shows me his dark red eye socket. The partisans are all '*na sluzhba*', in service in Leningrad, they told me. Seems the Russians are assembling everyone who still has two legs and is able to squeeze a trigger up there in Leningrad.

Thursday, 31 July 1941

11.00: Uninterrupted sleep until 08.00. Yesterday we sat together until 21.30, celebrating Hille's birthday. By chance Theo Langenbruch had arrived in the evening with some paperwork from Glässgen and at the same he had brought a box with 100 half-litre bottles of beer from Riga! What a joy! Hille had secured ten bottles for us and in addition a bottle of cognac supplied by the Spiess. He then had a big pan of fried potatoes made. At 21.30 all platoon leaders had assembled in the farmer's parlour which we had nicely tidied up for the occasion. On a table there was a quietly hissing samovar and there was excellent music on the radio. The potatoes tasted amazing and we could take a lot of them. All washed down with half a litre of Riga's best, which was very good indeed. Good enough to match our German beer. Then we passed the cognac bottle around, together with my schnapps glass, the only one the company possesses. A wild collection of cups and mugs stood ready on the table to be filled with steaming hot tea. I need to get myself one of those samovars. They work far better than the modern coffee apparatus owned by Zangenmeister. Hille tells us that we'll be staying here for eight days before the attack on Leningrad begins. The Oberst has told him that.

We notice that the old houses here, so close to Leningrad, show more traces of culture than those we have come past further to the south-west. Here the wooden constructions rest on stone foundations, while inside there are sometimes two or three rooms. Inside we often find traces, small items like photographs, which link to a bygone time of culture before 1917. There are no traces of any cultural achievements of the Soviet period. The people here are also slightly better dressed than in the villages and don't all have the bearing of the international proletariat. Many women still sport the short cut hairstyles which I remember seeing in Germany during Communist marches. In general, their clothing is that of Germany in 1926/27. When our propaganda claims that the Bolsheviks have proletarianised everyone out here, turning the people into a big herd of submissive cattle, it is entirely right. Their outward appearance alone proves it.

Besides we have noticed that the collectives and kolkhozes are either hiding all their cattle or they are driving them to the north, away from us. That puts us at quite a disadvantage, as that means that, in addition to petrol and ammunition, our supply units also have to drag huge amounts of food across enormous distances. But in general there is nothing to complain about. There is enough bread and crispbread and that is quite filling. We just have to be careful with what we have and take the rest from the land if we can find something. If only the potatoes were ready to harvest. Now the thoughtless infantrymen dig whole potato fields over just to find enough to fill one small basket with potatoes. And in the winter it is we who can feed the population. And we already have the whole of Europe hanging on our shirt tails.

Friday, 1 August 1941

17.00 – We slept until 08.00 as usual, washed ourselves, had breakfast and then assembled at 09.00. Letters from home were distributed. I already received mine yesterday evening and I read them all in the flickering light of a small candle before I went to bed.

Now as I am writing here my driver is testing our new brakes right in front of me. We just had new brake pads installed and now he is going back and forth with a howling engine and is distracting me quite severely. Particles of soot from the exhaust are raining down on the paper, but I am more than willing to tolerate that if only the old bucket can still take us to Leningrad. Strategic objective: Leningrad! Hille is in Lossoskina, where he is trying to educate the men about the situation. Bongardt and I were sitting in the adjoining room and a map was hanging in the doorway. 'So what do you think our strategic objectives here in the East are?' We are standing behind the map, our heads sticking out to the left and right and we both look into the empty faces of the Landsers in front of us. They are all quiet and are looking at us with big eyes. Hille loses patience and shouts: 'The Volga River!'

'The Volga?' someone asks. No one wants to believe it. Another states that 'with our old carts we'll be happy if we get to Leningrad. That will be it for us!'

When we were still in battle day after day, the same Landsers would have laughed and replied, 'Consider it done, and then to the Urals if it has to be.'

And now the lazy brothers are lying around all day, being professionally tired, making trouble, becoming mutinous and wailing into one another's ears. It is an ancient truth. Too much rest dissatisfies the troops. Even Oswald now starts to get fickle. Since the day when he finished off the tank with the petrol can he feels cheated of the Knight's Cross. Now he only wants to get a transfer back to the replacement section. Opetz is even worse. Having been shot up twice by anti-tank guns, he now doesn't want to enter a tank any more. His nerves can't take it, he says. I won't even mention Bartneck, the bloody coward. He certainly won't be earning his Iron Cross 1st Class in 5th Company. But the bearing of Oswald and Opetz has shaken me. Now, when they both have the EK1 and nothing else is in sight any more, they suddenly start shirking.

Matussek is a much better man. He already got this high award in France and continues to do his best here. Aures is showing his best side too. The only thing he mutinies about is the food, even though he has the biggest belly of them all. But apart from that he still goes at them hard. The only reason why even proven men behave in that manner is that they have nothing else to do. They sit together and drink beer and one word follows another: 'If only we were at home. Poor Schramm will never get back home now that he lies buried at Zvegiai like so many others. Only a matter of time until we bite the dust too.' And whamm, that's it for morale and doubt is setting in. And because they have slept through the day and didn't fight they can't sleep in the night and start telling ripping yarns, wearing one another down even more. Damn! Next week we'll be back in action, which will be the end of the miserable mood.

Today I witnessed a local family reunion. The house on the corner, next to our tank, at the exit of the village, is inhabited by several women with lots of little children. The old woman who lives there showed us the village well yesterday. Her son-in-law has just returned a short while ago, which caused a lot of joy among the women. One of our patrols had picked him up quite a few kilometres away. He claimed to come from Leningrad, where he worked and that he was trying to get here to Samoschje. Someone interrogated him and then supplied him with a handwritten passport which he had carefully folded into a bit of old newspaper. Armed with that, he arrived here in the sidecar of the motorbike of one of our dispatch riders. So much kissing, so many tears and so much hugging! I interrogated him as well as I could and then told him that at 20.00 he had to be at the church, where he would have to spend the night and that if he failed to comply he'd be shot. If he decided to flee, that would result in the arrest of his family. He said he'd come and then disappeared into the house with the women.

With my meagre knowledge of the Russian language I am usually forced to act as a translator. When some Landsers steal a cow from a woman's barn and she turns up to complain it will be me who has to tell her to bugger off. It was me who had to tell all the ancient Rasputins here in the village that they had to come to the church to spend the night there. I have to ask the people where the roads are leading and where to find water. By now that is working quite well as I am always using the same phrases. The problem comes when the Russians then start talking like waterfalls and I suddenly can't understand a word any more. Using hands and feet, I then usually manage to communicate in the way in which Robinson spoke to the cannibals. I do intend, however, to continue to study this language after the war.

Sunday, 2 August 1941

12.00 – Now then, the morning is over again. One day passes like another at the moment. Only our driver, who always works on the vehicle, has different things to fix every day. Just as commanders describe their days based on the action that happened, the drivers base their descriptions on the damage they had to repair. The day I describe as 'the one on which Oswald finished off the big tank at Zvegiai', my driver describes as 'the one on which my camouflage headlight was shot away'. We have long stopped counting the days and making notes of the villages and towns we reach. We only take note of the special events. And for the old Skoda drivers, these events are usually linked to the ever-increasing ailments of our 'Skoda Super Sports'. I hope we get rid of the old bangers soon. I stand in awe when I see the admirable and difficult work our maintenance and repair services are doing. The old Skodas in particular cause a huge amount of work, and in terms of vehicle strength we are way ahead of other divisions.

We made ourselves comfortable in the house next to our tank – after giving it a thorough clean. I have cobbled a makeshift lamp together and now I can continue to write here, more or less protected from the swarms of midges outside. I mounted the bulbous body of a glass bottle over the flame of the oil lamp. I have fashioned that myself by hammering it into shape with a horseshoe. The things one learns in the army. To replace Rink, my wireless operator who has been transferred to the war academy in Wünsdorf, and Lorenzi, the slimy coward, I have received two new men for my crew. My new wireless man is Mashäuser, who was in the trench with me at Jamkino when we were surrounded by Russians. The boy doesn't know fear and in general knows what needs to be done. He is also a trained gunner. Bussmann is my new loader. Seems to be a quiet and calm fellow. He has only seen one action so far, so is still a little bit inexperienced. No doubt that will change quickly now that he is with us. Both are Westphalians, which is quite okay with me. I can't stand any Rhinelanders. Except for a few of the old bulls like Willi Esser the tank driver. The Rhineland brothers talk too much and don't act correctly when they need to. But afterwards there is even more big talk. The same applies to the Saxons. A big contrast to the quiet Silesians. Here in the army one learns to judge one's people.

But here is a different story about a Rhinelander: a few weeks ago Schallenberg, an Obergefreiter with four years of service, drove a Büssing lorry loaded with petrol cans. But he doesn't 'drive' in the normal sense. He doesn't care for it, he doesn't maintain it, but uses it for racing. Someone, in his eternal wisdom, has decided to give our best and heaviest lorry to this lunatic. He then races down a road which has a deep ditch, of the kind commonly found in the Soviet Union, on the left and right sides of it and tries to overtake a car and just manages to squeeze past it! What he hasn't noticed, however, is that the car is that of the regimental commander and neither has he seen that, a few hundred metres ahead of him, there is a pile of stones on the left side of the road. In full view of the commander, he rams his lorry into and over the stone pile, rupturing the oil sump before ending up in the ditch. The commander gets out of the car and gives Schallenberg the bollocking of his life and later orders him to be detained for ten days! The punishment is read out in front of the company, but Schallenberg isn't present during or after the ceremony. He seems to have disappeared. We are told that he has been posted to Germany to drive stones around for the Organisation Todt. Our best and heaviest supply lorry is ruined and out of action for an unforeseeable time.

And then, when we were in the Russian bridgehead ten days or so later, a big lorry comes racing down the road, grinds to a halt with screeching brakes right in front of the company HQ and starts hooting and blowing the compression pipe. The driver is – of course – Schallenberg, who jumps out of the cabin to make his report to the Spiess who has just turned up with the field kitchens: 'Schallenberg! You do know what's waiting for you?' asks the Spiess, and Schallenberg, in his thick Cologne accent replies: 'Yes! You surely have a pile of letters for me!' When informed that there are ten days of detention waiting, Schallenberg seems heartbroken: 'Me? What? Never! And if I personally have to speak to the OKH!' And then he tells us about his adventure. While in Königsberg, he manages to get permission to get a new oil sump from the replacement vehicle park, to replace the one he shredded. They don't have one for him. For that, they say, he needs to go to Braunschweig. A phone call is made and, yes, he can collect one there. He gets permission and train tickets and travels to the Büssing company in Braunschweig. When he arrives there, it is already closed for the night, so he spends his time in the inns of the city and returns the following morning. But there is no oil sump for the heavy lorry available. Now Schallenberg goes ballistic and puts on a show as only a Rhinelander from Cologne can do. There is a lorry full of tank ammunition at the front, he says, and states that he has been ordered to find a replacement part, come what may, and if necessary he'll take one out of a new vehicle. By then the director of the company is personally involved and promises Schallenberg a custom-made replacement which he can collect the following day. A day later a shiny new oil sump with all its fittings is waiting for him there. All is parcelled up and paperwork for priority, express delivery is issued for it. Well, thinks Schallenberg, if that parcel is getting prioritised so should I! As such he installs himself in a second-class wagon on the journey back. There he makes the acquaintance of a Leutnant of the Luftwaffe, who listens eagerly to Schallenberg's adventures and the quest for a new oil sump. Whereabouts does Schallenberg need to go? asks the Leutnant. First he needs to go to Rossitten, says Schallenberg. What follows is quite exceptional, as the Leutnant agrees to fly Schallenberg and oil sump from

Königsberg to Rossitten in a Junkers 52. Once in Königsberg, Schallenberg and oil sump have to wait for two hours before the big bird arrives. But that's nothing for an Obergefreiter with four years of service. For the first time in his life, Schallenberg travels in an aircraft. As 'Operation Oil Sump' is urgent, the Leutnant, once landed, organises a car which takes Schallenberg and his parcel to Repair Shop 2 in Pskov, where, after an hour of work, the big Büssing is repaired and ready to go. And now poor Schallenberg proudly arrives back here to learn that his few days' leave in Germany have been extended by ten days of detention* in Russia. The poor bugger.

3 August 1941

Sunday. One like the one before. Slept until 08.00, drank lots of coffee and wrote a few letters home. At 11.00, a platoon leader meeting. Wünsche and Oswald acting as troublemakers again. One man of my crew is down in the woods to help build a new thunderbox. I have brushed my uniform a little and while I am sitting here, I can hear Eggert loudly blathering about all his heroic deeds. What a damned blowhard this man is. Only when he needs to be brave, all of his vehicles suddenly bog down in a swamp, just as happened when we were down at Hill 98 at the railway line behind Karamyshewo. I am already tired again. Going to sleep some more.

14.00 – Woken up by Bongardt, who asks if I want to go bathing. Well sure! So I quickly brush my hair with my dirty fingers, cap and jacket on, don't forget the pistol, quickly grab the Russian towel and then hop into the car. Spiekermann doesn't want to join us. He suspects Glässgen is going to arrive today. Well, never mind, we'll go without him. Eggert is joining us. We drive through the woods adjoining the village, across a small bridge spanning a small stream and down a dusty road. I still think that we are heading to the small lake nearby which is the area where our regimental staff is based. But no, Bongardt and Eggert want to drive to Saruschtje. What

---

* Here Sander has stapled a squashed bedbug to the page and added a note to the upper margin: 'Here on the page sticks a deceased enemy bedbug from Samoshje. This is what they look like.'

idiocy. Sure, I'd love a bathe, but not if that means driving 50 kilometres to where II. Abteilung is based. All that for a quick dunk in the water before the 50-kilometre return journey starts along the roads 'of best Russian quality'. We are driving past an airfield where deep bomb craters and the smouldering remains of houses point to lively Russian aerial activity.

Two hours later we arrive. I can't feel my legs any more and also put my back out. On a more positive side we are informed that II. Abteilung has got our mail and – even better – Eggers has brought a nice pack of 'North State' cigarettes. What a nice surprise. We go down to the water and learn that Glässgen wouldn't come to see Spiekermann today, as he was down in the lake having a bathe. The Ozero Dolgoje lake is about 6 kilometres long and 1 kilometre wide. And I have to admit that the beautiful scenery and the lovely, clear water made up for the terrible journey. There is a nice sandy beach too. The ground gently drops into the water, before suddenly dropping to a depth of about 10 metres. By using German and Russian tent squares, several Landsers have turned some of the local fishing boats into sailing yachts, going back and forth from one bank to the other. There is a lot of traffic on the water. Rafts made from roof beams, also mostly equipped with sails, but also old rubber tyres and inner tubes had been taken into naval service. Some pioneers, more posh than the others, have two proper German rubber paddle boats with which they are speeding across the lake. A wonderful place which could make one forget that we are at war. Oh, to have a holiday house at a lake like this. One finds it hard to believe that Russia has beautiful places like this to offer, at least after all the hardship we have been through. Masses of Landsers are swimming and crowding the beaches, the air is filled with laughter.

A bit further down there is a group of men from our reconnaissance platoon. They are sitting on a wooden beam on the beach and are enjoying sunbathing. They very much remind me of a group of penguins. Out here, one does, of course, bathe in the nude and that means that our arses, which last saw the sun at Freystadt, shine bright like the sun, while the rest of our skin is dark brown. I run into many old acquaintances and after bathing we all sit down in the sun to dry ourselves. Kessler of 1st Platoon supplies Eggert and me with a nice and very tasty fish sandwich. Then another comrade brings hot tea and crispbread with honey, it is so good that we finish off most of Glässgen's crispbread supplies. After that, at about 18.00 we drove back, spending a lot of time stuck in columns of heavy supply lorries. When we arrived back at Samoschje we were so dirty and covered with dust that we had to wash ourselves again. After reading the letters we brought with us, I volunteered to fry the potatoes for the evening. By turning them over personally, I can at least make sure that none of them looks like charcoal. Everyone agrees that my fried potatoes are the best. I am very proud of that. Later in the tent, however, we noticed that we had eaten too many onions in the previous days. Just now my petroleum lamp toppled over and the glass cylinder has smashed. I need to get candles tomorrow.

Wednesday, 6 August 1941

17.00 – We are still in the idyllic woodland village of Samoschje. I feel as if I am a spa guest in the Soviet Union. Except for a few aircraft and the boom of the artillery in the distance there are no signs of war here at all. Our infantry has closed up, the artillery is in position. Now the Finns only need to shake hands with our eastern wing and when that has happened we can launch the hammer blow in the middle. I haven't got much to say about the general situation, but it isn't too bad for us. It is far worse for the Russians. Only recently the numbers of Russian tanks and heavy weapons destroyed by XXXXI. Armee-Korps and our division have been published. We are proud to have done so well. Today Hauptmann Fara has arrived. He is supposed to stay with our reinforced company. He is an odd fellow. He has overheard me talking about him, but I don't care. At 14.00 he ordered a vehicle muster of the company troop and of my platoon. That's fine with me. Even the best drivers often overlook small problems. The drivers of my platoon are all good and Benno Albert, my own chauffeur, is the best of them all. Spilken, the red-haired mutineer is also very good. When I first met him, I was sure that he was an old Communist or SPD man, but then it turned out that he had been an old Hitler Youth fighter. He will get his promotion to Unteroffizier soon.

Sounds of wild firing from the direction of the airfield. Hard to say what exactly is going on there. It's the same every day. Just now I could hear some of our Messerschmitts fly overhead. They make a high-pitched, whistling, jingling sound. The Russians, on the other hand, emit a muffled buzzing, gurgling sound. Their Ratas have a squat, thick shape, while our Mes are slim, have a longer wingspan and fly faster. The Russians also have a type which looks similar to our Ju 88s, but its cockpit sticks out longer than the two engines in the wings, just like the middle finger is longer than the index and ring finger. Their bomber types are all hard to tell apart. By now not many of them come over any more, even though there are eight big airfields around Leningrad. In the morning hours it's now our fighters and bombers flying over towards the Russians. This morning, early at 03.30, I was woken by a closed formation of our bombers, twenty-six of them, heading towards the north. In these moments, when we see our Luftwaffe, our feelings are similar to that of the infantry when they see us going into action. They cheer and laugh and wave their hands excitedly. When we tankers see our aircraft going into action, we feel the same. Only they can't hear us shouting or see us waving.

Yesterday evening we ate like kings. Enz had slaughtered a cow; the meat was distributed to the crews and until deep in the night there was frying, stewing and cooking going on. The whole village smelled wonderful. Before that, however, something typical happened: a fellow of the supply train had, in a moment in which Enz was distracted, cut the tongue from the briefly unguarded cow's head. Always the same with these guys. It can only have been Bartneck! And yes, when it was announced that there would be no meat distribution before the tongue had been returned, Bartneck stood at exactly the same spot where ten minutes later the tongue was found in a bucket. Uncomradely *Schweinehunde*. As a side we had boiled potatoes with peas, prepared by Mashäuser and Unteroffizier Albert with extra gravy for everyone. Baumann and I had organised the peas. The farmers here have several large fields full of them. It was a boring job to sift through all the peas and to pick out those which were riddled with worms, but I know how to do it; after all, I always had to help my mother when she did it. I can take care of myself, I have no need to marry. Today we'll have peas again, this time, however, with fried potatoes as all the meat has been eaten. But that will be nice too.

Other than those rather boring details there is nothing new. Glässgen visited yesterday and brought a big pile of cigarettes which Ritgen had organised in Riga. For a non-smoker like me, nothing to become excited about. I wonder what we'll be able to pull out of Leningrad once that has been cleared. Won't be long now.

Thursday, 7 August 1941

Samoschje, 11.40 – Platoon leader meeting with Hille soon. Earlier I have been down at the regiment to visit some old comrades. Robert Gläser wasn't there, only Najdkowski and Beese were with their vehicles and Klüsener the nipper. The regiment, which means Koll and his staff, are based in a hospital at the Samro lake which had once been a cloister. We looked into the church, which was still fully furnished with images of the saints and a beautiful wooden altar. Piles of chasubles of the clergy were also still in there. Then Hauptmann Fara and I climbed up the spire, from where we had a fantastic view across the lake. For a moment we both felt like schoolboys on a sightseeing tour. One hour left until we march out. Mood is excellent. Everyone is looking forward to tomorrow when we'll finally advance on Leningrad.

Lossoskina, 17.30 – Our company is waiting at the crossroads where Tamschick was wounded and where the nine artillerymen were killed by bombs. And damn yes! It is already getting busy! The Russians seem to want to reconnoitre our assembly! Finally it's kicking off again, thank God for that! No more endless waiting! Here at the crossroads we are waiting for the artillery section with its Nebelwerfer, to which we have been attached today. I remember when we saw their rockets detonating at Raseiniai, howling across us towards the Dubysa. Many Landsers threw themselves to the ground, our knees trembling, and it was an eerie feeling when we saw the detonation clouds rising up ahead. I hope I can witness the spectacle again today. At the moment the flyers are busy again. A Russian bomber flew over towards the airfield and was immediately taken under heavy and well-aimed Flak fire. The bugger didn't fall, though. The aircraft of the Russians are all well armoured, that we all know by now, and they don't fall easily. Two of our fighters gave chase and down here the whole assembly climbed out of their vehicles to see the spectacle unfold through their binoculars, cheering and taking bets. The three aircraft, however, soon pulled out of sight. What a shame, but by then we all had to hurry back into our tanks as all the Flak splinters came raining down just where we were standing and it is not nice to get one of those stuck in your head.

The Russians here have started harvesting the rye. Yesterday there was a great commotion when an assembly of old women marched towards us while we were having a sunbathe and started babbling about sickles, scythes, rye and harvesting. It took a long time before I understood that they were asking for permission to walk to an uninhabited house near the village to fetch some sickles for the rye harvest. The women said they were too old and frail to use the scythe and the crop-cutting machine had broken down. After the war I will study this language properly.

11.30, Friday, 8 August 1941, in front of the Luga bridge

The attack has been rolling for two hours now. At 09.00 our artillery barrage started and at the same time our infantry attacked. We are standing about 1 kilometre away in a forest clearing to protect one of our Nebelwerfer batteries. During the night our rifle companies have been pulled out of their positions along the riverbank and are participating in the attack. We are basically doing their job now; making sure that any Russian elements who might be pushed across the Luga by our attack don't end up capturing the valuable Nebelwerfers. At the moment our own fire has ceased, but Russian long-range artillery is sending its shells here towards the Luga bridge. The shells impact about 500 to 800 metres ahead of us – 15- and 21-cm calibres. The heavy shells are to make sure that we are staying where we are – at least that's my guess. It's a shame. I can't make contact with anybody and I would love to learn what's going on in front and how the infantry attack is going. The intensity of the fire was incredible. I wonder if the big bridge has survived. And if not, will we be able to cross over the small one? Why haven't we silenced their heavy batteries first? After all, our flyers are over there all the time. But the Luftwaffe might be up at Kingissepp and Weymarn now, attacking the railway line there. We can hear the howl of the shells before they fall around the bridge. The reports of the Russian guns can be clearly heard as well. There is a sound-ranging section here as well, also with valuable equipment. We are guarding those guys as well.

Now our artillery is firing again. I just noticed that I can also hear machine-gun fire ahead. Seems that they haven't advanced that far yet. I doubt anything will be coming our way. Well, except for their artillery fire. But so far, thank God, nothing came down anywhere close. This is unexpected because the rocket projectiles of the Nebelwerfer battery leave long smoke trails in the sky which usually mark their position clearly. But now the rain is coming down in streams and that seems to be pushing the smoke down again, quite effectively hiding the Nebelwerfer position from the Russian artillery observers on the other side. We, on the other hand, just need to stick to scheduled fire plans. Down at Bol'shoy Sabsk, where 1. Panzer-Division is attacking, it's rumbling quite considerably. They probably have more artillery down there. Whamm! That was a close one. If after the war they ever need a sound imitator for the movies, I will volunteer as a howling shell. Since Jamkino I have become quite adept in judging those sounds. Too close, too far away – I can hear that quite clearly.

I was just informed that the Nebelwerfer are going to fire another salvo, which means another 108 rockets! That spectacle will last two or three minutes – I have to correct myself, it didn't even last that long. We are lucky that it's raining so heavily.

The Nebelwerfer chaps are taking the camouflage off their launchers again. Seems the infernal spectacle is going to repeat itself a third time. I wonder how long it will take until the Russians pinpoint our location. I am not keen to see these big Russian shells coming down here.

Miserable weather. Rainfall is so dense that I am quite happy now that we didn't have to lead the attack. No chance to see or aim through our optics in this monsoon. And I am tired. Hardly slept during the night. Only arrived here at 04.00; there was just no going forward on the vehicle-clogged roads. Horse-drawn vehicles on the left and right side of the road, all surging forward and we in the middle squeezing past the oncoming traffic. I really have had enough of this. Today I am in a bad mood, I think. But a bit of moaning should be allowed.

Now it's lunchtime and, quite laudably, Enz has materialised up here with the field kitchen. He is now distributing food, not minding the artillery fire. The infantry chaps at the front don't have that luxury today. I really want to know how far they have advanced by now. I can still hear machine-pistol and machine-gun fire, I think. I might be wrong, though. Maybe Hille knows? I am going to eat first.

It feels odd. The fire has moved further and further northwards and we are still sitting here in the same spot, with the knowledge that the great offensive on Leningrad has started. This will be a day for the history books and I can't take part in it in the furthermost line. The men are similarly depressed. 'Herr Leutnant, when are we buggering off?', 'Herr Leutnant, the infantry should be way past the anti-tank positions now, shouldn't we form the lead now for the next 50 kilometres?' It makes one want to cry.

Feldwebel Funk, the leader of the tank mechanics, is here to take a look at my tank. The engine is losing oil. Six litres alone yesterday! I really hope the old bucket won't die under me. Funk also informed me that the infantry advanced about 6 kilometres. The only thing I can say from here is that the heavy Russian guns are still firing. If they had advanced more than 10 kilometres these guns would be on the run by now. It's now 15.00 and still no one really knows what's going on.

Saturday, 9 August 1941

At the Luga, 18.00 – I am a little shaken at the moment. Our offensive has stalled in heavy Russian fire at Jurki. The 1. Infanterie-Division has managed to advance about 6 kilometres towards Kingissepp. These are the results of two days of fighting! For us that means that we are now only 500 to 600 metres ahead of where we started! There is absolutely nothing 6. Panzer-Division can do, even with tanks, as, in addition to deep anti-tank ditches, the Russians have also placed mine barriers. Directly on the road just in front of the first Russian positions alone, our men have dug up more than eighty mines! Two tanks of Hoffmeyer's company were completely destroyed, one dead, six wounded. Our company has three wounded. One of the Luga bridges has been considerably damaged; it can now only take cars and motorbikes. It's sagging between the piers too. The other bridge was only scratched. Kradschützen 6, of which two companies had been deployed at the front, had twelve dead and many more wounded. Schützen 4 has severe casualties too. For now I remain sceptic about the rumours that they suffered 30 per cent casualties. 1. Infanterie-Division has managed to reach Srednje Selo, with its batteries now standing on Point 61, at the entrance to the village. That's what you get when you give the Russians three weeks of time to dig themselves in! In addition there is a division of Red Guards there as well, mostly made up of Party members and well known for the fact that its soldiers don't surrender. Now it's 20.10 and the Russians are giving us the evening blessings, sending shell upon shell into the gun limbers and artillery positions along the road.

Shells are falling closer and closer to where we are. I am getting slightly concerned. It'll soon get interesting if that continues. Still those pesky heavy Russian batteries. I can faintly hear the reports of their guns in the distance. Some of the Nebelwerfer guys who were once regular artillerymen tell me that these are 21-cm shells. Bloody hell, they are really hitting us hard now. I hope they don't shift their fire on us during the night. They are surely going for the bridge now. They are nearly smashed to bits already. Some of our vehicles down at the river seem to be damaged. My vehicles are just taking their night-time positions between the rocket launchers. I hope that the Russians don't dare to cross the river tonight.

Sunday, 10 August 1941

On the Luga, 11.00 – We are in the process of driving down to the bank of the Luga. The Nebelwerfer are changing positions and my platoon is still tasked to protect them. I wonder if we'll draw artillery fire down there, because it's right in the range of the Russian mortars. At the moment we are traversing a forest which has been very much hacked to pieces by the Russian artillery. I have already been down at the Luga to get an impression about the situation there. We'll have to dig ourselves in there, no question about that. The weather is wonderful now and the flyers make full use of it. A Messerschmitt returned from chasing a pair of Russian bombers drawing a thick trail of smoke. While it was flying over us, its cockpit canopy flew off and tumbled to the ground. It seems to have flown on without further problem, however. The Nebelwerfers are already moving out, our tanks will follow when they have gone. If we drove in front, our tracks would make the already bad road unusable for their light vehicles.

My driver, Unteroffizier Albert, has caught a cold or something like that. Probably due to the wet weather. What exactly is wrong with him he can't describe. He can feel something in his bones, he says, there is something wrong with his stomach and he feels like he needs to puke. I can't tell if he's just pretending or not. I hope he doesn't come up with a story about 'his nerves', just like Opetz and others did. Then I'll really lose my patience. Unteroffizier Eich of the light platoon, who was only just decorated, has now decided that the intestinal ulcer that had already caused him trouble in France has reappeared. I can't stand people like that.

At 16.00 the launchers were supposed to fire again. If they continue to move at that speed, there is no way they can fire another salvo today. Just now a group of our bombers flew over. Junkers 88 and Heinkel 111, fifteen aircraft in total. Our best wishes go with them. Baumann says that they are able to cause a lot of damage. Well, I hope they do. Hille has informed me that a tank of the 1st Company has been knocked out. Direct hit by a Russian bomb. Its parts now lie spread across a field near the second Luga bridge. Two men were killed. Now, war is certainly no life insurance. The Red Army is offering stiff resistance here.

Monday, 11 August

Luga, 9.00 – Launcher battery, Verza estuary.

I am in my tent which has been half dug into the ground. Weather outside is still abysmal.

At 07.30 the launcher battery fired its first salvo into the morning mist. When the first rocket streaked into the grey sky the first drops had begun to fall and at the time the hundredth round was fired it was already raining quite heavily. I would really like to see the effect of a barrage of that kind from nearby and it was already so impressive at Raseiniai.

Damn! I nearly wet myself again, as just now another salvo howled into the sky. There will be several more coming today, I guess. Even though I have now heard this infernal howling and hissing multiple times I seem to be unable to get used to it. It terrifies me every time. Three hundred metres on my right are Dahlmann and Aures with their tanks, directly on the bank of the Luga. With them is a group of our pioneer platoon under Mack. They have set up a machine gun there. About 600 to 700 metres further downriver, exactly at the Verza estuary, there is Oswald with five Skodas and Wilhelm Lope with two Panzer IVs. Since the morning they have been busy taking the opposite bank with their fire. I can't help laughing about it. I suppose that they still have a few crew members among them who are trying to get the tank assault badge by trying to force some kind of engagement in that manner. Maybe I should recommend myself for the infantry assault badge. The amount of time I have spent on reconnaissance patrols on foot recently beggars description. But what choice do I have with my indigent protection platoon, than to grab a machine pistol and to head out with another of my men to take a look at the surroundings myself? There is no one else to do the job. My shitty mood is not being improved by the pouring rain.

In general today's situation is as follows: from our bridgehead 1. Infanterie-Division attacks towards the north-west towards Kingissepp–Narva; the 6. Panzer-Division thrusts towards the north-east to Krasnoye Selo. A battalion of IR118 advances on the road running parallel to the northern bank on the right of the Luga towards the 36. Infanterie-Division (mot.), which is approaching from the bridgehead at Sabsk. 1 Panzer-Division attacks from the Sabsk bridgehead towards the north-west and then – linking up with us – turns towards Krasnoye Selo and the coast of the Gulf of Finland. The 1. Infanterie-Division and the 1. Panzer-Division advanced towards one another and formed a cauldron in which they encircle the 1st Red Guards Division and other Red Army elements at the Luga. The 6. Panzer-Division, we are only advancing slowly in face of the tough resistance offered by the elite divisions of the Reds at Jurki. On the first day of the offensive 1.ID managed to capture the positions and anti-tank obstacles at Srednje Selo and immediately positioned their artillery on Point 61, where it had already opened fire the same day. How far they have advanced now, on the fourth day, I do not know. Our division, however, the battalion of 118, is stuck in the forest in front of Krutyje Rutschji. The enemy is still sitting on the opposite bank of the Luga. That surely includes the observation post which is spotting for the long-range railway guns which the Russians have about 15 kilometres away from here near Weymarn.

But the Russian will surely be beaten soon. Just a short time and then the whole drama will be over.

13 August 1941

06.45, on the road in front of the bridgehead.

Our defensive task at the river has ended. The Nebelwerfer-Abteilung has been shifted forward into the bridgehead and my platoon, as well as those of Lope and Oswald, who had been standing further downriver, and that of Wünsche, who had been defending the bridge, have now reunited under Hille. They are waiting along the road in front of the bridge until the division has passed by. We are to attach ourselves to the staff, as we are now directly subordinated to the commander of the division. Only yesterday Hille remarked that this way not much is going to happen to us any more! And he is right, as General Landgraf is nothing like the old Kempf, who could always be found in the furthermost line inside his half-track. But never mind that now, I am sure there'll be enough tasks to fulfil. Today, on the fifth day of the offensive, the Russian force has withdrawn towards the next village behind Jurki, from where he is now defending himself behind a large anti-tank obstacle with the usual tenacity. Yesterday my old comrade Edi Brüggemann was killed during the fighting for this obstacle. He had only just arrived here from the Ersatz-Abteilung in Paderborn. Just like Rudi Daun, Brüggemann was an old boy of the 5th Company and had been with me on Christian Schmidt's training course. He had been in action in Poland and France and now, after having been promoted to Leutnant, he has been keenly looking forward to his first deployment at the head of the service arm at whose side he had been raised in Sennelager.

Now we are standing here alongside the road watching the vehicles of the divisions as they drive past us. The armoured half-track in which General Kempf used to lead, has just driven past too. Soon we'll also cross the bridge, on which men of the Organisation Todt are currently repairing the damage caused by Russian long-distance battery fire. Aircraft have tried to hit the bridge as well; there are huge craters which surely have been carved into the ground by Russian 1,000-kilo bombs. I remember that morning when we drove back from the bridgehead, when everything was shrouded in dense fog. The black bridge girders rising wraithlike into the sky, the ground pockmarked with bomb and shell craters and the road lined with the white birchwood crosses marking the graves of fallen comrades and the mass graves of the Russians. Then the sight of the burned woodland, the scorched heathland and the shot-up houses! Through all that we withdrew and then had to wait until the other army wings here in the north-west had closed in on Leningrad. In those four weeks of waiting, the Russians had entrenched themselves so well that each of his excellent positions could only be captured with great casualties.

We have now found shelter in a forest near Jurki. The boss has just been down to see the commander of the division and asked him for new orders. There were none, but he was issued with a fortification map showing all Red positions up to the railway line from Kingissepp to Leningrad. What it shows is quite tremendous. A defensive system which will give us a lot to chew on. The only good thing is that we more or less rid ourselves of the Red artillery, especially the railway guns which kept pounding our rearward areas with high-explosive and flame-oil shells. Yesterday in the darkness our own 15-cm long barrels passed by and, damn, they do fire some enormous coffers. And the effect of the Russian fire in our area? Well, these 21- or 28-cm shells uproot even the biggest tree. One has grazed the bridge and even that has caused the whole construct to sag. But this morning already, our 28-ton tanks could cross it again.

And still the Russians construct good bunkers wherever they can and they are not taking any chances. Right next to the village there is one of those wood and sand bunkers to which the German artillery inflicted a total of zero damage. One needs to crack these in close combat and by lobbing hand grenades through the firing slits. And the anti-tank trenches these chaps have shovelled are simply enormous. There is no way one of our Skodas could cross those in a rush. On the far side the steep wall is about 2 metres high while from the other side the run-up towards this wall only drops gently. Often these trench obstacles run along rivers and streams while in front of those there are often additional wire obstacles. They can also be found behind the anti-tank trench. In the forest of Jurki, long before the actual anti-tank obstacle, there were several trench lines and the whole area was littered with foxholes. That the attack is gaining ground at a slower pace than that right after crossing the border, where the troops were inferior in numbers and quality compared to the Red Guard Division we are facing here, comes as no surprise. We have taken heavy casualties in front of these cunningly constructed defences. Even though the campaign has been a great success so far, we are paying a high price for it. Only yesterday in front of Sabsk 1. Panzer-Division destroyed seventy tanks. The Wehrmachtsbericht reported that yesterday evening. They face far less resistance than we do here.

Many dead lie in our bridgehead. In the cemetery of the main dressing station at Wolovo lie over 100 more. The Russians, however, have left thousands dead in front of our lines.

Thursday, 14 August 1941

Rollbahn Kingissepp–Leningrad, 18.00

It is raining again and thick clouds are hanging low in the sky. Really not looking great. The weather chaps of the division have stated that night frosts aren't rare in this area of Russia from about mid-August onwards. From Schmauch I have received a thick overcoat and from Unteroffizier Albert I have collected a thin Russian blanket of which he has several on his vehicle. As far as I am concerned, frost can set in now.

From Jurki we have moved to Wypolsova. We are now a few kilometres north of that village in a forest in front of an anti-tank trench. From the road, which can be barred with concrete obstacles, the steep 2-metre deep trench runs 500 metres through the fields, where it meets a stretch of high forest. Bongardt and his company, together with the Kradschützen, are in the next village, which is closest to the Luga woodlands, and thus in a position to bar the withdrawal of Russian troops flooding back from there. Will have to be seen if any of them make an appearance there.

Yesterday evening I spent quite some time with Theo Langenbruch who is now acting divisional orderly of the regiment. We talked about a number of subjects. We both wish that the boss returns soon, very soon, to take over the company again. Surely it won't be long until we are being deployed again. No one in the company enjoys all this loitering around. It feels shit to pass all these bunkers and defensive positions with the knowledge that one has done absolutely nothing to aid the capture of them!

We live like battlefield tourists on summer holiday, they should really charge us money for it.

The division has just interrogated a few prisoners and I was able to listen in on some of them. An Oberleutnant of the staff of I./11, the right hand of the Ic of the division,* stood behind the prisoners and made notes. The prisoners were interrogated by Sonderführer Stein, who is a German from Ukraine. I had some mints in my pocket and offered some to Stein, to the Oberleutnant and also to the prisoner. Stein laughed and said to the Russian: Yes, see? These are bullets with which we Germans will shoot you. The Russian had to laugh. The interrogation had the following result:

The Russian was 30 years old and a foundry worker from Leningrad. In 1933 he had served one year in the Red Army and he was not a Party member. On 14 July he had suddenly been drafted and was brought to Krasnoye Selo. He had been there up until about two days ago. They had nothing to do there. They just shovelled some foxholes. At one time there had been firing practice where every Red Army soldier had been allowed to fire three whole cartridges (ammunition shortage). Two days ago they had been quickly formed into a battalion and subordinated to the 1st Red Guards Division, which had had great losses in the previous fighting. He knew that that division was commanded by a General, but he had never seen or met the battalion or regimental commander. They then travelled 30 kilometres by train and 70 kilometres on foot to reach the Luga. Without any rest they had then been deployed in combat, came under heavy German fire and had been forced to withdraw. He and eight other men had decided to go over to the Germans. The fire had been so

---

* The third General Staff officer of the division, responsible for military intelligence.

heavy that they had crawled towards the German lines on their bellies and once they had been close enough they had stood up, raised their arms and had been taken prisoner. – The prisoner made a good impression on me. He was also quite clean. So it is clear that the brothers are short of ammunition; he also told us that he had seen lots of tanks, artillery and Flak batteries. All in all quite interesting.

10.30, Friday, 15 August 1941, formerly Gorki Farm

Just been visited by Feldwebel Ulrich of Neuling's company. His group is deployed not far away from here. We are still waiting to be deployed. The situation is as follows: Koll has taken command of the leading Kampfgruppe and his unit was the only one in the whole Korps to reach its objective of the day. For that he was mentioned in dispatches. Koll is now furthest in front and well beyond the main railway line. On our left the 36.ID is making good progress. On the right the 1.Pz.Div. had encountered heavy resistance which soon stalled its advance. Kampfgruppe Raus is now tasked to hit the Reds from the flank in an attempt to take pressure off 1.Pz.Div. We might participate in this flanking thrust together with the recon section and two companies of Kradschützen. Hille has informed us that we might get a deployment order by 12.00. I hope it will come through.

Yesterday evening I drove to the rear to where Martin Loock and his fuel columns are, or rather, should have been. He wasn't there. Seems he is still down at Wolovo. On my way I came past several bunkers and anti-tank trenches. This I found highly interesting. Along a small stream and on quite soggy ground, the Russian had expertly dug an anti-tank ditch which ended once it reached the road. That was covered with a minefield. On the other side of the road the trench continued. Further behind the trench, behind an area covered with foxholes, they had built several cleverly camouflaged artillery bunkers which impressed me a lot. Some of them were even made of concrete! To do so, they had used concrete slabs, which they produce somewhere in their hinterland. These slabs only weigh 100 kilos or so each and are then put together with the use of cement. Each slab is about 25 centimetres high, about 1 metre thick, and made in a manner which allows the construction of several different bunker types. The Russians also have several types of wooden bunkers here. They are virtually shellproof, if not hit directly on one of the vision slits.

Just now there has been an exciting interruption. Eight Ratas were chasing one of our Henschel observation aircraft. The Henschel flew a tight turn and then flew across the edge of the forest at an altitude of only about 10 metres, two of the Ratas right behind it! I could see how the first Rata fired a burst into the Henschel and how flames erupted from its back when the Russian explosive rounds hit. During the show I stood behind the tank. One has to be careful, as the Ratas very often strafe our columns with their guns and drop small 2-kilo high-explosive bombs as well. After the wild chase had raced over our heads, one could hear rapturous cheering from one corner of the woods from which there was a better view of what happened next. One of the Ratas crashed into the ground right behind the woods while the other broke off its attack and headed back. A pillar of thick, black smoke rose up from where the Red fighter had come down. I started running to the spot to take some photographs, when suddenly four more Ratas appeared out of nowhere and started raking the ground with machine guns and 2-kilo bombs. I threw myself into a foxhole when one flew directly towards me, its projectiles detonating all around. Damn, I really had a lot of luck there. Our Flak could well have fired too, but the crews had all run into cover.

Coincidentally we had some good food today. A few Feldwebel had gone 'organising'. Opetz is now to take charge of the field kitchen, because Enz – the chef – is of the opinion that he is too well decorated and that he doesn't need to put in any work to keep other men fed. There is always just enough for himself, though. Swines like that are no rarity. Today we had cabbage and carrot stew, with a few bits of potato in it. In addition a tin of plums, half a bar of chocolate and half a lemon each. Also half a cup of sugar each. To that we can add the basketful of cucumbers and beetroot which the Feldwebels had supplied. Nothing to complain about.

I just heard that 1.Pz.Div. has broken the resistance and is advancing again. We are now part of Koll's lot!

for the Red artillery observer who, all through the evening, had expertly guided the fire of the Russian artillery.

After we had set fire to the village we, together with the infantry, set out to establish a defensive position in it. I was deployed at the exit of the village near the road. A platoon of Kradschützen of the Jonas Company was there, Feldwebel Westhoff among them. We had four of our tanks there. Next to me there was Matussek, Goßler and Aures. All old, experienced Feldwebel. After I had distributed our tanks as well as possible in the darkness, I took the first watch up until midnight when Wittkötter, my little gunner, was to take over. After him Wrenger and Pusch the driver. We had piled up some hay behind the tank which made a more comfortable place to rest than the bare ground. Wrenger was sleeping in the tank as usual. He claims it is the safest place to be and, as it is also a lot better for his nerves, I am not going to disagree. Towards the end of my watch the moon was rising, a huge glowing red crescent. Then there was the blood-red glow of all the burning villages in the area – quite a sight to behold. When I saw the moon, I had to think of Hamburg, all the good days I spent there when on leave from the army, and the nightly trips back from the bar. Yes, all that is gone; it is all over. And should I, one day, be back in Hamburg and walk back home, I will have to think about these hours here in Russia …

When my watch was over, I went to take some photographs of the fires. I am looking forward to seeing if the photos will be usable. I then took Wittkötter's place and went to sleep. Before that I had shown Oberleutnant Jonas the location of the hay bales. In this regard the riflemen are far less fortunate than we are. They are in their foxholes, on the naked ground, without coats, blankets or tent squares. No chance to even think of catching some sleep in that manner. At 4 a.m. the Russian artillery began to harass us. At 04.30 I took over the watch from Pusch and climbed into the turret. Cannon and machine guns ready, loaded pistol in my pocket. Time and experience have taught me to be careful. We were now all inside the tank, and the driver and the radio operator both began to snore loudly. But one gets used to that kind of experience in the army and it didn't really bother me. Then, in the distance, I could hear the sound of motorbike engines and the clatter of hooves – Russians! And only a minute later a machine gun starts barking and an anti-tank gun started firing. One shot, another shot, and another. 'Cease fire!' someone shouts and I hear the words 'Ruki werch!' I climb out of the tank to see what's going on to the right – in the field of fire of Matussek's tank. Three Red Army soldiers had walked up, all pretty ancient fellows, with a horse pulling a two-wheeled cart. Our Landsers welcomed them. On the road there was another, similar cart which had tried to turn around when the first shots were fired and was then shot up by the anti-tank gun. I send one of the Russians and a couple of our men back to collect the Russian rifles. The three old fellows tell us that there is a fourth, wounded man, still on the cart. Our Landsers shot the wounded horse and left the Russian, who pretended to be dead, where he was. They had just returned when the 'dead' Russian suddenly stood up and made a sprint towards some nearby bushes. Our machine guns started firing but didn't manage to hit him. That's what 'dead Russians' do, at least those who are not stiff and cold.

By then it was **Sunday, 17 August**. I let the men sleep and climbed back into the turret. The sun was already rising and I started scanning the edge of the forest ahead with my binoculars when I suddenly heard angry shouts of magpies in the bushes ahead and then several crows rose up from their sleeping places, crowing terribly. Two hundred metres in front a single Russian had made an appearance and was slowly walking towards us. A bit further behind there were more, a good dozen of them. A Russian patrol. Just at that moment one of our recon patrols returned from scouting the area ahead. The German and the Russian reconnaissance patrols stared at one another through their binoculars and then the Russians beat a hasty retreat. As a direct result the armoured recon section sent out an armoured car which very carefully drove up to the edge of the forest in the far distance where a man got out to reconnoitre a further 50 metres ahead on foot. Then they drove back to our position at breakneck speed. They had cut a Russian telephone cable and had established that the village down there was occupied by the enemy. That village we were now supposed to attack. By then everyone was awake, we had some breakfast and I had had a wash. The Russian artillery then opened up and a dud shell bounced off the ground, punched through a pasture fence, overturned several times in the air, howled past across our heads and then, after hitting the ground again, rolled out right in front of one of the infantry's machine-gun positions.

We had just finished breakfast, when a runner came from the boss and told us that the whole platoon was to assemble in the centre of the village. That was right where most of the shells were falling and we all cursed that we had to give up our old position. When we came to the village centre there was no sign of anyone else. Only a single Panzer IV stood there. 'Where is the boss?' Jupp Wellinghoff, a former classmate from Osnabrück, was kneeling in cover behind the rear of that vehicle, looked at me and then replied, 'Under the tank!' And indeed, they were all there, under the tank, flat on their bellies: Oberleutnant Hille, a Hauptmann of the infantry, Wilhelm Lope and several other men. I was told to get out and join them under the tank, where I then received a situational briefing for the coming attack. We were to drive to the corner of the forest which we had observed from our old position, pick up the riflemen and then advance on the village of Konochowizy which was occupied by the enemy. We were warned that we would probably receive flanking fire from Pleschtschewizy – that was all. There was now huge chaos on the road as, on the orders of the boss, all platoons had left their defensive positions to come and see him in the village centre. And now they were all being shelled by Soviet heavy artillery. It is a miracle that no one was seriously hurt.* Two of the riflemen had been standing right on the spot on which a Russian heavy shell exploded. Not a single scrap of them could be found. A third one had both his legs blown off.

We drove down to our assembly point at the forest, where we calmly waited for the artillery observers; the infantry climbed on our tanks and we slowly rolled towards our objective. Again one of the Panzer IVs had a technical problem, so all the other Panzer IVs stopped as well and we had to wait until Lope's lot were ready to roll. During the attack I was on the right wing, Wünsche was behind the road. One Panzer IV with me, two more left of the road. We had advanced about 1 kilometre through the rye and oat fields when the enemy defensive fire became so heavy that the infantry had to dismount. They then advanced behind our tanks, using them as cover against the hail of projectiles poured at us from the Russian defensive positions. The Russians were well entrenched in several lines.

---

* Sander means none *of his own men* was seriously hurt. As shown in the subsequent sentences, he does not see infantrymen in the same light.

One had to get very close before it was possible to locate the excellently camouflaged foxholes and dugouts. I fired high-explosive shells into each of the many bushes in the field in front of us, while at the same time we used our machine guns to suppress the Russians in the foxholes until our infantry had caught up. Soon a wild close combat ensued. I had to hand a few of our hand grenades to the infantry. They were needed to take out the bunkers. The wretches would not surrender; I guess they thought we were going to shoot them anyway. The left wing couldn't advance any further. On our side it went quite well. I particularly noticed one machine-gunner who advanced towards the enemy positions without wearing a steel helmet, firing his machine gun from the hip. We were always 20 metres or so in front of the infantry or directly with them. That way we could pin the Russians down, until the infantry could take them out in close combat. To keep the closest Russians away from us, I often had to make use of my pistol, shooting down several fellows in foxholes close to my tank. Alongside a road, leading into the direction of our attack, there was a group of twenty or so Russians who surrendered when we pulled up. The infantry took them prisoner. Everyone is delighted, our progress is excellent. Then suddenly, another group of ten Russians slowly rose from the tall grass. The Reds got on their knees and raised their hands. But among them there was one swine, who suddenly pulls out a hand grenade and throws it at my tank. While I shoot the man with my pistol, a machine gun opens up and mows the whole group down.

The wretches have Molotov cocktails in every foxhole. I think to myself that once the first bottle has been thrown, I won't be taking prisoners any more. Slowly we are advancing on the hedgerows in front of the village. The first houses are clearly visible behind it, but in front the Russians have a dense screen of foxholes and dugouts. Soon we are running out of ammunition. I am sending one high-explosive shell after another into the dugouts. A Russian machine gun is firing on the left and one of my explosive shells tears it to shreds. The infantry now advances at speed, charging the Russians with fixed bayonets. These Kradschützen are a good bunch to work with. They are hard fighters and know that they can trust the 5th Company. We work together well. On the left the Panzer IVs are engaging the bunkers. Suddenly Feldwebel Westhoff falls headlong into the potato field. He can't walk any more. Shot through the hip. From the ground he urges his men forward. I can't do anything, however, and have to focus on what's going on in front. Through a gap in the hedgerow a Russian tank appears. With both turret hatches open, it is rolling into our field of fire. Five hundred metres. Armour-piercing! I eject a high-explosive round from the breech and load an AP shell. Wittkötter is feeding the last belt into the Skoda V.Z. Five rounds of armour-piercing into the Russian tank. Via the radio, Wrenger indicates the target to Matussek, who also opens up on it. Suddenly a burst of armour-piercing machine-gun bullets slams into the turret and the tiny shards of paint flying into my face remind me that there are still plenty of Russian infantrymen ahead. I send an explosive shell into a foxhole and two men crawl out. Before they can get away they are gunned down with the machine pistol. The infantry is clearing the last foxholes.

We can now enter the village itself. I advance slowly, five or six infantrymen are still behind my tank. The houses in front hold no threat any more as they are burning brightly. Alongside the main road there are several Russian lorries, also on fire. While I am driving through the village, I suddenly spot three Russian tanks trying to disappear through the cornfield on the left. I inform the platoon via the radio. At that moment I heard Wünsche's voice in my headphones, I would hear a lot more of him later – but that is only a side note. Soon the whole company is firing on the three green buckets. The one in the middle, on which I had fired several shells, suddenly comes to a stop. I am overjoyed and think to myself that I have destroyed it. But then the beast suddenly lurches forward and disappears from sight into the nearby forest. Now the Russian artillery starts firing and is sending 10.5-cm shells into the village. Whamm! One of them slams right into the engine of Vollmer's tank, and in this case it was really a classic piece of soldier's luck that he is still alive. The shell was a dud, or rather some kind of exercise shell filled with a concrete-like substance. The top half with the fuse on it broke off while the bottom half, with the base of the shell, smashed through the armour before being stopped by the engine block! If that had been a live shell, not much would have been left of the tank!

Fighting my way forward alongside the Kradschützen I finally reach the other end of the village. Barn by barn and house by house has to be captured. In the last house at the far end of the village, I alone take ten prisoners. We also capture two mortars and one machine gun. Then it suddenly goes quiet and I deploy my tanks for the defence. I send Aures over to the right while

Matussek, Grawe and Goßler are to stay with me. We then rouse a few more Russians from the cornfield ahead of us before I send the whole lot, together with one guard, towards the rear. That guard is also ordered to report to Hille that we have run out of ammunition. When some Russian bombers and Ratas appear above us we start camouflaging our tanks. The wretches are so low that one can easily spot the red stars on their fuselages and underneath their wings. On my right Aures is rolling forward. What is he up to? We scan the terrain ahead of us. There is a group of German infantry in the distance. They are walking towards our position, but now and then they halt. I can also hear the sound of shooting: something or someone is shooting at that group. Ahead Aures is driving towards a dense clump of bushes from which, all of a sudden, several Russian soldiers rise up with raised hands. They start running towards our position. Aures has roused ten, twenty and then thirty and more than fifty Russians from their hiding place. Mostly older fellows, 40 to 50 years old, former factory workers from Leningrad. No officers or commissars with them. We let them keep their possessions, coats and rucksacks – that way we don't have to supply them with those essentials once they arrive in the Reich.

Just on the right of my tank, at the corner of a house, there is a dead body. The whole upper skull of the corpse has been shaved off. The 3.7 is pretty effective.

There are still single bullets whizzing past our heads. There are more Russians in the field ahead of us. Slowly but steadily and assisted by the infantry, we pick up about thirty prisoners. Wittkötter has gone with the infantry in an attempt to find himself a piece of soap in one of the Russian rucksacks. I decided to join him and, armed only with our pistols, we approach another group of Russians, armed with at least one machine gun and a couple of scoped rifles. After searching them we let them pick up their coats and rucksacks and then assemble all their weapons in a big pile. Two machine guns, one machine pistol, two mortars and ten scoped rifles and a large pile of other rifles, all of them brand new, made in 1941.

Accompanied by Wittkötter, I then set out in the search of some water and it is Wittkötter who discovers a number of wooden boxes which are filled with bottles. All secretive and full of joy he walks up to me: 'Herr Leutnant, vodka!' – but it didn't take us long to find out that this was just wishful thinking, they were Molotov cocktails! We take a few of those bottles to try them out. They burn beautifully and for a long time. One can also throw them very well. The things work thus: a bottle, filled with a highly combustible liquid, closed with a cork and with two rubber bands stretched around it. The rubber bands hold a sturdy matchstick, the top 10 centimetres covered with a phosphorus substance. The matchstick is ignited with a special striking surface, one of which is attached to each bottle with a piece of string. Once the match is ignited, the bottle can be thrown against a tank. Once the glass breaks, the burning phosphorus mass ignites the liquid inside. The contents keep burning for about two minutes!

By 16.00 we still hadn't received any food, fuel or ammunition. Wittkötter had captured a live chicken which he had stored in a pillowcase. The two chickens we already had, plucked and cut into pieces, in a pot on the rear of the tank, had been too shot up, and had sadly become inedible. We had to throw them away. What a waste of work and beautiful food. I went down to Hille to inform him that we had still received nothing to eat and – much worse – no ammunition. But I had just climbed out of the turret when the order arrived to prepare for another attack – we would advance further! I mutinied and told Hille that I would not follow that order. That worked and he told me to follow up as a reserve platoon. He then drove off and I waited until the ammunition lorry and the field kitchen had appeared. In the meantime another group of prisoners had been assembled in the village. They were chewing on roots and raw potatoes which they had picked from the fields and were looking quite satisfied with the general situation. For them, the war was over and they hadn't been shot by the 'Germanskis'. What more could they have wished for?

After resupplying ourselves with ammunition and having eaten something, we followed the rest of our group towards Terspilizy. Our riflemen mounted up too and we drove off together. We didn't have any further enemy contact on the way, but we passed one of the three Russian tanks, which was burning brightly. Once we had reached the farm at Rekkesko, we found that the road had been blocked with a barricade of farming equipment. The commander of our Kampfgruppe drove past in his armoured car to evaluate the situation himself. We made good progress. Terspilizy had already been captured by 1.Pz.Div. We went past several Russian tanks and artillery pieces which had been shot up by 1. Panzer and then also linked up with the outer perimeter defences of that division. To rest, we moved into a small piece of woodland, in which we could have become quite comfortable – but no, we had just made a fire and organised a new pot to cook our chicken in, when we were ordered to prepare to move out again. So we packed our tents up, stored our kit away, moved our platoons forward towards the road.

The commander wanted us to advance on Pankowizy, but he gave the wrong instructions and that meant that we were heading in the wrong direction. Instead of attacking towards the enemy, we found ourselves rolling down a nicely cobbled road to the right towards the centre of the sector of 1. Panzer-Division. The Ostmeckerer* Limbrunn was even then talking big in his silly dialect: 'I will send an armoured vanguard ahead of the lead tanks; that'll offer the gentlemen some extra security' – and then the look on his face, when after a long drive we didn't encounter any Russians, but instead ran into a Kampfgruppe of 1. Panzer-Division! We were ordered to turn around immediately and raced back to Terspilizy at breakneck speed. That our Skodas and especially the Panzer IVs suffered from that kind of handling doesn't need to be explained. On the same evening still, we were then to advance towards Pankowizy – this time in the right direction – but this was something we could not agree to. Together with Hille we went to see Limbrunn and then told the man that something like that wouldn't make any sense at all. If Hille had gone alone, he'd probably have fallen for this stupid idea and would have returned to us entirely convinced of it being the right thing to do. I was supported by the commander of the Kradschützen recon platoon, who didn't want to participate in such a folly either. It was then decided that we would attack Pankowizy at dawn on the following morning. As we were to set out at 03.45, we tried to catch some sleep for the four hours that remained.

On **Monday, 18 August**, we were woken up at 03.00 and immediately set about preparing our vehicles. When we rolled out, Wünsche's platoon had the lead, then came the Panzer IVs, followed by Oswald and me – with Matussek and Aures – forming the rear. Goßler's tank had suffered a breakdown. The riflemen were riding on our tanks and together we rolled into what appeared to be the start of a beautiful morning. First through a

---

* Lit: 'eastern grouch', a derogatory form of 'Ostmärker' (Austrians).

small village, where the farmers stood, their belongings packed onto little carts, ready to rush into and hide in the forests as soon as the first shots were fired. Then we drive through dense forest and suddenly, ahead of us, contact with the enemy. The riflemen dismount and advance on foot. Enemy tanks in front. Three of them, big buckets, are reported to be standing next to a barn. One of the Panzer IVs opens fire. Wünsche is sending one radio message after another! All the Panzer IVs now roll to the edge of the forest and start firing shot after shot in the direction of the barn and one of the big Russian tanks. Another one, according to Feldwebel Wünsche, has been withdrawn. A few Russians have escaped, running across the field to the right. Then suddenly Wünsche reports that there is an anti-tank gun firing from the bushes on the right. Oswald rolls forward and opens fire on the bushes where enemy movement has now reportedly been observed. No one realises that they are firing on our own advancing riflemen. And because of that, they direct a hail of fire on them. Hauptmann Knaust is angrily calling on us to cease firing on the bushes, and when I run over to Oswald to tell him that, the swine gives me lip. He says that I should concentrate on running my platoon; he wouldn't be firing towards the right!

Later I learned that down there on the right German soldiers had been killed and wounded by our tanks. Well, and the anti-tank gun later turned out to be a mine obstacle – in which Wünsche's tank had nearly ended up. Wooden box mines, buried in the ground and covered with turf – easy to overlook if you're not very careful. And if one had been careful, one could have seen that the tank in the barn was actually a threshing machine! Over 1,000 Reichsmarks worth of ammunition wasted firing on bleeding farming equipment! And all because of Wünsche's idiocy.

In front of the mine barrier we turn into the open field on the right. We advanced on the village from the right, Lope and Oswald on my right flank. While doing so, one of them ran over a beehive and we suddenly had to cope with the damned bees, which had quite a nasty sting! Alongside some houses, we took up a defensive position. A few girls fetched some drinking water for us and I used the time to wash myself. A shave was badly needed as well. One of the girls mended my tunic which had a large, triangular tear in one of the sleeves. In the evening we had to return to the forest where Oswald had fired on our own men. We did so because the Soviet artillery had started shelling the village. The villagers, by the way, were mostly Protestant Finns and Estonians! In a house near to where Wilhelm Lope was standing with his tank, the owner proudly showed me his German-language edition of the Lutheran Bible. The Estonians also print their newspapers in normal letters like we use in Germany. The man offered me some milk too. The houses were all clean and the girls weren't ugly either. One realises how long it has been since our Landsers have seen some nice girls. Everyone gathered around to ogle at the *Marjells.**

We found a good home among the shrubs and started cooking our chicken in a pot borrowed from another crew. Then I had a shave. Nearby a few German batteries were firing and the Russians were replying in kind with counter-battery fire. No wonder that a good amount of what was meant to hit our artillery came down very close to where we were. We also received mail – twelve letters for me too! Everything is well at home. Nothing new from Hamburg. More important was a parcel with some lemons and several films which Clara had sent. In return I packed a few parcels for her, containing some films to develop and some dirty laundry. Then it started to rain and when that had passed over, we had to move out again. I was supposed to lead the company back to the village. And when we had crossed over the meadow and then turned towards the road, Pusch's tank collided with mine so violently that Wenger and I were thrown off onto the road. Before I landed, however, both of my arms slammed on the cannon barrel while my face made full contact with one of the storage containers. It was a miracle that our tank, which had slipped into the roadside ditch at an oblique angle, didn't overturn and squash us beneath it. The pain was so bad that I could hardly raise my arms any more, let alone talk.

In Ronkowizy, riflemen climbed up on our tanks and then we drove, through the artillery fire, towards Klopizy, from where we had an overview of the terrain we'd have to traverse during the attack on Muratowo. We had to expect to be attacked from the left, from the direction of a Russian airfield, and my platoon was deployed to guard that flank in case something like that happened. I was unfortunate, however, as this meant working with

---

* Prussian slang for 'girls'.

the Aufklärungs-Abteilung, which wasn't as attuned to fighting at our side as the Kradschützen who had been fighting alongside the regiment since Poland and France. Our four Skodas, with Dahlmann being furthest left; next to him is Mattusek; then me and Aures on my right. Behind us is a Panzer IV, supposed to offer us fire support. Ahead on the left are some bushes, from where something was pouring fire on us.

Behind us, two self-propelled 2-cm quad-Flaks and a platoon of 2-cm Flak guns started taking these bushes under fire. The effect was quite spectacular and very effective. In the meantime we started clearing out the foxholes ahead. A shell inside each of them and then a hail of machine-gun fire – again with good effect. The first Russians started running. Over the radio we were ordered to drive faster. 'I am not advancing without my riflemen!' I replied to Hille. Our infantry was already more than 500 metres behind my tank. Hille repeated his order at least four times more, but in the end I stopped replying. On my right there was a car with a limber behind it. Just enough time to fire a few shots at it – at that moment all our focus lay ahead of us – we were now right among the Russians. Damn, my vehicles on the left flank are not following up! I take a moment to take a look at my surroundings and find that there are two Russian soldiers in a foxhole right next to my tank. I drag my pistol out and shout: 'Bros' tebe oruzhiye! Ruki werch!' – One of them is raising his rifle, however. I make short work of the two and empty a whole pistol magazine into them. They won't harm anyone any more.

In front of us there are more foxholes. High-explosive shells into them, and then I notice that the two comrades on my left are not there any more?! I turn around and – damn, one tank is burning: it is Matussek. Dahlmann is standing there too, but is then driving up to me. I advance further and report the loss to Hille. Ahead on my left another Russian is playing dead. I take the machine pistol from inside the turret and fire a few rounds into the back of his head. The swine! As he bites the dust, a hand grenade rolls out of his hand. While we are firing our machine guns at a few brown-coated shapes in the distance, I notice that Dahlmann's tank is burning too! I can see the silhouette of four men in the grass behind it and think to myself 'at least they all managed to bail in one piece'. No sign of our riflemen. The area is still bristling with Russians and it is a miracle that I haven't been hit yet. With my aching arms, I try to lob some hand grenades into a bush on the right. Seven grenades, a few bursts of machine-gun fire and one high-explosive shell and suddenly I have some space to breathe again and at the same time the Panzer IV is finishing off some fleeing Russians on the left. I turn to the right and with Aures on my left, I drive along a row of tall pine trees. The Panzer IV is following behind. In the village some of our Kradschützen are clearing the last pockets of resistance in fierce house-to-house fighting. It is actually more like a farm with a lot of crumbling barns and sheds and huts. I briefly halt next to a house with shuttered windows and for a moment I have a weird feeling standing there. When we roll forward again I realise why. When the Panzer IV rolls past the house, hand grenades are lobbed from inside and their detonations force the riflemen to dismount. The house is then completely obliterated by combined fire of the Panzer IV and the riflemen. There is not much more for us to do and as such we advance further and, after traversing a huge cornfield, link up with the rest of the company.

All platoon leaders to the boss. I report the loss of my two tanks and ask Hauptmann Knaust to send a dispatch rider to find out what has become of my two crews. In the meantime we are supposed to advance on Mulatovo along a narrow forest path. The riflemen mount up and together we crawl through the dark forest. No sign of any Russians. A whole mortar crew is travelling on my tank. They are happy that they don't have to walk with their heavy weapon. The road is bad and very muddy and I am expecting to hear the bang which denotes that the lead vehicle has run over a mine. But there is no bang, no rifle fire, not even a single shot – we continue to roll slowly forward. When we exit the forest and assemble for the attack on the next village it is pitch dark. One can hardly see a thing, let alone whether the ground ahead is covered with mines. Well – it has to be done. Together with the riflemen we advance on the village. This time with me in the centre of the attacking line. The tanks then halt 200 metres in front of the village and wait until the infantry has combed through the houses. Then white signal flares rise into the sky at the end of the village and we move forward to secure positions alongside the road of advance. Wilhelm Lope is down there too; he also has only two vehicles left. We set up our tents and lie down to sleep, but not before we have camouflaged our tanks with a few house doors and a bunch of shrubs and designated the sentries who will spend the night in the tanks.

On **Tuesday, 19 August** we are woken by the sounds of wild shooting. Alarm! Enemy tanks! Alarm! Enemy tanks! We stumble out of the tent, but by then an anti-tank gun on the left has made short work of the Russian tank. It is already burning. It is becoming quiet again, so we crawl back into the tent to catch some more sleep. Half an hour later, however, the shooting starts again. This time it's an anti-tank gun in an advanced position which is firing. Out of the tent again. There is a civilian car in the field about 500 metres away. It was shot up by Lope's Panzer IV, who at the time had taken fire from a hidden anti-tank gun in the forest on the other side of the field. The combined fire of everything the company has to offer seems to have silenced that Russian gun, but it has to be pointed out that our scouts had reported that the forest was free of the enemy. After they had left, the Russians had seemingly moved back in. Now we could catch up with some much-needed sleep until 8 o'clock. It was a beautiful day. I couldn't help thinking that yesterday's attack had cost another young and flourishing life. The dispatch rider had found Matussek and had brought him back to the company where he reported that his crew was unhurt. In the other crew, however, Unteroffizier Dahlmann had been slightly wounded and Bussmann, his gunner, severely wounded. Gefreiter Mashäuser had been killed. Albert had been lucky and was completely unharmed. There had been Russians lying in the grass only 15 metres ahead of their tank. As soon as Mashäuser had bailed out, he had been shot through the head and was killed immediately. A firefight developed in which Dahlmann and Albert desperately tried to defend themselves with their pistols and it was only when Albert gunned down one the Russians that the situation changed. The Russian had been in the process of throwing a grenade, and after he had been shot down this detonated in his hand, shredding his lower abdomen and causing the others to withdraw.

More mail arrived on Tuesday. We were staying in an old barn which we had furnished to quite a comfortable standard. Later that day, after having drawn rations from the field kitchens, Aures and I walked down to where the two destroyed tanks were standing to find and bury Mashäuser. A recovery vehicle had arrived from the field workshop and Koppmann and Korn had already wrapped Mashäuser's body in a tent square, removed some private items from his pockets and had broken his dog tag. We carried Mashäuser back to the road and then dug him a grave under a tree, next to a bunker. One of the tank mechanics had found a few flowers in one of the shot-up houses at Klopizy. Each of us threw three shovels of earth onto the grave. We then placed his black cap on top of the birchwood cross and thus added to the many such monuments which adorn the graves of bold and brave Panzer gunners. It compels us to further, relentless, commitment. His death will not remain unpunished.

In one of the bushes there were the dead bodies of a Russian Captain, that of a First Lieutenant and that of a commissar. In total more than twenty corpses lay around the destroyed tank. A wounded Russian was also lying there, still with his rifle in his hand. He didn't react when I ordered him to raise his arms. I shot him myself. I did the same to another who was lying in a foxhole closer to the tank and who pretended to be dead when I told him to stand up. Are they acting in that manner because they are afraid of us? Or out of deceit? If it's the first reason, then the commissars are to blame for the death of those men. If it's the latter, well, they deserve it. I remember the incident with Oberleutnant Bethke a few weeks ago.

We had just finished decorating Mashäuser's grave with the flowers and the cross when six Russian fighters flew in, accompanied by a few bombers. Then we witnessed how one of the bombers was shot down and a minute later a Rata came flying back, trailing a thick cloud of smoke. That Rata then seemed to be going down on the airfield which we had passed by a day earlier. For a moment we were cheering the event, but not for long as, soon after, a whole swarm of Ratas plunged down from the sky and came at us in a low-level attack. That didn't have any effect and they flew away. All except one, which returned, flew a few turns and then initiated a landing on the airfield, after which it vanished from sight behind a hedgerow. He was obviously trying to pick up his comrade, so we rushed down there as quickly as we could. Most men headed there on the half-tracked recovery vehicle, while Aures had hitched a ride on a dispatch rider's motorbike that had been standing on the side of the road. I ran over using my long legs.

Upon arrival we could see that the first machine was standing way too far away, while the second one was already in the process of taking off again. At that moment I heard a bang from the direction of the road, from around a bend where – according to some nearby infantry – Aures had headed with his motorbike. Albert, Koppe, Voss and I started running down the road towards the bend. From a distance already we could see a small black spot on the road. That had to be his motorbike! I was carrying a Russian machine pistol, while the others all had their pistols, and together we now advanced carefully up the roadside. The first thing that caught my eye were several dead Russians and I realised immediately that these men had stepped on mines! Now we had to be very careful! Now, only a short while later, all that feels unreal to me, so distant and improbable. But the sight of those Russian corpses, unburied by their comrades and only hastily covered with a few branches due to the fear of mines, somehow increased the gravity and seriousness of the situation. Albert Berscheid and Wrenger, who had been following behind, crossed over to the right side of the road. Slowly and with crouched bodies we walked through the minefield, our eyes peeled on the ground and watching every step, getting closer and closer to the motorbike. There was a man lying there, he was waving to us. Now we had to be fast. Quick help was needed. We started running. No one was firing on us. Only a day before there had been heavy fighting at this spot. When we had finally reached the motorbike we could see the whole mess before us. The dispatch rider and Aures had driven over a mine. The whole road was covered with mines. There was no sign of Aures, only his cap and his pistol were lying on the ground, together with some parts of the motorbike. And the driver himself, I could hardly look at him, so ghastly was the wound on the poor boy's leg. The mangled bones of his lower leg were sticking out of a lump of shredded flesh and the whole bloody mass was attached to his upper leg only by a thin strip of sinew and flesh. He had deep wounds on his arms as well, all of them full of splinters and his artery had been cut as well. With the leather strap of the machine pistol and a muslin bandage I first created a makeshift ligature for his leg and hurried to finish before the blood vessels, contracted by shock, started bleeding again. I also started bandaging the wounds on his arms, but then I ran out of bandages. Koppe, Albert and Voss didn't want to help binding his wounds. Their nerves couldn't take it.

And admittedly, the sight of the blood-covered soldier was anything but nice. It was, to put it simply, absolutely horrible. The boy conducted himself impeccably. He said that he would be happy if he'd be allowed to keep his hands and the one leg. He remained conscious throughout and his pain must have been terrible. He asked me to cut off the lower leg. I only had a pocket knife with me, but I tried it nevertheless. The wounded boy watched me doing it, but as it hurt him too much I gave up the attempts to amputate with my primitive tools.

Voss was white as a corpse when he watched me bandaging the boy. There are many people out there who can't bear watching something like this. We then placed the wounded boy on a blanket, which we unbuckled from his motorbike and then started carrying him to the recovery vehicle, which stood waiting behind the bend of the road, quite some distance away. But then 'Wham!' – damn it to hell! The recovery vehicle had also hit a mine. A crash, a huge cloud of dust, and the vehicle stood still. We had failed to spot the anti-tank mine barrier up there when we had advanced on foot. With three carriers and a distance of over 1 kilometre to cover, a wounded man can get very heavy indeed. But we were lucky and managed to reach the recovery vehicle. We carefully placed the wounded boy on the vehicle and secured his body with rubber straps. Unteroffizier Albert then carefully dug up a mine located behind the vehicle, which allowed it to reverse. It was still in working order, although the driver had a deep cut in his scalp.

Albert, Koppe and I then went back to look for Feldwebel Aures, or at least some traces of him. We searched everything as well as we could, even walked to the airfield to search the buildings located on it. There was no sign of Aures. When we walked back we took a pile of blankets from a Russian artillery limber which had run onto a mine. We were concerned about Aures, fearing that he had fallen into the hands of the Reds. But, knowing Aures, there was always the possibility that he had fought his way back to the road himself.

As we walked back we suddenly heard a fusillade of shots in front of us from the right side of the road. Carefully we advanced through the undergrowth on the left roadside until we spotted a group of men on the road. Matussek, Hauptmann Fara and a few of my men. Lots of talking followed: what had happened to the recovery vehicle, and how lucky its crew had been when it had run over the mine. But it was mostly Hauptmann Fara who did the talking. It was also Fara who, after looking at the Russian machine pistol that I was carrying, suddenly told me to get away from him. One of those things had just gone off in his hand, all by itself. He then asked why the hell I had walked into the minefield?! By then I was livid with anger and replied that all those who had seen their fair share of action from the start would know the answer to that question and that everyone else would be better advised to shut up! In the aftermath, that reply led to a joint meeting with Hille, where Fara withdrew his accusation and even offered me his hand in friendship. I ended it there as I had no intention of taking this any further.

Saturday, 23 August 1941

I am sitting in a cottage which is owned by an old Estonian woman. We have to stay here all night. I don't know what the plan for tomorrow will be, but we know that we will be deployed somewhere else. The current situation is as follows: together with Vorausabteilung Limbrunn, our 5th Company has driven the advance of the division further towards the north-east, where it is now only 45 kilometres away from Leningrad and only 35 kilometres from the coast. We are not advancing any further north, as the main road ahead of us is already in range of the Russian coastal artillery. That we want to avoid having our hides tanned by those big buggers, which can rotate their guns 360 degrees, is pretty clear. We'll defeat the Russians anyway. Our attack stalled in front of Luga. There the 8.Pz.Div. has turned south-east towards the Luga while 1. and 6.Pz.Div. are defending towards the north for as long as it takes to clear the situation and to get rid of the Russian divisions there. Some of our recce squads have managed to advance within 5 kilometres of Peterhof. The only Russian soldier they could find there was a courier, who was of course taken prisoner by them. He had been on the way from Luga to Leningrad.

All along the defensive line, the Russians launch regular, small-unit attacks. That is all. Some tiny village nearby was suddenly attacked by four tanks and 250 Russians. Four tanks were destroyed and 160 Russians finished off. We can also feel the effect of the many airfields in this region. Bombers and Ratas come to visit often. Only 500 metres from here some Ratas have only recently strafed a vehicle of the artillery. Of the twelve Ratas not a single one was shot down, but they in turn nearly sent one of our Messerschmitts to the ground, which had been escorting one of our Focke-Wulf reconnaissance aircraft. Today I. Abteilung and Abteilung 65 came through the village. I. Abteilung had a Russian tank with them – weight 48 tons, armed with a 7.62-cm gun and two more guns in smaller turrets. A huge bucket!

We just received supplies including ½ litre of schnapps, chocolate and 150 litres of beer for the company. Not bad at all. But let me talk about what else happened in the last few days.

On **Wednesday, 20 August 1941** we moved into a defensive position, but nothing happened. We rolled back into a forest behind Gorki, where we settled down and made our home for the next eight days. We dug a square-shaped hole and covered it with wooden beams which would serve as protection against shell splinters. We also gathered some fresh hay, which smelled wonderful, and on which we then had a good night's sleep. But on **Thursday, 21 August** Oberst Koll ordered us to move. We were all feeling very sorry for ourselves. We moved into a forest outside Kaladeri, tall pine trees without any undergrowth. It started to rain. No Russians in sight. On that evening Oberst Koll briefed us about the situation here in the East. Even if I am not at home by 31 August, we will surely have taken Leningrad soon. On **Friday, 22 August** we moved from the high forest to another place nearby, where – together with the riflemen – we formed the mobile reserve of Kampfgruppe von Seckendorff. In the worst case our tanks could carry a whole company of riflemen. During the night we heard the sound of intense shooting in the distance, but were not committed ourselves.

Sunday, 24 August 1941, Puljewo

I am again sitting in the house of the old Estonian woman. Our tank is parked right next to it. Thunderstorms and rain have driven us all indoors. In one corner of the room another woman is delousing a child; she does so with a kind of religious devotion. Glässgen and Ritgen have just been over and shortly before that, Theo Langenbruch was here to collect his mail. An Unteroffizier of the Flak was here too, he wanted to have me as witness for his destruction of a Po-2 aircraft. He is stationed 50 metres away from here. The Flak is now firing armour-piercing shot at some of the more heavily armoured Russian aircraft. Several new types have made an appearance, including some modern bombers and fighters. Now that it's raining, we won't get any more visitors. No one really knows what we'll do next. The general situation isn't too bad for us. Voroshilov has issued a statement in which he orders his people to stock up on food supplies. The circle around Leningrad is slowly closing. Again we are the division which is at the forefront of it all.

Otherwise nothing new. Last night was freezing cold. Just now six Russian fighters zoomed over, even though it was raining. Everything and everyone opened up on them. Since Werdecker has brought down that Russian fighter with his Russian gun, everyone else seems to be determined to copy that feat.

10.30, Monday, 25 August 1941, Puljewo

Our rest has come to an end. We have just been subordinated to 8. Panzer-Division and are to march out at 11.00 together with Battalion Zollenkopf* and a light artillery unit. There seems to be work for us again. I wonder where. I hope it will help to close the door of this shop a bit sooner. Yesterday evening it was reported that Luga had fallen. I don't know yet if that is true. I wish it was; it would be nice. The entire sky in that direction was illuminated by huge fires last night. The horizon was bathed in blood-red colours. It is only good that the war isn't waged on German soil, as it was in the Thirty Years War.

Last night was very cold again. Makes me wonder how the weather will develop in the future. I hope there will be less rain than we had during the last few days. The daytime heat is much better to bear than the freezing cold of the nights; one can't find any sleep – just tossing and turning in

---

* I./Schützen-Regiment 4.

an attempt to keep warm. Today is the 25th, and I personally doubt that Leningrad will be fully encircled in six days. Maybe that's what they'll be employing us for. Maybe it is us who are supposed to close the lock. But I need to stop thinking about ifs and whens. There is no sense in that.

Yesterday evening I washed my clothes in a waterhole nearby and the results were better than those usually achieved by the Russian women and it didn't need the usual payment of a loaf of army bread. While I was doing that, Feldwebel Ulrich came to see me to say goodbye. He is being transferred to Neuling's company. Since the time at Gdov, I really came to like Ulrich. Before that, I had hardly known him. I cannot help thinking about the fighting for the field positions at Konochowizy, Chimosowo and Muratowo. I wonder where comrade Bongardt is now. Two months we have been out here now, and who knows how much longer it is going to take? In the future we have to watch that not so many houses go up in flames during the firefights. Otherwise we won't have anywhere to sleep. There are now broadsheets on the wells and other public places with calls to bring in the harvest. The farmers here were already busy harvesting before the damned rain started.

My platoon has five vehicles again. Feldwebel Goßler joined us yesterday, together with Feldwebel Engelhardt. My other commanders are Unteroffizier Grawe and Albert. The company now has eighteen Skodas and the radio vehicle of the regiment. Three platoons of five Skodas each, two in the company squad, the said radio vehicle and Wilhelm Lope's platoon of three Panzer IVs. We are now waiting in Nikolskoye. The vehicles are lined up alongside the houses and are well camouflaged. The boss has driven off to find out what he is supposed to do with us.

Earlier we drove through a village, Natsashjewka, which was inhabited by a strikingly northern-type of people. Most certainly Finns or Germans. Women and children with long, beautiful faces, light blue eyes and white-blonde hair. Clearly not of Russian or Slavic descent. We were astounded to see gardens, even beautifully kept gardens, with nicely painted fences. I wonder how these people managed to survive out here. Their fields were the best we had seen in the whole region.

Nikolskoye has been virtually abandoned by the people, but it is a clean village with a neat church made from stone. On its spire, of which half is sadly missing, sits our artillery observer, who is guiding the fire of our 15-cm guns onto some Russian railway stations ahead of us. Not much else going on here. We are to establish a defensive line, what is our next task, we don't yet know. I wonder what news the boss will bring.

Wednesday, 27 August 1941, Pokrowka, in front of Krasnogwardiejsk

Yesterday I couldn't write any more. Hille, Fara, Lope, me and the other platoon leaders had been called to a briefing with Oberst Zollenkopf to discuss the further deployment of our company. We are defending a line facing beaten Russian troops flooding back from Luga. Our positions are widely dispersed. In the gaps between, Spieckermann – the leader of Zollenkopf's pioneer platoon – has installed a number of 'treats': mines, booby-traps, spring guns. Yesterday evening, after a strong artillery preparation, about 600 Russians attacked from the direction of Krasnogwardiejsk. As usual they were repelled and suffered heavy casualties. In general, the casualties of the Reds are absolutely enormous! And when one speaks to the workers here – well, they think in the same way as our workers do. In a lost war, the working population suffers most. Am I too much of a materialist, if I claim that the upper levels of the population can bear the loss of their ideational values much better than the working class can bear their material loss? That's saying it carefully – I don't want to be classed as a Bolshevist. But my socialist Weltanschauung is only strengthened by this war! Only, when it comes to me, the international social ideology is replaced by a strong nationalist direction with an emphasis on the racial stance. The political perspective of the Landsers has been much widened, by this campaign in particular.

I have now left the front porch and fled outside. Even though it is a bit draughty out here, I have escaped the company of the mutineers in my platoon. Spilken, Grawe, Schweinsberg – Obergefreiter with four years of service, Koch the roofer – all as bad as each other. Grawe in particular is one of the eternally colourless. Quite a good comrade, but politically not quite plus and not quite minus either. People such as this, without a clear position, have always existed, especially after the last war. They have quickly taken advantage of a secure bourgeois existence, but they have gained just as much as they have dared – not much at all. Particularly so when it comes to intellectual matters.

In contrast, men like Bill Veit, Peter Coolhaas and Rudi Gerke have spent fourteen years of their lives with one foot in a fortress prison cell. They have been despised by the glutted citizens, while they themselves were forced to live from hand to mouth, marked down by society as 'failed existences'. But it was them who helped to shape and create a new, enormous Reich, and that monumental thought, and the satisfaction that arises from it, is worth so much more than quietly munching one's middle-class cabbage bought with a secure union wage.

Now then, enough of politics. We have to move out soon. I have just seen the boss – we'll have to shift our positions a little bit further to the right. Why? – Only the stars know the answer. This kind of thing doesn't bother me any more, I have become just as stubborn as all the other Landsers have become. Yesterday evening, when it had just become dark, we had to move houses, even though we had only just moved into what seemed to be the only waterproof house in the village. And now, just because the battered riflemen need something to lean on, I have to move my five laughable tanks. And then they were still so jumpy that one of their sentries opened fire on one of my men when he was busy following a call of nature that night. Good that the comrade wasn't able to hit anything and even better that most of our Landsers are a lot more relaxed.

It is strange how one can write down all the little details one experiences on quiet days. What we experience on days of combat, however – those details one does remember, but somehow it is hard to write them down. The faces of the Russians who surrendered after the close fighting during the attack on Konochowizy. The expression of the man who lay next to my tank and threw the hand grenade, even though he was already looking into the barrel of my pistol and only a fleeting second before I shot him dead. One cannot really express all this on paper.

Then the Russian tanks appeared; I warned Wenger via the radio. Eject the high-explosive shell, load armour-piercing – the deadly serious face of Wittkötter when the gun suddenly jammed – three enemy tanks ahead which could have ended us then and there. I will never be able to forget that. The expressions on the faces of the riflemen, weapons in hand, machine guns ready, riding on the tank during some fighting advance through a forest. The constant watch for Ratas in the sky. All this I will not forget. But I can't describe it properly either. I have seen photographs of men attacking across a river in assault boats. They looked like our own riflemen when they advanced towards the Russian bunkers at Arokjuly. Feldwebel Westhoff of the Kradschützen with his small moustache and the machine-gunner of his platoon, who just stood there in front of the foxholes, his machine gun at the hip, keeping the heads of the Russians down with his scything fire. The two men I supplied with hand grenades which they then used to smoke out a Russian bunker. They all had the same hard, stoney faces and tense expression. The same as mine, I guess, when we stood in front of the Russians and our guns failed to work.

This evening I was visited by Oberleutnant Schneider, the Adjutant of Nebel-Abteilung III/52 and former member of IR37. After the episode at Poretschje, where we guarded his position, he was decorated with the EK1. He deserves it and the award is not begrudged by anyone; he does a fantastic job as a forward observer for his unit.

Leonhardt has informed me that Oberleutnant Bethke is going to be transferred as an instructor to the Waffenschule in Wünsdorf. The ideal job for him! There he'll be reunited with Ashauer, Rink and the other boys of our company. I wonder how they feel, now that they are freshly baked Unteroffiziere! We have supplied them all with the attestations needed for the assault badge.

Currently there is a very peaceful atmosphere here. Just like in one of those forest villages near Hamburg at this time of year. The Russian artillery is silent and smoke from the evening fires rises into the clear evening sky from the chimneys of the clean, wooden houses. I can't help thinking about Jochen Möllenberg, about Kleinjung, Vielbaum and Günther Eggers. They will walk with us, be among us again – I still can't reconcile myself with it all.

Thursday, 28 August 1941, Siwioskaya

[*Blank*]

Friday, 29 August 1941, Kuriza

After the Russian night attack on Siwioskaya, we have been deployed here to the 3rd Company of the riflemen. Now I sit here in the doorway of a big, stone-built barn, which offers some protection against splinters. I am dog-tired, but I do want to try to describe what has happened. At 8 p.m. I was called to the boss for a briefing; although he was still away with Zollenkopf, he had left a whole bunch of instructions for us. We were supposed to move our whole defence unit further towards the south into the wake of the advancing 8. Panzer-Division. The crews stood at their vehicles and were ready to move out, but I had to wait for Hille, who only arrived back at 10 p.m. But when he arrived he brought us the news that we had been given more time and were only to march out at 03.15, before the break of dawn. Then we would drive to Siwioskaya to relieve elements of 8. Panzer-Division. After having slept from 11 p.m. to 3 a.m., we then marched out into the pouring rain. Totally tired and soaking wet, we arrived at Siwiosk and were lucky enough to find quarters in an empty and quite exquisite house. The house was uninhabited. Using the hay from an adjacent barn, we made beds for ourselves and the crews in the rooms on both floors of the house and then caught up with some much-needed sleep. I made my bed on a quite excellent sofa in the living room. Before that we had lit the stove and then slept wonderfully well, even though we were roused from it several times by the usual interruptions: 'Platoon leaders to the boss!', 'Vehicle strength report requested!' and similar malarkey. At 13.00 we inspected the positions of the rifle company and then, accompanied by Lope and his tanks, drove to the glass factory – the name of which I have forgotten. It is located alongside a lake and was once built by Germans. A Leutnant of the Geheime Feldpolizei who had been born in that village was just then visiting the house he had been born in. The section there is held by Oberleutnant Stöcker, who was still asleep when we arrived because it had taken him and his vehicles the whole night to get there. One of his vehicles had driven into a roadside ditch and had become stuck there. He didn't see the need to get up when we appeared and greeted us like some old dame, lying on the bed. He has always been a little braggart.

We left Lope's lot in another small village and then drove to another place where Fara and Hille wanted to organise some 'meat'. But there was no livestock and not even a single egg to be had, as the population of the village with the glass factory, who were all factory workers and did not own any ground or livestock, had to be supplied by the surrounding villages. The situation in the area was similar to famine. Hundreds of people were queuing for hours in front of vehicles from which bread was being distributed. In stark contrast to our situation at home, no one in Russia has wasted even a thought about securing the provision of the non-combatant population. We talked to a worker who spoke fluent German. He said that of the original German workforce only an old man in his seventies remained. Until recently he had still been the best-paid worker. Now he received a pension of 102 rubles, but then he had earned 700 rubles. That's 70 Marks in German currency.

We took a look at a church in a neighbouring village which had been turned into some kind of dance club. That was also something the worker had also told us about. Only the old people were still living their Orthodox religion. The young were growing up without any religion at all and felt good about it. Inside the Red Club they had hung big cloths with the faces of Stalin, Lenin, Woroschilow, Kalinin and other Soviet dignitaries. They were hanging right above the old and much smaller images of the saints. I was shocked at the scruffy appearance of the workers. Even before 1933 no one in Germany had looked that shabby. We then drove back to the glass factory, stopping briefly at Lope's position, where someone had managed to source a few scraps on fresh veal of which some was handed to Hille. I took the time to rummage through some of the nearby houses. Communal kitchen, sports hall, a food and housekeeping shop all grouped together there. All very practical and, in my opinion, the right thing to do from a socialist perspective. Maybe it's because of the army that I am such a friend of communal cooking. Just the right thing for the employed – communal kitchen and cooperative society – but there is no space for individualism, just one of many arguments against all this. On our way back we were overtaken by Zollenkopf's Adjutant, who told us that there was something brewing in Siwiosk. We drove back as fast as we could, but not without bartering half a dozen eggs from a Finnish woman in return for half an army loaf.

Everyone is on high alert. The stolen chicken is out of the pots, the fried potatoes taken off the fire and then to the vehicles on high alert. After we had waited for a while, however, we unpacked all of the food again and ate it all nevertheless. Then it got dark and we deployed the sentries. Then the first news came in. A Finn had reported that he had seen large numbers of Russian troops advancing through the forest towards our position. Soon after, a Russian defector was brought in and with him came more important information. He told us that at first they had wanted to defect with the entire company. His comrades, however, had been too scared of their superiors and had, at the last moment, decided to stay behind. Everyone had been in a depressed mood, but that morning at 04.00, they would be attacking the village. One Russian battalion would attack from the left while another would bypass the village and then attack from the right. A third Russian battalion would be kept in reserve. There were no tanks, but they had been promised artillery support.

Based on that report, all rifle pickets were withdrawn, in the cover of darkness the baggage was sent to the rear and then our tanks, anti-tank guns, Flak and riflemen were formed into a main defensive line on both sides of the river near the road. My platoon, together with Feldwebel Dreyer, was deployed on the left. Section commander was Oberleutnant Prinz. Trying to get through the vehicles of the withdrawing baggage train, it took us from 11.00 to 11.45 to cover a distance of only 1 kilometre. Obergefreiter Koch, a man of Albert's crew, was caught between two tanks, badly bruised on the hips, and as such hors de combat. We placed him on a bed in one of the houses where he remained until dawn, shortly before the Russian attack, when a dispatch rider of the riflemen took him to a doctor.

Even though it was dark, we had found good positions where, well camouflaged, we remained until the daybreak. Feldwebel Dreyer's tank had to pull the vehicles of the Flak from the wet and soggy field and then took position on our right wing, leaning against the edge of the village. On my right, next to a house, there were Feldwebel Goßler and next to him – linking up with Dreyer – Feldwebel Albert. On my left there was Feldwebel Engelhardt, who secured the road towards the left and behind him; to prevent any attempt to bypass and flank us, there was Unteroffizier Grawe. The gaps between our vehicles were filled by one 5-cm and three 3.7-cm anti-tank guns, several heavy machine guns, a platoon of 3.7-cm Flak and a couple of additional 2-cm, self-propelled Flak guns. The Russians could come if they wished to do so. And as it slowly got light, they came!

All of a sudden my wet trouser legs and the freezing cold were forgotten. I was physically totally exhausted, I had been shivering all over in the freezing wet cold and my already tired eyes had been hurting from staring into the darkness through my binoculars. But then, when I spotted dense waves of attacking Soviet infantry from a distance of 1 to 2 kilometres, all of that was suddenly forgotten. Weapons ready and one final check. Wittkötter was arming and sorting the ammunition, Wenger was busy working on the radio. I again checked all the weapons, unlocked the turret and continued observing through my binoculars. And damn, there they came, huge numbers of them. One could see how the individual Russian companies stepped out of the forest, from where they advanced, in an oblique angle, towards the village on the left. They advance in wide lines. Due to the rain most had tent squares hanging over their heads and shoulders and many were holding their rifles with one hand on the carrying straps. On the far right of the Russian line, one company stepped out of the forest a moment later, directly opposite us, but they also swerved towards the centre of the village. Everything was quiet, when suddenly a few single Russian soldiers appeared about 300 metres in front of us. And I don't know which idiot was so unnerved by it all that he decided to open fire on them, as it had been agreed that we'd only open fire at closest range.

An MG 34 started hammering away and then the infantry guns on our right, possibly on someone's order, also joined the untimely concert. Then the 3.7 Flak started firing on some distant targets while Unteroffizier Albert, somehow enticed by Hauptmann Fara, started firing on some single Russians. I was really angry! That way we had given away our new positions before having clipped even a single Russian hair. The effects of that folly could be felt shortly afterwards when Russian artillery started falling around us – at least one 15-cm and a battery of 7.62-cms. Some Russians were now approaching and entering the village and our artillery started shelling it. Soon the house of our neighbour there, the carpenter, started burning. A pity – the man had been very kind to us. Most of the Russians had withdrawn when the firing started and now, slowly but surely, the fire of both sides got weaker and Hauptmann Fara appeared next to my tank. My radio, receiver and transmitter, had stopped working and he informed me that a battalion of tanks of 8. Panzer-Division and a battalion of Kradschützen were on the way to kick the Russians out of the village. On the horizon one could see a company of Russians laying mines in a potato field on the edge of the forest. I could clearly see one man holding a large white object, probably a map, who seemed to be guiding the operation.

I am now sitting in the building housing the children's home, waiting for the things that are lying ahead. The rainfall has become weaker and – at least at the moment – the same applies to the artillery fire. I was interrupted several times while writing the above lines when heavy shells detonated nearby. I hope they'll spare us in the coming night.

At 15.00 Unteroffizier Enz was here with the field kitchens. He brought news from Hille. After clearing the village, the tanks of 8. Panzer had pulled out again. Forty prisoners had been rounded up there. They told us that a Russian recce squad in civilian clothing had been in the village yesterday and had come back with a detailed report. They had known that we were there and with what strength, they had even known the location of Zollenkopf's command post. Feldwebel Giersig has been wounded by shell splinters and has to go to hospital. Another of our soldiers was sitting on the turret of a tank when a shell splinter tore through his trouser pocket and ripped away his wallet. Such luck!

The Russians are firing again at the moment. 15-cm calibre. I am out of here.

18.00, Saturday, 30 August 1941, Kurobizy

Up until now, the Russian artillery hasn't fired on this place. Our troops must have captured Wirizy and thus probably forced the Red batteries to withdraw from there. Thank God! – that's the only thing one can say. Yesterday, during the barrage, the infantry gun platoon of the riflemen suffered casualties, two killed and four severely wounded. And when I visited the communal smithy and the attached carpenter's workshop this morning,

The old people have a mirror here in the house, and looking into it I can't help noticing how much hair I have lost during this campaign. How did that happen? With my twenty-five years, I can't say I am particularly happy about it. I have to admit now that here in Russia they do have some really pretty girls. One of the refugee girls, who after staying in the village here for several days, came out of the bathhouse here this morning, is just my type. She is not Russian, more of the Finnish-Estonian type which is common here in the region of Leningrad – I wonder if there will be time to eat the potatoes which the old woman is kindly and voluntarily preparing. What will they have in store for us today? Who knows – will probably turn out to be one of those after-dinner surprises again.

Surprise, surprise! As expected, we are to drive back to Nikolskoye. The job has been done here. We were just in the process of eating the potatoes, Wittkötter had fetched a tin of fish from the tank, when Engelhardt brought the news from Hille. Now it is getting dark again and we'll have to cross that deep ford. That sounds really great!

We are just rolling through the village of Staraja Possjolok and I have to say that the people here are very clean and not too fond of the Bolsheviks. They have welcomed us with bunches of flowers! And everywhere people are waving when we roll past! The populace astonishes me!

Something that doesn't happen every day: ten prisoners are standing at the roadside and want to hitch a ride! We gave each of them a slice of army bread and then loaded them on the Panzer IVs. The hungry locals are standing nearby and are also asking for bread, so we get a few loaves from the leading tank and quickly distribute them. We have taken plenty more prisoners today, by the way.

Tuesday 2 September 1941

We are standing on the road between Wiriza and Kurowiza. Not a soul knows why we are standing here so long. We were supposed to reach Wyra, which lies on the main road, yesterday night already. But first we had to pull our vehicles across the Wiriza ford. Wünsche and his platoon had been designated for that job. On the path leading to the ford there were mines which had been cleared and placed by the side by pioneers of the 8. Panzer-Division, but which hadn't been defused and not even marked with barrier tape. In total there were fourteen of them piled up there. And when Jörgens's tank rolled towards the ford it hit a picket fence, which fell over right onto one of those mines. It exploded at once and ignited the other thirteen mines. The effect doesn't need to be described. Obergefreiter Berhorst, one of the old men of our company, with forty-two attacks under his belt, was killed. And that – to protect the sensitive nerves of possible future readers – is describing it mildly. Jörgens, the driver, suffered a concussion of the brain and related other things from the blast. Unteroffizier Steffen, the commander of the tank, and his radio operator Zurhausen, who both had been walking a bit in front of the tank, were lucky and remained unscathed. Of course it's the pioneers who are to blame for this – they have negligently violated their duties and a lot more could have happened. Then, just as the first of our vehicles rolled past the brickworks, another mine went off down at the ford. And all that only because of the pioneers! Wilhelm Lope addressed a few of them who had taken part in clearing the mines at the ford and asked why they had only been dug out without defusing them too. 'Our orders were to clear a path. No one ordered us to defuse anything!' – yes, understood – just like us, when we point our weapons at the Russians in a close-combat situation and then we don't pull the trigger because no one has ordered us to do so! We loaded the body of Berhorst on our tank. The poor boy had been torn up terribly, so we had to wrap him tightly into a tent square before we could do so. The detonation had killed him immediately. Near a barn, on the grounds of the collective where we spent the night, there were a few trees. We dug his grave below them and decorated it nicely. Just as we did for the graves of so many other comrades, we made a cross from birchwood and placed it on the grave. In the meantime, some comrades had brought potted flowers from one of the nearby cottages. Those were also put on the grave. After a silent tribute, we walked back to our vehicles and to tasks that still lay ahead of us.

From today we have been assigned to Gruppe Limbrunn, but for now we are still in Staraja with the baggage, where our vehicles are undergoing some much-needed maintenance. What will become of us then, I don't know yet. Seems we'll be forming the vanguard again. Our company is billeted in a huge building, a former workers' convalescent home. We are now in the region of the forest belt around Leningrad. Yesterday the old man said that if we went a bit further north, there would be wide, open terrain. Siwerskaya, just like Wirza, is surrounded by woodland. There must be an airfield in the distance, or some industrial site with a lot of large, hangar-like structures. I have never seen so many railway lines before in Russia. Since the beginning of the campaign, from the very first day, we are now in the first village and in the first house with electric lighting and not only that – it is still working.

And they even have running water in the house! The wash basin, however, is blocked.

Outside there is a deep Russian trench and in that there is a thunderbox designed in a way which makes it impossible to use it quickly. The reason for that is that it is unavoidable to spend at least ten minutes laughing before business can commence. The beam has been fastened to the sides of the trench and has been furnished with a backrest, but it is clear that the designers didn't care much for the practicality of it all. Anyone trying to relieve himself on the contraption looks a bit like a monkey sitting on a sharpening wheel. And just to make sure that the 'cacktuses' who perform on it are protected against the rain, some clever dick has decided to install two glasshouse roof panels above it. That way, anyone sitting there while the bombs are splintering is guaranteed to get an additional hail of glass splinters into his face.

Another peculiar thing here is the wide use of hammocks, which can be found in every house. Also the women do not walk barefoot or with wooden or bast fibre shoes any more. Here they often wear leather shoes with high heels and thin socks. Both men and women, however, wear the 'quilted standard jackets' of the kind the Red Army soldiers are wearing too. Nearly every worker wears a thick wool pullover, a torn pair of trousers and a flat cap. And with their mouths filled with cigarettes rolled with newspaper or sunflower seeds they are now standing around without employment. All the large factories around Leningrad have stopped working, and that gives them time to talk to the German soldiers, marvel at the weapons and to listen to them when they talk about a different Europe and of German socialism. And they are genuinely interested, asking about the German working hours and the wages, if we can buy everything and for what prices, the living conditions of the workers. The kolkhoz farmers want to know how much livestock and ground our farmers own. Questions of that kind come up again and again and we notice the great joy with which they welcome us here, especially the older people who remember life in the old Russia and those who have been prisoners of war in Germany.

Wednesday, 3 September 1941

Hille was with the Oberst yesterday. Now he has also received his assault badge. There is also news about our new task. Today we'll stay here and concentrate on servicing the vehicles. Tomorrow we drive to II./Pz.11 which has been restructured and is now under command of Knight's Cross holder Hauptmann Stern. Together with them we are going to be subordinated to 36.ID which is launching the attack on Leningrad, together with 6. Panzer-Division. The 1. and 8. Panzer-Division are being pulled out of the line and will form the army reserve. That means that the old 5th Company is not going to the scrapyard to gather rust there. Instead we'll fight the final battle for Leningrad alongside the infantrymen with whom we have already fought at Lake Peipus. I am glad that Glässgen doesn't have the company any more, and that it is now in the hands of the businesslike and calm Hauptmann Stern who is taking over. I wonder what else we'll experience in the coming days. The fortifications in front of the city are not shabby and have been prepared long beforehand. But then the artillery of the 36.ID is most excellent. Since we received mail yesterday my mood has changed. There was a letter from home containing developed photos of the tank battle at Raseiniai and from the first days of the war in the East. The pictures, which my mother has sent me, are all very good. The letters from the Heimat have blown my bad mood away entirely.

Last night I sat down with the boys of 6th Company for a while. They had set up a radio and played some really good music. Serious music from Belgrade. It felt like a festival hour – simple radio music! As soon as I am back in Hamburg I can finally go to concerts again! Into the theatre, just like Herbert did when he was on leave there. Just a short while longer and then I will have an even greater right to enjoy these pleasures. Hille is said to have received a bollocking from Koll because he has missed some appointments. I have no idea what exactly. Now then, I want to take a look at what mail has arrived in the makeshift orderly room here. The technical servicing of the vehicles is mostly finished. The men are doing their laundry and cleaning their weapons. Wittkötter had the watch last night and is now lying sleeping on a Russian folding bed which someone has organised. We have all slept as much as we could last night, it was a real treat –

I have now slept a couple of hours more. What else am I supposed to do without trousers – I have given mine to Ischer and Metgen, our company artificers, to have them mended. They have set up their shop here. My trousers are slowly falling apart and new ones are a scarce commodity. Vellner with his lorry is in Germany at the military clothing office. We are expecting him back in about two or three weeks. And I expect that the war here will still be ongoing then. At least I will be getting a new uniform. Due to all the things I have been through on foot over time, I now look scruffier than the tank gunners do and because of the oily main gun, my trousers are constantly dirty too. When Leningrad has fallen I will wash them in petrol again. The crew has lost my washing bowl and has mislaid my coat. It's a disgrace how the brothers care for my things. I have replaced Wenger with my old radio operator Schweinsberg. I hope that from now on my tank's radio will be working without fault.

The brothers of the baggage train are always bragging loudly about all the fighting they have been in. I hate that like the plague. My men, even the youngest of them, always roar with laughter when they hear such talk from the baggage men.

Today at 18.00 roll call. Metgen and Ischer, the artificers, have received their promotions to Unteroffizier. For bravery in the face of the enemy Wittkötter, Lauer, Kawilk, Laufermann, Mundt and Kortly have been promoted to Gefreiter. Several of the older men of the baggage train as well. One of them even has the assault badge, but had been kicked out of a combat formation because he was afraid of the enemy. It's funny, I can spot people like this just by looking at their faces; I can see it in their eyes if they are useful in combat or not.

A whole bunch of assault badges were awarded and Unteroffizier Wiesner, the driver of the fuel truck, received the War Merit Cross.

In the morning wake-up call at 05.00, leaving at 06.00. Then drive to II. Abteilung where we'll have another day of rest and then we attack Leningrad together with 36.ID (mot.).

Thursday, 4 September 1941, near Krasnogwardiejsk

It has rained the whole morning. Across Nikolskoye and Balschoja we have ended up in a little Finnish village where the Russians resided before us. Steel helmets, machine guns, Molotov cocktails, ammunition – all kinds of stuff is littering the ground. In the past we would not even have considered entering a Russian cottage and now we are happy if we can take shelter from the cold rain and grateful if we can find a warm stove on which we can fry our potatoes. Outside my tank is parked next to a sauna. On the other side of it is Grawe's tank; he has set up a tent there. Pusch, Wittkötter and my new radio operator Schweinsberg want to sleep in the antechamber of that sauna – the *banja*, as they call it here. There is plenty of clean straw nearby. I have moved into the bug-free cottage of a Finn. His wife is currently doing the laundry and it is a bit smelly, but still better than outside in the rain.

I wish I could see into the future to find out our fate up here at Leningrad. The Ic of the division has informed us that the 36.ID and the 6. Panzer-Division will attack west past Krasnogwardiejsk towards the coast, which means we'll end up somewhere near Peterhof on the Gulf of Finland. And 1. and 8.Pz.Div are indeed being pulled out to form a reserve – for now at least. On our left the 1. and 58. Infanterie-Division will advance. How long will the whole malarkey here continue? I am expecting there will be a hard winter, just like last year. And it is coming early too, the potato leaves have already frozen. We may as well expect the worst. The only good things is that I have got the rubber boots – at least my feet won't be wet all the time.

Damn, if only this damn rain would stop. Outside a few men of the reconnaissance platoon are dragging two large glass panels through the mud. They have taken them from a greenhouse and are now bringing them to

Hille. He has moved into a house in which the window glass is missing and the glass panels will now be leaned against the windows from the outside.

A few Finnish girls walk past carrying sickles. Why are they not using scythes, at least, when even the threshing machines are not working? But now I do at least know why the Bolsheviks chose the sickle as one of their symbols – sickles are used everywhere and by everyone here; scythes are rarely seen and machinery is unknown. Most tractors have been taken away by Red Army troops and the last horses were taken by the partisans. Earlier I spoke to one of the farmers here, his name is Hokannen, Andrey Philipp, and in his passport his nationality is indeed recorded as 'Finnish'. And he told me that whereas all the Russian men in the region had been drafted, the Estonians and Finns were not.

Here in front of the house is a very deep well. I have looked down the shaft right now and it seems to be full of ice at the bottom. Enz can get that out to make ice cream for us. They had tried to do the same in Puljewo, but didn't manage to get the cream and sugar mix to thicken up. Instead they poured a whole bottle of schnapps and lemon juice into it and then distributed the vile stuff as 'lemon ice cream liquor'.

Turausky has been placed under five days of arrest because he told Enz, who is an Unteroffizier, to 'shut his face'. Poor Hugo. Now that I am sitting here, looking out of the window, all the odd characters are walking past. The old fighters of II. Abteilung, who haven't heard a shot fired in anger for two months, since Jamkino, and who have spent all the time away at the rear with the baggage train. Yesterday Wilhelm Lope said that by now everyone of us has more attacks under his belt than these guys had in Poland, France and Russia combined. I wonder if Neuling will lose his nerve in the coming engagements. Only sad that such people, who with their lack of tactical understanding have the fate of men like Jochen Möllenberg and Kleinjung on their conscience, can't be dragged in front of a court martial. There is no way I will stay in the army longer than required. Since Jochen, Günther, Vielbaum and Kleinjung have been killed and Theo Langenbruch and Bongardt have left us, I have fully withdrawn into the little world of my platoon and I feel quite well in that environment. Now then, I will arm myself with a map and then I am heading to Hille to a platoon leaders' meeting. I wonder what news he will have.

Friday, 5 September 1941

This morning I have really earned my lunch. I was in charge of the search operation inside the forest here in the sector of 5th Company. I can only repeat – only good that I have my rubber boots! It rained heavily when we walked out, but no one pretended to have painful feet or related ailments. We stomped down the forest path towards the road where the artillery is located, and divided the men into groups, three men and one NCO in each. The groups found all kinds of propaganda leaflets which were very well designed. We gathered them all up and burned them once we came back. The men also found several excellently camouflaged wooden bunkers, all abandoned and empty except for a few hand grenades, which we took with us after defusing them. Slowly we are getting used to handling Russian weapons. Here on the outskirts of the village we found piles of gas masks, rifles, steel helmets, machine-gun belts and spare barrels. Anyway, we have spent the whole morning rummaging through the wet undergrowth and now we have to see how we can somehow dry our uniforms again.

It was Hauptmann Stern who ordered us to search the forest. During the briefing he also informed us that our division would be deployed in the Schwerpunkt of the attack on Leningrad and the fortifications west of Krasnogwardiejsk. Using thousands of workers, the Russians have built good fortifications there: concrete and wooden bunkers, all well camouflaged, minefields, mine barriers, anti-tank trenches, stake obstacles, barbed-wire barricades and other wire entanglements – all that is waiting for us there. I wonder how we will fare. In front of Leningrad the Russians will surely field large numbers of tanks too. No doubt they have managed to save a few hundred. But anyhow, I must not be too negative. When our buckets have broken down, been shot to pieces and have been blown up by mines – well, then we'll have to attack on foot and get ourselves the infantry assault badge in addition to our Panzer badges.

Here in the East one meets the old comrades of II. Abteilung again; they have been at the rear through most of the time during which we have been on defensive duties. Walther Leckenbusch and his men, in charge of the two radio tanks – Klein, Schmaldt, Lorries, Oberfunkmeister Middelmann and the two recruits, who now have been with us for nearly a year. Spahr is also running around here, and getting fatter by the hour, Jupp Heitmann too – with my hair loss I will soon be as bald as he is. And then there are the old, unsympathetic Feldwebel of the staff company and staff – men like Dettenbach, Falk, Lenz, Oberschirrmeister Naundorf and the old Unteroffiziere who joined up with me like Franz Dilling, Meger. 7th Company is also based here, yesterday during the briefing I ran into Ulrich and Leutnant Knust.

16.00

I slept for a few hours. Outside the weather has cleared up a little and now and then a bit of blue sky makes a brief appearance between the clouds. Even though the rain has only ceased a short while ago, the road leading through the village has already dried up a little. Fockel, the driver of 'Hauptmann' Fara, is standing around there. The stupid twat has got stuck again with his car. There are some people who never learn. In a civilian job, one would just fire them, but here in the army, one needs to learn to cope with them. Yes, the army! I have to admit that I did indeed reach a low point recently, probably fostered by the trouble on my birthday, to which I had been looking forward since the campaign started. And I guess that the relentless rainfall and all that sitting around also plays a role. The campaign has to be over soon – one way or another. But for me there is only one option now: to stick it out until the Endsieg has been achieved! One must not think that the wounded are better off, or 'If I had a wound like this, I could at least get out of these uncomfortable, dirty surroundings'. I am past all that now. Only today, a few letters from good and much-loved friends in the Heimat, a few photos and the thought of my mother's upcoming birthday have brought me back to my senses. I am not giving up, now that the end is already in sight. And what a sight Leningrad is! The thought of the Endsieg, and the knowledge that the people in the Heimat are watching and relying on us; all that will now spur us on during the final thrust on the Red metropolis, on the cradle of the Red Revolution, on Leningrad.

18.30

I have just had a bath in the *banja* and it was so hot that I nearly collapsed. The whole platoon had to go to the bathhouse to sweat out all the bad flu germs. Looking at how basic the little bathhouse here is, it is not bad at all. Only good that I was able to pop my head through a broken window now and then to avoid suffocation. After I had poured a few handfuls of water over the red-hot stones, it became really hot in the low-roofed room. I closed my eyes and soon I really started to sweat. Then I worked myself over with the brushwood twig, so all my pores were opened, and after I was really sweaty, I started soaping myself up. After that, everything was washed off with ice-cold water. That will surely have helped against the flu and colds.

Our attack has been postponed by twenty-four hours!!!

Saturday, 6 September 1941, Pigkelewo

The attack has been postponed by another twenty-four hours. It is now not taking place tomorrow, on Sunday, but on Monday. This morning all platoon leaders met with the boss and were issued with maps of the terrain we will have to attack across. There is something wrong with my stomach, so I went into the fields to relieve myself before the briefing. Would not have been ideal, if I had been forced to do so while the meeting was ongoing. Wonderful to have stomach problems here – and as a free bonus there is always the chance to catch some bugs, dysentery, a cold, kidney pains or crabs – the blessings of Russia. I have to pop out again now … I am feeling miserable.

Only yesterday evening I was still sitting with the comrades drinking mulled wine and chatting about the recent fighting. We have time for that now.

A Primus stove detonated in Schweinsberg's face. Schweinsberg, our best technician, had started to repair it and while he was doing so, the burning stove exploded and the flames burned his neck and right ear. Now he is lying in the porch with the medic and is moaning. Very painful burns, poor chap. He'll probably be transported to the rear, he can hardly move at the moment.

Sunday, 7 September 1941

The latest news is that the advance of the far left wing is making good progress. The 'Reval' business seems to have been sorted out and now the infantry is rapidly moving into the wedge that we have driven towards Leningrad. In the south and in the centre it's also working well, but there is something wrong at Wjasma. Wjasma had already been reported to have been taken by us. We are still standing 50 kilometres away from it, however. Schweinsberg, my radio operator, is feeling a bit better today. He isn't hurting as much as he did yesterday either. Maybe he won't have to go to hospital.

Yesterday several EK2s were awarded in the company. Leutnant Bongardt got one and Hero Spiekermann. In our company Meyer the medic and Obergefreiter Werdecker, who shot down the Rata with the Russian rifle and who is now in hospital after the mine explosion at the ford. Wilhelm Lope and I then went over to see Spiekermann to congratulate him. He was sitting in the house with Glässgen and Rudi Schöner. I am not too sure what's up with the latter. Is it the influence of the woman who had herself transferred from Hamburg to see him when he was in hospital in Magdeburg? Or is he depressed because he was posted to the baggage train in the leadership reserve? They haven't even given him a light platoon – that had gone to Knust, the reservist. I have made the start of the Sunday morning as comfortable as possible. Slept until 8.30 a.m., then washed my whole upper body properly with lots of water – not like the Finns, with three drops from the valve outlet next to the door. And now I sit in the tidy room, write and eat a bit of chocolate – out here, it can't get much better.

I have been ordered to see the boss. I wonder what it could be about, maybe an invitation to dinner?

So much for the dinner invitation! I have been ordered to inform my crews, immediately and without delay, that they must always salute me, except when in battle. Discipline in my gang has become too lackadaisical – yes, that is the influence of the snappy II. Abteilung. And when I step outside, there are Tutasz, Oberholz and Turonski, the youngest man of the company, taking the piss out of me and practising 'saluting'. Three in line abreast, one doing the German salute, number two is standing to attention and the third in line is saluting me with the traditional hand to the cap. I did have to laugh about the three ugly bastards.

Monday, 8 September 1941

Nothing new today, so I have just gone to visit the minister's son to report to him that there is nothing new to report. He probably didn't sleep very well, the face he made wasn't too friendly. When I think about it, it never is when he is looking at me. But I am certainly not reliant on his good mood!

In the night we were woken by the harsh singing of old songs coming from the where the staff is billeted. Schmauch, officer of the day, was sent over to ask them to shut up. When he got there he found all the staff officers and the Hauptmann sitting there, so he returned without having fulfilled his task. When one is awake at night, one constantly hears the shells howling outside. An aircraft just dropped some bombs here. Now, having drunk coffee, we are back in the parlour, waiting, chatting and writing.

Tuesday, 9 September 1941, Pigkelewo

Today at 9.30 a.m. the attack on Red positions at Salesi started. Since 07.00 our flyers had been busy bombing the villages and positions in front of us. At 08.00 the artillery barrage began and at 09.20 a group of Ju 88s appeared, dived down on the Red positions and dropped their blessings. Just when we had climbed from the observation post, two groups of Stukas flew in from two sides. On the north-north-west side of our section of attack an observation balloon hung in the sky, similar in shape to our barrage balloons. On the horizon one could see the spires of Krasnogwardiejsk and behind it, towards the west, a range of hills. These hills were the objective of our division. At 11.00, a group of Ju 88s bombed Krasnogwardiejsk.

And then things happened at great speed: from the hill here at the village, where there is a big children's swing, we could see that the entire horizon was shrouded in clouds. On the heights of Tayzy a locomotive or railway train was trying to escape, but our bombers got there on time. At first the spires of Krasnogwardiejsk had been well visible, but then they were also covered by thick clouds of smoke and started to burn. A gigantic picture! On the left wing, where our I. Abteilung is fighting with 36.ID, the Nebelwerfer-Abteilung is firing several times. The 10.5 and 15-cm artillery is firing shell after shell from the barrels. And again the Nebelwerfer fire! And just when we decide to leave, the wave of aircraft flies over and a whole series of new detonation clouds rises up in the distance. One of the bombers returns at low altitude and trailing smoke. Then it suddenly starts burning. Through my binoculars I can see the flames licking from the fuselage. What a pity, the Russian Flak seems to have got this one, possibly even with a gun delivered by us. The Russian 8.8-cms are firing quite precisely, but our aircraft drone stubbornly onwards and ignore the bellow from below. Until they can answer in their own language! The howl when our machines dive down, and then one hears the bursting crashes and sees the detonation clouds, black, white and dirty-yellow rising up on the horizon. The burning aircraft, a Junkers 88, is landing in a field not far away. From up a tree we can see how the machine is being consumed by the flames. One has to acknowledge the cool-bloodedness of the pilot, who managed to bring his burning kite back until, far away from the Russians, he found a place to land his death-stricken machine. I just hope the boys got out all right. We get an idea about the meaning of the term 'rolling operation'. Quite a spectacle that we are allowed to witness here. The beautiful landscape here stood sharply divided from the scene in front by a long curtain of fiery smoke. Burning villages in between, and here and there, but especially when our formations were flying in, our white signal flares: 'We are here!'

Yes, there they are, the comrades of Panzer-Abteilung 65. Already quite far ahead – that we have to admit. But we have to stay calm, when Raus can't advance any further, they will deploy us and Koll. That can happen very soon.

I suppose the weather is going to improve. The smoke of the burning villages is rising vertically into the sky. I hope this rainy period is over now. Hauptmann Stern was standing next to me just now and told me that, due to the fact that more divisions have been committed, our section of attack has narrowed from 12 to only 4 kilometres. That isn't too bad at all. At 11.30 a Focke-Wulf dropped a message for the division, which we then passed on via the telephone. According to this our tanks were only 100 metres in front of Salesi, the artillery has ceased firing and no traffic could be observed on the road from Krasnogwardiejsk to Salesi and on the other side of Leningrad.

Evening and no news. More aircraft attacked, the artillery is firing; everywhere smoke is rising into the sky. The white signal flares, however, can only be seen in the far distance now. We will have to spend the night here and should be joining the attack tomorrow. The division's task is to advance to the second defensive line around Leningrad and then to break through it – if possible together with the Russian troops that are flooding back from the first line towards the city.

This evening Enz, with the field kitchen, had been ordered to make goulash and noodles, while we, by platoons, were to prepare the potatoes ourselves. And what did we get to eat? A brown glue in which a few overbaked scraps of meat were hidden. None of the Landsers wanted to eat the stuff. We were mutinous, so I went to the boss and gave him a piece of my mind. The boss, in his customary manner, gets a daily special dish prepared for him and, with Hauptmann Fara and selected men of other companies, doesn't ever go hungry. But the vast majority of the men run around with empty stomachs and have to rely on a few sandwiches. The guys serving with the field kitchens are living quite well too. They don't have to cook their potatoes in coffee just to save some fat. The boss was much affected when I talked of chicken murder and extra portions. But even though he didn't accept any personal responsibility, he accepted my demand that Enz needs to be punished. He has been relieved of his duty with immediate effect. And I will get him demoted too; after all, he has only been promoted to Unteroffizier because of his role as First Chef and because he is not good for anything else. At 18.00 there is a platoon leaders' briefing.

Unteroffizier Enz has been punished with three days' detention because he didn't follow the order to cook a second meal and with a further ten days of close arrest for having withheld a 25-litre canister of cooking fat.

Wednesday, 10 September 1941

Prepared to move out at 5.30 a.m. and then marched towards Sabino. We are now in a forest to the north of it. Soon we are supposed to advance on the long defensive line from which we are still being shelled by artillery. We had some bad luck today – Oberstleutnant von Seckendorff wounded and his Adjutant too. The commander of the I. Abteilung of Artillerie-Regiment 76, a Major, has been killed. Oberst Zollenkopf was also wounded, as was the commander of the Kradschützen, Hauptmann Knaust. In addition a large number of the rank and file were lost. We didn't see much of that, however. Even though the Russians were shelling Sabino, our tanks offered us good protection, as did the houses. But a little bit further to the front, where the staff of the Kradschützen and that of 114 is, there is wide open ground in full view of the Russians, and there it was a lot more violent. Even here in the forest there are too many distractions. Just now a whole group of Henschel Stukas attacked the Russian positions. We can only be happy about this operational deployment of our Luftwaffe, as it takes a lot of work off our shoulders. In forest fighting it's often hard to tell who is doing the shooting: are these our shells or theirs? Stukas are howling again now. The Russian isn't giving up easily now that he knows there is not much left to fall back upon, being so close to Leningrad. The positions at Sabino were grimly defended. The whole forefield was covered with mines, and four Panzer IVs and two Panzer IIs are said to have been lost. Two of the heavy tanks of Abteilung 65 I have seen myself. They were standing nearby. Next to them stood an artillery tractor with an anti-tank gun, or better 'lay an artillery tractor', as it had run onto a mine and the detonation had flicked the heavy vehicle onto its back. In the tanks two men had been killed.

Just now a few Ratas were chasing one of our Focke-Wulf recon birds. It came in very low right across the treetops and there, when they were over our lines, the Ratas turned back towards the Russian side. Yesterday I only once saw some Ratas, a group of six of them – other than that not a single Russian aircraft made an appearance. Our good Messerschmitts even flew ground attacks with guns and bombs.

Looking on the map, we have just noticed that our whole flank is still open. Down at Korpikowo the Russians are still clinging stubbornly to their anti-tank defences. That's the objective of the SS-Polizei-Division and from there the enemy has a field of fire towards Salesi. Wilhelm Lope was here to see me. He thinks that we won't capture these tank obstacles. He thinks it's better just to close the shop here and then simply starve Leningrad out. Even though that would take a bit longer, it would cause us far fewer casualties. We have already lost enough men. I don't know what to think, better to attack now, smoke the enemy out and then halt our infantry formations on the line of Krasnoye Selo, until the Russians come over with their hands raised. If only we could look into the future!

Sunday, 28 September 1941, near Demidow

We are still lying in front of the little village in front of Demidow. We spent the night in the Russian cottage again, with the sixteen men and a complete Russian family. Yesterday night I finally received a new pair of trousers. Today I put on fresh underwear while the woman here washed my dirty laundry. Who knows when we'll have time to wash our laundry properly again? The Russians always make big eyes when they see us washing our naked upper bodies in the morning. When they saw me standing there with bare feet today, some of the Russians remarked that I might freeze if I continued doing so. It wasn't even that cold. Not even frosty as in the previous nights. This morning we had potato fritters. It's Tutasz's birthday, so Pause and Oberholz peeled and grated the potatoes and the women prepared the fritters for us, worked the pans, later assisted by Oberholz and Wiegand. Lovely things with lots of fat and bacon. These were then dipped into a bowl full of cream and they tasted heavenly. We save one portion for later, because at the moment our regular supplies do not suffice.

I finished the interrogation report of Unteroffizier Krone and his lot – I just signed it and now it's done. What a spectacular case: a crew which has been 'fighting' at a farmhouse in Latvia for the entire period of the campaign against Leningrad. Certainly, he has informed the repair shop, one has to give him that. But he certainly didn't do his utmost to get away from there.

Oberleutnant Ritgen has become regimental Adjutant. Nothing new.

20.00

Just back from the regiment. Sad news: one of our good officers, Hauptmann Saalbach, is leaving us tomorrow because he has fallen ill. Even though he looks healthy enough, he has severe breathing problems, probably severe asthma. He can't cope with the climate. He is leaving tomorrow morning. Very sad. Very good and very fair superior. I have experienced myself how important that is out here. Koll has taken over the brigade, Ritgen is Adjutant. Theo is taking over the 7th Company. II. Abteilung is being disbanded and one company each is going to Abteilung 65. The heavy platoons are being distributed among the companies.

I am sitting with Goßler, Engelhardt and Albert, who have been sitting here since the morning playing a relentless game of cards. This evening is one of those where the army really pisses me off.

Tuesday, 30 September 1941

We are waiting alongside the road until the company can fall in line behind the staff. 09.30 – today we are driving towards the deployment area for the brigade attack. I have taken my old place in the turret and quickly scribble down a few lines; my hands have turned blue in the cold. We are all wearing our coats. Just now we have said farewell to our Russian hosts. They are looking forward to the day when we will finish the Bolsheviks off. Wherever we have to say goodbye, the farewell is usually quite jovial. Yesterday night the old farmer gave us some schnapps, which we of course shared with him. He solemnly stood up and raised the glass to Hitler and his good soldiers. We were flabbergasted! And when I left this morning and I shook hands with him and his wife, they both wished us a good homecoming and expressed their hopes that we'd end our business in Moscow soon. The old fellow in Hille's quarters conducted himself even more wildly, he tried to hug and kiss the Spiess and his expressions of gratitude and wishes of well-being were never-ending.

We are now standing on the road behind Sporki and wait until it is 17.00. We are not to reach our deployment area before nightfall. On the way here we only saw a few graves and little actual traces of fighting. The fighting here has been as hard as it was closer to Leningrad. In Demidow, about 40 kilometres away, we have seen the last graves. They had been dug right in the middle of the village, near the church, at the foot of a large wooden cross. They looked very nice and dignified.

The path of our division has in recent days been turned into a log-road; otherwise it would have been impassable. All the women from the nearby villages had to help to get that work done. All the men seem to have been drafted. One can see only boys and the ancient Rasputins at work here. The roads are very much the same as in the area of Leningrad. Now then, off we go! Away with the diary, the advance continues further towards the east. Our objective being the positions along the upper reaches of the Dnieper.

Just now the medical squadron rolled past. I hope they won't be as busy as they have been so far.

A few guys from Wuppertal are currently taking the piss out of Feldwebel Müller, the husband, in their native dialect. At least the men of the Organisation Todt are not being entirely weaned off the experiences of married life and have plenty of opportunity to keep in training with the girls during road construction. And the banter continues. Müller states that he has learned patience in that regard too, even though he had once been quite a stud – which had forced him to marry when he was only 20. Now they have wagered a crate of beer on whether the war will be over by 20 October. Maybe we are done with it all in a month or in early November. As long as there is no snow or ice then, there is still a chance.

I now have to think about coming home. The good and healthy return which the Russians have denied me so far. How will it be, back at home in Hamburg? Do I go back to school? To university? Or do I find a job? One is better off not to think about things like that here, there are far too many things to get done first.

Wednesday, 1 October 1941, in the deployment area

The weird coincidences one experiences on campaign. We are in the deployment area, right next to where the II./AR6 from Osnabrück have set up their guns. My old SS-comrade and schoolmate Helmut Boockhoff is serving as a Leutnant in their 9th Battery. A shame that I could not leave my position here, I would have liked to visit that hulk of a man. One can't help but marvel about how busy it is here in the deployment area. Boy, oh boy, what an enormous amount of troops we Germans have drawn together here! I hope it all goes smoothly tomorrow. How long will it take us to reach the Dnieper? Will the Russians face us with tanks? How many days will the whole thing go on for? These are my thoughts today, the day before the attack on Moscow.

On 8 August we launched the breakout from the Luga bridgehead. On 9 September the attack on the line of Krasnogwardiejsk started. And now, on 1 October, we stand in front of Wasma and as such, in front of Moscow. Will that be our last deployment in Russia? Everyone would be delighted if so.

The whole plain is full of tanks, one right next to another, towards the left and towards the right, for as far as the eye can see. The Russians are shelling the area with 15-cm shells and in front the Russians are blasting away with all calibres imaginable. They have clearly got wind of our deployment here.

the following spring. After the stabilisation of the front, Panzer-Regiment 11 was deployed in the Rzhev area and in May 1942 it was transferred to France to be refreshed. In the coming months Sander not only married, but also decided to study economics and applied for leave to commence his studies in Berlin. Leave was granted and was to last from 23 October 1942 to 2 April 1943. It was cut short on 8 November, when he was recalled to his regiment for its upcoming employment on the Eastern Front.

*　*　*

Thursday, 2 October 1941, before the attack

From our deployment area both regiments (11 and 25) first rolled in the wrong direction, which took us too far towards the north. But then the scene that unfolded before our eyes was tremendous. Hundreds of tanks attacked and rolled across the open plain. Shells detonated between us, forcing us to pull our heads in and button up. When we rolled over the first line of enemy positions, which had already been traversed by our infantry, we were eagerly fired upon by wounded and single hiding Russians. The furthermost Russian position consisted of well-constructed trench systems. We then approached a wide open bush terrain, one of the kind so typical for Russia, and then fanned out into a broad wedge formation. After that we stopped and waited to be marshalled in to attack a hill north-east of our position 'marked by two leafless trees and a steep peak on the left side of the hill'. We climb back into our tanks, wait until the order to attack is given and roll forward. I am in the first wave with my platoon, Aures is on the left and Oswald is forming the reserve. I had lost Grawe to a breakdown and he was now slowly catching up from the rear; as a result I had only four tanks. While we are traversing the first dense bushes, going stubbornly forward without being able to observe the enemy, we are called to turn to the right. 'Head towards the sun!' That is always nice, driving into the sun, with squinting eyes and unable to see anything ahead. Not even mentioning that it's impossible to see anything through the Czech optics if there was the need to fire. I stubbornly roll forward through the dense bushes. I don't give a crap, it's pretty clear that someone 'at the top' made a bullshit decision when marshalling us in.

273

Feldwebel Engelhardt is rolling forward on my left, Feldwebel Goßler on the right and Unteroffizier Albert next to him. Suddenly the vehicle is shaken by an enormous bang, so violent that my microphone, headphones and cap are blown off my head. For a moment I can't hear anything and clumps of earth rain down through the open turret hatch. The tank stands still. For a moment I think we have been hit by artillery, but when I lift my head out of the turret to see what has happened, I notice a big hole in the ground under the track. 'Mines!!' I shout to the radio operator, so he can pass it on to the rest of the company before they all snuff it in the minefield. But it's already too late. A bang on our left side and one on the right, followed by another one. The radio operator is shouting back that the apparatus isn't working. The enormous pressure has blown the receiver out of its socket.

Screams and groans on the left and right. It did have a greater effect there than it had on us. I dismount and first run over to the left to Engelhardt. Otto Müller is just being lowered into the grass. Trauthoff is sitting on the ground groaning. Engelhardt himself is bleeding on the forehead. Only Endermann is unscathed. First of all I start uncovering the mine system in the close vicinity around us. We learned how to handle that at Leningrad. One can roughly estimate where the things lie buried. These damned green wooden boxes filled with what looks like small rolls of shaving soap. Suddenly the ground gives way below one of my feet. For a moment I am frozen stiff with shock and my heart skips a beat. Below the thin layer of grass the green wood of a box mine becomes visible. But nothing happens – I haven't broken the thin shear pin of the mine. The shock, however, has shaken me to the bone.

Otto Müller is groaning and groaning. He must be in terrible pain. I start to help the poor boy as well as I can. With my pocket knife I cut the trousers from his body. Engelhardt is helping and carefully pulls one boot off the one foot; the other is totally shredded. The kneecap of one leg is mostly gone and thick blood is oozing from a wound in the thigh of the other. I remove a few scraps of fabric from the wound before we apply a tourniquet. His testicles are all bloody. I ask him if he can feel pain there. He doesn't know. I carefully examine him. He seems to have some major bruising there, but otherwise everything looks intact. Thank God.

Trauthoff's calf is swelling up a lot. It isn't life threatening so we'll have to check him over later. First we have to help Goßler, who is still in the vehicle. While we are heading there, I uncover a few more mines to make sure no one runs into them which could potentially endanger us too. Right beside the right track of my vehicle there is another mine which has already been slightly pushed in. I can feel my heart beating in my throat while I remove its grass cover. It has to be done.

Stabsarzt Möschler is already at work at Goßler's vehicle. On this tank the mine hasn't exerted its force towards the side as it did on ours, where it just blew off a track and a roller. Instead it has smashed in the underside of the hull with the floor hatch and shredded everything inside. They have managed to pull Goßler out alive, but both his legs are badly torn up. The surgeon and I apply tourniquets. Both legs are only attached to the body by thin strips of sinew and flesh. Goßler doesn't want to stay still, he has gone insane. He has started to sing with a slurring voice, so great is his pain. He can't see us any more. His left eye has turned pallid and lost its colour while the nerve of the right one seems to have been damaged by a splinter in his brow. With a knife and a pair of scissors the doctor and I cut away the remains of his trousers so we can apply the rubber tourniquets. The doctor wants to move on and follow the regiment. I am to call for Oberarzt Menke and an armoured personnel carrier over the radio. Krautwig, the orderly officer, pulls up with his vehicle and tries to help as well as he can. All the tanks of Abteilung 65 and I. Abteilung which are rolling past have no connection, or can only reach the company. I send two of my men, Wilhelm Müller and Tutasz, to the advance road to stop and fetch a Sanka. Möschler doesn't even have a stretcher with him. I dress Goßler's head. Korte is also standing with us; he is wounded in the arm. With two wooden poles which I found at the boundary of the minefield and a Russian tent square, I fashioned a crude stretcher for Goßler. We carefully rest him on it and then carry him to a farm track on which our tanks are rolling past. His face is already turning yellow. He probably won't survive.

Next I have to take care of Oberholz. He is still sitting in the driver's seat of his tank and is unable to move. He doesn't want us to touch him and demands to stay in the tank. He doesn't care about anything any more. Two men then carefully lift him out anyway. His spine is broken and he is totally paralysed. He can hardly speak any longer. We place a rolled-up coat under his head. 'Leutnant Sander, I don't lie properly! My head is too low! Leutnant Sander, my head is up too high!' It is just awful! I briefly jump onto the tank to look at Wiegand. I have had enough. I want to scream. I just want to scream it all away. My nerves can't take it any more.

Nearby Unteroffizier Albert uncovers a cartridge box which has been filled with explosives and buried as a mine. It is a cursed, shitty work. Any moment you can step on one. Müller and Tutasz return with stretchers. In the meantime Goßler's suffering has ended. He is dead. We cover his horribly mangled corpse with a Russian tent square and then place Otto Müller on a stretcher. His whole body is shaking and trembling from limb to limb. A symptom of blood loss. While we are dressing his wounds, I place a small piece of wood between his teeth and tell him to bite down hard on it, should the pain get too much to bear. But he is too weak to do even that. Finally we carry Trauthoff to the Sanka on a Russian stretcher. On the way I step on another mine right beside Engelhardt's tank.

When we had carried all the wounded to the Sanka, which couldn't come nearer than 500 metres, we began to remove Wiegand's body from the tank. The boy didn't have to suffer long. Life must have left the totally destroyed body in an instant. Little Zimmerman placed the recovery belt around Wiegand's remains, but we couldn't pull him out as his feet were stuck somewhere. I had to take a pickaxe from the tank and began to free the mangled body. The battery had been pushed into his lower abdomen, a foot lay between the wooden ammunition boxes, his body was torn open and the flesh was hanging down his leg. The stench of the warm blood was mixing with that of the battery acid. Everything I touched was slick with blood. His head has been caved in. Tell me again about dying a hero's death! This war is the most horrible of things! There is nothing beautiful or grand about it, only the hard and cold necessity, the damned duty and obligation and the idea of a greater Reich and the security of our families at home which is standing behind everything. On the desks of the pencil pushers this is of course very different, no whistling bullets and explosions. 'No sweeter death than to die in the face of the enemy.' Is that really true?

All of a sudden Vedder appeared and in the meantime Müller had repaired the radio and established a connection to Hille. I told Hille that I would go back with Vedder's tank, so Paul got out and remained with my crew while I took command of his tank in which, after loading it up with my things and changing the radio over, I followed the regiment. Saying farewell to my men was incredibly hard.

A last salute to the two fallen comrades who lay at the roadside covered with tent squares and then I followed the enemy, humming the first stanza of the 'Panzerlied'.

In the evening we caught up with the rest of the company; most of them had already crossed the Kokosch. I can't help being impressed by the enormous number of troops here. We traversed the Russian artillery positions. Shortly before reaching the Kokosch, Hauptmann Hagemann came towards us. But damn, isn't that Aures's tank? What the hell has happened? 'We have Feldwebel Aures in the tank, he was shot in the head!' Zervas shouted over. I quickly climbed on the other tank to take a quick look at Aures. He knelt inside the fighting compartment, resting his bleeding, bandaged head against a machine-gun ammunition box. One man was holding and supporting him. Aures couldn't speak, his larynx had been hurt as well.

We then rolled through the furthermost lines of the infantry and crossed the Kokosch via a ford. Soon I was back with my lot and took command of 3rd Platoon, which was made up of the crews of Fröhlich, Krone and Hünecker, so there were four tanks in total. Nearby stood a 15-cm gun, its towing tractor had burned out. A few men are fumbling around with the breech and I give them a proper bollocking. I have seen something similar at Tawtusze in Lithuania, where one of those Rushkas was still loaded and suddenly went off. A barrel burst of that calibre has quite an effect!

An advancing group of infantrymen is suddenly taken under fire from some foxholes near the street, not 20 metres away from us. After we have thrown a hand grenade into one of the holes, five stagger out. One has a foot torn off by the grenade. He is shot dead by the infantry. Our Panzer men would have gunned down the other Russians too, but I managed to stop them.

At about the same moment a whole Kette of Stukas flew over and dived downwards just ahead of us. Our guys fired white signal flares and ignited yellow smoke charges, but one of those idiots still dropped his three bombs.

Our infantry – now mistaking them for Russians – opened fire on the Stukas. And just as they had disappeared, some Russian Curtisses appeared. I was sitting in the turret writing my diary when suddenly explosive rounds detonated on and among the vehicles. What a mess.

During the night our advance continued down a wide, new road. At Bykowa we deployed for all-round defence, while ahead the sky was illuminated by the four burning villages which were being pounded by artillery. A bit further away an ammunition dump exploded.

3 October 1941

09.00: The attack is rolling. Should our sister regiment encounter no resistance in the forests here, we will push past Cholm towards the Dnieper. If they do meet resistance, we'll move into the forest on the left. Our Abteilung is rolling forward now. I spent the night sleeping in the tank, and I am quite refreshed. My nerves were completely wrecked. It was incredibly difficult to just change into Vedder's tank and continue rolling forward. Of what use is Hille's praise? Apart from the boss, the only other company officer left is Willem Lope, and he is a Panzer IV. It was my fucking duty and obligation to drive at the front. I have to leave nerve problems to men like Zangenmeister, Neuling, Baum, Dermin and others. The end! I am not thinking about all this any more. Even the staff surgeon with his EK1 turned pale, and, no longer professional, was driven mad when he saw the shredded bodies, and Oberholz couldn't move any more with his broken back. And Otto Müller lying there, moaning, groaning and asking for a Sanka. I hope that Oberholz won't be injured any further on transport. His nerves were wrecked too, and he always asked me to reposition his head. Poor little Wiegand. I am starting to weep again when I think about him. One of those moments when the only thing one can do is to take a deep breath and keep calm. After my experiences, I would now, if I wasn't too old, choose to become a doctor after the war.

While I was treating the wounded yesterday I kept calm. But afterwards, when I saw the sad remains of my platoon and the wounded, I could not help breaking into tears. How terribly hard this war is.

We are rolling. I have just written a few lines to Mother and Father, telling them that I am still well and healthy. Will I cross the Dnieper today?

We drove south and it dawned on us that we were forming the Schwerpunkt of the attack, due to the fact that this time, the light of the burning villages was way behind our leading tanks. The roads were terrible. Röhlen is my driver, Brune is operating the radio, Müller III is my gunner. On the way here we have rolled over a Russian ammunition supply column, now the draught horses are standing grazing at the roadside. A group of Stukas is coming back from a bombing raid, flying low over the treetops. We wave at them and then it goes on, crossing over open terrain past Danilova and other villages on the way to the Dnieper. Behind Pustoshka the Russians had dug an anti-tank trench which ran alongside a stream – similar to the defences they had erected at Cholm. Abteilung 65 crossed that trench near Romaniki and Weselova and soon after ran into enemy tanks which had already been reported by our flyers. Nevertheless the lead element lost four Skodas and a Panzer IV to the Russians and was forced to withdraw as quickly as possible when Russian infantry attempted to cut off their line of retreat towards the bridgehead. My platoon and Lope's Panzer IV were then employed to keep the Russian infantry in the trench in check. Oswald's platoon was covering our flank. We were successful and the rats in the trench withdrew towards their main position at Cholm.

In the evening my platoon was only three tanks strong as Uffz. Kollne's vehicle had broken down again. We spent the night sleeping beneath our tanks to be safe from the ongoing fire of Russian mortars and artillery. At 21.15 we were woken by a false alarm. A nervous Unteroffizier has mistaken a Russian shepherd and his herd for Russian infantry. He had seen movement and when he had called upon the shepherd to identify himself, the man – instead of doing so – had thrown himself to the ground.

Saturday, 4 October 1941

All tanks were ready by 5.30 a.m.; only the rest of the Abteilung wasn't, and a bridge was still under construction. After sunrise we advanced, 7. Abteilung with Feldwebel Ulrich in the lead. The sun had just come up on the horizon and thus we could hardly see anything. From the south we bypassed the village of Romaniki and then squeezed past the village and began to cross the small stream from which yesterday the Russian tanks had attacked. While we were doing so we were taken under a raging defensive fire. I used my machine gun to return fire. A terrible situation, standing on open ground, not being able to see properly against the glow of the rising sun and the two tanks next to one's own have already been destroyed. In addition, the steering of my own Skoda Super Sport wasn't working properly. I was lucky that I got through this. Fröhlich's vehicle suffered engine breakdown somewhere. Hille sat in H31 of Unteroffizier Hagemann. The lead of the 7th Company then clashed with Russian tanks. Feldwebel Ulrich stood only 2 metres away from a Christie, which fired a round directly into the machine gun of the Skoda's loader. The shell went right through his body. Another Christie rolled up from the right, was hit by one of our tanks and erupted into flames. Then Ulrich used his gun to finish off the Russian at this unprecedented firing distance. Three hundred metres away, I spotted another Russian which was firing on us. But how was I to hit it, with my miserable Czech optics and aiming against the sun? We don't even have tracer ammunition in our buckets and, when firing without optics, couldn't even observe the fall of our shot. I gave up firing on this target.

What happened next was utter chaos. No orders from the Abteilung, and only requests from the company. Oswald was issuing orders to his platoon, but then forgot to switch off the transmitter. One after the other, our tanks started going up in flames. In front of me, Feldwebel Ulrich and his crew were running around between the tanks. His wild hair had fallen into his face and his blue neckerchief was hanging down his jacket. Heuck, his driver, was with him. I won't forget the expressions on their faces anytime soon. Oberleutnant Hille and his tank were right behind me. Again and again, tank shells slammed into the dirt around us. As there were no orders coming from the Abteilung, Hille enquired what we were supposed to do. Hauptmann Stern bluntly replied: 'The 5th is to break through!' and Hille passed the order on to the company. Oberfeldwebel Oswald realised the foolishness of the order and just ignored it, while I was still combing the edge of the forest with machine-gun fire. I told Röhlen, the driver, to fire up the engine. The men inside a vehicle often don't realise that they are in a dangerous situation – which is good – but I decided to inform them that this was an 'all or nothing' moment and that we would need a lot of luck to avoid being shot up. The many burning tanks all around me didn't do much to raise my confidence. The engine didn't pull properly and the steering on the left didn't work properly. I drove towards Leonhardt's Panzer IV, which was standing behind a bush, and then straight ahead across the boggy ground. The old bucket churned itself through the mud at a snail's speed.

Five hundred metres away, in the shade of the forest's edge, I identified a Russian tank which fired its gun into the mass of assembled vehicles on our side. I fired one useless shot at it, but with less than 1 per cent chance of a hit, one has to ignore even such a fat target and conserve ammunition. The other vehicles, however, instead of following up as ordered, were now slowly withdrawing! I stood completely alone in front, near a narrow road, while some hidden Russians fired a hail of machine-gun bullets against my turret. Using my own machine gun, I managed to silence them for a moment. They had holed all the full fuel cans, tent squares and rolled-up coats and blankets we carried on the rear, but it seemed that the Russians had withdrawn or at least pulled their heads down into their foxholes. At that moment I watched my surroundings like a hawk as, in my exposed position, I didn't want to make the acquaintance of their hand grenades and Molotov cocktails. Wilhelm Lope had now realised that I was in a tight spot and he and his loader fired their machine guns into the bushes next to me. When I looked to the rear I could see at least three burning tanks. In the bushes next to me another one was burning and the black smoke it emitted drifted across the street. Not a nice feeling one has in such a situation. But then Hille called me and ordered us to withdraw from the unseen enemy!

But how am I to do that, with the shitty bucket in which I and my three men are sitting, when that route is so terrible that the other tanks didn't even manage to cross in forward gear! I was livid. But it's of no use: an order is an order. Now it's up to the driver, and to me in particular, to get the bucket back as well as possible. Between us and the bush where Leonhardt is standing there is a large open plain across which fire from both sides is raging. The 4.7-cm of the Russians perforates our buckets as if they were made of paper. I let Röhlen climb up into the turret so that he can take a look at the route which will lead us over the treacherous terrain. There is a big waterhole there which we must stay away from. If we ended up in it, there is no way anyone could pull us out again. So we started reversing until we reached the bush where Leonhardt had his Panzer IV. We had done it. I can't describe how delighted I was. All the things that came next are hard to describe with words.

As soon as the Panzer IV had given way, we could make another jump towards the rear. While we were doing so, some unseen enemy fired a few shots at us from the left flank. This was getting serious! And the old Skoda can't pull itself through the dirt! It makes one want to cry. Standing on a tray, ready to be hit by the shell which destiny has reserved for us. One tank standing next to us is hit by whatever is firing there. At that moment Briede calls on us to take some of the wounded with us to the rear. The doctor is running around; he has been wounded in the arm. A shell splinter. I climb out of the tank. Unteroffizier Möller is lying on the ground. One of his legs is missing, the other is badly shot up. The doctor has already applied rubber tourniquets. It's a familiar image: Möller's face has already turned yellow. He won't survive the transport. Uffz. Walter Bethke is also lying there. He was more lucky. Only one of his legs is full of splinters – 'only'. Assisted by Zimmermann, Dreyer's driver, I placed Möller on the engine deck of our tank. Bethke can still move and climbs up by himself. The staff surgeon, however, has already jumped back into his Panzer II and is trying to get away. That makes me incredibly angry. 'Where the hell are you going?' – he points hectically towards the rear, and off he goes. He has just disappeared, when Oberfeldwebel Busse, Jupp Wellinghoff – who was a classmate of mine at the Caroli Gymnasium – and a small Gefreiter named Thieshuis jump out of their Panzer IV and into a rainwater ditch on the side of the field. At the same moment I hear how their Panzer IV takes several direct hits before it bursts into flames. The Russians then switch fire on us. Probably a 7.62-cm gun which is now firing shot upon shot into the field. Jupp has two badly burned hands and a scorched face. I can see the raw flesh through the strips of skin hanging off his hands. His left foot has been torn open by a grazing shot, the whole boot is torn to shreds. The little Gefreiter is also wounded. My tank, the last working one, is moving. I order Brune to fetch an armoured half-track to evacuate the wounded. Brune leaves us with his machine pistol and jogs off, following our tank.

I later learned that, after catching up with the tank, my chaps headed back to Bolshansk. On the way they were hit by a Russian anti-tank gun which failed to cause any lasting damage and only holed a few petrol cans on the back of the vehicle. It didn't hurt Bethke any further either. Once he arrived, Brune made sure that Bethke was transported to hospital, and then approached Hauptmann Stern, asking him to send a few tanks back to assist us. This was denied, so Brune decided to turn back to help us himself. As he was doing so, he was spotted by Hauptmann Burgstaller and immediately sent back into the village. Bad luck.

On the field, which is now full of our burning tanks, I give first aid to the little Gefreiter, pulling a few scraps of fabric from the wound in his hip before applying a dressing. Nobody carries any more dressings, so I have to use a piece of string to apply a tourniquet to the wound of Jupp Wellinghoff, who is bleeding heavily. Oberfeldwebel Bunse is also moaning, something wrong with his foot. He is moaning quite loudly and I take a closer look. Nothing is visible other than a small flesh wound. I give him a bollocking for making such a show for crap like that. To distract him, I press the machine pistol into his hand and tell him to make sure that we are not surprised by Russian infantry. At that moment the Panzer IV explodes and we are showered with a rain of metal lumps. And because the 7.62 is still firing, I then decide that we three need to get away on foot. Jupp is pulling himself together and, with his badly mangled foot, is able to walk. I am astounded that little Thieshuis is still so mobile even though the wound in his hip is rather deep. I have forgotten to mention that before that, Obergefreiter Thiemeyer from Herford, also a member of Bunse's Panzer IV crew, and the Obergefreiter Grothuis of 7th Company had come past us and in the wild chaos I sent the two, together with Zimmermann, towards the rear.

I took Jupp Wellinghoff under my arm and together we hobbled towards Bolshansk. We hadn't come very far when suddenly we were taken under machine-gun fire from the left, and from the forest on our right. We threw ourselves onto the ground and continued to crawl forward. I had to marvel at Jupp's conduct and how he managed to do all that with his badly burned hands, which by that time were shedding bloody water. Not even mentioning the bad wound on his foot. Bunse and the little Gefreiter also managed to keep up with us. We continued to crawl forward, further and further, and as soon as anyone raised his head, the bullets whistled across our heads. That way we managed to get to a position about 400 metres in front of Bolshansk, which was still burning and smoking. Then, 300 metres in front of us on the left, I spotted several people. They were wearing steel helmets – but our men didn't wear such big greatcoats! I used Bunse's binoculars and, damn, they are Russians! A terrible tightening feeling in my chest and my lower abdomen, when I suddenly realised that we had been cut off from our regiment! Surrounded! What a mess!

So what shall we do? I think about it; the situation is as bad as it gets. We four decide to stay low where we are. We will wait for a while. I am scanning the surroundings with the binoculars. The Russians are spread out in a line, across the route we have to take, toward the right. The Russian artillery is firing into the area even further to the right. That means that this is still our territory. On the road to the rear, next to where we were recently standing, several columns of Russian infantry are marching now. Russian tanks are rolling towards the forest in front of Cholm. A few others, turrets turned towards the rear, roll towards Romaniki. Now we can also see the Russian tank which had fired on us earlier on. A shitty situation – we are cut off on both sides. The only hope now is that the Russian positions, which we had taken under fire yesterday with my platoon and Lope's Panzer IV, are still unoccupied. But first I crawl back with the intention to reach a burned-out Skoda tank standing on the road on the right. Maybe the wounded can hide below it. Or should we surrender? I am an officer and as such the chances that I would survive a surrender are meagre. The others, though, might get out unhurt. I know Jupp Wellinghoff's wife in Osnabrück. That is what I am thinking about at this moment. No, I won't surrender to the Russians as long as I still have bullets in my pistol. While I am crawling towards the Skoda, I see Groothuis of 7th Company running back. He is standing behind the burned-out tank. And then Zimmermann follows. Both have still got their pistols, so they can still defend themselves. The face of Groothuis is black and scorched. I approach them and then send them back. Jupp is behind me and asks what he is supposed to do now. I tell him to pull himself together once more and to join the others, who are now withdrawing along a row of bushes. On the field ahead, I have spotted a group of Russian infantry who are examining the bodies of some fallen German soldiers. It is time now!

I shout over to Bunse and tell him to give me fire support. Zimmermann, Groothuis, Jupp and Thieshuis have reached a shallow ditch 200 metres behind us and are now preparing to reach the forest in front of Cholm. Are they mad? I told them to head towards the area on the right, which is being shelled by the Russian artillery. And yes, that has drawn the attention of a group of Russians who immediately take us under fire and now the situation is getting hairy for me.

The Russians ahead take cover behind the burned-out tank and open fire on me and Bunse, who is returning fire with his machine pistol. I crawl back towards the bushes and then cover Bunse when he jumps back to join me. Bunse has emptied the first magazine. Someone is firing on us from the left too. We have to get back as quickly as possible. Bunse's machine pistol jams! The magazine is stuck! Russians are only 50 metres away now. The brothers are throwing hand grenades. I can see clearly the green fragmentation rings of their stick grenades as they wheel through the air. Five metres too short – thank God. Bunse has jumped further back, I have to follow. On my stomach I crawl through the shallow ditch. Bushes 50 metres away. That is where I need to go. By now I don't give a shit any more. I have just run 10 metres when the Russians start firing like mad. I am standing on a serving tray. I throw myself into the grass and pull my exhausted body forward. I can't breathe any more. Then suddenly a hard blow to my head. That came from behind. I take off my cap and touch my skull, which is suddenly hurting mightily. No blood! Nothing has happened! But the cap has a hole in it where the bullet has passed through. My eyes start to flicker in a red light. But then I can go on. Once I reach the bushes, I rush as fast as I can to another ditch on the field. The Russians on the right are getting frighteningly close. Closer to the ditch ahead, I see a few men clad in black. Thank God, they are already that far ahead. But I have to think about myself now. I just start running, as fast as I can, across the rye field. The soil is clinging to my boots, weighing my feet down. But that doesn't matter. What follows now is the worst and most terrible 1,000-metre sprint of my life. Behind me the Russians, who are now screaming and shouting. When they shoot at me, they have to stand still for a moment. Something is firing at me from the left, but soon I am putting a distance between me and the Russians. Three hundred metres now. With long strides I race across the field. When I can't breathe any more I throw myself onto the ground for the briefest of moments! Then I continue. The pistol in my right, the binoculars in my left hand. At that moment I am past caring. Around me bullets are smacking into the ground and others whizz and swish past my head. Never mind, never mind – I have to go on. I reach a hollow in which I throw myself down again, just deep enough to get out of my coat. I take the spare magazines out of the pockets. I cram the maps into my trouser pockets and then do the same with my calendar, notebook and diary. In my grey turtleneck pullover I then start running again. I am tempted when I see a few horses running around in the field. But I have no clue how to handle them and it's better to rely on my own legs.

I walk the next 100 to 200 metres, I have to save my stamina. The Russians haven't kept up with me, but when I walk through a sunflower field, the volume of fire from the left is increasing again. Shit on them! They can't hit anything anyway and I have to conserve my strength. In front I see the position which I have taken under fire only a day before. I stare into the trees and cannot see a single Russian. The positions have been abandoned! I jump over a trench and approach a small stream running along the valley floor. A few big steps and I am across the water. Another 100 metres, I climb over a fence and disappear among the trees. The Russians send a few machine-gun volleys in my direction, but now I am safe.

Deeper into the undergrowth, just to avoid the possibility of running into a Russian reconnaissance squad. Once inside the undergrowth I feel safe and protected. Experiences gathered while playing 'Cowboys and Indians' in the forests of my hometown and later, from the time in the boy scouts, now comes in handy. I am quite proud that I am not making a sound while I am sneaking from bush to bush. I have to think about home and whether my father ever experienced shit like this. After the war I will marry! If I had at least had a boy at home, even if only a toddler, I would be a lot calmer. I also have to think about sports during my army time in Freystadt. As a young Leutnant I always wondered about the complete lack of sporting exercise among the officers. Not a single one of the officers in the Abteilung would have been able to match my pace today.

Soon I reach a small valley. A small stream runs through it and nearby there is a pasture. How peaceful it is. On the other side the colourful leaves of birch and nut trees and the occasional pine. It's like a nice autumn stroll and suddenly my eyes fill with tears, I don't know why. I think about the huge amount of luck I have enjoyed in the previous days and I can't help putting my hands together and take a grateful look above the treetops into the bright blue sky. I am praying! Not like Christian would; I am not thinking about Christ for having saved my life. I think Wilhelm Lope once said to me that everyone who is standing on our side out here has to be at peace with himself, must consider his life finished and must never rely on help from any side. Man is not big enough to hope for the assistance and help of a higher being. The experiences here show us daily how small and meaningless our lives are and how grateful we have to be that we exist at all. This knowledge must drive us to great accomplishment, as only that way can we make ourselves worthy of that existence. I have now learned of how little importance the threat of death is in serious moments like this. How little I cared about death. I didn't care any more.

I took off my cap and looked at the long tear the bullet had left in it. A few millimetres further down and my name would have been added to those of the other seventeen officers killed during the campaign in Russia, to that of the Prinz of Ratibor in the campaign in Poland, and to that of Schlegell in France. How small we humans are and how little is lost when we die! At that moment I touch my lucky charm medallion, my talisman.

When I look at it now, it gives me a feeling of strength and warmth. Everything around and inside me has been shaken up. I can't wait to get back home.

When I step out of the forest I check whether I can spot any tanks in the village of Pastoschka. If they have gone, then I have to find Kampfgruppe Raus behind the forest. From the forest edge I can see the rooftops of Pastoschka and also the Russians at Bolshansk. I have to move on. I withdraw into the undergrowth. It is too dangerous alongside the forest edge. Then suddenly there is a lorry, a licence-built Ford, standing in front of me. It's right inside the forest, the engine is running. I approach it cautiously; the crew must be around somewhere. But there is not a single soul to be seen. Maybe there are weapons inside it? There is a parachute and a leather flying cap on the load bed. They are German! No chance for the pilot if he has fallen into the hands of the Reds! There is a box with sausages too and another with cutlery. I take five small sausages in case I require rations for a longer walk. I also take the flying cap as a souvenir. The white silk of the parachute is tempting me too – would make a nice wedding dress and would give me something to wave about when I run into German troops. Our riflemen shoot on anything that moves. Rubbish! I leave the silk and climb up a tree to have a look at the surroundings. Tanks roll up the road towards Cholm and Russian infantry is there too. I walk for another thirty minutes and step out of the forest again. Now I have a view on Pastoschka and, yes indeed – there are tanks there and men are walking and standing between the trees. They are ours! Hurrah! I have made it! I run into the field, waving like mad to avoid being shot down by some idiot. But damn, what is that? There is a Russian lying in the field. Have they surrounded the village? But then I see tank tracks and realise that these are the corpses of the Russians who were mown down by Wassmuth yesterday evening.

Now our men are approaching me. No one can believe it. Everyone is patting my back and congratulating me. So many hands to shake. All the officers come to see me, Lope and Theo Langenbruch among them. They had already given me up! Willem Lope's nerves are clearly wrecked. He is close to tears. I try to make a joke to cheer him up and make him laugh. In the end I fail to hide the bitter seriousness in my voice when I ask him if he really believed that I would leave him alone among this assembly of cyclists and no-hopers. Anyway, all has turned out well. Röhlen and Brune, the loyal souls, and Müller with the old comrades of the signals platoon. They all come to say some kind words. Feldwebel Ulrich is there with his driver. I have to tell the whole story to Major Löwe and I don't spare him the accusation that no tanks had been sent back to us. I can't hide my feeling about this whole fuck-up of an attack. He can read all that in my face. He is trying to make sense of it all by telling the little Leutnant, and all his other subordinates who are now his judges, that we have tied down the 101st Red Armoured Division here at Bolshansk and thus kept the path towards the Dnieper bridgeheads open for our troops. In the end, a little man like me can't give a Knight's Cross holder like him a fitting reply other than to congratulate him on his 'prestigious success'.

As such Willem Lope and I headed to a well and washed ourselves. Then a bit of food. And after we had watched how the Russians used their

Christie tanks to pull their broken tanks and our wrecked Skodas from the field, including the command tanks of 5th and 7th Company with their valuable radio documents, I went to visit the wounded.

Sunday, 12 October 1941, in front of Cholm, Alferkovo

A brief comment: by now Oberst Siebert has returned from Semmering and, during the cosy and comfortable evening that followed, has showered Hille with praise and kind words. We always used to say that only 1 kilometre behind the furthermost tanks true comradeship makes way for chicken roasting and arse kissing. Now we are even further at the rear, behind the field postal service and the supply train. But this foul spirit doesn't bother us. Theo, Willem and I are sticking together.

On Sunday morning, a week ago, Zimmermann returned from the forest in one piece! Thieshuis and Groothuis as well! Jupp Wellinghoff, however, was found shot dead in the Red positions and there was no sign of Bunse. He was probably taken prisoner. They told us that he didn't want to follow the others; he had been afraid and wanted to stay where he was. We have buried Jupp Wellinghoff, Tiemeyer, Snake-Otto, Feldwebel Zieschang, Unteroffizier Müller and several other men whom I didn't know alongside the road to Cholm. Lots of dead Russians are still lying up there on the hill.

Our division didn't stop at the Dnieper, but pushed further towards the south behind Wjasma and from there to Gshatsk. A vanguard is now advancing on Kalinin. How long will the struggle for Moscow last? The supply of fuel and ammunition is now conducted by the Luftwaffe with Junkers 52 and large gliders. The ammunition for a 21-cm mortar battery was dropped by parachute. Our II. Abteilung is now fully unemployed, as we had to give our last working tanks to Abteilung 65. On 9 October, after my commendation on 10 July, I was decorated with the Iron Cross, 1st Class. But until Willem Lope has received his, I will not wear mine. And even then it is doubtful if I am going to wear this thing, which has turned into some kind of a membership badge for professional officers. Not in this regiment. I already got a bollocking from Siebert because of this. I am pig-headed, he says.

Monday, 13 October 1941

Yesterday I was told that I will take command of the divisional security platoon. A nice job!

The tanks which are now coming out of the repair shop will not be deployed at the front any more. At the moment at least. That also means that the Führer's 'Secret Weapon' isn't going to be deployed either! That is our name for Leutnant Walzer – he is known as this because you can't see him at the front. I wonder where I will meet the Ib of the division. That is where the security platoon will be.

20.00

I am on my way to the division. We are sitting in a Russian cottage in some dump alongside the divisional route of advance. We have become quite modest and call it 'route', not 'road', as it leads across fields, straight on over hills, through meadows and shrubs – yes, that is the route of advance. There were still plenty of Russians lying there in the Dnieper region, many of them unburied. And who of us would have time to do so, when we are busy burying our own comrades, who lie under the turf kilometre after kilometre under their birchwood crosses. The many Russian prisoners which are marching along the roads, don't care about their fallen either. White Russians and Ukrainians have become just as apathetic as the national Russians. Finns don't serve among them, at least one never finds any. Estonians, Latvians, Lithuanians have long since defected and have returned home. And the Armenians and Caucasians, the ones who form the intelligentsia here in Russia, care only for their own wounded comrades. I don't understand these people; here in front of Moscow a large number of Mongolians are fighting. Behind us at the Dnieper the Russians had a large concentration of armour. And what kind of armour that was! We looked at a 7.62-armed tank of the most modern design of a kind which could well be fielded by us too! But still our Landsers shot it to pieces, even though it was heavily armoured, even though it was of the most modern design and even though it was carrying a gun twice as long as that in our Panzer IVs.

The daughter of our host, Katya Stepanova, said to me that with Russian soldiers and German technology one could dominate Europe. Little does she know! I have chatted a lot with the girl. Tomorrow they have a bank holiday here. Just a day in the week where no one does any work.

Tuesday, 14 October 1941, Prjetschisloje

Yesterday Voss and I drove until it was dark. And today, at about noon, we reached the division. Always the same old tune when one reaches the staff. It is easier to find a place to sleep with the rank and file. Today there was still fighting at Kalinin. In the village of Prjetschisloje there are the graves of twenty-one soldiers of the 14.ID who were killed in the fighting at the anti-tank trench. I am feeling quite well. The swaying in a driving car is much better to bear than that in a rolling tank.

The division has run out of fuel! The roads on the way are lined with vehicles which can't go on because they have run out of fuel. Zurhausen, who has got our rifles on his lorry, has run out as well and in addition one of its wheel hubs has broken in two. It is now 17.00 and it is already dark.

Just then a few girls have been visiting – relatives of the 100-year-old woman. They have immediately been drafted for potato-peeling duties. One of them looked like the movie actress Christina Söderbaum. They are quite naughty, these girls. They pretend not to understand what we are saying and then they continually talk about us. I have been invited to dinner with the Ib, Hauptmann Holzmann.

Wednesday, 15 October – Wjasma

I was out all day today. At 09.00 I went to see Hauptmann Holzmann and at 10.00 I drove off. Through the snowstorm I managed to get here, until Voss, the old slob, somehow managed to break the windscreen on the driver's side, and the gust of snow and wind hitting his face ended any chance of getting any further. The snow crystals have cut our eyes quite badly and now I can hardly write because of the pain. Here in Wjasma, I first visited the 78.ID to enquire about the local road conditions, and when it got dark there was no use continuing our journey. That means that, due to an incompetent orderly driver, I am now losing up to two days before I can fulfil my task to bring a big bag full of orders from the Ib to Siebert. Instead I am sitting here.

Saturday, 18 October 1941

With my Kübelwagen I am standing in front of the Dnieper bridge on the road to Moscow. The big concrete Russian bridge has been blown up and there are masses of traffic queuing in front of the new crossing. Supplies for the front have priority while I, a little sausage of a liaison officer, am forced to wait for hours before I can resume my journey. I am in the middle of three rows of queuing vehicles. Three days ago I came from the other direction and since then I have hardly slept or eaten and I am dog-tired. And I had taken my task so seriously. When I reached Werkstatt 1 of the division, Hauptmann Schreiber had already arrived before me and done most of the jobs. Hauptmann Schlothmann does a lot of work in that workshop for the Ib; he knows of his concerns and understands them well. I'd better not tell him what Siebert said, or he might commit suicide out of despair for the 'desolate' fuel supply situation. 'Desolate' is a new favourite word of Hauptmann Schmöle, whom I met on the way. God, the man has some problems! And he doesn't even realise when one is taking the piss out of him.

With all the jobs the Ib gave me I returned to Siebert, after I had visited W1. Guckel, the Adjutant, informed me that Oberstleutnant Siebert has been transferred to take command of Regiment 33. The regiment was based in the Ostmark, in Vienna-Mödling and was equipped with Panzer IIIs and IVs. The young crew are also mainly Austrians and I am sure that our old 'Papa Siebert' knows who to cope with them. He surely had to be more stern with us Prussians. We are now getting Hauptmann Stern and I am sure I will feel the 'new wind from above' once I return to the old company. Many of our officers don't realise how good our old commanders have been. Siebert is leaving. Yesterday night he invited us, the old men of the Abteilung, to have dinner with him. It was quite nice and comfy there – the usual experience when one sits down with Siebert. He even had some absinth for us, and later some proper burping-water: Russian champagne.

Siebert will marry after the war. Krautwig and I, Hille, the pastor's son, are the only ones who still have to do so. Before the war we laughed about Wilts, Leonhardt, Glässgen and all the others, and today we are all very serious about it. The war surely does change people. I wonder who will be the first of us three to marry. When they asked me about it, I joked and replied that I would run a contact ad in a newspaper 'adventurous young man is seeking …' Hille seems to have cheated on his sixth-form girl. Anyway – enough of this. Time will tell and I can't look into the future.

It has taken me the whole day to travel 56 kilometres and I have to find accommodation before I reach Wjasma, which is another 60 kilometres away. These roads are just terrible. It's now pitch dark, I have to come to an end.

Sunday, 19 October 1941

Yesterday we nearly reached the area of Wjasma. At about midday, Voss slid the car sideways down a slope where it collided with an oncoming car. The blacked-out headlamp on the front bumper was torn off. Thus we could see little in the dark and didn't really make any progress.

Now I'm sitting in the parlour with the divisional clerks. I stayed here previously. There are two little girls here. One of the little lasses is called Njura, a deviation of Anna, and the other is called Katya. I have just asked about their names, so I don't have to call them *panienka* all the time.

I have also been in the postal office to sort out the mail for the company. It is based a couple of villages away in an old church, inside which they are currently sorting 300 sacks of mail. One of Hauptmann Baum's lorries had brought another 150 sacks. If there is nothing for me in there, it must be the devil's work or I have been forgotten. I am really excited about it. The divisional staff has twice received mail today! Well, they are sitting at the source. Mail! That is a subject of the greatest importance, especially when there was none for several weeks. I really hope that there will be a few nice letters for me tomorrow.

While I am writing here, the Unteroffiziere of the divisional staff are starting to make some music. One, a very sympathetic-looking guy, who would have made a good frontline soldier, plays the violin. Another, with a strong chin and cheekbones, who doesn't look stupid either, is accompanying him on the accordion. I can't wait to go to a concert in Hamburg again. Music! – How long has it been since I heard good music, even via the radio? They often play the song of the sentry under the lantern at the barrack gate and every Landser will sing along when it's blaring out of the wireless – but long term, that is nothing for me. No one can eat pastries and sweet dishes all the time; it makes one feel sick.

I had a chat with the medical orderly here and I found out that in his civilian life he had been a clerk in the Melitta company. I like to talk to people to find out more about them and what they do. It helps me to judge them and that is quite important out here. Voss, for example, who is sitting next to me at the moment, would also make a good combat soldier – even though he is not very bright. But he has a certain kind of character that would work well alongside Oswald, Engelhardt and Albert.

Lots of changes in the company. Steinbusch and Zimmermann, who was with me when the drama behind the Russian lines unfolded, were decorated with the EK2. Unteroffizier Albert, who was in my platoon, and Unteroffizier Wilhelm, the old companion of the boss, are to be promoted to Feldwebel for cowardice in the face of the enemy. Franz and Krautwurst are getting the same promotion according to schedule. Several new officers have arrived. Siegel is among them. He was with us in Wünsdorf and there he told the other Unteroffiziere not to address him in the informal manner, as he had already conducted officer's training in Putlos. He also played up when he was shown the graves of Jupp and the other comrades – he is, simply said, still an idiot. He ended up in 7th Company with Theo Langenbruch.

Hillenkamp, a very calm and quiet man, a lawyer, has joined 5th Company. Soon, however, they will either be transferred to the Panje column or to the workshops of the division. The latter will surely be the solution preferred by the Ib. There are over a hundred vehicles waiting for repair there and they need someone to hold all the crews at bay.

Next to the W1 workshop in Cholm there is a prisoner-of-war camp, or a collection point of some kind. The Russians there have to camp in the open and in the previous days many of them didn't wake up when the morning came. These were then fully undressed by their comrades, who then distributed the clothing among them. They are being fed with the meat of slaughtered Panje horses. I have seen how the ravenous Russians swarmed, like a pack of starving wolves, over the carcass of a dead and half-decayed cow. The sentries are armed with long sticks which they use to batter the prisoners, to stop them catching diseases from eating the rotten stuff. I feel sorry for the prisoners – but on the other side the Russians show such a laziness and lack of organisational talent that it does make me angry too. In Alferkovo, for example, they let the potatoes rot in the field and they didn't go to cut firewood, but broke down the village fences and barns instead. The men, mostly old Rasputins, don't work at all. They just sit there and look at us. In the best case they find the energy to complain that they have nothing to eat, no firewood, that they are cold, hungry and lacking everything. What a tragedy, but if the lazy pigs were working instead of complaining they would be in a better situation. They cross themselves ten times and then start blathering in such a manner that we can only understand half of what they are saying, and when we tell them to sweep the houses and wash the muddy floors – nooo! That would be work and work that means 'rabota' and that comes from the word 'rab' and that means 'slave'! That is what the Russians think about working. How different the German thinks about working, earning and spending.

Monday, 20 October 1941

I have had employment as an animal catcher! Last night I caught nineteen bugs! It was really exciting for me, as I was lying right next to the wall and suddenly noticed that my entire coat and the blanket were covered with the little beasts. Well anyway, due to last night's bug-hunt I have become more careful and will make sure to make more use of my field bed. I am not interested in either of the diseases spread by the little buggers.

Soon Voss and I will collect our mail. I am looking forward to seeing the faces of the clerks here when they see me with my pile of letters. There will be a lot after four weeks! At 09.00 I saw Hauptmann Holzmann, but there was nothing new for me. Within the next few days, our Abteilung will move to Wjasma and I am not giving up my duties as orderly any time soon, because otherwise I might also end up in the workshop company as a crew overseer. I dread to think about the enormous vehicle columns on the Rollbahn. I, the little worm, will have to spend many hours queuing again. There is still no better place than with the furthermost tanks at the front. When one catches a chicken in an abandoned village and chucks it into the pan, or when one catches a cow for the field kitchens, that isn't a problem there. It only gets complicated once they clock that I speak and understand a bit of Russian. Then the wailing women gather in a crowd, counting with their fingers the number of their many children who used to be fed with that cow's milk – and who will now starve to death. The Russian women here look more like Eskimos than Europeans. With their felt boots, sheepskin skirts and thick headscarves, they make a totally uncivilised impression. And their main job during winter time seems to be the creation of more and more babies.

Wednesday, 22 October 1941, alongside the Rollbahn

Nothing new under the sun. As in the days of the stagecoach we stand here with a broken wheel and all the mail and the orders for the workshops have to wait with us, until the damage has been fixed. Voss, my driver, has been right after all when he always drove so slowly. The suspension would probably have broken a long time ago otherwise. We felt really struck down by our bad luck. With the broken wheel, we managed to roll into a nearby village, where we found cover from the infernal rain inside a small cottage and where we attempted to fix the damage ourselves. But there wasn't much we could do, but when I talked to a Hauptmann from the vehicle park he pointed me towards a vehicle repair shop. 'Repair shop? What kind of repair shop?' – 'Well, one where they repair cars!' That reply took a load off my mind. There is a car repair shop of the 35.ID in the village! I quickly seek out the artificer and, if our cart is able to roll into the village, it can surely make its way to the workshop too. And Voss does indeed manage to move the car to the workshop, where it is now standing under a tent square to be repaired tomorrow.

Now I sit here in a cottage where an old woman is lying on her deathbed. She is suffering from consumption and is coughing all the time.

We soldiers are not bothered by that; just one of many ways to die. We have seen a lot worse.

Yesterday night there were still a lot of Landsers of 35.ID in the village. All troops from the supply services. That was crystal clear. Only the Feldwebel there had only just been transferred there. He was 36 years old and had once been a member of a student association. Not stupid at all. I learned that he was a cultural historian, born in Leipzig in Saxony and now, in his civilian life, the director of the town archive in Stuttgart. I enjoyed our chat and learned a lot from him. Today these men are gone and I doubt that we can continue our drive to Wjasma today. A shame, as we can't get out of here quick enough. The roads are completely driven to ruin. It is hard even to recognise the Rollbahn. Bumps and deep furrows, but certainly no 'run'-way there any more. The infantry supply columns on the big runway are incredibly long. Horse-drawn vehicles travel on both sides of it. If one tries to avoid running over the horses, it is virtually impossible to move forward in a motor vehicle. There is not much I can do to assist in the repair of my car, which means that I have more time to write. Yesterday a piece of loose metal from the chassis had ripped apart the oil supply hose for the foot brake. We just ignored that and drove on without brakes. Whenever we needed to stop, Voss just pulled out the ignition key and the car immediately became stuck in the muddy road.

Outside a bit of autumn sun is shining through the clouds. If there was peace, one could take a lovely walk through the leafless forest. I can't help wondering if in the future, Theo Langenbruch or Willem Lope are taking a weekend stroll with their wife and children, will they ask 'Is that forest clear of the enemy?' or 'Are you sure there is no anti-tank gun in there?' That makes me laugh. I am sure that Willem will teach his son how to deploy his troops properly, what is the right way to approach a forest, how to make use of the terrain and what a good defensive position looks like.

But when will that be? When will we drive on German ground again and when will I get my next period of leave? If it continues like this, we will have to celebrate Christmas with the Russian families. Or will our division be spent enough to be pulled out of the line? The artillery has already been fused together. S4 has been combined with 114 and K6 with AA57. And our regiment has been turned into 'Kampfgruppe Löwe'. The

28. Infanterie-Division has only recently withdrawn over the Rollbahn and is now to be transported to Smolensk. And when will our turn come? Hauptmann Anhalt is on the way to Gzhatsk to find quarters there. Our Oberst with his now unemployed staff has been made town commander of Kalinin and our division is securing the area there. The left wing cannot advance any further because there is no fuel. There we were with Reinhardt, while Guderian – also without fuel – was forced to watch the Russians pack up their stuff and evacuate Moscow. The infantry is putting its trust on the motorised troops, while the motorised troops trust that the infantry will sort it all out. The infantry, however, with its horse-drawn units, is not making much progress either. When will the ring about Moscow be closed and who is going to close it? Now then, little man with great concerns, it will all work out and it is going to happen soon. When will the real winter come and when will I be returning home?

Thursday, 23 October 1941, runway

Just now there are four girls sitting in the farmer's wife's parlour. They have kept me from writing. One of them had been a Young Communist. A typical Slav, but the sprightliest of them all and she even knows a few words of German. Damn, now I can't really write any more. One of them is Ukrainian from the Kharkov district. What a beauty she is, one can't deny that. A face from which Bolshevism hasn't yet taken the noble features. Her build, slim and tall. Ah well, how shall I fall in love with such a dream. She is a Russian. I am German – the end.

Saturday, 25 October 1941 W1, Cholm

Today I am sitting in the divisional workshop 1/57 and had my car repaired. It needed a new brake cable and the forward tie bar had to be bent down. The things one gets as mail and divisional courier. Neither are we losing any sleep over our provisions. There is enough for us everywhere. Well – what else shall I write in my book now? That I am sharing a table with some mechanics who are playing Russian Bank. That is not exactly setting the world on fire. These war mechanics have had enough of the business here. Day after day they have to run up and down through the mud outside between the vehicles, which they have to watch like hawks to protect them from having parts salvaged from them by members of the plethora of units which descend on the workshop. Everyone has his own sorrows. Hauptmann Nowag, who runs the assembly here, is looking for an officer to supervise the 'guests' of the workshop, i.e. the drivers and crews of the vehicles which arrive here.

Hauptman Schomburgk didn't get enough fuel to continue his journey and as his vehicle was damaged too, he resumed his journey with Oberleutnant Marx. Yes, Marx, this crablouse, is now an Oberleutnant. Marx is the swine who has spoiled the career path of my good fellow combatant in Bad Lippspringe days, SS-Lt. Werner of the Sicherheitsdienst, here in the Panzer-Regiment. The beggar still has eggshells sticking to his bum, but wants to write assessments of old men!

I went on a short stroll with Theo and we had a bit of a chat. We talked about his marriage and what he'll do for a living after the war – after all, he is probably Germany's best stenographer. Wilhelm Lose is out and about with Hauptmann Anhalt and both are staying over. Leutnant Hillenkamp, Doctor of Law and a little bit cumbersome, is off to Smolensk to collect some fuel. In Kotelki I ran into Leutnant Siegel, who was on the way to Rogetschinskaya to find some oil and had become stuck with his vehicle. He had to be towed out by a tank. While that was ongoing, he looked at the tank of Uffz. Möller, which still held the charred remains of three Panzer men whom Hille, the pastor's son, didn't want to recover. I will probably have to do that job myself. When it is about the recovery of a comrade's body, I don't want to hear excuses about ptomaine and other things. The only thing we can do is to create a proper grave for their mortal remains … if only we could do more.

Now I am sitting here watching the mechanics. Voss has fixed the car and one can hope that the foot brake is now actually working. Slowly but steadily we are fixing the old sled. In the workshop of the Fish-Division,*

---

* 35. Infantry-Division.

where I was made very welcome, they didn't have the plethora of different vehicle types that we have, but then they are a new formation. Here in the W1 there is much more to do than over in their place. I am just thinking about the types of people one runs into out here. In Lagotschi I stayed in a house together with a 103-year-old woman. Down at the workshop I stayed with a lunger who was on her deathbed while just behind the Dnieper Voss and I shared a house with a bunch of released convicts. Near workshop 65 I was staying in the bug-ridden hovel of a Cossack when a woman rushed in and asked who of us could speak Russian. And then she shared her troubles with me: her husband had been imprisoned for six years. Her father had been in prison for over ten years and now, aged 79 and broken in body and spirit, he could not work any more. She didn't look bad and her four children weren't exactly starving either.

I have to think about yesterday night, when we stood at the Dnieper and how we cheated our way past the 12-kilometre-long column of vehicles queuing up on the bridge. I had taken off my coat and stood on the footboard in my black uniform and with all gongs well visible. I had the pistol in my trouser pocket and the handle of the 08 was sticking out. And thus all the pursers and NCOs must have thought: 'Oh, this guy comes from the front and might just be rough mannered enough to shoot me down when he feels angered.' Whatever the case, no one dared to stop me and let me pass, even if it took a lot of shouting and cursing. That way I even managed to get to the front without asking the bridge commander, a Hauptmann of the infantry. I just crossed by joining Nebel-Regiment 52 which was just going over at the same time. In the darkness I then drove towards the north, continued for about 5 kilometres and found myself a place to stay. Anyway, enough for now, the electric light will be switched off soon, the generator is needed for charging.

Sunday, 26 October 1941, near Cholm

Last night it started to rain and since then the pitter-patter has not stopped. Dear me! I am stuck here and can't go any further! Just like that, the roads have become unusable. There I was yesterday, claiming that one slowly gets used to the conditions in Russia and now, all of a sudden, a new chapter for new experiences has opened. And I am in luck, however, as there is fuel to be had here at the airfield at Cholm, where I have driven on the advice of Hauptmann Nowag. I have now taken quarters with a very clean Russian family and I intend to stay here for as long as my supplies last, the roads have dried up or frost is setting in again. That might take until the end of the week. At the moment there is a waxing moon which is visible during the day. That will change in about seven days.

Voss tried to park the vehicle near a house and while doing so ended up in a foxhole. While he was trying to sort this out, I left him alone, angry because he had decided to ignore my advice and drove as he liked. I went inside, sat down at a table and began reading the *Das Reich* newspaper. Cultural news, theatre play reviews and so on. There is a photo of a play in the Deutsches Theater in Berlin, Schiller's *Die Räuber*. The actress in the role of Amalia is Ursula Burg! Uschi-Kampe Burg from Osnabrück, whose mother was at our national theatre in around 1934. Damn, I had to think about those days, when I was friends with Peter Burg and when Friedel Marschall and Otto Soestmayer had fallen in love with Uschi Burg. She was one year younger than I, and went to the Lyceum. Friedel and Otto failed to connect with her. From the beginning Uschi had been a member of the Nationalsozialistischer Schülerbund and in the BDM.* When you come to Osnabrück today, all the girls in our age are either married or already widowed. Like the wife of Klaus Hilmer. Waldemar Heckmann has been killed too and who knows who else of our age group. Yes, and Uschi Burg is in Berlin and is getting famous. She surely will; after all, her old lady wasn't bad either. I have to tell that to Marschall when the war is over. I am already looking forward to seeing his face when I tell him that. I also have to think about old Himmelmann, the pacifist: I wonder what he is up to nowadays. I have to think about Remarque and his sister. Will I not be returning with the same feelings which he held after the World War? Only for me there will be no Ilse and no war profiteer like Bartscher.† When I

---

* Bund Deutscher Mädel – League of German Girls.

† Ilse is a reference to Erich Maria Remarque's wife Ilse Jutta Zambona. Bartscher is a reference to a character in Remarque's novel *Der Weg zurück* (*The Road Back*), published in 1930.

go home, the gymnasium will still be 'in der Wueste'* and the gas lanterns will still be burning.† Ah well, I don't want to think about all this any more; for me there will only be work after the war, work and then some more work. Think about Jupp Wellinghoff, who also won't be with us any more. I wonder if 'Rabbit' Kommerich is still alive? And Otto Soestmeyer? And all the other class mates?

Now then, an end to thoughts like this! We are still in Russia and there is still a lot to do here. The road to the Volga at Yaroslavl is long and there is no way we can get there without fuel, oil and bread. I wonder how we are going to sort out the supply problem. Surely not before frost sets in.

Tuesday, 28 October 1941, airfield at Cholm

Now we are in the nineteenth week out here. In fourteen days it will be 9 November! And our division is still at Kalinin and not at the Volga at Yaroslavl where it is supposed to be by now!

When will all this come to an end? Outside there is still mud and dirt which is impossible to get through. How long is this going to continue? How long? But then, what about the soldiers down in Norway or other remote places cut off from the world, places dark as night and covered by snow. Compared to what they are facing, it is better for us here, so I will stop moaning. There is still the chance that we might get back to Germany in the foreseeable future. How will the infantry feel when they arrive here to relieve us?! How will those boys feel?

Voss has buggered off to deliver mail to the aircraft which is currently standing on the airfield to take the wounded on board. He also wants to refuel while he is there – C3 with engine oil supplement. That way we might have a chance of getting out of this area where everyone is craving fuel. I can't really write at the moment. I am obviously homesick. In summer the mosquitoes were dancing outside and now, when I am looking out of the window it is the snowflakes doing the same. I have to think about Hamburg

---

* The grammar school in Osnabrück.
† A veiled reference to Erich Mühsam's satirical song 'Der Revoluzzer'.

and the bachelor's den I plan to set up there. When I have my own den one day it has to have an open fireplace next to which one can sit in the evenings. The house would have to have a thatched roof – a low building with only one floor like those behind the dykes and on the heath at home. One like the cottage of the 'Communist' Lücke. One like this, or a similar one, I want to own later. But it has to be far away from the city, far out where nobody can disturb me and where only my best friends can find me.

Yes – friends! I can't imagine a life without comrades any more. Outside there is a blue sky now and the sun is shining through the clouds. Will it continue to smile for me? Me the daydreamer and Spökenkieker.* A motor tractor of the 7. Panzer-Division is rolling past. The sound calls me back to reality and is reminding me that today we'll launch another attempt to get through. I wonder if Stern is still there and if there will be mail waiting for me. As soon as the laundry has dried I am out of here. I would really like to receive some mail – maybe something has arrived.

I have now sat here at the table throughout the whole morning and looked outside where at one moment the sun is shining and in the next moment the snowflakes are drifting. Very slowly I put one piece of chocolate after the other into my mouth and let it melt slowly on my tongue while relishing in doing absolutely nothing, except to again think about home. Oh, the things I will do on my next period of leave! I will definitely go skiing. I wonder if Frau Goldmann will be at the 'Frohe Heimat'† again. I really need to write to the vigorous little woman and her husband again. I am thinking about Martin Loock and his silly, pointed red silk hat, and how he tried to pair me off with the Dutch girl. Such a clever dick; good that I have never danced! I am thinking about our tour to the Alps in Kitzbuhel and the grandiose mountain scenery there. By God, how beautiful that was. And now I am here in Russia in all the mud and dirt!

Now there are some infantrymen in the other room who are warming themselves up. What a bunch of pigs these brothers are! One of them has blown up a rubber condom and knotted it up with a piece of string so that the air can't escape. And then they have given that thing to the Russian

---

* A Low German term for someone who has the power of clairvoyance, or extrasensory perception.
† A ski hotel in Hinterglemm in Austria.

children to play with! I am sure that the mastermind behind this operation is a Catholic! The typical piggishness as I have already experienced it in Westerode. I really had to laugh when Major Dr Topf pulled several products of the most recent 'erotic handicraft hour' out of the reporting pouch of Müller of the recon platoon.

Incidentally the farmer here in the house has taken part in the campaign in Poland, where he was wounded in the leg by shrapnel. As such, he doesn't have to serve any more and has been spared the grief and concern about his family. His neighbour is my age. During the Winter War with Finland he was badly wounded by a shot to the stomach. Those two veterans are now sitting here and want to know when the war will be over. They were surprised to learn that Timoschenko isn't in charge of the central sector any more and has been cashiered by Stalin. That was news for them. They are both wearing quilted jackets and thick fur caps. I showed them our ear-muffs, which were unknown to them. The Russians here also photograph and pin the photos to their walls. Now they have started heating the room up to speed up the drying of our laundry. It is nice and white. The woman has washed it well.

It's now dark outside. I have finished a long letter to Karl Bongardt and I am sharing the table with the Russian family. They are currently eating. I have accustomed myself to the champing and slurping. That is the custom in all Russian families. First a big bowl filled with some kind of meat and potato stew and bread is put on the table. The father then cuts the bread and distributes it among his children who are sitting on the bench in order of age. Katja first, then the boys Widja and Wasja. All of them have big wooden spoons of the kind which is popular all over Russia. I have also found these spoons on most Russian soldiers, often shoved into their boot shafts or into their puttees. I noticed that the breads are decorated with a cross, the same one can be found on the breads of our farmers' families in Westphalia and surroundings. I asked one of the boys about the meaning of it and he replied that it symbolised making the sign of the cross at prayer. If the soup is finished before the bread cut by the father has been eaten, a bowl of milk is placed on the table and spooned out using pieces of the dark rye-bread until it is empty. I have noticed that the women, while eating – and in general really – keep their headscarves on. The children keep their caps on as well. No one seems to see anything wrong with that. The people also sleep with the same clothing they have worn throughout the daytime. Now and then they take a bath in the *banja*. These things can be found everywhere.

A moment ago a 56-year-old kolkhoznik was here on a visit. In the last war he fought against us. He can even read a few German letters. He told me that in the old days he owned 25 acres of land, two cows, two horses and several pigs. And now he was a kolkhoznik, and worked and worked, but owned absolutely nothing. Our host laughed when I asked him if he had been a 'Kulak' once. No, he answered, he didn't have the 9 acres required, but he didn't have to give anything away. They are all happy that we'll reintroduce private property. But for now, we have to continue living off the land and to be a burden to the Russians. The Russians live damn simple lives. Always potato soup and bread, and there is never much of the latter. They only have little petroleum and don't have the faintest notion about other cultural assets. They are in awe of our writing paper, our pocket lamps and all the other stuff. The woman is delighted when she gets our empty food tins, as metalware of all kinds is a rarity in the Soviet Union. The army had priority. These are the effects of Stalinism and its five-year plans. Anyway, we can make good use of the large amounts of flax that is produced in this area. And with a bit of synthetic fertiliser one could surely also take a large amount of grain out of the Dnieper region. Damn, if they'd give me 10,000 acres of land over here – I could turn that into something.

Thursday, 30 October 1941, W1, Cholm

The front and rear differential of my car are broken! Has probably been caused by the sudden frost in the night from Tuesday to Wednesday. All the parts have frozen together. A Russian-made 4x4 car of the W1 workshop has towed me to the village 3 kilometres away where I am now comfortably quartered as their guest. This morning I was served a cup of bean coffee in bed!!! Yes – in bed!! I share a large room with the artificers and they have made themselves nice foldable metal beds which they can take anywhere. For me a standard folding field bed – an 'accordion' – used to be the height of luxury, but what I found here really takes the biscuit! The artificers have brought several copper-pots with them from the region of Leningrad. I have seen that kind of ancient, hand-made copper crockery there in all the farms. I like that a lot, even though it is a lot less practical than enamelled aluminium crockery. The copper stuff would be ideal to furnish my weekend cottage. Anyway, I am not a war profiteer.

Currently Hauptmann Nowag is here. Everyone is already a bit distressed because of the two broken-down prime movers they have here, and just now an Oberfeldwebel of the artillery has arrived who towed two more broken prime movers into the yard. What a joy! One needs to make sure that this Oberfeldwebel doesn't realise what plans we have for his beloved prime movers. If he knew that we'll scavenge them for parts, he'd surely take them away with him again, broken as they are.

It is evening. I have bimbled around like this all day. The Stabsfeldwebel is in bed with a burned foot. I have kept him company for a while and shown him some of the pictures I have been sent from home. He wants to go home too, but for now prefers to stay with his lot as that is much better than being in a hospital somewhere. I have witnessed that here on the airfield when Junkers 52s arrived to take away the wounded. The heavily loaded machines were then unable to take off from the soft and wet ground and were forced to unload their sad cargo again. No, this way I can't endure the war any more, here in the rear area with hospitals and prisoner camps. All the heart-rending scenes that play out here, I can't stand it any more. I am close to tears now, I just can't bear it any more.

Sunday, 2 November 1941, W1, Cholm

The twentieth Sunday here in the Russian campaign. The mood is just like the weather: dim, very dim. Hemmenbach is singing a Zarah Leander song at the moment. The one from the film *Zu neuen Ufern* which has a text along the lines of 'I am standing in the rain, waiting for you'. In the next room I can hear the loud voice of Hilgenstöhler who is sitting with the Hauptmann. Outside in the big room in which the men of the guest company* and the Russians who are employed as mechanics are staying, the

---

* Personnel waiting to have vehicles repaired.

tall, pale Obergefreite who was once in the DBP* is playing the banjo. He is accompanied by a man from the workshop who is playing the harmonica. Yesterday when I took a look into that room the Russians were dancing to the wild and yet monotonous sounds of the balalaika. Yesterday I would really have liked to join their dance. Just for the joy of moving. What are we still doing here, a mangled division like ours?

Yesterday I bathed in the *banja*. The steam really did me good and has reduced the effects of my cold a little bit. It didn't hurt my ears, as I had expected it would. We took the water from a small shell hole – that way we didn't have to worry about contaminants. Otherwise all the streams and larger craters are full with the bodies of Russians who haven't been buried. Because of the ptomaine one really has to be careful here. The water supply situation here is extremely bad. There are no wells in Cholm; all water has to be sourced in the neighbourhood.

Tuesday, 4 November 1941, W1, Cholm

I still can't get out of here. There has still been no proper frost. And even if there had been, I couldn't have left yesterday, as I wasn't feeling well at all. On Saturday I had somehow upset my stomach, probably due to the plentiful liquor consumption. The boss had arrived just at the moment in which the artificers, the disbursing officer Quattek and I were emptying a bottle of bitter orange liqueur. He then ordered us, and that was at midnight, to organise a couple more bottles. And I guess we emptied those two too quickly, at least too quickly for my stomach. Together with the artificers, I persevered until 4 a.m., until the last drop had been drunk and then I went to bed. For warmth, I am sleeping right next to the oven; the stuff did have maximum effect. I was properly poisoned. Hauptmann Nowag had ordered me to drink several extra glasses, filled to the rim, and said that that allowed him to judge my character properly. That didn't quite work out, however, as he had become drunk a lot more quickly than I did. Anyway, one has to experience something like that. Today I am feeling a bit better, and in a moment Hilgenstöhler and I will go

---

* Deutsche Bauern Party – German Farmers' Party.

to the airfield to order a Storch. Adalbert is supposed to fly to the Ib to make a report about the terrible situation the workshop companies are in. Now it's evening and we haven't been able to get a Storch. The Staffel to which it belongs is based in Kalinin and the last Storch to arrive today only brought supplies and soap. No one knows when it will return.

When we were heading down the main road in Ssanovo, I noticed a grave on the side of the road between the houses. I walk down to it and read: 6./Pz.11. I can hardly believe my eyes! It is the grave of our missing Oberfeldwebel Bunse! So the Russian did shoot him too. At least we know now that he hasn't been dragged away by them, but has died a soldier's death by their hand. I can still see him, lying next to me in the shallow enemy trench, firing his machine pistol until it jammed after the second magazine. When I think about those terrible hours my heart convulses. Right now I can still feel the same indescribable fear which I felt in that trench and when a bullet went right through my cap. Damn, I don't want to experience such a situation again.

Wednesday, 5 November 1941, W1, Cholm

This morning Voss and I drove down to Ssanovo to photograph Bunse's grave. We'll send the photographs to Bunse's parents so they have an idea of where their son is resting. We first tidied up the grave as well as we could and then decorated it with fir twigs. The infantrymen who had buried him had done a very good job in designing the grave in a dignified manner. The tumulus, however, had collapsed a little. Voss and I repaired everything and also removed the withered flowers. The dark green of the fir twigs contrasted nicely with the white of the birchwood cross.

When we left the village we saw that an aeroplane had landed alongside the road leading to Cholm. The pilot was visiting someone in the village. My hope that he could maybe take me as a passenger was quickly destroyed as he only had thirty minutes to spare. He did, however, take my report and promised to pass it on. In it I reported that I would leave here on 7 November together with the vehicles of Kolonne 10. I wonder how far I will get with this lot. There are about twenty-eight different vehicle types, mostly MAN lorries. Now the real work and the real trouble starts. The boss is here and is debating the supply situation with Quattek. I was outside to check the practicability of the roads. Today we somehow have to organise fuel and tomorrow I have to signpost the route. I am certainly not inexperienced in the leadership of such columns, but the size of this rabble of men will make it difficult to find accommodation. The big troubles of little men.

Yesterday Hauptmann Nowag sent a dispatch rider out to take a message to the division. He returned this evening, by foot, with the remains of a ripped transmission chain. He had driven right into a frozen and straw-covered bog-hole and – with his motorbike – had sunk down into the mud up to his belly button. When he, with the help of some locals, pulled the bike out, he found that the chain had broken. We are lucky that I managed to send a report out with the aeroplane.

Wednesday, 19 November 1941, Gzhatsk

For me a new stage has begun. I have returned to my old lot, the 5th Company. While I was stuck in the repair shop, the company moved from Fjedina on the Dnieper to Gzhatsk, where it is now resting as part of the lot commanded by Hauptmann Stern. Here we are waiting for our transfer to Germany. It is unlikely that we can expect new employment as our last attack, from Kalinin on the Volga reservoir, was carried forward by only thirty-six Skodas, ten Panzer IVs and twelve Panzer IIs. Of those, several had broken down, so the regiment does not have sufficient numerical strength any more. Here in Gzhatsk I have reunited with my old gunner Wittkötter and Kappruch, a new guy allocated to me by Hille. We are staying in a relatively clean Russian house, without any bugs, fleas and lice. There is nothing to do. The company sleeps until 8 a.m. and there is no sense in running any kind of training activity for so few men.

I have led a column of repaired vehicles from the workshop to Prjetschisloje. My gang has covered the route through the swamps from Cholm to Katelky, or more precisely Kasulina, in two days. In that village we had to stay for two days, as we had to conduct repairs on the MAN-Diesel and because fuel and supplies were running low and we were also out of aether for the

Diesels. In Petrinina I found a bakery column which supplied us with 120 bread loaves, and in Wjasma we organised further supplies, which included tobacco. The roads leading to the Rollbahn were indescribably bad. Without doubt the worst I have experienced in Russia so far. On many segments on the route from Cholm to Katelky and beyond, the vehicles needed to be pulled through the bottomless mud by a half-tracked pioneer prime mover. Whatever wasn't worth that effort we just abandoned on the open road. May the carts hibernate there over the winter.

In the villages along the roads we couldn't find any accommodation. Everything was full of troops who had previously been stuck at Cholm and which were now using the favourable weather to make their way to the Rollbahn. Between Kasulina and Fjedina I ran into Hauptmann Nowag and his lot. One of his Russians, who had been born in Hamburg, and who was a cabaret tap dancer, ran up to me and shook both my hands for a final farewell. News had spread among the Russian prisoners that I was finally leaving the workshop and they were now shouting words of farewell and wishes of well-being in German and Russian. I have to admit that this made me marvel.

Thursday, 20 November 1941, Gzhatsk

Today I have derusted a semi-automatic rifle and made it usable. I had taken the dirty and totally rusted old shooter from a pile of rifles in the captured goods collection point at Cholm. I had also sourced myself a matching scope which I have just mounted. Now I only need to sight it in. This is the second semi-automatic rifle I have restored in that manner. It is worth the effort and gives one the feeling of having achieved something.

The woman of the house in which I am staying is quite clean and knows how to make herself useful. Today and yesterday, however, she didn't make the beds. Damn, I thought, where has the tart disappeared to? When I went down to Hille and the company today, I discovered why the woman hardly comes back to the house. Nearby, at the station, some infantrymen had torn down a shed for firewood. And that's where I found Natasha, who was busy assisting them. All the nice wood then ended up in her house. The busy bee had been working for two full days to source firewood. She was so busy that she even left her two small children to fend for themselves for most of the day. And now she was standing in front of me laughing, and proudly showed me the huge pile of stolen firewood she had sourced. All fine by me; at least it will be warm if I have to stay here any longer.

Otherwise, no news here. The division has captured the dam of the Volga and the canal – without us! Now the Russians are launching heavy counterattacks there, just as they did on the Luga. Today four tanks of the 7th Company rolled towards the front. The only four tanks which were ready to use in the area of Gzhatsk. Another of our companies, under Hoffmeyer, is also at the front. Everyone else is down here, including the Oberst, who until recently had served as town commander of Kalinin, and Löwe, who up until recently had commanded I. Abteilung. Seems that our once-mighty regiment of three Abteilungen has shrunk to the size of a single full company. Mostly due to technical breakdowns. The old buckets just can't take any more.

Friday, 21 November 1941, Gzhatsk

So, what did I do today after getting up at 7.30 a.m.? I have had my hair cut, read through some orders, have visited Hille for a bit of a chat and after lunch I popped down to the captured goods collection point to get myself a Russian sabre, another semi-automatic rifle and two stretchers. Then I visited Theo Langenbruch and after that I instructed the guards. I am on duty as officer of the day today. I don't quite know how that came to be. There seems to be a lack of unemployed Feldwebels in the companies, so they have made use of me instead. Well, except here I can't complain about it. After all, it's only a gesture to us old officers that we are not usually enlisted for such services. At the moment I am a bit groggy.

Monday, 24 November 1941

On the 21st there was a practice alarm which resulted in all kinds of mayhem. Yesterday, when I was with Willem to teach him some Russian, there was a fire alarm. The house in which Willem had stayed until recently had suddenly started burning due to a chimney fire. There was a Panzer IV Ausf. E parked next to it.

A bucket with fuel, in which the men had deloused their uniforms, stood right next to the wall of the house. The heat of the chimney fire made the wood of the wall glow red hot and soon the bucket outside had caught fire. A Russian then came running with a bucket of water, which he emptied onto the burning fuel, which caused the fire to spread rapidly. When the men inside the house (there were thirty men of the 6th Company staying in it) realised what was going on, it was already too late. The flames had started to engulf the whole wooden building so quickly that the Landsers didn't even have time to save their belongings. Leutnant Diercks has lost all his clothing, all of his equipment and a film camera. The things he was wearing were the only belongings he was left with. With the help of two lorries we tried to tow the Panzer IV away from the burning building. The heavy beast, however, had gearbox damage caused by a hit of an anti-tank gun and its tracks had lodged themselves firmly in the soft ground. There was nothing we could do. The tank was full of fuel and ammunition and we had to be very careful in case it exploded. And that is what happened once the house was burning brightly. First the rubber of the Panzer IV's wheels caught fire and then it all happened in the usual manner: fuel tank I, fuel tank II, fuel tank III, then the machine-gun ammunition ignited and then the cannon shells. And with the latter the whole vehicle violently exploded; the turret was thrown off and the frontal armour plate was blown off and came down 200 metres away. That the metal lump didn't decapitate anyone was pure luck. We could hear the heavy metal plate whizzing through the air. In the meantime all the neighbouring houses had been doused in water, to stop them from catching fire as well.

The Panzer IV has been blown apart. When Hauptmann Stern arrived later in his command tank, he didn't allow us to tow the still-glowing and smouldering remains away. There was a real danger that more houses would catch fire if we pulled the tank, which still held unexploded ammunition, down the road. Only now I realise why the Russians leave those big spaces between their houses. And the numerous firefighting ponds along the roads, which had never been of any significance to us, now made sense. Who of us, in the early days, had cared about a burning house? A burning cottage was far better for us than one that wasn't on fire. No Russians would shoot at us from a burning house. Where we are now there are strict orders that every building is important and valuable as winter quarters.

I went to the collection point again and picked up two more semi-automatic rifles. One for Oberleutnant Bethke and one for myself. In case we are getting away from here, I at least have a present for my old boss. The latest shithouse rumour: the Oberst is flying to Berlin to support his request to have the regiment pulled out to equip it with new tanks. The division has already approved and passed the request on to the Gruppe. The request includes the wish that the regiment – after reorganisation – will again be subordinated to 6. Panzer-Division. We still have the prospect of getting out of here before Christmas. We are all living in hope at the moment. I remember that we all looked forward to a big parade of the type which follows a campaign of this kind. And how does that look in reality? Our company has not a single operational tank left. They have all run onto mines or burned out. And the remainder has been repaired and repaired again and is now lying somewhere on the roads and fields north of Moscow, total breakdowns, cannibalised for parts. Someone has spread the rumour that we'll be equipped with captured Russian tanks! Well – I hope so! In the best case 52-ton ones. We'll take those into the Urals!

Tuesday, 25 November 1941

Today Natasha has read the cards for me. She said: *Khoroshiy karty! Khoroshiy karty!* It seems that my luck will keep up in the future. I seemingly have several female admirers too. Well, that's news to me. My path is blessed with three kinds of luck and I will soon be back at home. What more could I wish for? I was expecting that Natasha would also prophesy that I will have four children. And now I am waiting for what 'big stretch of water' I'll be crossing and my happy return home. Who knows what's going to happen. At least the whole thing let the time pass quickly. We heated water in the samovar for peppermint tea. Into that I poured the little sugar I had left and a good amount of schnapps. Natasha and her niece drank that too, and soon we all started sweating profusely from the potent, hot mix. I had to laugh when they started fanning their faces with a folded newspaper. Natasha, who is a good few years older than me, poured a good quarter of a litre of clear vodka into herself, which seemingly remained without any effect. Natasha's husband had been in prison because he had, like so many other Russians, made critical remarks about the government. From there he had been drafted into the army. If only the Red Army command knew how much the Russian women and children living in German-occupied territory are waiting for the fall of Leningrad and Moscow and the downfall of the government. The old people still remember a life without communism and commissars. In the Baltic provinces, in White Russia and in Ukraine everyone is already living under German civil administration.

It's amusing really. It's the same situation the old Romans had been in. There every official was sent to the provinces once during his career. The soldiers had to stay there as occupation forces while foreign workers were brought in to do the manual labour at home. Our human resources are only used for specialised work. Isn't that also some kind of pan-European union? I wonder what the result of the anniversary of the Anti-Comintern Pact will be which is celebrated in Berlin today. The Spiess, who owns a radio, told me about it when we saw one another a moment ago. He also told me that next to Udet, Mölders and Hauptmann von Werra, another flying hero – a General whose name I have forgotten – has given his life for the Fatherland. After this war we'll have plenty of heroes whom we can honour and pay our respects to. Let's just hope that all these great sacrifices have not been made in vain, in the same way in which those of the World War were.

Wednesday, 26 November 1941

I have now fulfilled the requirements for the assault badge twenty times over. Have just made some minute calculations based on my diary, as well as I possibly could. Twenty large-scale attacks as part of a major formation. Quite incredible. If I add all the smaller tasks I fulfilled, the actual total is over fifty. Good thing that I am always keeping a calendar.

Friday, 28 November 1941

Time is passing quickly these days. Between 2 and 4 in the afternoon I always visit Wilhelm Lope to learn Russian with the help of Wolja and Olga Lensinova. In the morning I practise my vocabulary, and after dinner, when it is dark, the day is already over again. In the evenings I usually sit down with Wilhelm and Diercks and these last days we have been joined by Binam the Armenian student and ingenious Semite. Wolja is the typical northern Slavic Russian, Olga an eastern Slav and in the case of Binam one can clearly see that he is not a European. The first two are from what I call the class of 'proletarian intelligentsia'. Wolja's father had been a senior buyer in a department store while Olga's father, who passed away twelve years ago, had been director of a textile factory which had been taken over by the Soviets. Olga is intelligent, but twitchy, the typical revolutionary type. Wolja, however, is far more thorough and also has a better grasp of grammar. She is a very calm and feminine type. Olga I could imagine in some military role, wearing a Basque beret and carrying a rifle. The women in the Russian female battalions are of the same type. It is weird that the people, who in the days of the tsars had jobs which required a certain amount of intelligence, were of the same long-skulled Slavic type as Wolja and the Polish girl who came to visit Tamara yesterday.

Saturday, 29 November 1941, Sovkhoz, Molaschno Gigant

We have been out and about the whole day. Panzer soldiers have turned into infantrymen. We are to be deployed as a protection battalion in the furthermost line near Klin. But one thing after another. The news hit us like a lightning strike right in the moment in which our thoughts had focused on 'going home' and on a Christmas under the tree in the circle of our families. The men of the Panzer-Regiment are to form an infantry battalion under command of Hauptmann Stern. Hille takes command of the 1st, Eggert of the 2nd Company. Wilhelm Lope and I are part of the rabble. I am in command of Hille's 1st Platoon, Lope has Eggert's 1st Platoon. The two other companies are being supplied by some other unlucky unit. We are supposed to move to Klin, into the furthermost line.

Sunday, 30 November 1941, Urossova, south of Latschino

My eyes are running and hurting because Voss and Steinbusch have put wet wood onto the fire. We sit in the hazy light of a lamp and the mood is where the temperatures are, below zero. Panzer soldiers are now infantry. The new experiences which are assaulting us all now are hard to put into words. Today I have returned to the company with my twenty-five men. When I drove past Wilhelm Lope, who was standing on the roadside with his broken-down car, I didn't realise that only thirty minutes later I would do the same, being forced to fix a flat tyre in ice and snow. A lorry full of freezing 'infantrymen', myself jumping from one leg to the other to somehow keep my feet warm, the driver with hands so cold that he can't take the fingers off the wheel any more.

The deeply furrowed gullies which make up most of the roads here in Russia after the bad weather period are now totally frozen. The lorry, which we had been given by 6./Transport-Regiment 602, had Russian tyres on. They are much weaker than German-made tyres, which haven't been delivered for a long time. With them the axle is only 11 cm above the ground and as such, during the journey, it regularly scraped over and through the frozen earth. No way to avoid the men having to dismount again and again to push the vehicle when it had run aground again. And when we had reached a waypoint, 30 kilometres away from our destination, the injection pump of our Diesel broke. Suddenly there was a hole in the metal and the Diesel oil spurted out of it. We repaired that by simply ramming a piece of wood into the hole and securing it with some wire. Fixed – simple!

We drove through Volokolamsk. There they had hanged eight partisans, two of them women, on a gallows. A big sign announced that these people had taken up arms against the German military. Eight people on one gallows, that's a sight one doesn't see often. Today a column of prisoners came our way. There were quite a large number of guards, about twenty men for over 500 Russians. Usually in the Vyazma region, you'd see six or so guards for 1,000 Russians. When we drove along the road they had come down, we found the bodies of many Russians who hadn't been able to walk further and had been shot by the guards. I myself alone counted fifteen men who were lying in a ditch who had been shot in the back of the neck. Personally, a sight like this troubles me. The Volksdeutsche in Poland can say what they want. I have seen crueller things here in the East.

Many destroyed Panzer IIIs and III Bs were standing on the roadside. Finished off by enemy fire and mines. Yesterday a woman told me that the Russians had laid out huge numbers of mines in the regions around Moscow. That will be interesting. Our division has crossed the Volga–Moscow Canal and assembled around Dimitrov, north of Moscow. Bypassing Tula, our troops are standing 30 kilometres north and south in front of Moscow.

Monday, 1 December 1941

We have ended up in Klin! The temperatures have dropped to below -20 degrees and I am amazed that no one has frozen feet yet. My platoon has taken shelter in a settlement that once had electric light, so clearly the inhabitants were once used to a higher standard of living. I have moved into a house which is quite nice. We are the first soldiers to move in and the people are falling over themselves to accommodate us. They have brought us mattresses so we don't have to sleep in straw. If they are bug-free we'll use them. Two of the women here in the house speak a little German. One looks like she's a German or a Finn with beautiful blonde hair of a kind I have never seen on a Russian. I have to stop romanticising; after all, I don't want to fall in love with a Russian woman.

Have to think about a boy I met when we were staying at Molaschno Gigant, who offered me the use of the family bed. When I refused to sleep in the bug-ridden bed, he said: 'Germanski nix Kultura' and then blew his nose into his hand, through his thumb and index finger.

Thursday, 4 December 1941, Klin

The situation is unchanged. We are still in Klin to supply ourselves with ammunition and to wait for the other companies. Wilhelm Lope with his big lorry full of men has also arrived after a long Odyssey. I'll visit him later to see how he is doing. From Klin we'll march on foot to the positions which we are to take over from 14.ID (mot.).

We are now subordinated to this division and our companies are supposed to relieve one of its battalions in this area. The place is 25 kilometres away. We are planning to load our weapons and kit onto a hand-drawn sledge. Secretly I am still hoping that we'll be back on the road before Christmas. Last Friday at 08.45 our last tank died on us. Panzer-Regiment without Panzer!

With seven men we are currently sitting around a table in the house and writing. Koprusch and another nipper of the 3rd Company are attempting to draw Christmas cards. At 11.00 an aircraft is supposed to take the mail to Germany. I have no idea what to write home. I don't give a crap about anything any more. Yesterday I was so apathetic that I went to sleep at 16.00 already. I really don't know what to do. This morning Wittkötter found four lice and one flea in his underwear. They tormented him during the night. This sparked a general bug-hunt and after a thorough wash I put on fresh undergarments myself. I didn't find any bugs, however.

Here in Klin there was once a large gunpowder factory while on our side of the river there were two glass factories. From one of those Obergefreiter Konkol has organised some baubles. I wonder if we'll have time to make use of them. I really don't understand why 'Infanterie-Bataillon Stern' should still be deployed operationally, even though Koll did have the confirmation from the OKH that the regiment would be pulled out to be reformed in the Heimat. Rumours said that this could happen between 1 and 8 December already. But who cares about rumours; orders are there to be executed.

Here in the house there is a Russian with his wife, daughter and son, who once worked in one of the glass factories. During the Revolution he fought against Wrangel and Pilsudski. That makes me think about Kozlowsky, my tailor back in Thorn, who fought with Pilsudski against the Russians. Let's hope that this current armed confrontation will be the last for a long time. There has been enough bloodshed in the first half of this century!

One of the women in the house is a doctor and used to earn 300 rubles per month. Her 50-year-old mother originates from the social class of the old intelligentsia. She speaks German, which was once taught in the schools. The doctor has got two handsome boys. Bright and squeaky clean, they are. Then there is the young blonde woman and her daughter. The first woman with manicured hands I have encountered in Russia. She looks enchanting in her black fur coat and the black cap on her shining hair. Damn, it is about time that we got back into the Reich, especially for me. I need to get back on the bachelor's path, one where I don't have to look into dull Russian faces. I want to listen to some proper music in the Alster Pavilion and I want to listen to concerts in the theatre, and not through the radio of the Feldwebel. I have to admit that in the last few days I have really started yearning for the civilian life. I can't help thinking about the things I have achieved in my life. Up until now that is very, very little. The time in the army has been a time of decline for me. There is no gratitude and recognition is only given to the bootlickers. I have seen that when Oswald was put in for the German Cross.

Should I have a son later in life, he won't join the army and if I have a daughter she won't join the female labour service! Our generation has had enough insight into those associations. All of my comrades refuse to join any military organisation created by the SA after the war. I, however, would still be interested in joining the SS again. But then, when I am back home, I will need time to study and will probably think differently.

Friday, 5 December 1941, Dortschewo

Hoofed it over a distance of 25 kilometres, through temperatures below -25 degrees and on roads frozen smooth as glass. Result: 50 per cent of the men have taken some kind of damage. Frozen feet, toes, heels, noses, cheeks and ears. Several of them have severely swollen lymph nodes in the groin and blisters on the feet. Many now feel the effects of old wounds which don't allow them to move like they would have wanted to. Yesterday evening we learned that we would go on the march today. We still didn't receive any ammunition and the company of artillerymen hasn't got any warm clothing. A walk through hell of a kind which can't have been any worse than that of the remnants of Napoleon's beaten army. Enough for today, the lamps need to be switched off. There are fourteen of us in a small farmer's hovel. Who knows what the future holds for us?

Saturday, 6 December 1941, St Nicholas's Day

We are waiting again. We are sitting in the farmer's cottage in Dortschewo and it was supposed to continue at 09.30. After the exhausting march we all slept well. It was fairly warm too. In a corner the young woman is breastfeeding her baby. She is performing this deeply human task without any shame. The Russian doesn't know that, just like he doesn't know any stimulation of his senses through pictures of more or less clothed women of the kind which is published in certain magazines. I have also never heard a debauched joke of any kind.

Yesterday Hoffmeyer's company came our way. They had been relieved after they had lost their last tank. 'Poor devils!' they called us when they learned that we had been demoted to foot-sloggers. I really don't want to complain, but all this is infernal beyond comparison. I have recuperated a little, but my legs, overstrained from walking on the slippery roads, still hurt quite a lot. At the moment Enz and another man are distributing the totally frozen rations. The bread loaves have turned into lumps of ice. It makes me want to puke.

Sunday, 7 December 1941, in front of Rogachevo

It was a brutally cold night. There was an alarm because the Russians had attacked on the right and in turn had broken through the line across the road to Dmitrov. We now expected them to attack in our section as well. The whole night we had been waiting in our reinforced machine-gun positions. And then in the morning we were thrown into the village about a kilometre further west. We, with our company and an anti-tank section, are supposed to defend it. The tank hunters are telling us that the whole front line from Dmitrov to Kalinin–Klin is being pulled back! In the front they are blowing up all the vehicles which we can't take with us. All our sacrifices have been in vain. On the march from Dortschevo to Rogachevo we had come past the graves of Unteroffizier Speckorius and Gefreiter Preuss of 6th Company. Incidentally, if I didn't know that there will always be wars and armed conflicts between the people, then I would certainly be marching under the banner of the pacifists – people of the same sort as the reconciliation prophets of which we had so many after the World War. I don't think there is much hope of that being successful, however. In the past days alone I have seen enough suffering and inhumanity to know that such efforts are futile.

Last night the Russians broke into Rogachevo from the east and set fire to several houses. They were Siberian riflemen, formations of which we are facing here. From the north, where we are holding the line, they have not attacked yet. But that can still happen. Yesterday Stukas flew overhead, plastering an invisible target in front of us. We are lucky that the wind has died down. We already have more than enough casualties due to frostbite in my platoon. That the feet of our sentry posts didn't freeze last night is only due to the fact that we had found enough hay in our sector on which we could stand. When Rogachevo stood in flames yesterday night, the church looked absolutely amazing. Like a fairytale castle of Arabian Nights, the sight of the white spires with their oriental decoration and the blood-red, golden onion-shaped domes eerily illuminated against the dark, night sky. An infernal, but glorious spectacle. In an infernal concert, the Russian 'Gittara' sent their incendiary oil shells towards us while the Russian flyers dropped magnesium bombs and all kinds of other ordnance on our heads. The Russians clearly have aerial superiority here. Over our sector we have Spanish fighter pilots while on the Russian side there are cheeky English pilots in bomber aircraft.

At the moment baggage trains of the infantry move past. They are falling back on Klin. It is 13.00 now and I am deployed as a reserve platoon until 18.00. I hope that by then we'll be on the march as well. Our artillery has redeployed to the rear as well. Who knows what they'll have in store for us poor foot-sloggers in the coming night? Today our rations included a whole bar of chocolate. That reminded us that this is the second Sunday of Advent. At the moment Russian bombers are pounding our withdrawal routes in strength. A Russian tank attack was ongoing as well and the anti-tank guns had been redeployed. Captive Russians have reported that six Russian divisions are attacking us here! I didn't quite enjoy dinner today, pearl barley every day!

The Russian inhabitants of this god-forsaken place are fleeing too. A clear sign that it will get uncomfortable here soon. I worry about our wounded and the sick who can't walk any more.

04.00, Tuesday, 9 December 1941, at Woronina near Klin

Since yesterday, I have been feeling a great amount of compassion for the great Napoleon who, undefeated as he was, was forced to withdraw from Russia! I have now lived to see a similar withdrawal, a smaller version maybe, but one that couldn't have been much worse in his days. My mother used to tell me stories about the French and their allies, how they were forced to wrap rags around their feet and how they put on women's skirts just to keep warm. Well, now I have had that experience myself! Yesterday we were morally defeated, just like Napoleon's victorious troops were. We were forced to retreat. We, the former Panzer men, had been sent from Gzhatsk to this place, to cover our retreat and to torch villages! Yes, we have turned into proper murderous arsonists. Fucking hell, I have had enough of this. But one thing after another, this time I can't even calm my anger through writing.

Our divisions operating on the left flank who, still motorised before the mud period set in, had managed to reach the Dmitrov Canal and crossed – together with our 6. Panzer-Division – had been forced to fall back to a defensive line in front of Klin. Six fresh Russian divisions then pressed towards our bridgehead at Klin and south of it, all of them excellently equipped Siberian formations. The 30th Russian Army is pressing towards Spaskoye along the Rollbahn. Klin, Rogachevo, where we stood in the previous nights and the river crossing at Woronina. That's all I know of the general situation here, north of Moscow.

On Sunday we were relieved during a fierce snowstorm. At about midday we were ordered to prepare the village for burning and to make ourselves ready to withdraw to Woronina. A distance of more than 20 kilometres which we would have to cover. I only realised in the afternoon that it was a Sunday, and it felt like mockery when I informed the men about it. Rogachevo and the villages in front of it had changed hands several times in the previous night. Now they were still defended by our rearguard. Any vehicles we couldn't take with us any more were blown up and all houses were put to the torch. We received the order to do the latter to our village as well.

At 15.30 it was getting dark and we started loading our baggage onto the lorries of the company. At 16.00 the first vehicles set out from Bogdanabo towards the rear. Stern remained in the village for a while and during the night requested support from one of our platoons because 6th Company had reported that Russians were advancing from the north. As such only two of our platoons remained in the small village, while Matussek and his men were sent to Bogdanabo. Wünsche, I and our platoons remained in our small village. We were supposed to withdraw during the course of the night, at the latest in the early morning at 06.00, after the infantry companies with their baggage had passed through. Then the houses were to be torched and I, with my platoon, was to form the rearguard until we had reached Ssafregino, from which 6th Company would withdraw once we had passed.

Everything went as planned, until Hille panicked and, in his fear, torched the house that had been allocated to him early, just in the moment when the first self-propelled anti-tank gun rolled into the village. What a stupid thing to do! Hille didn't want to lose connection to the infantry, no matter at what cost, and had then quickly driven away in his Kübel. The house was burning so fiercely that the horses of the columns moving into the village would not walk past and were forced to wait until the fire had died down. But that didn't happen. The strong wind fanned the flames and soon all the other houses, which had been allocated to our platoon, and had already been packed with hay and doused with petrol, were burning brightly as well.

We walked in between the burning houses, and through lines of wailing women and children, towards the end of the village, where Hille was waiting, anxious to get to Ssafregino as quickly as possible. In Ssafregino it was Eggers who panicked, and set fire to the houses way too soon, long before we had even managed to march through the village.

In school we learned about the Vikings, how they had put whole fishing villages to the torch. We have learned about the Thirty Years War, and the suffering of the population whose cities, towns and villages were burned by inhuman, marauding soldiery. So many fires that the whole night sky was illuminated by their blood-red glow. In East Prussia the people still remember how the Russians burned down the villages during the World War. All that we have now lived through ourselves. We have seen the horrified faces of the wailing women and heard the miserable cries for help of the old men. We have seen the livestock running around in fear, heard cattle and horses screaming in terror. We have seen mothers with their children, too terrified even to speak – and now we know how a German soldier feels when he, according to the hard laws of war, <u>is forced to commit such brutalities himself</u>!

18.20
Just now the Russian artillery has placed a few big lumps right in front of our noses, so close that we could hear the splinters whistling. Then we all had some aquavit, the most excellent vodka. Matj Mamm, or 'Matka' as she is called here, lit a fire which emits volcanic heat. And now I sit here at the table with the card players near the petroleum lamp. What shall I write about? Yes, I forgot to write about the march to Woronina. The wind blew the snow into our eyes …

Alarm!

11 December 1941; Bol. Schtschapavo.

'What is actually going on here?' – that is the question we all ask ourselves here in Sicherungs-Bataillon Stern. Watchword: total sugar! (if one doesn't want to use the other, more familiar quotation). Morale? Just like the temperature, always more or less below zero!

Outside on the street infantry march past, they are just as exhausted as we were. The pressure was released a little when a message came through from Klin informing us that we were not surrounded any more and that the danger that the 'Siberiaks' would turn south behind Klin and thus close the pocket had passed for the time being. During the briefing, Wünsche clearly stated there might be a chance for us to get through south of Klin. By doing so he openly voiced the thought of fleeing. This is what we had come to!

Yesterday night the Ib of the division had radioed in to report that our baggage vehicles had managed to get past Klin and across the road threatened by the Russians. A great relief for us that our meagre belongings, the few blankets and tent squares, and our wounded comrades were safe. Stubborn and numb, with tired faces and exhausted limbs, the men outside slog through the snow to man the machine guns at the barns in the field. It is snowing heavily and freezing cold and every single man is happy when his hour outside is over and he can come in again.

Grawe has just told me that he has seen a construction battalion move through outside. An Oberfeldwebel of that unit had told him that, with their 45-year-old men, they had defended their positions against Russian attacks in the north of Woronina. Thirty of their men and an old Oberleutnant had been taken prisoner. They had then been replaced by Kradschützen of 36. or 14. Infanterie-Division (mot.) who had managed to bail the prisoners out by force. All except the old Oberleutnant, who had been shot by the Russians. That again confirms what's always been happening. In a situation of the kind we find ourselves in here, during the withdrawal to Klin, all old platitudes crumble and all the masks come off. Out here there is only one thing that can help the Landser to survive: he has to take the stance 'may the whole world lick me in the arse!' And if he manages to do that, he'll be able to act like the men of IR53 who, while being flanked, and marching through villages which were already half occupied by the enemy, replied to calls of 'Ruki werch!' by throwing a bunch of hand grenades in front of the Russian's feet.

Now it is 10.00 am and I am with the boss. He has been called to see Hauptmann Stern and has called us to him before he went there. Soon he'll return, take off his glasses and announce that we'll have to leave our boiling potatoes and the meat, which has been expertly prepared by Unteroffizier Enz, to move into a new position. What are we supposed to eat then? We have become rather modest in our wishes and we were happy as children under the Christmas tree when yesterday, Feldwebel Lahr made an appearance with a stale old loaf.

My old orderly Erdweg has taken up a guitar, and even though we are all in a poxy mood we have all raised our voices to sing the 'wild goose song', a song which our fathers sang out here in the east and for which I have had a soft spot since my time in the Bündische Jugend. More fitting to our mood, our longing for home and what we hold dear, are the songs that he is playing now and to which we are singing too. In moments like this it is the eyes of those Landsers who went through the thick of it that are the first to fill up with tears.

Outside our artillery is firing, and we hardly look up any more when the Russians send some of their shells over to us. They have put a few layers down on our rearguard positions, and up in Klin there has been some plastering as well. Quite substantial plastering even. We don't give a crap about it. The last two days have been worse than this.

High command is urging us not to give up and to hold out a bit longer and is telling us that large reserves are being diverted up here. But of what use are reserves which are in the same bad shape that we are? Motorised regiments with five or ten working lorries. The others have been blown up or, where we have failed to do that, have been taken for a drive by the Russians.

Now we are singing 'During a Day in Spring' and when we reach the bit where it goes 'wo Fortuna winke-winke macht',* we all think just how much luck we have had so far and in the previous days.

Oberleutnant Hille has returned with news. The situation is serious but not hopeless. 2. Panzer-Division is to come from the south to clear the Rollbahn up again. The positions along the Sestra and at Woronina are supposed to be held by those divisions which have been deployed to secure the withdrawal. These positions will become the main combat line this winter. In the north it runs behind Spaskoye towards the motorway and the crossing of the storage reservoir. In the south it runs towards the road systems captured by our Panzer-Division, which means that here, north of Moscow, the line runs from south-south-east to north-north-west. With sorrow we remember those who have fallen in combat for the canal bridgeheads.

In the summer, when one by one, our motorised vehicles started ending up on the vehicle graveyards, the Landsers began to organise Panje wagons to transport their stuff. One horse pulling and another led on behind, and the advance could continue. One could find hay everywhere, and if not there

---

* 'Where Fortune is waving'.

was usually oat straw or something similar. Now we have all switched over to sledges. My platoon has two horse and sledge teams which have been supplied by Brune, the great 'organiser'. Our machine-gun boxes and the guys with bad feet travel on them. They are simple things, taken from some kolkhoz or farmer's barn. They have no iron runners and as such they don't run as smoothly as those that we are used to in Germany. Anyhow, we can make some headway with them.

It is now 14.00. It will soon get dark again. A battery of heavy mortars is rolling past; 21-cm calibre. 'I wonder where they are going,' asks a man who is also looking out of the window. There are three men lying in the corner to my right who are humming old Schlager melodies. Ohlemeyer, Königshofen and Schäfer. Schäfer is a proper tango lad. He is from Krefeld and a technical draughtsman. Ohlemeyer is also a very young warrior. The bunch is not complete, however, as Kopunik is not around at the moment. He is also a guy who still displays certain childish mannerisms. All of them have only recently been sent from the replacement battalion and joined up shortly before we were reformed to become the Stern-Battalion. But what else, but this infantile stuff, are these young lads supposed to talk about, they haven't seen anything else yet.

Brune claimed to have found a few ropes and a quilted blanket in a Russian bunker. But then the woman of the house started screaming blue murder. I have told Brune to give her her blanket back …

Saturday, 13 December 1941, Opalevo, in front of Klin

In the coming night the defensive line will be pulled back to Klin! Yet further back! More men will fall into Russian hands, vehicles, cannon and tanks that will have to be blown up and more villages going up in flames. To cover the retreat they now have at least sent the last working tanks down here. All of what was still running in 1., 2. and 7. Panzer-Division. From those three divisions we now have about forty-five to fifty tanks of all types, from Skoda 38(t) to the German Panzer III B. It is a calming feeling to know that these weapon systems, to which one has such a close bond, are in close vicinity! In the last days these tanks have destroyed quite a lot of

Russian ordnance in counter-thrusts, which has given us a bit of breather. The Russians are still plastering us quite nicely here, but they are not as dangerous any more. They are now unable to put coordinated fire on all of the villages along the road of withdrawal, of which they have excellent, flanking views At the moment there is lively aerial activity. The Russians are operating some new types here, Curtiss and Spitfire fighters. The Rata bumble-bees are still around too. On the airfield at Klin, tanks of 1. Panzer-Division have recaptured over thirty Messerschmitt machines.

Sunday, 14 December 1941, Teterino

Withdrawal route
Teterino → Sselinsk → Gotschokowa → main road south of Njekrassino-Wysokowski → Petrovokoye → Paveljzova → Jelgosina

Hans Koch, ⚔ 13.XII.1941

Oblt. Böttcher with Siegel and Walstaff drove by.

Wednesday, 16 December 1941, Davidovo

[*Blank*]

Saturday, 20 December 1941, Schachowskaja station

In four days it will be Christmas. Our 'withdrawal' of those divisions that had advanced too far east has ended according to the programme. The 6. Panzer-Division has covered the withdrawal of LVI. Armee-Korps towards the Lama position and has now become Korps reserve in the area of Schachowskaja. With Sicherungs-Bataillon Stern we are now based close to the Ib of the division. How long we are going to be in reserve I don't know. That can change quickly up until Christmas.

We survived the withdrawal. I am unable to describe all the cruel days, the hardships and the drudgery. I can summarise it thus: it was the worst thing we soldiers experienced in the whole of the campaign. Now that I sit here at the table with the skat players again, I can't help thinking that it is Christmas soon and that we are still here in this paradise. Four military policemen were staying here before us and have left a dried-out Advent wreath here. Yes, those brothers had the time to think about stuff like this.

On the march today I walked at the head of the company on the right side of the road, when a large car pulled up next to me and a monocled General looked out of the rear window. I turned around and made my report. When seeing the clean-shaven face with the monocle, the two stars on the braided shoulder boards, I realised at once that this was none other than General Reinhardt, the commander of the Panzer-Gruppe. '5th Company, Panzer-Regiment 11 – currently on foot, on the march to the assembly area of 6. Panzer-Division at Schachowskaja!' He asked me a few questions relating to our deployment and then raced on.

This afternoon Tutasz and Müller, my old comrades in arms, came round. Soon our whole old 5th Company sat in the room together. With a bottle of schnapps and a few of champagne we toasted the successful withdrawal. Like that we sat there for a long time chatting away. I can't keep my eyes open any more, I am too tired. Last night's march is having an effect. I wish I could switch positions with Unteroffizier Geyer, who is again unable to sleep today.

That's it, I've had enough for today. Brauchitsch is said to have resigned!!!

Sunday, 21 December 1941

This morning I first enjoyed a nice cup of coffee. I received a few parcels with the post two days ago and the contents reminded me and the comrades in the old manner that yet another week had passed. It is also the fourth Sunday of Advent, the last before Christmas. Wittkötter, my old loader, had been sent a few pieces of ham from home and used some of it to make a sandwich for me. It tasted wonderful. Then I was called to Hille.

Always the same old story. One always has to say farewell when it's most comfortable. An advance party has just set out to secure new quarters for us in a different village. And I had just given my laundry to the woman here in the house! Damn! And my laundry is in dire need of a wash. The morning's control sweep had located a range of lice and nits! It makes me want to cry! One has done the utmost to keep as clean as possible. With my naked arse I have stood outside every morning brushing out the impractical, black trousers. I have washed and groomed myself. And now, during this lousy withdrawal, where there was no time to wash, the beasts immediately move into one's pants. It helps to know that I am not alone; all Landsers search their clothing in the mornings and most of them with results. It will get better one day.

Yesterday Tutasz and Müller were here with a bottle of schnapps. We have invited them to come over again and to spend Christmas with us. Now that has fallen through completely as it looks we'll be back in action over Christmas. There are rumours making the rounds that Brauchitsch has resigned. I don't know if that is true. In the last few days there have been plenty of rumours. Tobruk hasn't been lost after all and Singapore hasn't either. I am wondering what will become of us.

During the withdrawal we were forced to burn the mail of other divisions as there was no way we could have taken it with us. In other cases starving Landsers have torn open the parcels on abandoned mail transports in the hope of finding something edible in the contents. The letters were just stomped into the snow. Disgusting. Just as disgusting is that they abandoned a baggage lorry. I saw how the Landsers ripped open the officers' chests, surgical and medicine boxes in the search for food. Many just took things which in that moment might have appeared valuable to them and only a few days later, when the things had shown themselves to be useless, they too were trampled into the dirt.

I will not talk about this withdrawal. I am not diplomatic enough to smooth these events, the greatest mess I have ever experienced, over with words, and I want to avoid being court-martialled as a mutineer. On Monday morning in Tarochowa, I was so mentally and physically broken that I collapsed. After that night's march I couldn't go on any more and after I had reached the house of the Ib I just fell over. Even with lots of bean coffee and Röchter's 97 per cent vol. schnapps, I only regained my feet after two days.

The field gendarmes also failed miserably during the withdrawal. They should focus on regulating sexual intercourse instead of the vehicle traffic of an entire Korps. Without the help of officers and old pursers of combat units, they would have failed miserably to organise and guide the wild columns. In many cases the gendarmes just ran away when they feared they would be cut off. The worst swinishness, however, was that the 23. Infanterie-Division never held its rearguard positions and always withdrew prematurely. This allowed the Russians to encircle us afresh every day while the horse-drawn vehicles of this 'Sprinters-Guard' then fell back on the same road which our Korps was withdrawing on, thus greatly adding to the traffic chaos. And when the sledges and carts attempted to cut past the traffic across the fields they very often ran into mines. While I was lying flat in Tachorowa, at least ten mines exploded. The withdrawal was conducted with such speed and haste that the dead remained mostly unburied – we had all become so apathetic.

Often I had come past the corpses of fallen comrades who had been killed by bomb splinters and strafing. When the Ratas and Curtiss came, the soldiers didn't even bother to return fire any more. That is hardly surprising, if one has an empty stomach in this kind of freezing cold. All the more astonishing and laudable is the conduct of our riflemen who covered the withdrawal as a last-ditch rearguard. Always surrounded, with frozen limbs, nothing to eat and little ammunition, they halted the exploiting Russian forces and inflicted severe casualties on them in counter-thrusts.

Schützen-Regiment 2 is said to have suffered great casualties at Teterino and the two commanders and the Adjutant who relieved us at 24.00 were killed at 06.00 in the morning when the Russians attacked the village with a whole regiment and seventeen tanks. There we can see how much luck we have had. Hille says it's only due to Hauptmann Stern that we didn't have casualties like Hans Koch during attacks and counter-attacks.

Monday, 22 December 1941, Rshischtsche

It was just typical that we were forced to leave our quarters in Schachowskaja in the dead of the night to make room for some staff formation of the Gruppe. Only rarely have I cursed so much as in this night when we set out in the darkness and a snowstorm. We were hardly able to find our route and I, being the translator, had to go and ask some Russians for the way. We all felt like we had been banished to Siberia and shared the hate for all those above company command level, who sat with their fat bellies at a warm stove.

As we stomped through the snow, which is already lying at knee height, we came past another group of men, wrapped up into their coats, bracing the freezing snow with gritted teeth just like we were. We shouted over to them, loudly cursing the snow, the roads and the whole war in general. First they didn't reply, but then one man among the group shouted back: 'Woina nix gutt!'* Now we realised that these comrades in suffering, deep in the snow on the other side, were Russian prisoners.

This march gave me ample time to again think about the reason why there are always, always two groups of men, cursing and execrating the war, moving through the world. On one side we now have kolkhoz farmers, metal workers and butchers, on the other fitters, farmers' sons, merchants and craftsmen. Both sides share the same amount of suffering and grief, and every day it is this or the other group which has to bleed more. I tell my men that this is about the reshaping of Europe, the creation and protection of German Lebensraum, the absolute defeat of 'Bolshevism', the enemy of the people. But have I myself really taken these slogans to heart? Am I myself convinced by what I try to explain to my men so convincingly? Again and again it is damn hard to get my own head around the fact that everything we are being ordered to do here is right and for the benefit of not only our people. It is true that such a war is an eye-opener, even more so when one has experienced the bad sides of a campaign and when the war drags on and on. But I can't help saying to myself, in moments when I profoundly fail to make sense of it all, that Hitler, when he let us loose on the Russians, had already been through the same kind of crap himself, which didn't make a lot of sense then. On the face of it, it is all quite obvious and from the perspective of the beer-table strategists, those deferred from military service and Ortsgruppenleiter, all this here makes sense. But ask a serious man who doesn't just repeat the slogans and who has repeatedly put his own neck on the line, if he at times didn't have the same thought. As far as I can tell, all of them did so!

---

* 'War isn't good'.

Now we only have the wish that they will leave us alone at Christmas! Again and again, this is what I hear from the men. Otherwise we're all only thinking from one day to the other, but in this particular instance we are all thinking three days ahead. We are now under command of Oberstleutnant Limbrunn, who has already given us plenty to be angry about in the summer. It was also due to him that we had to set out into the freezing night. This damned East Front whinger who completely misdeployed us at Leningrad and repeatedly sent us on night attacks.

The whole platoon is sitting in a nice, clean farm cottage together with the company squad. It has already been announced that this fifteen-house village will also serve as quarters for the staff company. Seems we'll all have to move closer together. But the most important thing is that on Christmas we'll have a roof over our heads. How frugal we have become. We don't even think about celebrating with our families any more and don't waste a thought about going home at the start of the new year.

Funny, I am writing here like I am the little tank gunner Pimpelhofer and not a Prussian Leutnant who can look back on such a great number of soldier ancestors that it puts even antiquity to shame. Am I really such a little philistine that the experiences here are turning me into a pacifist? And even in the face of all these great role models – the Prussian Leutnants and the Frederician Fähnrichs who all knew how to die so nobly – this isn't my ideal. A hero's death? That is a fraud! A hero's life! That's what it should be! There is nothing heroic in death! Only life, lived until the final beat of the heart, can be heroic – dying is the easiest of things! I have often secretly wished for such a deliverance, when I was morally broken, up to the neck in the dirt, only to abandon the thought again. It's this little spark, which reignites me in the last moment, reminds me of my duty and obligation and pushes me back onto the path of true Prussian tradition.

First day of Christmas 1941, Rshischtsche

I have thrown some work at the boss's feet, and that was in relation to the distribution of Iron Crosses. We have received eight Iron Crosses which are supposed to go to those men who have distinguished themselves during the withdrawal where, thanks to Stern's tactics, we had no contact with the enemy as we used to have in the old days.

Second day of Christmas, 26 December 1941, Rshischtsche

Soon we are supposed to head outside to shovel snow. But the coffee isn't ready yet, it is just too cold. Even the field kitchen doesn't heat properly any more with temperatures below -30 degrees. In addition there is a howling snowstorm. Well, it will surely be fun when our bones start to freeze. But Stern, so it appears to me at least, is keen to keep us occupied. When we have finished with the snow, we'll probably be transferred away. At the moment Oberst Koll with 1,000 men is on the way here. He is supposed to build a supply road for the Korps and to establish a second defensive line. Just like during the World War, we are building bunkers and positions like the Hindenburg Line. I would like to know how the gentlemen see that happening during this frost and with the ground being as hard as stone. In the furthermost line the Organisation Todt is working with several battalions. We are now supposed to spend winter here. One really has to switch to stubborn mode when thinking about the coming period. I try to say to myself that there have been generations who have been through even worse times. And what they managed to do, we can do as well. One day there will be peace again, peace on Earth, of the kind the angels pray for on Holy Night. Can one even imagine this after two years of war: nights without blackout, no more war on all fronts?

At least we could properly celebrate Christmas. In the morning we had to clear a path through the snow, a task which we finished at 13.00. Then we went home, where Laufenberg and Mischa, the owner of the house, had hewn a Christmas tree out of a fir tree 10 metres tall. None of us had ever seen a more glorious one. A wonderful tree, hung thickly with fir cones which we then started to decorate in a simple and tasteful manner. Our supply officer Bethke issued an extra ration and in addition cognac and liquor. From some recently arrived parcels I had saved a few sweets and a package of sugar from home to make a proper grog with. Small trifles like this reminded the whole platoon that at home the season of affectionate secrecies had begun. I had only managed to prepare a small parcel for Erich Lehmann and for my old loader and batman Wittkötter. For the latter I had added a 20-Mark note for his loyal services, which he ogled with great delight once he had eaten his way to the bottom of the box. Wrenger the wireless operator had managed to save an accordion through the withdrawal. Lauer knew how to play it and the music, together with Unteroffizier Greger's baritone voice, added much to the festivity of the evening. Actually the evening passed way too quickly. Amid the singing, the grog and the liquor under the beautiful Christmas tree one hardly noticed how quickly the time passed.

I didn't want to launch into a long speech, I had said that to the men too. But I nevertheless said a few words, particularly as we hadn't expected such large quantities of alcohol. I wanted to avoid some of the men drowning their sorrows with alcohol, and indeed we did not manage to avoid the usual piss-up. We did, however, manage to get over the fact that we couldn't be with our families on the day which is so deeply important for us Germans. The village, by the way, is ideally situated for the event, like in a fairy tale, deep in a forest. The tiny area of arable land is surrounded by tall, dark fir trees while the dozen or so small cottages along the road are also nestled into the shadows of the enormous trees, as if they were trying to find shelter from the howling snowstorm. A proper Christmas village, this Rshischtsche, although Father Christmas did surely have a tough time getting there using the snow-covered roads. To make sure he at least stood a chance of doing so we had to spend Christmas morning outside, shovelling snow. Many Russian aircraft were about, Ratas and bombers. What happened to our aerial superiority? I can't help thinking about the Spanish pilots who let the expensive and now much desired Messerschmitts fall into Russian hands. Damn this withdrawal; losses were catastrophic.

I wonder if the story about Brauchitsch is true. As I have only recently met Reinhardt, the commander of the LVI. Korps, I know that he hasn't been relieved of his post. So whose fault is all this? On 22 December General Raus had issued an order which hinted at spending the winter here and asked for increased readiness. A similar order came down from the division which stated the need to build a defensive system and to switch over to sledge traffic. We have used sledges for a while already, but our two horses apparently froze to death when the team was out to collect petrol. Somewhere one of our carts loaded with fuel had got stuck in the snow and so all the sledges of the Abteilung were sent out to collect the petrol cans. The snowstorm that's raging today was so bad that even the Panje horses perished in it. We humans could hardly survive out there, it is simply horrible. Faces frozen, hands, feet as well and that way we are supposed to work and clear the roads which snow covers again as soon as one is finished. There are always several men who are sick. In recent days mostly stomach ailments. We are all suffering from the damned runs, but there is nothing we can do against that. We did, however, construct a proper privy back here in the barn, but some of the sick men can't even get as far as that. At the moment Obergefreiter Kronke is lying next to me in the corner here with a temperature of 40.2 degrees. On the floor next to the barrack oven, Röhlen is lying on the floor squirming with pain. I am just waiting for the day when the lice will give us typhus. At the moment we are only struggling with dysentery and influenza. If we get typhus on top of that it will get really bad. Just now Stabsarzt Möschler was here to check in on Kronke and the other sick men. If only we had proper clothing! In his leather footwear the German Landser is literally freezing his feet off. In this cold the Russians are wearing useful felt boots which they can pull up over their knees. That way they can make their way through the snow which so easily enters our lace-up shoes and the shafts of our jackboots. The thick headscarves of the women and the earflap caps of the men are the only useful headgear, and while we were amused to see the Russians on the Leningrad front wearing quilted jackets and trousers in summer, now we would be happy to have them. None of the Russian pieces of clothing look nice, but they are all practical. And if all our transport units replaced their motor vehicles with sledges we'd surely make better progress. Instead they are all stuck somewhere in the landscape, leaving us to find other means of supplying us with ammunition, food and petrol. At the moment no one knows where our luggage is either – it's a mystery.

Saturday, 27 December 1941, Rshischtsche

Mischa, the muzhik and master of the house, speaks German! He seems to have a few words picked up from us and I had to laugh and he came to me to ask for their meaning: '*Wassili Wassiljewitsch, kak po russki*: "Verdammter Schlamassel das ist, Gottverdammt"?'*

During the night I had to consider that we are supposed to stay here through the entire winter. Surely we'll get replacements and new vehicles, and when new operations are possible again in the coming spring, we'll launch attacks which will destroy the Siberian Army of the East. I will be there, until an anti-tank gun, an aerial bomb, a shell or a mine puts a full stop after the last sentence of my life's story. If I could see into the future! Wilhelm Lope is gone too now and I am the only friend and officer who has been with me since the start of the campaign. But I will continue to do my duty, I will be as 'stubborn as a cartridge pouch', up to the final outage. Then I will have had my campaign, for which I have yelled so much after Poland and France. Gosh, at the moment I am so fed up again. There is no way our division will get out of Russia anytime soon; now the only thing we can do is to endure it.

My new motto is 'The Front clicks, and the Heimat is happy'.† Although clicking here is done with two thumbnails, and between them there is a tiny animal. Our new Schlager: 'I want a photo of yourself, no matter if it's small. Always yours, always yours …' – a wonderfully corny song. We are singing it, with fanatical stupidity, at any possible opportunity.

---

* 'How do you say this in Russian: "Bloody mess that is, God damn it"?'
† A marketing slogan for Adox film.

31 December 1941 [*entry in Sander's lost pocket calendar – extracts published in Michael Schadewitz's history of Panzer-Regiment 11*]

Defence in the kolkhoz barn at Timkowo. More -30 degrees cold. Russian attack with four 52-ton tanks. Night to New Year's Eve in position. We have to stick it out!

1 January 1942

Flight from Timkowo/Kolkhoz. fourteen dead, twenty-two missing, twenty-five wounded. Fit for action: one Oberleutnant, twelve men.

2 January 1942

We have warm food. Doctor is sending me to the rear. There are Christmas rations. Nightly march to the baggage train.

3 January 1942

March to Schachowskaja/station. Entrained and roll off towards Rshev. Bombs. Oven.

4 January 1942

Still rolling, brief halt, flipping cold, petrol barrel oven proves to be successful. The woe of the wounded.

5 January 1942

Arrival in Wjasma in the morning. Friendly reception by the Oberst. On foot to Theo Langenbruch and the company.

6 January 1942

Arrival at the company which is just pulling out. Can't endure travelling in a vehicle and have to take up quarters. Friendly Russians.

7 January 1942

With Olga I drive to Duchowschtschina. For 4 km of snow-covered road – five hours. Find shelter with a Luftwaffe radio unit behind the Dnieper.

8 January 1942

Arrive in the village of Tretjakova. Nice quarters in a little house alongside the road. Lots of mail.

9 January 1942

With Theo Langenbruch until evening. Siegel is ranting about the Nazis.

10 January 1942

Invited Theo to have dinner at mine. Chicken fricassée and sugared rice. Living like kings.

11 January 1942

Nothing special. Writing some letters.

12 January 1942

Nothing special. As above.

13 January 1942

Advance party is off to Jarsevo. Evening with Theo.

14 January 1942

Staying in Tretjakova for the time being. We have no fuel. New quarters don't have window panes yet. Russians are said to be 10 kilometres in front of Lytschevka!! About to form a pocket.

14 January 1942, Tretjakova

We have many visitors here in the Russian cottage, in which I am now staying with Wittkötter after my return to the remains of our 5th Company. As it's comfortably close to the road they come in to warm themselves up. They are a good source of news. One thing they told me is that three days ago the Russians were 10 kilometres away from Lytschevka, approaching the dump from two sides! I have to admit that this shocked me. Does it still make any sense to preserve the whole drama here for posterity in my diary? Even if we manage, against my expectations, to stop the Russian advance, then no one needs to know more than necessary about the hammering we have received here in the central sector of the front. And if we fail to stop them, even with the troops currently arriving from France, and if the Russians close the pocket at Wjasma, advance further and take all that territory from us, then this will be the beginning of the end. This is how I see it at least, with my December mood which isn't very rosy. I hope I am wrong with the second prognosis. That would be just horrible. All, all our sacrifices, would have been in vain!

I find it hard even to try to explain how this setback had come about. I have thought about it several times and if it wasn't the urgent desire of the Party, then surely they were forced into the attempt to achieve a prestigious victory at all cost by the pressure of press and propaganda. And then it all got out of hand when winter set in early while at the same time their army from the far east made an appearance in front of our weakened divisions. We all struggle to explain this outright failure of those 'above' in any other way. And what else could one call it but outright 'failure'. Hopefully, hopefully I am looking too much at the black side!

These days we old fighters have ample time to sit together and babble about this messy situation. After the chaotic days around the new year, I have ended up here with the remains of II. Abteilung, currently led by Theo Langenbruch. I am trying to recover a bit from the days of our infantry-style deployment in December. But that will turn sour should all the staff of AOK 9, which has fled from Rhev, try to spread out here in the village. Even Oberst Koll can't do much for us any more as he himself has been burdened with the role of traffic officer and, with all his staff, is going to be deployed at Smolensk. In addition we are supposed to be some kind of palace guard for the staff of AOK 3 (Pz.Gr.3), guard company together with the remains of 4/65. OLt. Baum, however, who used to command 4/65 and is well connected, is being transferred to the Führer-Begleit-Bataillon to take command of its tank company. He is the same kind of character as Zangenmeister. The other companies of 65 under Hauptmann Anhalt have been deployed to build supply roads and bunker lines.

As it turns out, there haven't been so many missing as we thought when we were at Timkowo at New Year. Now there are fifteen men classed as missing; they are unlikely to return. The company had fourteen dead, most of whom could not be buried, and the graves of those who were, are now in Russian hands since Birkino on the Lama and Anamino have been given up. Funny, as it's just there where they started building a line of bunkers. It's pathetic! Where do they want to stop the Russians now once they are past those villages? They can just march through now where there is no more line to stop them. I can't follow it all any more.

The Russians here in the villages are disgusting and evil-minded. For the whole time they have been friendly like kittens and now when they realise that the Russians have been reinforced for the defence of Moscow the rabble is getting brazen. Well, I can change my tune as well! Time to introduce a tougher regime for the scum.

Wittkötter is lying here on a stretcher next to me and is groaning in his sleep. In his dreams he might still be fighting the Russians at Timkowo. I think I am also groaning in my sleep again, just as I did after 4 October. But that is just a reaction of my nerves. A Prussian Leutnant has to carry on regardless. Nerves? That's something only people like Zangenmeister and Neuling can afford to have. And even if Hille tried to pull himself together, that was over in Timkowo. Bleeding hell, I mustn't even think about those hours in the Kolkhoz any more. Of our nineteen men inside the barn in Timkowo, only seven managed to come out alive and of those several were wounded: Hase (lower arm shattered), Unteroffizier Weil shot through both of his legs and both hands frozen. Weskamp was hit by a splinter and is in hospital. Only Röhlen, Liesmann, Lauer and I were unscathed. I am amazed that Liesmann had already felt the dramatic events on the morning of the New Year approaching while we were sitting around that tiny fire in the bitter cold night. Bechberger, Dreher, Endermann, Heine – what has become of them? I hope they didn't have a fate like that Unteroffizier of 106.ID who had been so kind to take us in, and who was shot off the sledge the following morning, and was left lying in the snow with freezing arms and legs! I hope that all our wounded got out of Birkino. The hours we spent there in Timkowo, which we were to hold at all cost, are now again passing by my mind's eye in all their horrible detail. The night in the potato cellar, the artillery and mortar fire, the Russian tanks which were running in exactly those conditions which we use as an excuse for the failure of our own buckets. The terrible yelling of the attacking Russians, the many unburied fallen, the wounded at the collection points, Werner, shot through the lung, lying on the sled next to the dead man. The moment when Stabsarzt Prinz and the Oberfeldwebel medic Schulenburg were trying to skedaddle. Esser and Geyer, my dear good Corporals! Both wounded but facing the enemy until their final moment came. Laufenberg, who ran out to recover the wounded infantrymen on the corner of the barn and was shot through the head while doing so. That's the end of it – I hope, for the men and myself, hours such as this will never, never come again.

Fallen in Timkowo, 6 kilometres west of Volokolamsk, 30 December 1941 to 1 January 1942

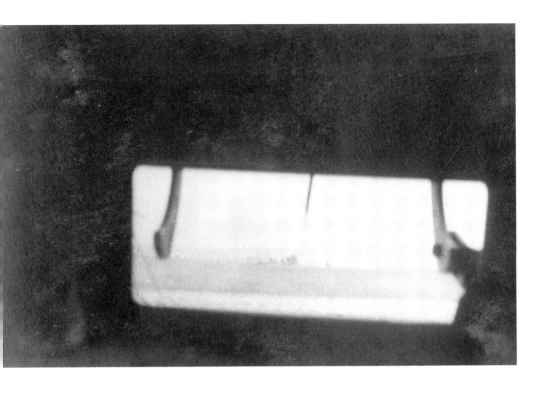

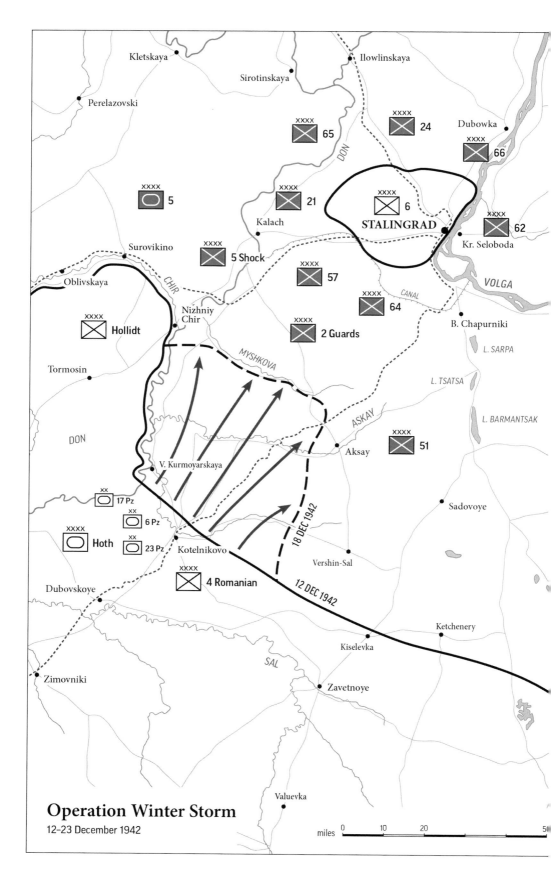

Kletskaya
Sirotinskaya
Ilowlinskaya
Perelazovski
XXXX 65
XXXX 24
Dubowka
XXXX 66
DON
XXXX 5
XXXX 21
XXXX 6
STALINGRAD
XXXX 62
Kalach
Kr. Seloboda
Surovikino
XXXX 5 Shock
XXXX 57
VOLGA
Oblivskaya
CHIR
Nizhniy Chir
CANAL
XXXX 64
B. Chapurniki
XXXX Hollidt
MYSHKOVA
2 Guards
L. SARPA
Tormosin
L. TSATSA
ASKAY
L. BARMANTSAK
DON
XXXX 51
V. Kurmoyarskaya
Aksay
Sadovoye
XX 17 Pz
XX 6 Pz
18 DEC 1942
Hoth
XX 23 Pz
Kotelnikovo
Dubovskoye
XXXX 4 Romanian
Vershin-Sal
12 DEC 1942
Ketchenery
Zimovniki
Kiselevka
SAL
Zavetnoye
Valuevka

Operation Winter Storm
12–23 December 1942

miles 0   10   20   5[0]

4

15 November 1942–8 April 1943

Rested and refitted, 6. Panzer-Division, and with it Panzer-Regiment 11, returned to Russia on 14 November 1942. On 19 November, the Soviets launched 'Operation Uranus', a two-pronged attack targeting the Romanian armies protecting the long flanks of 6th Army at Stalingrad, cutting off and surrounding it in and around the ruined city. To relieve the trapped German troops, an attack was to be launched by Army Group Don under Erich von Manstein, whose most powerful armoured formation was the newly arrived 6. Panzer-Division. Immediately after his arrival at Kotelnikovo, Sander – now commanding officer of 5th Company – was thrown into action, fighting side by side with one of Germany's most famous 'Panzer aces', Major Franz Bäke, then in command of I. Abteilung/Panzer-Regiment 11 in an action which led to the destruction of a mixed brigade of Soviet armour and cavalry. 'Unternehmen Wintergewitter' ('Operation Winter Storm') commenced on 12 December 1942 and within the first two days, with close support by the Luftwaffe, 6. Panzer-Division made good progress, but found resistance continually stiffening. With its modern tank complement of the latest Panzer IIIs, long-barrelled Panzer IVs and attached assault guns, the division was as powerful as it could be. The problem was that the three German divisions launching the 'winter storm' were facing not ten to twenty motorised Russian divisions as it had been expected, but fifty to sixty. In total the Red Army had 185 major combat formations between the German front line and the Stalingrad pocket. And while a Russian division was much inferior to a German one, at least on paper, in the winter of 1942 that was no longer always the reality. On 15 December the German thrust towards Stalingrad had ground to a halt, yet nevertheless 6. Panzer-Division had advanced to within 48 kilometres of the city. The German army had lost the numbers game and the fate of the 6th Army had been sealed. On 23 December the division withdrew to face yet another Soviet offensive between the Don and the Donets where, after breaking through the lines of the Italian 8th Army, the Red Army now threatened to cut off all German forces south of the Don and in the Caucasus. Within four weeks Panzer-Regiment 11 had again lost the bulk of its tanks plus thirty-five officers and 400 men. Wounded by a shell splinter on 28/29 December, Oberleutnant Sander left Panzer-Regiment 11 forever. A long period of hospitalisation and convalescence followed, from which he would ultimately be discharged as unfit for frontline service.

* * *

Sunday, 15 November 1942, from Brittany towards the east

My beloved Ruth!
Now during the journey it is a bit difficult to write you a letter, but it's possible to make entries into the diary, as the handwriting doesn't matter that much. In the late evenings, when you and Ernst and Mother sit at the dining table, at which I have sat so often in those wonderful hours in which we were together, then you can – one day – read this little diary. It will show you that all my thoughts and all my longing are with you in every hour, on every day and in every night. Here I want to tell you about all my experiences, and when you read these lines, then you can be with me in thought. The description of the sights we see over here and of the fighting we experience and of the tribulations we face here can thus be a bridge on which our thoughts can meet. In the letters we write, we can focus on our own little selves and all immediate and domestic matters.

We left Guer yesterday night. We were lucky and could already load up in the evening. The 6th Company of the Abteilung was less lucky and had to manoeuvre their heavy tanks onto the transport carriages in the dark. We have received extra-wide winter tracks for our tanks and had to manhandle the heavy things onto the railway carriage ourselves. A devil of a job, which took us a long time to finish. And then, once we arrive at our destination and when the snow lies thick enough, then we still have to mount these wide tracks! This will be another bone-breaking job.

Yesterday night we had one last good meal in the Hotel de la Gare in Guer! The day before that we had another good meal in Loutehel, where we were billeted. A proper portion of 'Pommfritz' with meat was our farewell to the pleasures of France. In the future we'll be back to the days of 'Matka u tebya yest' kartoshka?' and if the Matka then has some potatoes to fill the stomachs of the hungry Landsers will need to be seen. In Russia, even fried potatoes are a delicacy.

Let me tell you about what happened after saying farewell to you in Berlin. Just like you, I was somehow relieved that there was so little time for goodbyes at the station. In all the haste one didn't really realise the whole tragedy of separating. Only when I sat in the train did it dawn on me and I closed my eyes to somehow be together with you. The wheels rolled, but their clatter sounded only your name: 'My Ruth, my Ruth, my Ruth'. But I pulled myself together when I thought about how strong you had been, my dear, little soldier's wife! I am so proud of you.

Monday, 16 November 1942, Montherme

Just now, at 8.30 a.m., we are crossing the Meuse next to the village where our regiment crossed the river during the fighting in 1940. The landscape here is absolutely beautiful with the gently winding river and the hills covered with red autumn leaves. How I long for peace and the chance to witness such beauty with my beloved wife and maybe our future child. I pray that fate will give our souls the chance to live and to experience these sights without haste, without the sound of fighting and without the struggle and striving.

When I was a boy, on a trip with our school, I stared into the green waters of this river and I saw the fortresses of Namur and Huy. I couldn't get enough of all this beauty then, and now we just race past it in the blink of an eye.

There was a bit more time to enjoy the landscape of Brittany with its hedgerows and oaks, with the beautiful chateaus and the spectacular coastline. I am happy about this, for should I reach an old age and am not able to travel any more then I will have nice memories to look back on, and surely these memories will also serve me well when we're fighting and marching through the endless, snow-covered Russian plains.

Small grey villages nestle into the river valley and just now I can see the ruins of an old castle on a hill on the other side – a miracle of a distant past which saw just as much bitter fighting as our generation is experiencing today. It is the fate of the little human race to eternally fight and murder one another. And if I did not understand this principle, then I would be a pacifist.

11.00

Now on Belgian territory. There are bunkers here and a small bridge with the ruins of some houses next to it. The river is flanked on both sides by towering mountains, steep rock slopes of the kind in which the Belgian king, who deeply loved this landscape, had a climbing accident.

These slopes alone form a strong obstacle for any army, but if crowned by bunkers they become near impregnable. But our troops manage to cross the river and overcome these obstacles! And we'll finish our other tasks as well until the Endsieg is ours! We must and we will bring the Russian to his knees!

This is the Meuse valley, which I once crossed on a bicycle when I was still in the boy scouts. From Ypres to Kortrijk to Waterloo, and from there to Namur, where I arrived on a national holiday and was then locked up in a police station because my visa had expired.

Having passed Huy, we are now in the industrial heart of Belgium and when one looks out of the window one doesn't look into the face of the Walloon, or the Belgian, no – one looks into the international mask of the industrial worker. It has sharp and hard features and is worn by people of that kind all over the world. It reflects hardship, sorrow, hard labour, misery and hunger, and rarely do the eyes radiate happiness; instead they radiate the hate the modern slave feels towards all those who use and exploit him. In Russia I will see the mask everywhere. In Berlin one can still find them too, whereas in the rest of the Reich that mask of misery has mostly fallen since 1933. Here in the Belgian coal basin hardship and misery are visible even in the faces of the children who come to the windows of the train to beg.

Thursday, 19 November 1942, near Warsaw

We washed ourselves thoroughly before we had a good breakfast and then cleaned the rail cabin. Now everyone is pursuing their own individual interests. Young Lindenau, the General's son, is busy trying to accelerate the growth of facial hair by shaving quite enthusiastically, while Peter and I have opened a bottle of Benediktiner. This would have been wonderful to have at New Year's Eve! I wonder where I will be at the end of this year. But away with such thoughts – they lead to nothing.

When we were driving through Warsaw, one could still see a lot of traces of the fighting of 1939. All the houses are terribly grey and dirty and windows are crudely shut with cardboard and wood. The gardens are neglected, the streets full of dirt and rubbish – the Polish capital is decaying. The houses seemed to have been built without any system, some big places have been built right in the middle of some fields. All in American style, with flat roofs, while further beyond there are small Panje huts built of sheet metal and wood. Elsewhere there are houses which have been built before the World War. There is damage from shell impacts on many walls, which haven't been repaired yet. In that respect, Warsaw doesn't look much different from Thorn. There the Vistula is just as neglected and silted up. In general, however, the Vistula presents a pretty and picturesque picture no matter if it is near Warsaw, Thorn, Graudenz and in the area of Danzig. There is something a bit sad and maybe also 'hard' about this landscape.

We are not stopping in Warsaw but in the Praga suburbs, far outside at a large marshalling yard. There is also a train full of Luftwaffe infantry, but Herbert wasn't among them. We are rolling on. At a station in front of Warsaw, policemen are searching the Poles for hoarded wares and during the brief time we are standing there, they do find quite a lot. A woman is crying and beseeching one of the policemen: 'Nie Ma nie marsch do domu!' – if only there was no war and we'd be spared such scenes.

12.00
We are now rolling through an area where the soil is sandy and not very fertile. Most houses are small and made of wood. The only non-inflammable elements are the tin roofs and the stone chimneys. That is the same in Russia.

– Sometimes there are old men and boys with the typical square Polish caps – most trees have lost their leaves and lakes and rivers are covered with a thin layer of ice. About half of the journey lies behind us now. Once at Kharkov we need to march another 300 kilometres ourselves. It's already -25° C there, and there is lots of snow. I suppose we can mount our winter tracks as soon as we arrive.

There is a small Polish village here. It could well be Russian, with its little wooden houses.

Something is being loaded onto the train here. Probably just potatoes. The farmers are bringing them on long Panje carts which are sagging in the middle even though they are not too heavily loaded. They are all wearing high-shafted boots, thick jackets and caps, sometimes made of lambskin. There are large fuel depots here at the side of the tracks, and I just learned that this is Lidice. Lots of bomb craters here as well, not filled in since the beginning of the war.

15.00

Still standing in the marshalling yard at Lidice. We ate something and then got out of the train to catch some fresh air, but the warm railway compartment is still the best and most comfortable place to be. Waffen-Oberfeldwebel Raab lost our communal washing bowl at the station in Warsaw. He had gone forward to the locomotive to collect some water when the train suddenly started rolling. He ran back to the carriage, but had to drop the bowl in order to use his hands to pull himself in. Now we have to wash ourselves directly at the big tap behind the locomotive.

Peter Schulz is playing cards again. I can't understand his devotion to card games. It's pure fanaticism, nothing else. With the same kind of enthusiasm Unterfeldwebel Krone has climbed back into the uppermost luggage net. Shame that he is too senior to be put on aircraft observation duty and too young to act as duty officer. The man has to be kept busy, to take his mind off being homesick. I loathe such people, who are completely unable to pull themselves together and continue yammering for days on end. Come what may, that man needs to see some combat – that will do him the world of good. And if he bottles out there, well, then he can get his punishment for his cowardly behaviour in the previous year at the same time. I wonder when Schmauch, Opetz and Bartneck will come up with some kind of minor ailment.

There are several trains here in Lidice because somewhere the tracks have been blown up by partisans, who seem to be very lively in the Smolensk area. I suppose that the Luftwaffe infantry on the neighbouring trains will be deployed against them. Now then – we seem to be rolling again, the locomotive has blown its whistle. And off we go – into the approaching darkness, further and further east. It is only evening, but the glowing blood-red disc of the sun is already setting in the west. My mind is wandering west as well, to my beloved little wife. It is she who gives meaning to my existence out here.

Saturday, 21 November 1942

We are slowly rolling towards Minsk. The locomotive is now pushing a wagon loaded with sand – if the tracks are mined, it won't be the locomotive which will hit the first mine. Yesterday, when we had to wait at the station for so long, it was because a train full of soldiers on leave had been derailed by a mine.

Stolpce and Negoreloe, places in eastern Poland close to the old Russian border. Bomb craters and destroyed buildings on the sides of the tracks. A brief stop at a station which has been completely destroyed. A Russian ammunition train on the neighbouring track – destroyed by our Stukas in the previous year. The whole area is littered with iron scrap and wheels. This must once have been an infernal place. In front of the village the wreck of a Russian T-26 tank. We have finished quite a few of them off ourselves.

Tonight we'll have been on the tracks for a week already. It is snowing outside, but it's nice and warm inside the wagon where, as usual, I am sitting on my own. Our oil lantern is dangling from the luggage net, next to cameras, pistols, canteens, machine pistols in their carrying bags and wet towels hung up to dry. The luggage nets themselves are full of clothing brushes, drinking cups, maps, books, butter tins, packs of cigarettes and bread. Without doubt very picturesque, but a bit more order wouldn't hurt. Yesterday night Peter and I sat together in the flickering light of the lantern and talked about the war. Peter asked me why I was waging war – what I was fighting for. It is difficult to give a clear and simple answer to that question and it is one I begrudge answering.

13.00

We have passed through Minsk and are now rolling through the real, old Russia. From a distance Minsk is a city like all the others. Small, wooden houses with some big concrete structures between them. There seems to be more industry here than in Wjasma. Many of the big, modern, concrete structures seem to have burned out and even though the city is covered with a thin layer of snow, it does still look dirty. Russian prisoners are being guarded by Russians. The guards can also be Poles, but they are probably White Russians. They are of a different type from the East Russians with their Asian look. In Ukraine it is Russians who are deployed against the partisans. We'll surely be seeing some of those brothers sooner or later. Even though we are heading south, the land still looks wintery.

Saturday, 22 November 1942

One thing I can say: this was a short Saturday! It is only 15.00, but the sun has disappeared and it is getting dark. We are now rolling through the huge forests near Bryansk. The big towering clouds above trees in the west are glowing in the dark red hue. It all looks unreal somehow, but it radiates the kind of mood that makes one understand the old and tragic songs of longing in Russian folklore.

Having stopped briefly in Bryansk, we are now rolling towards Orel–Kursk–Kharkov. Outside there is more and more snow. I doubt that we will really be held in reserve until the coming spring, as the Russians are already pushing mightily at Voronezh in order to pinch off the salient at Stalingrad. They are also attacking from the south – but let them attack; this winter they are not going to surprise us like they did last year.

So far we have been lucky as far as the mines are concerned, but we passed several derailed and burned-out wagons along the route. The few line-keeper's lodges have been turned into little fortresses with thick walls made of wood and sand and surrounded by barbed-wire barriers. They are proper little bunkers and we are passing one every 1,000 metres or so.

Tuesday, 23 November 1942, south of Kursk

Just now we stopped at Kursk before turning south towards Kharkov. We have made good progress in the previous few days. We are classed as a rapid transport and wherever we stop we get prioritised treatment. Peter Schulz is sitting opposite and is trying hard to learn some Russian. I realise that I have not forgotten as much as I thought I had.

At the moment we are all hoping that we don't have to unload the train during the night, but if we continue at this speed, that is exactly what is going to happen. The tracks here are lined with snow fences and all the trees are decorated with a frosty layer of ice – it's all very much like Christmas. But what does that matter out here? Nothing. No matter how pretty something looks – it is war and we have to harden our hearts.

The houses here between Kursk and Kharkov are different from those at the central front and nothing like the grand, wooden constructs we have seen at Leningrad. Here they are small, one or two rooms, plastered with mud and often painted white. Most of the time the roofs are covered with straw. There are also far fewer trees here and instead of the large pine and fir forests, the land is covered with brushwood and a few deciduous trees. During the night it has become foggy and currently visibility is well below 500 metres. That is good for us, however, as it makes us hard to spot from the air. I have had more than enough of it during the air raid at Chartres and I certainly don't need any more of that. There will be enough excitement for everyone once we reach our destination. I still can't believe how quickly this week on the tracks passed by.

Tuesday, 24 November 1942, Belgorod station

12.00: We are still waiting to continue our journey. The mood isn't too bad, probably because there is a chance that we'll be deployed immediately.

The waiting would only have ruined our nerves. We are all amazed by the Russian women, who just came on board as passengers and are now travelling on an open wagon without any protection from the cold and the heavy snowfall. In Kharkov they'll be buying salt, a kilo for 7.50 RM, which they will then sell at Kursk and the surrounding areas for 20 RM. In Kursk they'll be buying rye and other grain which they will sell for profit elsewhere. With enormous sacks hanging over their shoulders, they trudge along the train just to climb onto a wagon at a moment when the Russian railwaymen are not watching. The Russians are all wearing many layers of warm clothing and are better used to the cold than we are, and I guess a little bit of a draughty ride on a train doesn't bother them too much.

We are now noticeably getting further south and even though everything is covered with a layer of snow, the temperature is rising. It is much warmer than it was at Bryansk. The fog is still protecting us from nasty surprises from the air. We have now been waiting for half a day.

This morning the commander of our Abteilung, Major Dr Bäke, joined us on our train. We had overtaken the staff at Brest and the commander had travelled on another train together with our General. Ours will now be the first Panzer company to disembark and I hope we'll be the first to get to grips with the enemy. Then our well-rested forces can show their full potential. The latest gossip is that we'll drive via Rostov on the Don.

Wednesday, 25 November 1942, Sloviansk

I am not feeling well. My stomach is giving me trouble.

17.00: I fasted until now and just had a bite of crispbread and a little bit of red wine. I am now feeling a bit better.

Peter and Lindenau have now abducted our commander and thus gained a third man to play skat with, and I have stayed in the compartment, so I am not alone any more. I have to admit that I quite enjoy being alone and undisturbed. We have just rolled past huge coking plants and on the other side there are giant grain silos, more than we have the entire port of Hamburg.

Thursday, 26 November 1942, Stalino region

I am feeling better again. Some coal pills and mulled wine have worked miracles. Last night the locomotive broke down and we had to wait on the tracks for quite some time. It was getting really cold, so I used my coat as an additional blanket. When we were rolling again, now pulled by three locomotives, and it was slowly getting warmer, it was as comfortable as if I was lying in the best of feather-beds. All through the night and at dawn we have rolled past enormous industrial plants, all of which are of no use to the Soviets any more. But to be honest, not of any use for us either, as they had all been destroyed by our bombs, just like most of the stations we rolled past. What better way to illustrate the futility of war.

We are now rolling through an area which shows the traces of bitter fighting. Anti-tank trenches are stretching into the distance with earthen bunkers and deep wire entanglements behind them. Scrap iron, burned-out tank hulks and wrecked artillery pieces stand alongside the tracks and in abandoned fighting positions.

They are transporting us pretty far south. There is heavy fighting at Stalingrad these days, so that is where we will be deployed – probably too late to strike any decisive blows ourselves, but there will be more than enough work for us too. The Russians are far from being beaten and are attacking all along the front with undiminished force. My estimate is that the Russians can still produce 600–800 tanks per month and in addition to that they have all the equipment which the Americans are shipping in via Murmansk and Arkhangelsk. I am of the opinion that we in Germany are probably producing 200–300 tanks per month. Of those a good part is going to Africa, where they will face whatever the English and Americans can produce.

Which will be victorious? Will it be spirit, morale and skill, or will it be the mass of their industrial output and their human resources? We'll see the result of that equation very soon – probably already next year. If the latter wins, it is over for us. Or maybe we will have to learn to organise a mass of the kind we are facing here in Russia.

We are rolling across endless plains and I am told that they used to grow wheat, maize and sunflowers here. Sometimes the tip of a high slag heap can be seen in the distance, the same kind we have seen in Belgium. There is value in and below that soil. If only we weren't rolling through this country to kill and destroy, but to rebuild, work and grow! If only the workers of all the warring sides would unite to work peacefully together for their own and for their children's future. Will we always stand against and never with one another? I hope I will live to see that day and that I'll be able to tell my children about all this.

Saturday, 28 November 1942, Rostov on the Don

Our train is slowly rolling up a slope alongside the Don river towards the city. The locomotive is hissing and puffing white smoke. If we don't reach the peak of this hill anytime soon, we will come to a complete stop.

We are now rolling into Rostov, for which we have fought so hard in spring and during the previous year. Since Novotscherkask our journey has taken us past a long line of destroyed freight trains. Hundreds of locomotives and thousands of railway wagons lined up behind one another. All destroyed by our bombing. It seems that they had planned to move the contents of all the factories in the Donez basin into the area east of the Volga. The wagons are loaded with electric engines, transmissions, steam boilers, pipes, turning lathes, industrial drills – too much to list it all here. In between are several ammunition transports which have blown up and shells and shell casings litter the area for miles around. An unforgettable, but also tragic scene.

We have entered a station. There are Romanians on the other side of the platform. Our Landsers are taunting them and making derogatory remarks. Some of them are shouting over in German, which makes our guys fall silent. There are Volksdeutsche among them who are enquiring where we are from and where we are going. While they are standing there talking to us, the Romanian train suddenly pulls out of the station, leaving the men behind. Their reaction is unexpected: 'Ah well, never mind!' The Romanians are wearing tall lambskin caps and in general look like Gypsies. Only rarely does one encounter one who is washed and clean. There are some Italian air force members here too. They leave a reasonably good impression.

We have just stood at Rostov main station, but now we are already across the Don. We crossed a gigantic bridge and from up there we had an excellent view across the city. A gigantic city with many large high-rise buildings. But most of the houses are destroyed. Burned out, collapsed during the bombings or shot up in some way or another. Lots of buildings are in an American style – rough, but enormous constructions. Many bomb craters around the bridge. On the other side of the Don lies Bataysk, and the land between Rostov and that town is a waterlogged floodplain, which is crossed by several bridges and criss-crossed by dams. A road is running alongside the railway, covered by an endless column of transport lorries bringing fuel and ammunition to the front. Next to the road, on both sides, large numbers of Russians on foot, pushing carts or on small Panje carts. They are carrying or transporting large sacks of grain which they have acquired in Ukraine and which they now hope to barter for salt.

By now our train is carrying more Russian women and men than German soldiers. A few are looking quite clean, but most look scruffy, dirty and unkempt. A woman has just walked through the carriage. She probably did her shopping in Rostov. Over her shoulder she was carrying a new broom on the end of which she had affixed a large wire sieve. Around her neck and hanging down her back she wore one of those pretty Ukrainian shawls. There was something wrapped into her bright-red headscarf which tightened the fabric and made its woven pattern stand out. We have taken up a Romanian Hauptmann and a few of his men as passengers, but in general we are all out of sorts with the Romanians after the recent developments in the Don salient.

Watching the traffic here is highly interesting. There are large numbers of Russian soldiers running around. They are armed with rifles and are wearing white armbands with the word 'Militia' written on them – these mark them as our fraternity brothers. All Russians in our employment are wearing these white armbands. Many have bags hung over their shoulders in which they transport their rations – similar to the way the French soldiers wore them. They are mostly stout fellows. I can't help noticing how the women here seem to be doing jobs which in Germany would be done by a strong man. For example, there are lots of girls and women swinging heavy pickaxes on construction sites alongside the railway. Some are carrying heavy railroad ties and planks, while others are working on the roads with shovels and picks. Since my days in Thorn, I have noticed that Slavic women do hard physical labour.

The train is now filling with comrades of other service branches who are hitching a ride to get back to their own units. There is no regular railway traffic to the Stalino region and from about here the hitchhiking begins. We have kicked all the Russians off the baggage wagons and now they are filled with German troops. All of them from frontline units – that is easy to tell by the casual manner in which they approach us officers. An old Landser knows exactly how far he can go and with whom.

I forgot to mention that we all had a wonderful bath in the morning. Inside an old railway repair shop at Novotscherkask station, the duty Unteroffizier had found a shower room with warm water and we took the opportunity to order the entire company to shower and that had worked very well. Putting on fresh underwear afterwards, we all felt fresh as new-born babies. I wonder how long that will have to last now. Tomorrow we will arrive at our destination and unload the train. Then the journey will be over and we'll have to say goodbye to our comfortable wagon. When, how and where will we go back in the other direction?

At the moment Lindenau and the old officer candidate Feldwebel Fink, the brother of our Fink of Abteilung 65, are playing chess. I am sure that Fink, with his thirty years, had hoped for a different employment than this one. The good doctor would have liked to become an officer at court and was not at all delighted when instead he was transferred into our fighting unit. Let's see how the brother will conduct himself. He might make a good soldier and he is not stupid.

We don't know when we'll continue our journey yet. Down here, everything is always either completely undecided or top secret. There is Flak fire above Rostov. Probably a Russian reconnaissance flyer. No one really knows what the situation in the Don salient is like and the army communique remains silent about it. Of course there are plenty of rumours making the rounds, but what is true and what is not, nobody knows. These latrine rumours are unavoidable; first one might believe them, then there will be arguing of some kind or another and then they are forgotten quickly enough. The candle here in the bottle doesn't give enough light. So

I'd better come to a stop now, I don't want to ruin my eyes. Tomorrow life will get a bit more interesting again.

On the other side some Unteroffiziere have started firing up our little wood stove. There is so much smoke now that I can hardly see anything.

But the smoke has made it better and has woken me up a little, so I can spend a bit more time with myself and my diary. There is not much else to do. There is just enough light to play cards or to have a snooze – reading only damages the eyes.

En route from Novotscherkask to Rostov we drove along a tributary river of the Don. On one side endless columns of destroyed vehicles and on the other side the glistening river. A man wearing a red cap and riding a sinewy horse is racing alongside us on the opposite bank. I have seen him before, not too long ago. He is the commander of the Russian militia who, in their silly uniforms, had been exercising on the station when our train pulled in. He has the appearance and looks of an old tsarist officer or NCO and he has got snow-white hair. He looks good in his uniform and his command style was not to be sneezed at. He counted out the steps of his men while they were doing a turn – 'Raz, dva, tri, chetyre!' and his colourful lot of White Russians marched along in good order. We all looked at what they were doing. Our allies, brothers at arms! – I could not help but think that we need many more of their kind. If we had 60,000 Circassians and Kalmyks to deploy on anti-partisan duties and to build bridges and railway lines, then that alone would free manpower for four good divisions, an entire corps. We Germans need human resources! A lot of them! I think that at the beginning we didn't do enough to get the Russian prisoners on our side and we didn't have enough food to feed those millions anyway. The newly conquered territories had yielded very little, because the Jews and the commissars destroyed everything of use. Not an ideal situation. But that is an unfruitful subject, so enough of that. How are our comrades who have been taken prisoner faring? That is the fundamental question.

Sunday, 29 November 1942, first of Advent, Kalmyk steppe, north-east of Bataysk/Don

Today is the third Sunday we have spent on rails. We are traversing the Kalmyk steppe. Lenin, the founder of the Soviet Union, originated from this area of Russia. If one wants to get a sense of endless vastness, then one has to come here. The steppe stretches as far as the eyes can see, now and then interrupted by a strung-out village. It is around those villages where one can spot the only trees in that landscape. If one can call them trees, because in fact they are just bushes, a bit taller than a man. The houses around which they are growing are not much taller. It is striking that, starting in Ukraine, the houses are that small. I guess that this is based on the fact that the people find it hard to source building materials. That is far easier in the forested terrain around Leningrad and in the central sector. In house construction in north and central Russia the logs are stacked horizontally upon one another. Here, however, the logs are placed next to one another vertically. The walls created that way are then covered with thin, wooden boards which are then smeared with a mixture of mud and straw. Once that has dried, the walls are limewashed.

We are now pulling into a station which belongs to a very modern village. This must be a good place to work. There is an enormous grain silo alongside the railway. On its sides there are several large suction lifters through which the grain can be sucked directly from the trains into the silo. All along the railway line there are large storage halls and wind-powered water pumps on tall steel frames.

Monday, 30 November 1942, Proletarskaya station

I saw lots of interesting things today. We stopped at Salsk and next to us there were several large armoured trains which we had captured from the Russians and which were now being stored there. They will be of great use in anti-partisan operations in the middle sector. The huge shoeboxes would also be useful in Serbia where the partisan situation is similar to that in central Russia. Sadly I was just in the process of washing and shaving when

I saw the trains, and I did not have the time to explore them on the inside. One locomotive had the name 'Kosomolz' painted on its side and the others too all bore similar names of the Red Revolution.

There are lots of Romanians here, all of whom have run away. Hundreds of them are queuing at our distribution points begging for some food. The bastards should be at the front. Now it is the German troops who can clean up for them.

I have been talking to a Volksdeutscher soldier of the Romanian army. He is a 32-year-old mechanic and a Banat Swabian. Before losing their Transylvanian territory Romania had a population of 18 million. In today's territory there are only 12 million, but still Romania has raised an army of 2 million men. Before the loss of Transylvania there were – according to Romanian official counts – 800,000 to 900,000 Germans living there. Now, the German foreign office counts over 1 million Germans, mainly living in the Banat.

There is a Romanian army in the northern part of the great bend of the Danube and another here in the Kalmyk steppe. The Romanian rankers get a monthly pay of 1 mark! Yes – one whole mark! Their families and relatives at home get no support at all. The Romanian superiors may beat and flog their men! The officers are supplied by their own kitchen, as are the NCOs. The enlisted men get an inedible gruel cooked up from what the officers and NCOs don't want to eat. But all that has improved somewhat now that they regularly receive German rations.

Romanian companies march everywhere accompanied by a retinue of chickens, geese, sheep, goats and cattle and as they have no regular motor pools they make use of any kind of vehicle they can get their hands on. A Romanian marching column is a sight to behold.

Even though this Volksdeutscher is a mechanic, he has been pressed into service in a horse hospital! There are 450 men serving in it and seventy of them are German. They arrived two weeks ago in covered railway freight wagons. Their commander and several of his leading officers and officials have brought their women and their own livestock with them! And just because of that, sixty-eight enlisted men had to cram into each of the wagons. His younger brother has crossed over into German territory and is now serving in a German pioneer unit.

I asked him if they could at least get items from the sutler. He didn't even know what that was! When I explained that we got items of individual request, like tobacco and extra rations, he told me that they had been promised to get three blank postcards per head. Three whole postcards! But they had never arrived.

The mood among the Romanians had once been quite good, he told me. But now they feel betrayed by their officers. He told me that in the unit in which one of his friends served, the commander and all the officers had driven away three days before the great Russian attack on 20 November. And they didn't drive west – they drove east! When the Russians attacked, not a single officer had been there to take charge. Ammunition hadn't been delivered and to make the few rounds they had count, their NCOs had told them to let the Russians come as close as possible before opening fire. Yet when the Russians came close they had decided to throw away their rifles and to run away.

Stories like that can be heard everywhere. At Obliaskaya, unarmed and dishevelled hordes of fleeing Romanian troops had blown up their ammunition stores and torched their fuel supplies. When they reached the Luftwaffe airfield there, a Romanian Major had ordered his men to burn a German supply train loaded with fuel. A Hauptmann of the Luftwaffe had to shoot the Romanian officer with his pistol. Here, near the town, a Romanian Major had struck a German Feldwebel with his riding whip. The German Feldwebel had then shot the Romanian officer dead. The case was brought in front of the liaison staff, where the Romanians got a rollicking and the Feldwebel went free. One does not beat a German.

The Romanians steal everything that isn't nailed to the floor. Bruno Gerlach, the Kriegsverwaltungsrat serving with the liaison staff, told me that he had been washing himself in a hospital train near Rostov. While he was doing so, he had placed his golden wristwatch on the bench next to him. A Romanian Leutnant and an Oberleutnant had walked past and when they had gone, so had Gerlach's watch. Gerlach, serving in an influential position, confronted the two officers, who denied everything. And after an official complaint to their superiors the statement remained the same – a Romanian officer does not steal. A great joke!

The train has stopped. Seems to have run out of steam. I lit a candle and popped it into the neck of an empty cognac bottle. That way I can continue to write a little bit longer. Next to me sits a young Leutnant of the infantry who is playing the harmonica. The sun has gone down, but there is still an orange glow over the horizon which is now slowly turning grey and thus melts the sky and the earth into one another. The light of the candle is quite cosy, so I have shifted into a more comfortable position while listening to the Leutnant from Düsseldorf who elicits one sad melody after the other from his harmonica.

He is not much more than a big boy, not dissimilar to our Lindenau, but maybe a bit more impertinent. My first impression was confirmed when I got to chat with him and learned that he had done some monkey business in his replacement unit in Belgium and had been punished with confinement to his room. He had found his old and stubborn company commander sitting in the officers' mess drinking champagne and had asked him if the acidity of the champagne was beneficial to his calcified brain. A bit later he had been sent to Namur and to get there he had been given a staff car which he had promptly rammed into a tree. That had been the final nail in the coffin, and he had been sent east. But now he has been driving around for sixteen days because the unit he has been transferred to is surrounded in Stalingrad. Many German soldiers here wander around in a similar manner and for the same reason.

The Romanians make use of all that chaos and withdraw across the Don towards the rear. The Gypsies have the discipline of a herd of pigs. Up until now the cooperation has been tolerable, but now they have suddenly turned feral. Their two armies here in the east are said to have suffered 200,000 casualties – all dead, not including the wounded. The Russians drop flyers over their lines which tell them to desert to the Russian side and that their rewards will be far higher if they fight at the side of the English and the Russians. But they are not defecting, they are just running away.

The Romanian soldiers are wearing tall fur caps, and I asked the Volksdeutsche why he wasn't wearing one. He told me that the Romanians don't feel well when they can't wear such caps, but that they were unpopular among the Germans. I noticed that his boots were shiny and clean and that his puttees were expertly bound. That is something you don't see when looking at the swineherds – which is the German soldier's nickname for the Romanians. The Romanian NCOs look just as bad as their men and the officers are absolutely repulsive. They are of the same type and character as was once represented by the Polish intelligentsia. Gallasch, who is forced to work with them in the liaison staff, tells me that the Romanian officers would never eat anything prepared by the field kitchens and that they were only satisfied if they could eat their three-course dinner and dessert at a table covered with a white table cloth. One will never find a Romanian officer in the furthermost positions fighting with the men. The Volksdeutsche confirmed that to me.

I asked him what he thought about resettlement, to the old Wathegau or to West Prussia. He replied that his ancestors had come to the Banat from the Schwarzwald and Alsace-Lorraine more than three centuries ago. They had worked the ground hard and it was only quite recently that it had reached maximum fertility. In East Germany, or elsewhere, they would have to get used to a new climate, new soil and would have to start all over.

War administrator Gallasch from Koblenz is a good Christian and academic, an eager hunter with his own hunting grounds in the Westerwald, blessed with five children, over 50 years old and very talkative, a bit of a pessimist and ideally suited to detect all the world's wickedness – this good gentleman has just sat down opposite me and is performing some cartomancy. He is laying out the cards in two rows and then removes all those which are lying next to, above or below one of equal value. If he lays out the whole deck without being able to remove any cards, it is a sign of bad luck. If he however manages to remove the whole deck by laying it out five times – then, he says, all of us will be going home soon. He does it to calm his nerves and I understand that. But the dear old administrator is talking too much without thinking about the corrosive character some of his words have.

It is now 5 p.m. and it has been pitch black outside for more than an hour. After the card laying, Gallasch entertained us with some card tricks, then we started telling one another some ancient jokes of Tünnes and Schäl* which, partially modernised and well prepared, caused great amusement and laughter, as did some more contemporary ones involving Jupp Göbbels.

Herr Schmitz is now telling us about his hunting experiences in the east. He claims to have seen and hunted wolves! I don't believe a word of that. I have seen none from the Volga–Moscow Canal all the way to the Dnieper.

---

* Fictional comedic characters, first introduced by a Cologne puppetry-theatre in 1803, who embody typical traits of Cologne people.

There were no wolves at Leningrad either and I have spent lots of time in deep forests, in all weathers and all hours of the day and night. Schmitz, however, has mostly spent his time in some staff orderly rooms. But at least they seem to have loads of time to spare. At one point someone really needs to clear out among them. Always out on the hunt, or on some major action with the aim of buying poultry or other supplies and never in any serious situation, but on the other hand Herr Schmitz swears like a trooper about those who remain in some comfy post in the Heimat. He is far better off where he is, but he doesn't seem to realise that. The Eternal Philistine.

In the morning we passed through the chain of lakes along the Manych River. The Russians dammed the river and the water reached the railway embankment which we were crossing. A gigantic scene and great natural spectacle, in front of which we humans looked small as ants.

Combat report of 5./Pz.11 of 3 December 1942

The company was deployed together with 1./Pz.11 under Hauptmann Hoffmeyer in the village of Nagolnij near Kotelnikovo. On Monday, 30 November, we disembarked at Ssemitschnaya, a little dump along the railroad from Rostov to Stalingrad. After the long train journey we started making the lorries frost-proof by using the supplied winter kits. The maintenance platoon was hard at work when at 11.00 a messenger of the armoured personnel carrier battalion arrived with orders for me to call the battalion staff. Of course the telephone was not working and a call to Kotelnikovo was impossible. The Adjutant of Hauptmann Küppers then informed me that the General had called and that we were to make ourselves ready for action. As our Hauptmann Hoffmeyer was away on a reconnaissance patrol, I was called to attend a staff briefing, where the Ia would brief us. The company, however, was to prepare to move out as soon as possible. I could do no more than to alert our group, which I was in command of during the absence of Hauptmann Bauer, and in which Peter Schulz was in command of 1st Platoon. This caused a great amount of excitement.

I ordered my luggage to be packed and then Krosch, the driver of the commander's Kübelwagen, took me and Voss to Kotelnikovo to see Oberst

Unrein, the commander of Panzergrenadier-Regiment 4 at the Staff HQ. There was a lot of commotion and lively activity there and it was clear that something big was on the programme. I reported that the company was preparing the vehicles and was waiting for further orders. I received a bollocking for not calling in via the phone.

After my return I led my company from Nagolnij to Kotelnikovo, where Hauptmann Hoffmeyer, who had by then returned from the General, led me to the western exit of the village. He was sitting on the turret of my Panzer III, Peter Schulz climbed up too, and he started explaining the tactical situation to us. This wasn't easy in the lashing wind and the dense snowfall which turned the map soaking wet. He informed us that in the morning the Russians had attacked the village of Pokhlebin and had overrun it. Most of the companies and all of our batteries there had fallen into Russian hands. Now the Russians were preparing to attack Kotelnikovo. They had at least twenty tanks and a large amount of cavalry – long columns of infantry were following behind them. Our SPW* battalion and our two companies were now tasked to annihilate these Russian forces.

At 13.30 our companies and the SPW assembled on the steppe to counter-attack. It was a glorious and great sight to behold. More than thirty armoured giants and behind them about 100 armoured personnel carriers carrying our grenadiers, racing across the snow-covered plain. My heart was beating with excitement – with a powerful force such as this our attack could only be crowned with success. Hauptmann Hoffmeyer was an excellent leader. The ideal man to lead an attack such as this, one where speed and flexibility mattered. We drove across the airfield and the road from Kotelnikovo to Mayorovskiy. In the distance we could see an assembly of vehicles on a hill – most probably Russian tanks.

In a hollow on our left more vehicles. A brief halt to observe to all sides through the binoculars, but damn – the snowfall is so heavy that we can hardly see anything. As such there is only one thing to do – a quick rush forward towards the enemy. Via the radio I tell Schulz, Opetz and Matussek to keep their eyes open and to report to me should they see anything.

---

* SPW: Schützenpanzerwagen, lit: 'armoured infantry vehicle', half-tracked Sd.Kfz. 251 or Sd.Kfz. 250 armoured personnel carriers.

I can now see that the vehicles on the hill are reversing into a reverse-slope position. Only two are not moving and remain where they are and these two are T-34s. The vehicles on our left seem to be German lorries and reconnaissance cars, no danger from that side – so the charge continues, directly towards the hill via the left flank, but for Hoffmeyer it suddenly comes to a halt in front of a balka,* half filled with water and as such an absolutely impassable barrier for their tanks. And at that moment, the dance begins. We are about 2,000 metres away from the Russians, who suddenly open up with all barrels – that was an eerie feeling after that peaceful time in France, where the only fire we had encountered had come in the form of a few puny rounds fired on exercise. A tracer shell howls over the turret and impacts the ground behind us. The brothers are serious. Time to get into a position where we can return fire!

Our artillery fires smoke into the Russian positions to at least give us some protection, but the wind is so strong that it is quickly dispersed and the Reds continue to give us hell. I order the 7.5-cm armed vehicles to fire a few smoke rounds directly at the Russian guns, but that also fails to have any effect. We have to get closer. Hoffmeyer's company should be attacking from the left now, but they are still blocked off by the balka. In the withering Russian fire, which was increasing in intensity, my men advanced a bit slower and I, instead of advancing with them, was slightly ahead, but in the heat of the moment I failed to realise this. But we had to close in, as our 5-cm guns could do no harm to the Russians at a range of 1,500 to 2,000 metres. But then we also ran into a branch of the same balka which was holding Hoffmeyer's company, which forced us to turn right where, driving alongside the rainwater ditch, we tried to find a place to get across.

Making a brief halt, we tried to take out one of the T-34s on the hill, but it was a futile gesture. I was still in the lead vehicle, and was spurring the platoons of Opetz and Schulz on to catch up with me. More and more shells were now slamming into the ground around my vehicle and suddenly, before the others had a chance to catch up with me, there was a mighty

---

* A Russian and Ukrainian term for a valley with grassy slopes around a dry or seasonal watercourse. In the steppe regions, a balka is a dried-up riverbed; it has a gently concave bottom, often without a pronounced channel, the slopes are convex, smoothly turning into watersheds.

blow against the tank, which ground to a halt. 'We've been hit!' Müller, the driver, shouted through my earpiece. Even in that situation I couldn't help grinning when I heard his comical Thuringian accent. A shell had broken our left track. We had been lucky and as we could still shoot, I gave the order to continue firing. I looked around to see what the rest of the company was doing and at precisely that moment the tank closest to me, Unteroffizier Steffen's 502, took a hit on its turret. I saw the crew bailing out just seconds before a second shell hit fuel canisters on the engine deck, ripping them open and dowsing the rear of the tank and its engine in flames. I could not see if all of them had managed to get out, but some men threw themselves into cover in the steppe.

I was boiling with anger. Being shot to bits at a range of 1,500 metres and no chance to retaliate with our 5-cm guns – it was enough to make you have kittens. Immobilised, my backing vehicle was destroyed, so I gave command of the company to Peter Schulz. He, however, together with the rest of his platoon, had driven to the far right to find a crossing over the balka. As I couldn't link up with Hoffmeyer on my left, I got out and sprinted the short distance towards him on foot, where I climbed up his tank to talk to him. Just then several shells detonated nearby and my head was nearly taken off by splinters. I clambered down again as quickly as I could, calling up to him instead and letting him know what had happened. I then enquired how he planned to handle this situation. My company was to give covering fire while our forces would fall back on Mayorovskiy. Once that had been done, I was to catch up with them there. We would then launch another attack from that new position on the following day. I got on board Opetz's tank and ordered Peter Schulz's platoon to fall back to the road leading to Mayorovskiy. I couldn't hear a word of what he was saying in reply, but he seemed to have understood and the vehicles started to move out. I remained behind the balka with the platoons of Matussek and Opetz until nightfall. In the meantime, Feldwebel Matussek and his men had assisted my crew to fix the track – tremendous work and right next to Steffen's brightly burning tank which, at regular intervals, was shaken by the force of exploding ammunition. Once they had done so we got back into my tank and joined the others on the road. Now and then I fired a signal flare, as it was nearly impossible to see in the snowfall and the pitch-black night. Reaching the far end of the balka, we managed to cross over all its small extensions before getting back on the road. On the way we overtook some of the grenadiers in their armoured half-tracks. At the end of the balka we had crossed an old weak bridge, which was the spot which we should have attacked over.

In the village we received orders from Oberst Zollenkopf and then, after waiting for a quite a while, rolled through the village and, leaning against its outermost houses, formed a half-circle for a defence supported by company Schäfer of the SPW battalion. In the village I found accommodation for me and my crew in a small house next to the one in which Hauptmann Schäfer was billeted. After a briefing by Oberst Zollenkopf I returned to my quarters and was soon fast asleep, guarded by a plethora of religious icons, who guaranteed that I wouldn't be tormented by my dreams.

4 December 1942

We have slept long, or what we call 'long' over here; after all, the sun rises about two hours earlier than it does in Germany. At 10 a.m. my company stood assembled on the hill north-west of Mayorovskiy, ready to attack Pokhlebin together with Abteilung Bäke. Right in the middle of the steppe Hoffmeyer was guarding the ford towards Kotelnikovo. He would attack the village from the south-east, while we would attack with Bäke from the west, and Abteilung Löwe – which had only just arrived – from the north-west. We had to wait for a while until the company was fully assembled for the attack. In the meantime I and the other platoon leaders had walked to the top of the hill where we could see smoke rising from distant Pokhlebin, which was being pounded by our artillery. From there we could also see long columns of Russians pulling out of the village and even some artillery pieces towed by camels. Several armoured cars of our reconnaissance platoon had driven towards them and were now taking these columns under fire.

To support them, I sent out 1st Platoon under Peter Schulz and to support them, I detached one of our heavy 7.5-cm armed tanks. My plan was to reunite with them once the attack on Pokhlebin had been launched. I sent out the platoon on my own personal responsibility, as Hauptmann

Hagenmeister, the most senior officer at the moment (before the arrival of Bäke), was not willing to take action. Before Schulz and his men had the chance to roll out, however, the three armoured cars were already coming back. Our company had to wait until 12.00 before it could attack, as we had to wait until Major Löwe had deployed and was in command of all the grenadiers and of Küpper's SPW battalion. When we finally rolled out across the frozen ground, I was on the right and – being the closest to Pokhlebin village – the most threatened flank. Staring through my binoculars I spot a battery of Russian guns on a rise south of Pokhlebin. They were firing on Hoffmeyer's company and were now turning their attention to us. As such my first objective had to be to suppress or, if possible, to annihilate this threat on our right flank.

We were 3,000 metres away and already the Russians were sending shell after shell towards us. Out Panzer IIIs were in no position to fire back and the commanders had more than enough work trying not to take any damage. In this instance we had good experiences with our long-barrelled Panzer IVs. While we were rolling towards the Russian battery positions, Wilhelm, Dr Fink and the other 'heavy' commanders gave us fire support. Via the radio Opetz informed me about his concerns and decided not to get any closer, yet we did have to get closer than 2,000 metres to do damage to the Russian guns. To save shells, we started engaging the larger targets with machine guns and that was done with good effect. The Russians began to pack in and were trying to change positions. All our fire didn't stop them from pulling most of their guns into the cover in the balkas. On ultra-shortwave radio we had long lost contact with our Abteilung so I sent one tank equipped with a transmitter, commanded by Oberfeldwebel Funk, towards the area where the other companies had disappeared from sight. He soon returned to us, however, and brought the news that Major Bäke and the companies of Hagemeister and Ranzinger were engaged in heavy combat with the Russian defenders in the village. They had all suffered casualties already.

Later on that evening I learned that we had fired 500 shells and 81,500 machine-gun rounds on the Russian batteries on the hill. With this enormous ammunition expenditure we had suppressed the Russians enough to stop them engaging our tanks fighting at the village. And they couldn't run away either as we had mown down most of the horse teams which tried to pull out the guns. Yet one team of six horses broke down in our fire, and the Russians limbered up on one of the guns. Accompanied by eight or ten Russian soldiers on foot, it was then set in motion towards the brightly burning village. I ordered the whole company to open fire on that gun. But the Russians, as if chased by the devil, continued on their course even though several of their number were shot down. The six horses, as if by a miracle, just raced on unhurt. They were heading straight towards a ravine and I felt my anger rising at the prospect that these stubborn Russians would quite probably be getting away. And indeed, after a few more seconds they had disappeared from sight. The same happened with a little car that drove up the hill towards the guns. Before we knew what was happening, a number of Russians had jumped out of their foxholes and had hitched one of the guns to the little American-made car which then raced towards the same ravine. We could see how our shells and machine-gun rounds impacted right next to it, but it raced on and then disappeared. Just like the horse-drawn gun, it didn't come out the other end – that much we could see. Soon we had silenced all the other guns. Only on the slope behind the batteries, from where Hauptmann Hoffmeyer's tanks with their white camouflage paint were now approaching towards us across the steppe, a few anti-tank guns were still firing on us.

While we were busy firing on these anti-tank guns, Major Bäke drove over to us in his tank and because we had no radio connection to him, I climbed out of my turret, and fetched new orders crouching on the engine deck of his vehicle. Not the best of places to have a sit-down while the Russians are firing with mortar shells. These are harmless for a tank and for those inside them, but now splinters were whizzing past my head and some smacked into the steel plates of Bäke's tank. I jumped down as quickly as possible and ran back across the field. My felt boots, however, were way too large and I had to slow down as otherwise they would have flown off my feet. It's a frightening experience when mortar and artillery shells are exploding and there is no protective armour plate between oneself and the splinters, and several times I was forced to throw myself down – a different way to express the principle of blood and soil.

When I was back in my tank I took a deep breath. On the slope in the distance we could still see the muzzle flashes of the Russian anti-tank guns, but the artillery had stopped firing. And then the order through the radio to launch one final attack on the village. Major Löwe and his group were already less than 400 metres away from the village. With Matussek's platoon on the right wing of the company, we raced towards the burning village of Pokhlebin, while the AT guns on the hill were still banging away but hitting nothing. The whole slope was still crawling with Russian infantry, in foxholes and trenches, which still kept firing on us. In front of the village I. and II. Abteilung had linked up and as such there was a large group of tanks assembled in front. I had no intention of adding to the numbers of this mess and led my lot towards the right where we found a small bridge across the ravine which allowed us to get to the other side where Hoffmeyer had attacked and where the fuel canisters carried by the tanks of 1st Company had been set on fire by the Russian infantry.

My intention was to scare the Russians out of their holes. The bridge was blocked by a lorry, which Leutnant Naumann of the light platoon of I. Abteilung pushed off with his tank. Everywhere on the slope and in the ditches were Russians who, now that we made an appearance, got on their feet and raised their hands. There were horses everywhere, some alive, most dead. Some were Cossack horses, with swords hanging from the saddles. Horses stood grazing peacefully between the bodies of Russian soldiers killed in the fighting. Dead bodies were everywhere, but also carts loaded with ammunition and equipment. There were anti-tank guns, small American cars, lorries and artillery pieces. We took a whole lot of Russians prisoner near the bridge and they were escorted away by Opetz, whose tank had suffered a barrel burst during the fighting and couldn't participate in any further operations. Some of my commanders stood in their turrets and kept the Russians in check with machine pistols, while others were throwing hand grenades into the trenches to rouse more of the brothers out of their hiding places. I really wanted to avoid any casualties among my men and gave them a right bollocking, as there were more than enough grenadiers around to do that job.

Then I started to engage the Russians on the opposite bank, but as soon as I had roused some out of their holes, there were more of them elsewhere. More and more of them, as far as the eye could see. Together with the grenadiers, we rounded up about 300 more, many of whom kept firing on us until the last moment. We then took all their felt boots, all German uniform parts they were wearing, and all the caps with earflaps we could find – all of which would be very useful for our company. We had assembled quite a pile of that stuff – enough to make sure that every man would have a warm cap the coming winter. We had captured at least a full battalion of these earth-brown fellows. For myself I got a Cossack's sword, which I affixed to the back of the tank, and a few leather straps which always come in handy when things need to be stored away. It was about 2 p.m., which meant that the sun would go down in about thirty minutes. We really had to hurry to get back to our old quarters. I couldn't reach the Abteilung via the radio and when we finally rolled south-west, back to where we had come from, it was nearly getting dark. We heard about our achievements and learned that we had annihilated an entire corps of cavalry. We had captured over 800 horses, 30 camels and taken more than 1,600 prisoners. Huge amounts of equipment, weapons and ammunition had fallen into our hands. The enemy dead were so numerous that they couldn't be counted.

After the battle a number of Landsers had come out of the houses dressed in Russian clothes; they had hidden since the Russians had captured the village on 3 December. After the battle the mood among the men was excellent. There had been no casualties in our company except Dygutsch who had broken his arm. Hauptmann Hagemeister, however, had been badly wounded and several men of his company had been killed. Ranzinger's company had lost several tanks. I am not sure how many men they lost, but compared to our successes, casualties will not be very high.

After a long drive we arrived back at Mayorovskiy and moved into our old quarters in the west of the village. During the debriefing with Oberst Zollenkopf I spoke to Bäke, who told me that Ranzinger had won himself the Iron Cross, 1st Class. My company was subordinated to Oberst Zollenkopf and would remain in a defensive posture in the west of the village. I had to find my way through the village in the pitch-black night. No moonlight and with the heavy fog forming over the steppes one could hardly see anything at all. In addition all the village roads had been turned into a quagmire by all the vehicles that had passed through.

As such, all the members of Zollenkopf's staff didn't even bother to leave their house, even if they had to take a piss. Instead they were pissing standing in the door, letting their water splash into the mud at the bottom of the stairs. Later that night I was called over by Zollenkopf who had received a call from the commander of the Schützen-Regiment.

Wednesday, 9 December 1942, Kotelnikovo

Together with the armoured half-tracks we have now conducted two attacks. The armoured attack of 3 December was my first since October 1941 when we were in the middle sector near Wjasma. My leadership brought success, which makes me very happy. On the evening after that first attack we moved into a defensive position which we held together with Oberleutnant Schäfer of the SPW battalion. We were lucky as the night remained quiet and later found a house with a room all for myself. The corners of the room with its dark wooden floor and walls were decorated with paintings of the saints and on the table and the shelves stood wooden crucifixes. The icons were all very old and larger than those we had encountered in north and central Russia. All kinds of saints are displayed on these wooden boards which have been covered with plaster, gilded with gold foil and then painted. The gold foil is mainly used to depict the large, glistening halos. They are mostly covered with old Russian lettering in some kind of symbolic writing. Similar to the IHS and the earlier IX monogram of the ancient Greek Christians.

18.45: Peter Schulz should be returning soon. He is with the Oberst at the moment from which he will receive his EK1. I recommended him for that award a few days ago. Ranzinger got his immediately after the fighting; I could congratulate him on the same evening at Zollenkopf's command post. I had to wait three months for mine after having been recommended for it.

Now then, Schulz has been here. I did indeed manage to surprise him. He came in and then put a bottle of champagne on the table. He knew that I put him in for the EK1 and that I already knew all about it. Leutnant Lindner of the company baggage train joined us and we then emptied the bottle together. Well, as leader of the baggage train, he can't earn any laurels. He will have to make do with that Romanian award the Oberst put him in for. It's supposed to be a very colourful one.

Another occurrence: Voss is an Unteroffizier again! Friedrich Wilhelm Voss, once the driver of Hauptmann Hille after he had been demoted and sentenced to two years' imprisonment by the court martial of our division. When we advanced through Lithuania he had, being completely pissed, checked the contents of the fuel tank of his motorbike with the help of a burning match. With that he had endangered the life of another Unteroffizier who had been riding on his bike and the punishment had been quite hard. Now, after he had proved himself at the front, I wrote an appeal to the court in which I asked to reinstate his rank and waive the outstanding punishment, and that had worked. He is wearing his braid again, and that makes me very happy indeed because I like Voss – he was my driver last year when I acted as a courier for the Ib who, at that time and due to the terrible road conditions, had been the most important man of the division. After he had been demoted, Voss became the driver of my Kübelwagen. Yes, yes – never join a drinking competition with Lithuanians, and when it's dark outside never try to illuminate the inside of your motorbike's fuel tank with a burning match! For the resulting fireworks, he got much more than the three days of arrest he had hoped for. But now he is an Unteroffizier again, and yesterday he penned a joyful letter to his young wife. Probably the first time I have seen him write a lengthy letter like this.

Up until now we have been subordinated to Oberst Zollenkopf, whom we got to know during the 1941 campaign. He is as cool as a cucumber and has often had command battlegroups on the Leningrad front and the central sector. He has never received the Knight's Cross, however, only the German Cross in Gold. They have treated him a bit shabbily in that respect, but that can happen to anyone out here.

I now have to report another little adventure which I experienced when we attempted to recover Rulisnski's body. The exploded tank was standing alongside a ravine near the road which lead from Kotelnikovo to Pokhlebin – 2 kilometres north of that road, to be precise. While we are approaching this location I spot movement on the slope. There are horses there, saddled and with swords hanging from their sides. When we are getting closer I jump off Klusen's half-track and walk towards the horses to find out what is happening there. In a crouch I get closer until I am about 50 metres away and only then do I realise that the whole area is full of dark-skinned, slant-eyed Cossacks! At first glance I count about twenty of them. I didn't see them at first, because they have tethered their horses and hunkered down at the stream, on the opposite bank. I am now closer to them than I am to my men in the half-track behind me. I turn around, shout, 'Everyone get out and arm yourself!' and throw myself into cover in a shallow depression in the ground. I then crawl closer towards the Russians and shout at them to drop their weapons and raise their hands. Fiddlesticks! They are swinging themselves into their saddles and taking their rifles off their shoulders. That is not good. Now I count over thirty of them, all armed and on horseback. We are only five men in an old half-track tractor. Not ideal odds. I had made my pistol ready but didn't open fire as I didn't want to 'annoy' these Cossacks more than they already were – I still wanted them to surrender. Not taking any risks, I ordered everyone to get back into the half-track and we drove back towards the road. In the meantime, the Cossack patrol had ridden off towards the north-east at breakneck speed. Five against thirty – that would have taken it a bit too far. And the Russians could decide to turn around.

As such we were glad when we saw the tank of Unteroffizier Picard on the road, waiting to be towed into the repair shop. It had suffered a barrel burst, but the machine guns were still working and with those we could have slaughtered the Russians. The tank had broken down in the water of the ford and could not be started again. There was no way we could chase the Russians, who we could see riding away across the ridgeline in the distance. A very picturesque scene, and a few minutes later they had disappeared from sight. We then drove to the destroyed tank and recovered our dead comrade, whom we then buried in the heroes' cemetery in Kotelnikovo, next to the grave of Hauptmann Hagemeister.

Thursday, 10 December 1942, Kotelnikovo

Today we are to fall back on Ssemitschnaya. It is now 10 a.m. and at 11.30 we are to move out, even though we had just got comfortable here after two nights. Our future quarters will be in a tiny village and we are supposed to move into the school building which also houses the hospital. So we are back on the road and we arrive in the dark again. And that is where the real trouble starts. The small tribulations of a company leader.

Today we learned the Russians have given up Budarka in the north-east and up at the Don they have cleared Wesely and Safronoff. I wonder what Timoschenko is planning. I can't make head or tail of it. The comrades at the Volga are deep in the shit. There will be no Christmas leave for them – that much is sure. I guess there won't be any for us either, but at least we are not surrounded and reliant on being supplied from the air.

Now I have fifteen vehicles in my company. Four of them are currently in the repair shop and the other eleven are fully operational. These consist of three 7.5-cm armed vehicles and eight armed with the long 5-cm gun. Not ideal, but now we must wage war with these machines; we did get by with less in previous years. Yesterday I took ten men to Pokhlebin, where we deinstalled the gun of Hauptmann Hagemeister's tank with the intention of installing it in Picard's tank. We captured two cows along the way which have been slaughtered by now. There is chaos in Pokhlebin. Our company alone has fired 500 shells and 21,350 machine-gun rounds to keep the artillery in check. That is quite a lot. The Russian had most excellent, interchangeable positions up there and as soon as we had identified a target by its muzzle flash, the Russians limbered up and – using the deep ravine – brought it to a different location. The Russian AT-gun crews – who we could see quite clearly through our binoculars – aimed their guns and fired, before jumping into foxholes which had been dug all around. Always quick enough to evade our retaliatory fire. All the Russian guns were excellently camouflaged and their small anti-tank guns in particular we found impossible to take out. They made the error, however, of opening fire on us too early. If they had waited until we had come within 500 or so metres of them, then they could have caught us in the flank. But being lucky has always been the most important thing at war. If one is not lucky, that will be the end. During the attack Peter Schulz got stuck in a rain-filled ditch. Bartneck's tank suffered an engine breakdown and Gefreiter Dygutsch, who had walked barefoot in France and had bent his watering can,* had suffered a broken arm after holding it too close to the gun deflector. That was – thank God – our only casualty that day.

---

* Slang phrase, meaning that he had had unprotected intercourse and caught an STD.

Friday, 11 December 1942, Ssemitschnaya school

Soon we'll be moving out to Kotelnikovo again. The company is already assembled. Peter Schulz and I are still sitting in our room while I am writing these lines into my diary. Thanks to the two cows we found in Pokhlebin, we had fried liver yesterday night. Having something as tasty as this after such a long time is a real treat – even though the flames of the big oven leaped into the pan and the liver was more black than brown in places, it tasted really good.

Back in Kotelnikovo, old quarters, near the road.

When we were rolling into Kotelnikovo some Russian bombers made an appearance and dropped their eggs on us. The Flak started firing like mad, but even though one of the seven Russian machines started trailing smoke, they all managed to get away.

'Kamerad, Kennst Du Knäckebrot?'* – at the moment this is the way the comrades greet one another. This is the slogan which is printed on the crispbread packages which form part of our rations here. In some of the platoons the men have memorised the entire advertising text on the package and then, out of fun, composed a tune to go with it. Now, whenever comrades meet one another or whenever a supply column or some other vehicle is pulling into the village, they are greeted by terrace songs and chants about crispbread. All the best funerals have humorous elements.

Now it is 14.30, and the sun is already setting. My tank crew is getting a new gunner – Unteroffizier Picard. He has just arrived with all his stuff. I was fed up with Bauckmann. He likes to bark, but doesn't know how to bite and worst of all, he never hits anything. In combat I don't have the time to correct and adjust the shots myself. I need a gunner who knows how to do the job on his own. Now Picard is standing here, lamenting the fact that his own tank had just been repaired when he was detached to join my crew. I can't help it now – he will soon have his own tank again. There will be plenty of vacancies should it kick off tomorrow.

---

* 'Comrade, do you know crispbread?'

I am waiting for the call from the Abteilung ordering me to join the briefing for tomorrow's attack. Are we really attacking towards Stalingrad? That would be a hard job indeed.

I can't stop thinking about our first two attacks here and how lucky we were. The muzzle flashes through the haze on the slope ahead – four, six, eight, sometimes all at once. Mortar shell impacts emit dark black clouds of smoke – having been fired over open sights, the Russian shells howl past in more or less the same moment in which one sees the muzzle flash. Kawham – kawham – kawham – in front of us, behind us, next to us – the hiss of the large splinters and the howl of the fuses and the projectile bases mixing into an unmelodic, threatening din.

I forgot to write about how – while clearing the foxholes after the attack – Scheunert and I took quite an unusual prisoner. A Russian soldier, but with nearly black skin and almond-shaped eyes and a long, seemingly Armenian skull shape. 'Otkuda ty rodom?' I asked him and he replied 'Turkmen!' The chap came from Turkmenistan! When we didn't shoot him, which he clearly expected us to do, he seemed to say a prayer in his language, but we didn't understand him and shoved him towards the other prisoners. Then he suddenly bent down and touched a lump of snow, admittedly I wasn't really taking notice of that, but suddenly he raised his hands and then lowered them again to cross them in front of his chest, and only when he then dropped down on his knees and then leaned forward to touch the ground with his brow, did I realise that we had captured a Muslim. For as long as I live I will not forget this scene. The man on his knees on the snow-covered ground, praying in the manner of his people, while around him the battle was still ongoing, taking no notice of the dead around him, the burning houses, hand grenades detonating nearby and the sharp reports of the guns of our tanks which still firing in front of the village. He prayed, probably to thank his god for having kept him alive.

Looking at the fact that we captured several camels and are facing troops from Mongolia and Turkmenistan, I guess we are not too far away from the real Asia.

There is a lovely smell of roast meat wafting through the room. Krosch, the driver of my Kübelwagen, has collected a large chunk of beef at the field kitchens and is currently preparing it for us. I hope he is quick enough

– there is a chance that we might have to leave in less than two hours. My wireless operator Steinbusch is having a discussion with Peter Schulz. The two big-mouths match one another well. Steinbusch, the electrical expert, and Schulz, a living pioneer fuse and master of explosives. Both are trying hard to make sure that the other understands that they know more about their respective fields than our good Lord himself. I am tired and in an hour, they will bore my pants off in yet another briefing. Good night!

12 December 1942

The whole company is assembled on the road to Kotelnikovo with the lead vehicles at the crossroads. The night is lively with activity, column upon column is hastening past our waiting men who are supposed to fall in line with the second wave. Nearby is a Romanian staff HQ and now and then, when illuminated by a badly screened-off vehicle, we can see the ghostly shapes of the Romanian sentries with their tall black fur caps. For fractions of a second the whitewashed walls of the Kalmyk houses flash up in the headlights of the passing vehicles and now and then one can see the divisional insignia on the back on the vehicle ahead, which happens when a driver, half asleep, get too close to the vehicle in front. A loud curse – a German sentry shouts: 'Lights out! Black out! Pull over to the right!' An army goes to battle.

We roll across the road which leads to Stalingrad and alongside which we are going to attack. Stalingrad! – What a name! Stalingrad on the Volga, this is what it's all about! More than 200,000 comrades are trapped there, and they are about to see that we have not forgotten them. Stalingrad! Since Adolf Hitler underlined that name in his speech, we have not forgotten it and now, at this hour, during our march into the assembly area, the name becomes a beacon. The comrades at the Volga rely on us. And it will be our men who, during this morning on which the first rays of the rising sun gently touch the endless steppe ahead of us, will launch the blow to bail them out, free them from the Russian grasp! In the previous winter, when we were deployed as infantry, we learned ourselves what it means to be cut off.

As we roll into the open steppe it is 4 a.m. In one hour the attack will begin. I see how some of the commanders, standing in the turret, are looking towards the sky. I follow their gaze and see a rain of falling stars, briefly lighting up and then going out. Some of these heralds of eternity are drawing a fiery tail. I start counting them and with every one, I wish that I will always have the power and strength to carry on until I am back home, with my first child, which my wife is pregnant with and which will be waiting for me in the Heimat. These falling stars, up there in the vast, black sky, show us once again how small and insignificant we are. In fact, each of us is comparable to such a little falling star coming out of the endless depths of space, briefly flashing up in a bright light only to disappear in endless darkness.

Some of us, however – only some of us – draw a long tail of fire behind them. The fire can be fuelled by their deeds in life, by their merit and its recognition and in death by the sorrow and grief of their friends, their comrades and the people they loved. But even this fire, as bright and hot as it may burn, will go out and disappear into nothingness. Maybe every falling star is the soul of a comrade, one who went before us and one who is now looking over us, or maybe they are the thoughts of our children and loved ones who remember us out here in this strange and foreign place, fighting against hordes of foes with Mongolian faces, speaking languages we don't understand. The thoughts of the women who hold us in loving memory and who will remember us when we fall in the fulfilment of our duty. This thought is strangely comforting as we roll into the blackness of the vast steppe ahead of us. The tank is swaying on its suspension and is softly rocking me back and forth, just like my thoughts are flicking back and forth – I have to pull myself out of it.

Does it make any sense to always try to evade and dodge one's inevitable fate? How often have I looked into the face of death right next to me. I am happy for all those comrades who have been proper men to the final minute of their lives. They have shown no doubt, no hesitation – we need to be like them. A coward will say, 'Pah, so what did he get from being brave? He is dead now and can take his courageous deeds with him to the grave!' – I, however, tell them this: 'One day your turn will come, and you will have nothing to show for yourself, no glory, no courage, nothing your comrades and brothers in arms will remember you by.' In addition, I have the responsibility for my men. None of them asked to be led by me. So I won't rest on my laurels at their cost, I will lead by example. I won't let them charge into certain death and I will do my utmost not to add to the ranks of the legions of the dead. I will protect them as best as I can. And then – when the dictates of the moment need to be obeyed, then they will follow me, to hell and back and no matter what the odds will be.

'Ever closer to death than the others, we knights in steely armour.'

I have let my mind drift and because of that we briefly lose our way, but that doesn't matter – we'll reach the assembly area well in time. We fuel up using the fuel canisters that each of our tank is carrying and chuck the empty containers to the side of the worn-out road. It is murderously cold and an evil wind is howling over the steppe. The frost of the previous days has refrozen the ground, which is now covered with a thin layer of glistening ice. That will be really great – we haven't mounted our ice cleats and the tracks have worn pretty smooth during all the exercises on the rocky ground of Brittany. They are lacking the grip required to manoeuvre properly on ground like this.

Major Löwe's I. Abteilung is going first, our II. Abteilung under Major Bäke is going second. The order is: regimental staff, 7th Company, staff II. Abteilung, 8th, 6th and 5th Company. I guess my lot was forming the rear as we already had two attacks under our belt. Behind us the observation vehicle of the light battery, then 3.7-cm Flak of the Lehr-Regiment, 10th Battery, then the regimental engineer Kärtgen with all the maintenance and repair services and the ambulances. Behind that the entire SPW battalion under Hauptmann Küppers, 2./SR114, the 6th and 9th Battery of Artillerie-Regiment 76, one battery 8.8-cm Flak with three guns, the 8th Battery of the Flak-Lehr-Regiment with 2-cm guns and behind them, the command Kübel.

Then followed the next group, commanded by none other than the 'Führer's Secret Weapon', Leutnant Walzer (can't be seen at the front) himself. He had the field kitchens, the lorries of the maintenance platoon, more Kübel and the dispatch riders.

The third group remained in Kotelnikovo, led by my comrade, Oberleutnant August Niemann, and consisting of support vehicles of II. Abteilung with the air defence platoon Pisug, fuel transports, supply column, paymaster's officer under Feldwebel Röchter, a Kfz.17 and the alternate crew, which hasn't been seen in our company since France, then the shoemaker and tailor and the whole baggage train. Also at the rear was the young Lindenau, the son of the General from Hamburg. He is so young that in France he was still eligible for an additional underage allowance and would have loved to be with us at the front. I can understand that, but we need reserves at the rear if one of us is taken out.

We followed behind Löwe, who had raced ahead and was already crawling up Hill 110.6 at Kurmojarksy. Our Abteilung had fanned out into a broad wedge, at the rear to the right 5th Company for flank protection. In my company Oberleutnant Peter Schulz led the 1st Platoon, Feldwebel Matussek 2nd Platoon and the always careful Stabsfeldwebel Opetz the 3rd Platoon.

Crossing 110.6 and a shallow balka, we drive towards 129.0, our first objective. We are to attack some foxholes defended by Russian infantry but on the wide hill platform they are impossible to detect. What I can see, however, is that even though our first tanks have managed to cross the balka, several tanks are still trying, again and again, to climb up the slippery, frozen slope. Damn! Are they drunk that they allow their tanks to slip sideways down the slope? They are lucky that none of their rollers have been bent or ripped off yet. To the devil with them, haven't they learned to drive!? As I am getting closer I can see the whole mess myself. The opposite bank is heavily frozen and the first tanks driving up it have compacted and polished the surface further. Now those following behind can't cross the glassy surface any more and either slide away backwards or to the side. There are even a couple of cases where some clod of a driver – and there are always some of those – leaves too little distance to the sliding tank in front. I can see at least two collisions caused in that manner. Soon there are a whole lot of tanks clumped together in front of the slope. I let my men wait until most of them have managed to climb up and then pick a spot, less steep, a bit further away. We then show the others how to do it; experience is everything. Climb down the one slope as slowly as possible in a low gear and then – with full throttle – up the opposite bank in the same gear and never, ever stop in between. The balkas here in the steppes of southern Russia form the same kind of tank obstacle which in the north and central sector was formed by those dense, primaeval forests. But a good tanker will always find a path – it just takes patience and experience.

Now that we have crossed that balka, we rush after the rest of our Abteilung. It is a breath-taking scene: how our tanks thunder across the steppe, how they race forward as if on attack exercise, and the whole experience grips me much more than any theatre play ever did. This here is real. This is our reality – a reality of steel and blood. The din of hundreds of engines fills the air, a sound drowning out the thundering hooves of the knights of old, louder than any battle in the ancient past. An armada of steel! What do we care for the Russians cowering in their foxholes up on the hill; we have long bypassed them. Our grenadiers, following behind on their armoured half-tracks, have already started to liquidate these pickets of the Red Army. We must go on, we are rolling to the Volga, we are rolling to Stalingrad, we are rushing through the icy wind howling over the steppe towards the railway line; to Grematschij!

Our I. Abteilung didn't even stop when it shot the Russian battery, the signalman's house and the Russian baggage trains to pieces. From the other side Romanian infantry attacks in wide lines – we have seen that picture often, but it has always been Russian infantry attacking in this manner. Wave after wave of infantry, rifles at the ready. We are passing fleeing Russian infantry and gun them down with our machine guns. Anyone who is not coming towards us with hands raced, is being mown down. But why waste ammunition on these few men, better to let them run. They will either starve or freeze in the steppe or surrender themselves at a later time. Two tanks of 6th Company have run over mines. I can see how the crews bail out, the wounded are recovered and the minefield is surveyed. We have lost two heavy tanks, at least for this attack. The Romanians have now reached the Russian positions, so our wounded are not in any danger of being attacked from the flank. The ambulances are following behind us. We must go on!

Via the radio I receive the order to count the spoils and the prisoners. I tell my radio operator to reply that we are not doing that – 'Leutnant Kallfelz is sorting this out.' He is just climbing back into his 2-cm tank and is waving over to me. Our medics are starting to work. More and more Romanians arrive who are herding the Russian prisoners together.

14 December 1942, Kalmyk steppe

We attack towards Point 147.0 about 3 kilometres west of Werchne Kumskji when the light platoon reports enemy armour, T-34s, near Sogotskot. We all mount up and behind our leader Dr Bäke west of the road to Salwiskij and then, turning east, in a broad wedge formation towards Sogotskot. With 5th and 6th Company in the lead, we traverse a hill, from the top of which we suddenly have an unexpected encounter. At a distance of about 1,000–1,100 metres, we can see a large assembly of armour, about forty tanks in total. They are painted white, like ours and through the binoculars I can clearly see that there are numbers painted onto the turrets. My commanders radio in – are these ours? Maybe Panzers of 23.Pz.Div.? Surely they are not Russians. Schulz and Matussek radio in: there are no cupolas on the turrets, the guns look a little bit too short. I am still not sure, but I do order everyone to pick a target and to make ready to fire on my command. The lead vehicles of our Abteilung are now about 700 metres away. If these were Russians they would long have opened fire on us. Or are they as uncertain about our identity as we are about theirs? The voice in my mind still tells me that these vehicles somehow look German. And then it all unfolded within minutes. Matussek's voice grates through my headphones: 'Some of them are turning their turrets' – and another voice, 'Achtung, two of them are heading towards us' – then a loud shout across the wavelength of the Abteilung: 'Russians! Fire!' In confirmation of this there are two muzzle flashes ahead as the two Russian tanks which are closest to us open fire. A shell is howling over our turret and I duck in and button up. They are only about 400 metres away now, but, firing on the move, they couldn't even hit a barn door.

And then the covering tanks of our companies open fire. The effect is spectacular. The two Russian T-34s are torn apart in violent explosions after a multitude of impacts. At ranges under 600 metres our long 5-cm guns are lethal even for a T-34 and with our higher rate of fire and our far superior training, the whole matter was over as quickly as it had begun. Half a dozen T-34s had turned around early trying to escape, but these were quickly finished off by the 7.5-cm tanks of the heavy company whose guns could crack them like a nut at ranges up to 1,200 metres. Standing in my turret about twenty minutes later I can see black smoke rising up from the wrecks of thirty-six

Russian tanks. At about 15.00 we headed back to Werchne Kumskij, where in the meantime another large group of Russian tanks, including several 52-ton giants, had attacked. They too had been repelled and eight had been destroyed. Our own losses have been low – two tanks lost and nine damaged, most of which will be operational again in a few days.

It is now 21.00 and I am sitting in the turret of my tank – I don't know what else to write. Outside the world seems to be on fire. Wherever one looks, the horizon is illuminated by the orange glow of countless fires. In the distance the faint rumble of artillery fire, while here – very close and at irregular intervals there is the rattle of machine-gun fire when one of our pickets sends a stream of tracer fire into the night. What they are firing on, I don't know. Probably the same apparitions which make dogs bark in the night. Or just to calm their own nerves and to reassure themselves with a display of their own power. I need to sleep now. *Gute Nacht.*

18.00, 28 December 1942, Tschernyschkow

I am sitting in the orderly room of the schoolhouse in Tschernyschkow. Outside temperatures have dropped to -25° to -30° and there is an icy wind howling from the east. Everything outside is covered in a layer of ice which is hard as crystal, but here in the house we are kept warm by two large, iron stoves. One needs to avoid sitting too close to the thin wooden walls and the windows, however, as they are still as cold as ice. It has been nearly two weeks since I last opened my diary and now that I sit here I don't know what to write. Finding the words to describe what I have experienced during that time – is that even possible? I don't know, but I will try – even if it's just to give myself some clarity and to unburden my mind. My head hurts and I am finding it hard to keep my eyes open, yet I can't find any sleep and if I do, the dreams come and I find no rest; even last time I had a full night's sleep was on 11 December.

The tank battle of Werchne Kumskji, the thrust towards Stalingrad, everything is over. No day on which there wasn't any fighting – light at first, so light that there was the faint hope that the Russians had not even realised that we were thrusting deep into their territory. An advance of nearly 40 kilometres in the first twenty-four hours. Then the inferno on Point 146.9 with our 5th Company attached in support of Gruppe Küper (II./SR114), the night march on Wassijewska and days of fighting in the bridgehead, low on fuel and nearly out of ammunition. Wassijewska, another name which has forever etched itself into my memory. Relentless Russian attacks, often at regimental strength and supported by armour, had to be repelled. No water, little food, the entire village in flames, our own casualties rising by the hour – attack and counter-attack, again and again. Only our Luftwaffe brought respite when our Ju 88s and Ju 87 dropped their eggs on the Reds.

Among those lost is Matussek, my dear old comrade and brother in arms; he was severely wounded when the shell of a T-34 penetrated the turret of his tank and the splinters injured him badly in the face, neck and shoulder. I saw how he bailed out of his stricken tank, but I could not aid him as I was myself engaged at the time. That was near Point 146.9 and we were attacked by fifteen or more T-34s who had opened up on us at long range and, even though they were firing on the move, one lucky shell found Matussek's tank. He lost one of his eyes; I don't know if he is still alive. The regiment now has only twenty-two operational tanks left. I am told that in total we have destroyed over 200 enemy tanks, but still they kept on coming.

On 25 December it was all over. We are hopelessly outnumbered and in many respects technically inferior. Superior leadership, morale and training alone is not sufficient without ammunition, fuel, food, water and spare parts. The Russians are wearing us down, the infantry here is already broken and the sole appearance of a Russian armoured car is enough to cause entire picket lines of tired, exhausted Landsers to fall back. It is, however, not over yet.

Tank alarm –

[*A day later Sander is wounded by AT-gun fire. A long period of hospitalisation follows, which is also documented in the form of a diary.*]

Friday, New Year, 1 January 1943, Taganrog

I am in the war hospital in Taganrog and have a shell splinter lodged in my right shin. I am lying here together with lots of wounded officers, several severe cases among them. I am feeling outrageously well, I just can't use my leg. I am lying in a white bed, I am washed, shaved and soon I'll be getting a good breakfast. Nina, the pretty Russian girl, is just washing the 'severe cases' and soon the doctor will be making his rounds. As such – that's it for now.

Saturday, 2 January 1943, war hospital, Taganrog

The doctors haven't made their round yet, so I have time to write a little more. The senior physician on duty is going the other way round today, so he'll be seeing me last. This morning they X-rayed me again and the nurse remarked that there seem to be no metal splinters in the leg any more, just bone splinters. I wonder what the doctor will tell me about that today. If that is true, then the metal splinter I have found in my boot and the one which I pulled out of the hole in my leg together with the shreds of my underpants must have been the only metal bits to get too close to my person in the iron-filled air. Maybe my wound isn't bad after all and I will be released sooner than I thought.

Yesterday I was given a small plywood board which, resting on my left knee, forms a sturdy base to write on. The sun is shining brightly through the large windows and outside one can see the frozen Sea of Azov glistening in the distance. It is very quiet here, only now and then the moans and cries of some of the badly wounded comrades break the silence. Some of them have terrible wounds – I am lucky that my 2-cm sized hole in the leg isn't giving me any serious trouble.

We are getting food now. Nina, the Russian girl, who had once been a student in the technical centre here in Taganrog, is serving us. She is a nimble and agile girl, while Fjodor – the general dogsbody – is the complete opposite. Is just slowly walking past my bed, in one hand a glass full of urine and in the other a glass of warm tea for another wounded comrade. Fjodor is a professional and as such he can carry two glasses at the same time and there is a good chance that he will not confuse the two. Sadly the 40-year-old illiterate and former collective farmer cares very little about hygiene; he is immune against even the nastiest dirt and grime and as such he is quite happy not to clean anything. It won't hurt him – but it might well hurt us!

Nurse Antonia has just come in. I christened her nurse Grethe before I knew her actual name, because she looks and sounds just like Grethe Weiser. I have noticed that the average nurse doesn't know a lot about medicine. But she has the key to the drug cabinet and access to the apple juice for the severely wounded. She can also tell the pills apart. She is from Saxony, by the way.

The bed on my left is occupied by an infantryman from Pomerania. Leutnant Krakow, 23 years old, battalion Adjutant and, more recently, company leader. A penetrating gunshot wound in each thigh. He seems to be a good soldier. His pain isn't too bad either. He is lying on his side and is reading a book. Must be quite an amusing one as he is regularly laughing out loud. He regularly does so when a badly wounded comrade is moaning in pain. This is painful for me to bear, but I can't blame him for it. It is not his fault and only I, in the bed next to him, can hear him laughing.

On my right side there lies the 21-year-old Leutnant Schmidt. One of the worst cases on this ward. He has been flown out of the Stalingrad cauldron on a He-111. Right shoulder, right arm and parts of his right side were completely squashed when a tank ran over him. His arm is gone now and his pain must be terrible. At the beginning he drank like a horse and soaked himself with juice, tea and coffee. He had lost a large amount of blood and the body needs lots of liquid to regenerate the blood. He is getting large amounts of painkillers and as such he has no appetite at all. Now he lies here, pale and with hollow cheeks and sunken eyes. With his current profile he is looking like a Jew. I have to get him the newspapers from the cupboard so he can read them to distract himself.

The doctor has told us that we – I and the comrade on my left – are on a list of those who will be transported back into the Heimat. The meals were again very good today!

Monday, 4 January 1943, Taganrog

Yesterday morning my leg was encased in a plaster cast. At the spot where the wound is, a piece has been cut out so the pus can flow out. To make sure that I don't move my injured leg at all they have plastered a wooden board horizontally into the bottom of the cast. Now I can't move at all any more. A dirty trick of the meanest kind! It makes me want to puke! In addition they have stretched the leg to assure that it is not healing in the wrong position – and because of that my knee and ankle have started hurting so badly that I find it hard to sleep at night. I have developed a fever, the wound is inflamed and is trying to discharge all the foreign matter inside it. It hurts like hell.

It is nearly midday now. Nina and Fjodor have gone to the kitchen to fetch lunch. Food is always good and there is plenty of it. In the morning we get bean coffee and jam sandwiches – as much of both as we want. For lunch there is always a good stew. As there are no potatoes, they cook it with rice or noodles. There is plenty of meat too. There is usually soup for dinner and pudding for dessert. In addition we get sandwiches, thick with butter, sausage or cheese. Again we can have as many of those as we like and I am sure that I have already gained some weight since I arrived here. Soon a proper hospital train is to transport us into the General Government. So we'll be out of the danger zone. Here in the hospital we have comrades from Stalingrad and the Caucasus. It seems that all the hospitals on the opposite side of the Sea of Azov up to the Caucasus are being evacuated. And it seems that supply depots and army offices towards the Caucasus up to beyond Rostov are also being withdrawn. I guess a Russian attack towards Rostov is expected and that has the potential to cut off everything between the city and the Caucasus.

On 2 January there was a report that we have taken 1 million prisoners in the great bend of the Don, and that we have destroyed such and such a number of enemy tanks. I don't believe any of that as currently it is our forces which have been surrounded there. There are several comrades here who have been evacuated from there and they have told me what is going on. Surely that report of 2 January is one of those collective results – all our successes of the previous year combined. I don't want to agitate anyone – no matter how much hot air Jupp Göbbels blows into these reports – but nowadays even the Wehrmachtsbericht isn't reliable any more. Or maybe we have to put more effort in to make it all more interesting again. We – or a different high command, one which deploys us in a more systematic manner than before. What else was our thrust on Stalingrad but a great failure? Why haven't they ordered SS-Reich, Brigade Hermann Göring and 7. Panzer-Division to attack together? Now they are following up and will be deployed piecemeal, just as we were. It makes me want to puke. But I am just a small man and maybe my horizon isn't wide enough to understand the actual, gigantic and enormous reasoning behind this total lack of plan. I need to change the subject.

Today we have eaten very well again and I have swallowed three pills against the pain and now find it somewhat easier to lie here. I will continue doing that in the future should the leg give me gyp again. Otherwise I am fine – looking forward to the hospital train.

Tuesday, 5 January 1943, Taganrog

A minute ago I went down to the operating room where they renewed my plaster. The wound hurts like hell since they have put that on. Last night I tried to help myself by taking more painkillers and sleeping pills – with success, but now I am feeling so sick that I could vomit. Somehow I have managed to get through that infernal night and the dreams. I don't know if I will ever be able to see snow as just that, or as something romantic like the snowfall at Christmas. Sledging children and snowball fights. The snow I dream about is black and red. There is a picture of that medic on his motorbike who tried to assist some of our wounded at Werchne Kumskji. The tank shell which hit him left no trace of the man. Just a black and dark brown furrow in soil below the snow cover and a corona of uniform scraps, bone, flesh and blood around it. The Russian soldier lying in the snow with mangled legs, his face contorted into a hate-filled, inhuman mask, firing round after round at my tank with his revolver. I didn't fire back. Standing in the open turret hatch I could only stare at him until he had spent all his rounds. Cursing, he then threw his revolver at us. It fell short. We left him there to die. I still dream of that terrible night in Timkowo on 31 December '41, the thump and crack of the mortar rounds, the tak-tak-tak-tak of the machine guns, the coarse howling and shouting of thousands of attacking Russians: 'Uraah! Uraah!' And then I see them falling again, again and again and their bodies are swallowed up by that terrible snow, poor Laufenberg, dear old Geyer, Esser, Schmid. My snow is red and black – but enough of that. The wound in my leg is seeping and is badly inflamed. I wonder how long it will go on like that. There are still scraps of my underpants and other bits of fabric in the wound and only when they have all oozed out is the whole thing going to heal.

Yesterday my old comrade and brother in arms Oberleutnant Schäfer of the armoured half-track battalion was brought here. Shot into the stomach with damage to the sigmoid colon. Soon the whole division will end up here. He said that there are hardly any vehicles left in his company either. He lies on the opposite side of the room and only spotted me in the morning. With him came a Leutnant of the Sturmgeschütz-Abteilung who told us that Bäke's Abteilung had destroyed thirty-seven Russian tanks in a single engagement. That is quite a feat and I am very pleased about it. One by one, so he told us, repaired tanks were coming back from the workshops, so that we could soon resume waging war. But I need to stop here, I am really not feeling very well. More later.

There was a heavy storm last night and the wind kept howling through the patched-up windows. It was arse-cold in the room and Fjodor, or 'Paulchen' as we call him, must have been freezing while he was sitting in his armchair on the night watch. I put my polo-neck jumper on which kept me warm quite nicely. It is a disgrace that our blankets and the bedding are full of lice and those who aren't tortured by these little pests are being bitten by bed bugs. I just hope that the bites don't cause us to fall sick with something – I have got more than enough to do with what I already have.

While I was down in the operating room I saw some severe cases waiting for surgery or to have their dressings changed. Horrible wounds and terrible suffering. I wish I could just keep it all away from me. I am sick of it all, so very sick and even Jupp and his lies can't change that any more.

Wednesday, 6 January, war hospital, Taganrog

Another new arrival in the night. A comrade who fought on the Terek and told us about the withdrawal there on the front. I must not indulge in guessing and hoping – yesterday we had a brief chat about the situation here in the East, but I have steered the conversation to a different, less dangerous subject. I only want to know what this war still holds in store for us. I am not relying on fortune-tellers, but on my own common sense and on what I can see with my own eyes. And I have seen a lot of things, and I thought about a lot of things – and it is not nice if one has to tell oneself again and again: 'Stop thinking about it! All will be good in the end.'

14.00: Even though I have swallowed a lot of pills the pain in the leg, and in the knee in particular, is still very bad. I am quite willing to bear it all if only I can still use my leg later! The Leutnant with his bloody leg stump, who lies right next to the wall on the opposite side, is suffering much more than I do. And the chap next to him, who has lost an eye and had his foot operated on for the fourth time now, is not much better off. The sight of them teaches me modesty and to stop moaning about my little problems. One of the medics has just turned up. We told him to get the war administrator up here to take a look at the hygiene situation in the room. Who knows if he'll turn up.

Now everyone is talking about whether we will be able to continue if the war drags on much longer and what we'll do if it suddenly comes to an end. No one seems to dare to think that thought through to the end.

Nurse 'Thermostatsia' has made an appearance – Lilo, the Russian girl with the admirably well-proportioned body, is taking our temperature. On her attractive body she is wearing a face which decent people would hide in their trouser pockets and her round skull is disfigured further by her short man's haircut. Something like that you can only see in Russia. She is entering our temperature in a zig-zag line on a board above our beds. These numbers will decide who will be allowed to return home and who will have to stay here and of course we all hope that we'll be fit enough to be transported to Germany. If only we could return to Germany – how wonderful the thought of not being surrounded by these ugly Russian types day after day.

The new comrade next to me is a pioneer. He has just shown me a medal which the Romanians have awarded to him. The Romanians award their trinkets in different classes, for the officers, the NCOs and the enlisted men. Comrade Vincke received his on a light blue ribbon.

Thursday, 7 January 1943, Taganrog

The previous night I slept without pain. I still woke up several times, but not because anything was hurting. I had to swallow sixteen pills – they call it a Eubasin shock-treatment. This is designed to combat inflammation and is quite brutal. I am feeling terribly sick. The wounded Oberarzt who shares our room says that this is not surprising after a drastic treatment like this. But it seems to have worked and I am more than happy about it.

Now it is 7 a.m. and I am washed, shaved, have a fresh haircut and hunted some lice.

10.15 now and I just had my bandages changed. If only I could get out of these halls of pain. Every day I witness scenes that make my blood run cold. This morning they carried me past my neighbour Schmidt who was getting a new plaster. His wounds, each about the size of a fist and oozing blood and pus, looked absolutely horrible. Next to me, on the other operating table, a man with more than a dozen bullet wounds in his body. They have just rolled him into our room – so far he hasn't said a word. Just now Krakow is raging. He is having a claustrophobic attack, triggered by all the Russians and Germans in the room. He tried to run out into the hallway. Now Antonia has given him an injection and he has calmed down. Next to him is the Leutnant of the Stug-Abteilung. In addition to his wounded thigh, his urethra has been cut by a splinter and he is in terrible pain.

Down in the operating room there was a new Oberstabsarzt, a professor of medicine and consulting physician who took a look at my leg and told me that I didn't need to worry. In about eight weeks or so it would all be healed up and I would not even have to go to Germany. My nerves were completely frazzled after this news. The leg is now hurting again. Inside the plaster cast my heel has started to hurt too, I need to ask them if they can't cut a hole into the plaster there. I need to get out of here, away from the stench of urine bottles, pus and shit.

13.45: Everything is quiet. Most of the comrades who had their bandages changed this morning are now asleep. The whole procedure is incredibly exhausting. I need to do my utmost to get into a German hospital in the Reich. Away from the many wounded and all the Russian auxiliaries, otherwise I will end up getting the same fits as Krakow. When I look at comrade Schmidt the fear is gripping me. I am suddenly terribly afraid and what about, I don't really know.

Several Ju 52s are flying overhead with their human freight. I must stop thinking. My nerves are more affected by all this than I thought. One more of those shrill and blood-curdling screams of pain from the operating rooms and I'll have a breakdown. Never mind the things I have seen and done, like on the day where I lifted Wiegand out of his tank, or when I dressed Goßler's wounds and those of the man who drove into the mine barrier with Aures – I can't do anything like that again, after all the things I have seen and heard here, I can't go on. I am finished with it all. My foot is hurting and there is a pulsating pain inside the wound. I will have to take some more pills. Willi, the Kazak Russian, is just taking another full pan outside. If only the hospital train would take me to Germany soon, so I don't have to look at that shit-carrier any more.

How lovely it would be to do some garden work during my sick leave in Germany. Is that going to happen? Will it become true that the baby's wicker basket will stand in our own garden, in the warm sunlight of a spring day? With Ruth and me standing next to it, hand in hand, it would be so so moving!

Saturday, 9 January 1943, Taganrog

I am feeling a bit better today and I have eaten something too. The sickness caused by the Eubasin has vanished, but the night was infernal and never before have I longed so much for home and the loving care of people dear to me. My patience has come to an end. The train needs to arrive. This morning the doctor told me that I am fit for transport and if the hospital train doesn't arrive, then I could be transported in an auxiliary one. That should happen in the next few days and until then I need to show some patience. It will be worth the wait.

Yesterday Farnbacher visited me to say goodbye. He was moving quite well on his crutches. He too was going home on one of these auxiliary hospital trains. I gave him my address in Osnabrück, so that he can write to me when I am in Germany. Farnbacher is a good soldier and if he becomes an officer, he will be an excellent one.

15.00: Just had another haircut. The Leutnant with the many gunshot wounds has a temperature of 40.5 °C and is sitting upright in bed to have his hair shaved off. We have told him that he shouldn't do that. He needs to rest. But there is nothing we can do, it is his decision. We told Willi-Fjodor to fetch the medic. Instead of doing that, he had stood outside, where he flirted with the Russian women. When he came back we gave him a proper rollicking. Now he is standing here with empty eyes and is picking his nose. Lembke, the Stug Leutnant with the shot-up urethra, remarked that this is the same hand with which he wipes our arses, empties the urine bottles, carries our tea glasses and picks up the pills which we have to swallow!

Sunday, 10 January 1943, Taganrog

Today is Sunday. A sabbath day, even for the Russians. It doesn't make any difference to our daily routine here, but it makes me think about home. Even during the fighting I always tried to make the Sunday feel a little different for me and my crews. I have done that from the very first day of the war and I believe that is one of things which makes us different from the beasts. We have a day for contemplation. This is good for the spirit and as such for morale as well. It helps us to focus on the really important things and not to lose ourselves thinking about nullities. Thinking about things which matter – always on a Sunday and often after some hard-won battle. When I was with my old crew, with Tutasz, Müller and Szepanski – we all lived by that rule. We would save some special food for Sunday, even if we only had some captured biscuits. Then on Saturday we would wash ourselves and clean up as well as we could and would read the mail from home or write letters to our loved ones. And on Sunday, the day on which the Christian goes to church, on that day I let my thoughts travel to the loved ones at home and offer strength and motivation, reminding us what we are fighting for so that we can carry on, even in the darkest of times. By focusing on all that is good I found the strength to continue where others committed suicide, gave themselves up as prisoners or went mad. Only through that could I be an example for my crew and my comrades.

I am sitting together with Ruth and Mother and later we all have a nice day out walking through some of Hamburg's beautiful parks. Accompanied by Ernst, I visit Osnabrück Zoo while the women are at church. Yes, the women – because my slim and elegant girl has now become a woman and soon she'll also be a mother. I wonder if I will get home in time to see our child, my son, being born. I need to get back to the Reich as quickly as possible – if only the train would arrive – we are all waiting for it.

18.00: Tomorrow we will be leaving this place with an auxiliary transport for the wounded. But into which direction and where to, no one knows. But at least we are getting out of this hole. No matter how far we get, it will be closer to the Heimat than we are now. Many are envious of us three lucky ones, the Doctor, Leutnant Krakow and me. I am scared about the stresses and strains of the journey, but I am happy to get away. Now then – I have to come to an end, maybe even for a few days. Here's to a good journey!

11 January 1943, hospital, Taganrog

Today we are supposed to leave with a BVZ.* No one knows where we'll be going. I have to admit that I am concerned. Will I be able to cope with the stress of the journey? How cold will it get and is there a chance to get

---

* Behelfsmäßiger Verwundetenzug, an improvised hospital train – passenger or freight trains were converted into makeshift transports for the wounded.

back to the Reich? And – for me in particular – there is the worry that there won't be enough food. I can't cope with hunger at all.

Just now Willi-Fjodor the Russian has said goodbye to us. Only yesterday he caused trouble again by claiming that the commander had exempted him from making the beds. That was women's work, he said. In reply to this I drew my captured sabre and pointed that at him while I cursed him in Russian as well as I could. He kept a respectful distance from my bed, but started helping the nurses to change the linen. Nina is off sick, so Lilo is now replacing her, serving the meals and washing the severely wounded. And currently Nurse Thermostatsia with her casserole face is doing the rounds, taking the comrades' temperatures. The powdered arse face would be well advised not even to attempt to touch me. Disgusting proletarian-type of a woman.

Everything is quiet. The Doctor has just finished shaving. I have done the same – who knows when we'll be able to do that again? I am really excited about the train ride now and hope that it will be more comfortable than that dreadful ride from Shakhovskaya to Wjasma.

The surgeon, Dr Kellhammer, has just been here to say goodbye. He has left a very good impression on all of us. We thanked him for what he has done for us and for the newspapers he supplied us with during our stay. I need to dress now and they will pack my toes in cotton wool so they won't freeze off during the journey. The medic is packing our things and, well, then we are ready to go!

12.45, Tuesday, 12 January 1942

This morning we left Taganrog at 10 a.m. after having spent the entire day in the station inside the wagon. It is a covered goods wagon, the interior lined with sacks of straw. We three from the hospital are the only passengers forced to lie down. There is also a nurse with us, together with nine more officers. The cattle wagon is rumbling and shaking and my wound is starting to hurt again. The train has halted. Outside I can hear Romanian voices talking, but I can't understand what they are saying. The medic here in the wagon is a Protestant minister. An oddly clumsy fellow.

And he is short-sighted too. He has just left to ask the scum outside where we are.

It is 120 kilometres to Stalino and 110 to Yasinovataya. Not one arse in here knows if that is actually true, but I guess that means that we can't reach either of those places today. Major Müller, who is from Saxony and forms part of the group here in the wagon, has got diabetes and looks like that too. Only fit for rearward-area duty. He was a war correspondent on the staff of Army Group Kleist and served as a movie camera operator. His camera has been shot to bits and he was recalled to Germany. The impression he leaves isn't too bad. He was once a proper soldier – an Oberfeldwebel in the Wachregiment nonetheless. He became known and 'famous' with the footage he shot during the campaign in Poland and was then transferred for special duties.

14.00: We are 3 kilometres from Verbinskaya. Krakow just had to go on the shitter, which is a nasty procedure on a transport of this kind. Unimaginable for anyone who has not experienced it himself. Now he is pestering me and just committed the ultimate sin by looking over my shoulder into my diary. As revenge I now have to write about this morning where he tried to piss into a bottle for over an hour, but failed to perform as he wished. The whole wagon supported him with a loud 'psss, psss, psss, psss' – like the Russian mothers do to motivate their kids to piss.

Outside the sun is setting. There was a brief stop at a small station to let another train pass by. The sky is clear, there are hardly any clouds and that means there is a very cold night ahead. The nurse prepared a few sandwiches for us. It will be a while before we can expect warm food again. Seems that our train is going to Makiivka.

Wednesday, 13 January 1943, war hospital, Makiivka

The 'Merry Three from Taganrog', with full bellies, washed and shaved, are lying in comfy and clean beds in War Hospital VII/533//39661. We are in Makiivka, in the region of Stalino. In a few days we'll be transported to Dnepropetrovsk and from there, if we are lucky, into the Reich via the

General Government. The journey here was wild indeed. In Taganrog a nurse and nine officers got on board our train. We three wounded soldiers, lying on the wagon floor, couldn't help noticing that these gentlemen joining our transport for the wounded were of the finest behind-the-lines stock. Among them an official with 'tonsillitis' and swollen lymphatic glands. Another official with jaundice and an Oberst of a Luftwaffe construction battalion suffering from the same ailment. Then the aforementioned Major Müller, branch of service: artillery and suffering from diabetes and with a huge amount of luggage. Initially he had hoped to be flown out, but due to the staggering amount of bags and suitcases he was travelling with, he was put on our train. And even here all his stuff is filling nearly half a wagon. Simply said, these chaps with their silly ailments made me so sick that I could have puked there and then. No chance of that kind of treatment in a fighting unit. An official sent home with rheumatic problems? Is that a joke? How can a man like this be allowed to just drop his work and go home? When we disembarked at Makiivka, the fine PK-Major and all his luggage were loaded onto a Luftwaffe ambulance van. When he climbed on board, Krakow and I drummed him out properly, using spoons and our empty mess tins while loudly whistling the 'Badonviller March'.

Friday, 15 January 1943, reserve war hospital, Makiivka/Stalino

Another morning in the hospital. We are washed, shaved and Lora, a Russian girl, has made our beds and supplied us with some thickly cut jam sandwiches which we have already eaten. The Doctor is reading a newspaper and Krakow is whistling some Schlager tunes and when it's one of the more popular ones the whole room joins him. Just now a guest who only arrived last night has said his farewell. A Leutnant of the army Flak from Stalingrad, who had a lot of interesting stories to tell.

There are about 240,000 men trapped in Stalingrad. To that number one has to add large numbers of Romanians and Croats who have been pushed into the city from the flanks. The Russians had attacked on 20 November 1942. They had come from the north and south and the Schwerpunkt of their attack at the Don near Kalatsch. Even before, the Russians had started to attack the German blocking positions from the north and – with less force – from the south, but all of those attacks had been repelled. The Russians only managed to hold on to the Volga itself and inside the steep-banked banjas in Stalingrad. Good Russian formations which defended themselves stubbornly. Particularly so in an industrial complex named 'Red October' where they fought so hard that our troops could not dislodge them. That bastion survived the relentless shelling, while the rest of the city around it sank into ashes. Never before had that comrade seen destruction of this scale.

In this wasteland of rubble the Russians had built command posts and posts in cellars and under the debris. There they now faced our troops, who were often not more than 10 or 20 metres away from them. This war about ruins and wasteland went on for weeks until, on 20 November, the Russians attacked from the north towards Kalatsch and from the south towards Tschinskaya. With that, the situation changed drastically. The Russians just smashed through the Romanian lines – and as I said before, that was not a difficult task. Kalatsch fell into Russian hands. The bridges hadn't been blown, the hospitals and supply depots hadn't been evacuated. Even the nurses and medical personnel fell into Russian hands. The Russians then charged on, from their bridgeheads up to Obliaskaya towards the west and their armies then linked up in Tschinskaya.

The blocking positions along the Volga in Stalingrad had held firm, but now a new front, facing west, had to be established. There were enough men to do so, but it had required lots of organisation. Some German troops had managed to break out of encirclement at the Don from where, after blowing up all their heavy weapons and equipment, they had managed to escape into Stalingrad. Over 100 tanks had been left behind and these would have been badly needed to avoid the catastrophe the Germans troops in the city were facing. But even tanks, self-propelled guns, artillery and heavy Flak are of no use without fuel and ammunition. The German western front is now under heavy pressure – two officers who were only flown out of there yesterday told us so.

The situation in the city is as follows:

Parts of Stalingrad are firmly in Russian hands, including the 'Red October' industrial complex where they are supplied across the now-frozen

Volga. The northern blocking position then runs north past Gorodishche (map 1:300,000) towards the west-north-west, from 48.70° alongside the Volga to 84.30°. From there towards the south the western front continues to the area of Betekovka south of Stalingrad. The other blocking position run along the line of Baburkie–Nizhny Alexejewskij–Sharnoklevskji–Karpovka–Rokotino–Krawzov–Zybenko. At Karpovka a salient had been driven towards the west deep into Russian territory up to Marinovka. The distance from Karpovka to Stalingrad is about 30 kilometres, which is the same distance as between the northern and southern blocking position. A near-perfect square, yet large amounts of the interior of that square are held by the Russians.

On 11 and 12 January the front lines in the north-west and south-west came under severe pressure again, but the salient was holding. It is expected, however, that the line there needs to be straightened out soon, and when that happens the airfield will come under threat and into the range of the enemy artillery. An enormous blow for the defence of the fortress Stalingrad. To keep the garrison alive, the Luftwaffe needs to fly at least 300 tons of supplies into the city on a daily basis. A Junkers 52 or a He-111 can carry about 2–3 tons, but there are larger aircraft available there, FW-200 and multi-engined Junkers types. Yet with each airfield falling into Russian hands, the supply problem is getting worse and when the stage is reached at which our machines cannot land any more and have to start dropping supplies from the air – well, then the wounded can't be evacuated any more either. Usually a soldier needs 500 to 600 grams of bread per day. In the fortress they can be lucky when they get 100 grams and often they get less than 50! That in turn means that they have started to slaughter the horses and these would be needed as draught animals to make up for the lack of fuel.

The Leutnant of the Flak told us that there are still countless numbers of Russian civilians in the city. They live in the sewage systems and in underground shelters. During a crackdown by our troops in one of the latter they found 250 tons of grain. The Russian civilians seem to live better lives than our Landsers. The few wounded Landsers which are being evacuated by air and then arrive here in the hospital look like walking corpses, so thin it is a miracle if they can still stand upright. No wonder, after having been in that cauldron for more than two months.

Even though I have eaten like a threshing machine since I arrived here, the wounded men need as much food as they can get to build their strength up again.

Together we have just calculated how much ammunition the comrades in the cauldron will require per day. That alone requires a whole fleet of aircraft. Some comrades told us that in Stalingrad they could hardly ever use the available artillery as rounds needed to be conserved to repel Russian attacks. The Leutnant of the army Flak – who had been in command of a 2-cm battery – told us that the Russians had been so used to not being shelled that they had started drilling their troops only 2,000 metres away from the German lines and in full sight. He, however, would not have that, and one day had ordered his men to fire three magazines into the Russians. The success had been spectacular, but he received the rollocking of a lifetime from the section commander for wasting valuable ammunition. A Leutnant of the artillery confirmed that they had not been allowed to fire on even the most valuable targets. They could easily have targeted the Russian supply columns on the frozen Volga, but never received permission to fire.

The air supply causes another problem, because the aircraft committed to it can't be employed in combat operations. In addition the distance to Stalingrad is too great. Now they have transferred thirty-five Stukas to an airfield somewhere south-west of the city. And they are supposed to be well supplied with bombs and fuel. That is unlikely, however, as so far they haven't flown a single attack. The Russian, though, knows that our Flak is out of ammunition and as such relentlessly bombs every sign of life on the ground. They even target individual men out on the streets. The Russian air force gives special attention to the airfield, disrupting our operations there. There is no sign of German fighter cover. Of the 240,000 men in the city 70,000 are remnants of annihilated rear area and supply units, like bakery and butcher columns, maintenance units and so on. None of their personnel have ever seen any actual combat. These are organised into so-called 'fortress' battalions and then thrown into battle across the city. I know from experience how useless such ragtag formations are.

Most men now have winter clothing, but warm quarters are rare and there is a chronic lack of firewood. There are no places to warm oneself up.

The only wood in Stalingrad comes from the house ruins and from several wood depots in the city. These, however, are under constant artillery and sniper fire and it is forbidden to forage for wood during the daylight hours. Most of the little wood that is available has to be sent to the field kitchens. No food without wood.

All this, the cold, no food, constant action, no sleep, no warmth and the constant extortion lets the men fall over by the hundreds. After a few weeks of combat even we looked haggard, tired and worn out, but we always had food and regular rations. The comrades in Stalingrad have nothing. The Russians there, however, have everything, mostly from German depots: tins of plums, peaches, peas with bacon and rice with beef. How the times have changed. The comrades have told me that they had known about our attack on 12 December from Kotelnikovo and that Flak and tanks had been amassed in the south-west of Stalingrad from where they had been supposed to fight their way towards us. They also told me about the great sadness that had befallen everyone when they learned that we had been forced to withdraw. Now they all hope that another relief attack will be launched via Kalatsch.

Well, that is all I learned about Stalingrad. Here in the hospital there are new admissions on a daily basis, new comrades to talk to. Leutnant Schmidt, whom I have come to like since I first met him at Taganrog, told me about the terrible mood in the encircled city. Some of his men had deserted to the Russians, where they had been given a bowl of food before being photographed. Then, after a further interrogation, they had been shot. At one point a man of 60.ID had deserted to the Russians and they had then made him broadcast messages to his former comrades by loudspeaker, telling them how well he was being treated by the Russians. There are certain elements who prefer treason of this kind to the noble death of a soldier. In well-led units, however, such cases are the exception.

An Uffz. of 100. Jäger-Division, a dashing and courageous young man, told us about the fighting in the 'Red October' factory and about the distances over which Russians and Germans fought one another there. He is from the Steiermark and a lot of his comrades serve as snipers. He told us how they had picked off the Russian teams collecting water from puddles and shell holes. Never had he seen such an enormous amount of hand grenades being used in the fighting among the ruins. He also told us how he had set a house on fire using bottles filled with fuel which he later ignited with hand grenades. It is highly interesting to listen to the comrades and I have made an observation. The soldier of a second-line unit, of the baggage train or something similar, will tell a story in a completely different manner from an experienced fighting man, 'one of us' (as I can proudly say). He will talk about the intensity of the artillery fire, the loud explosions and he will use general terms to tell a story which will mainly be about himself. The frontline fighter will tell a story about how he pulled off this or that thing and what weapons he used and so on. He has no need to describe the battle and the sounds and sights – we have all experienced that ourselves.

It is 15.00 now and we have already switched the lights on. Russian Lora has just brought us something to drink. Krakow and the Doctor are asleep since they finished eating at 14.30. Another hospital train has arrived and the new arrivals are being examined and bandaged at the moment. One of the nurses has just brought me some writing paper, so I can start writing a few letters again. The nurses here are all from the Palatinate and the Saar. They don't quite correspond to my ideals. The women from northern Germany are a different breed. And the Russian women we see here – good Lord, better not to waste a word about them. Lora surely is the most noble among them. They are all dressed in shabby clothing and Lora also has slit eyes like a Mongol and an oddly short haircut. We couldn't help noticing, however, that the girl speaks excellent German and, in stark contrast to her weird look, is damned clever. We have got used to her and only a short while ago she asked us, with a devious glint in her blue slanted eyes, if the Caucasus was still in German hands or if the Russians had repossessed it by now. Of course we told her that it was still German, but she – and the other Russians too – heard a lot from our Landsers and surely she has other, additional sources of information. She asked me on what front I had served before I arrived here.

She might look like a farmer's daughter, but she has studied medicine for two years and qualified as some kind of 'sub-surgeon'. This is all a bit different from in Germany; in the Soviet Union something like a private practice does not exist. Doctors of her qualification are being employed as company doctors for health control and in the villages as baby carers and so on. The doctors who study medicine properly and with a degree later work in hospitals. Here in the German hospital this 'sub-surgeon' is only allowed to do simple work, like serving food and making the beds and if they do anything else, like the time when Lora changed one of Krakow's bandages, she has to do so under supervision of a German nurse.

Saturday, 16 January 1943, Makiivka

Outside some craftsmen are hammering like mad on the window frames. Quite a farewell concert, as today another train is supposed to leave and we all hope that we'll be on board if it does. Yesterday evening we three had ourselves carried downstairs into the cinema where we watched a movie with Zarah Leander. That was quite a nice change, although the effort to get there was something else. After all that limping around and being carried up and down the stairs we were all exhausted and slept like babies right until the morning.

16.00: No train for us today. So far we have wasted nearly a week here and we have only travelled 150 kilometres. There was a BVZ to Dnepropetrovsk and if we had got on board we would at least have been a little closer to the Heimat. And now we lie in our beds and are annoyed. It is a shame that I don't have any Russian-language books with me, as I have noticed that I have forgotten quite a lot of words since the campaign in 1941. Today there was a female Volksdeutsche here in the room. She is working as a translator. It is terrible to hear our beautiful language coming across the lips of these disgusting Russian proletarian types. Here in Russia one learns to appreciate the advancement of the German workers in recent years. Krakow and the Doctor are downstairs again and are watching another movie. I just had my plaster changed. I was surprised how much I must have bled in the last few days. I have to make an effort to keep my leg still until the wound has healed properly. I am bored now.

Sunday, 17 January 1943, Makiivka/Stalino

The barber has just turned up and is now standing at Leutnant Krakow's bed. He greeted us by wiping his runny nose with the index finger and thumb of his right hand, then snorted the remains up and wiped the mess off on his moustache and the hair on his head. There followed a 'Goohd Morrrning' – with a much extended 'oo' and a long rolling 'r' – and then he started giving Krakow a shave. Krakow, by the way, can't even grow one of those. The barber is an older Russian with a deeply furrowed face and a martial looks, ice-grey moustache under his nose. The hair on his head, however, is pitch black with only some white strands on the sides. He is of typical Slavic stock, like Pidulski the Polish marshal. He is a big fellow, with a heavy build and with bony, yet dexterous fingers. The biggest difference to a German hairdresser, however, is that he keeps his mouth shut and doesn't try to force a conversation about the weather or politics on his customers. The nose incident aside, he is a very clean and cultured man. He is even wearing a white coat! The fellow is not your average barber. That the coat is, in the best case, 'infantry white' and has a large brown stain on the right pocket, well, who cares about that, 'nitchevo niet', 'that doesn't matterrr!'

Below the coat, from which most of the buttons have been ripped and which is fastened around his belly with a muslin bandage, he is wearing the typical torn and tattered Russian gown. The buttons on the end of his sleeves are missing too, but 'that doesn't materrr!' either, a couple more muslin bandages do the job just as well. That he is a long-standing employee of the German military is proven by the pair of thick, grey army socks he is wearing on his feet, which in turn he has planted into rubber slippers. He isn't wearing any other shoes. Indeed, our barber is a clean man. Before he starts working on his customer's face, he washes his hands, using water he has brought with him in an old, rusty tin. Then he dries his big hands in a page of newspaper, which he completely shreds to bits during the drying process. Yes, he is a very clean man.

With solemn movements he then begins to soap up Krakow's face with an old brush which is missing half its bristles. We can be quite sure that the missing bristles were lost while soaping the faces of the Red Army soldiers who had been in Makiivka before us. He is, one has to give him that, using hot water to shave Krakow! That is the old Russian school. From the dirty pocket of his once-white coat he pulls a bottle of spiritus, which he has stolen from the nurse, and then dowses a big swab of cotton wool, which he has obtained in the same manner, with the sharp liquid which the nurses use to rub into our legs to improve the circulation. The alcohol-soaked cotton wool is placed on a thin tin plate and set alight with a match. Once that is burning, he holds a small aluminium tray above the flame which he has filled with a tiny amount of water from his rusty tin. And even before the cotton swab has collapsed into itself the water in the tray is beginning to steam.

Hard to believe that in Germany barbers pay to have hot water boilers screwed to their walls. The Russkis just carry them in their pockets. Very convenient and practical! The stupid Germans should just copy the Russian patent which, with its open flame, also adds very much to the celebratory atmosphere. Now then, the dozen or so stubbles on Krakow's face have been thoroughly soaped up and the barber pulls out a Russian officer's belt of the kind I took as a souvenir last year. He then affixes that to one of the bedposts and, voila, a sharpening strop for his brand-new shaving knife has been created. The gleaming new knife fascinates me, and I can't help asking where he got that from; surely this is not a Soviet product. And I am right: he tells me that he has bought this in the German sutler's store. And while he is talking to me he starts sharpening the blade on the strop with the wide, sweeping, ritualistic movements of an Orthodox Russian priest. Well, it is a Sunday after all. He then checks the sharpness of the blade with his thumb and considers it sufficient to mow Krakow's stubble. But he is not ready to proceed with the shaving! No! First he wets another cotton swab with liquid from one of the five little bottles which he arranged, with military precision, on Krakow's bedside table and then wipes the blade with it.

And then, very solemnly, the blade is set to work on Krakow's face. The Leutnant has closed his eyes and has leaned back in expectation of the great event and has tied his towel like a bib around his neck. The Doctor remarks that the bib makes him look even younger and that he actually looks quite cute with it. Now the shaving has begun and the old barber is gathering momentum for each cut and swipe of the blade by turning his entire body.

Looking at him from the back, bent down over Krakow like that, one could think that he is a Muslim, repeatedly bowing down in prayer. After each stroke, he wipes off the excess soap in the palm of his left hand, as if paper has suddenly become a rarity, and soon the work is done! No, I was wrong, it is not done! With his fingers, with which in the meantime he has wiped his nose several times more, he now runs over Krakow's skin to find the spots where some more, thin stubble might be hiding. A few more swipes of his German blade and Krakow's face is as soft as a baby's bottom. And now, the next act of the great ceremony is going ahead: the washing of the face and the application of the lotion!

With another swab of cotton wool, which he wets in his rusty tin before pouring on some more alcohol, he now rubs down the sideburns, the lips and the neck of his patient. Then, the contents of a small red tin box are used to smear the master's hand with some gelatinous substance, probably to make them more slippery and then he rubs the contents of another small bottle slowly and very ceremoniously into Krakow's face. The whole grand procedure reminds me of the anointing during the administration of the last rites. And then, the sacred ceremony comes to an end. The bottles disappear into the coat pockets, he takes the little trays and bowls and bows down deeply when Krakow pays him with a few cigarettes: 'Goood byeeh!', the barber says and then raises his hand, which still holds the cigarettes, slightly above his head in a gesture which resembles a mixture of a German salute and a Papal blessing. Then the door closes and the high priest of the barber's profession has left our dormitory.

Our comrade, who is known among the nurses, themselves only just old enough to vote, as 'the little boy', is raising the baby-bottom soft skin of his face into the sunlight and looks mightily pleased with himself. And while the smell of perfume is slowly drifting away, we turn back to our usual pastimes: the Doctor is reading and I am writing.

Monday, 18 January 1943, war hospital, Makiivka/Stalino

On this day, one year ago, a Junkers flew me from Smolensk to Königsberg! A year ago today the war in the East had, for a little while, come to an end for me. Today, from my warm room I am again looking at the war from a distance. I and my two brothers in suffering are still stuck here! There is much traffic on the hallways and corridors outside because today another fifty comrades are being released. Only the 'bed-ridden' cases like us have to remain here. Now we have started crying havoc, demanding to be at least taken to Stalino and from there, together with the 'sitting cases', to Dnepropetrovsk. It was to no avail, the doctors here don't care about anything; they just want to be left in peace. Slowly but surely I am fed up with being wounded. The gratitude of the Fatherland is not very uplifting at all. Last night a Hauptmann serving on some Korps staff arrived to spend the night here. He told us some amusing stories about the Romanians. He himself had had a streak of bad luck recently. His staff headquarters had to run away from the Russians no fewer than six times and during the last time they managed to capture a staff motor coach full of top-secret documents and the best uniforms of the General in command of the Korps.

Tuesday, 19 January, still in Makiivka

Yes! Still in Makiivka! We have been here for so long that we have even been informed of the hospital gossip. This whole place is really getting on my nerves now. Yesterday Lora told us what an absolute mess this place is. Later Agnes, the little nurse, came in to cry on our shoulders, followed by Marie, who told us a free additional thing. I am well informed now. The next time I get to the front I will be doubly afraid of catching a bullet, as this will result in yet another Odyssey through war hospitals like this, where nothing is working as it should – unbelievable for anyone who hasn't experienced it himself. When Laura left and closed the door behind her she summarised it all by saying: 'This is not a hospital!'

It is very obvious that the Russians are soaking up all information of this kind and similar deficiencies of our medical services, and that includes Laura – we have to take far greater care to make sure everything is running smoothly and have to be far more suspicious about the Russians who work for us. The things which are happening here would be severely punished in a fighting unit. Here, however, they only result in a few days of arrest. But anyway, I don't want to warm up the gossip again.

Yesterday, after Hauptmann Holleben had made off to Stalino, a Leutnant was brought to our room suffering from severe frostbite on both hands. He is an infantryman, just like Leutnant Krakow, and originates from Pomerania, not far away from Krakow's Heimat. Now we have two bachelors in the room and a banter equilibrium has been established.

Friday, 22 January 1943, Makiivka

For the foreseeable future we'll have to stay in Makiivka as there is no transport available for us! It seems that troops are being concentrated somewhere in the area and that all the transport available is being deployed for that purpose. The new Unteroffizier in charge of our ward has informed us about it, followed by the measly assistant surgeon who told us the same. This month we are not getting back to the Reich. Question is if we will ever get back at all, or any further than Kiev. But what can I say, after a long night's sleep the world doesn't look as bad any more. I can't change it; I'll just wait until I can at least limp around without assistance.

15.30: Until a moment ago one could read without the electrical light and after shouting for about ten minutes, Nurse Gretel came in to switch it on for me. I am alone in our room. Flamme – our new man – the Doctor and Krakow are downstairs watching a movie. Flamme has given me a book to read and I am trying to kill time with it. It's wasted either way.

Saturday, 23 January 1943, Makiivka

Today we were informed that it is most likely that we'll be taken away from here in an express leave train. We are sitting fully dressed on our beds, waiting for what is going to happen. Seems that the 'having to stay here' story was nothing but a latrine rumour. We have received our rations and are now waiting to see if Leutnant Krakow, infantryman, unmarried, unblemished and unshaven, will be kissed goodbye by Nurse Marg. Margarethe has shown a lot of interest in our little boy – much to our amusement, I have to say. But later Nurse Laura told us that Marg has already given her heart to a 'tankist' downstairs but, who knows, she might still appear. At the moment it is a little chaotic here. All our packed bags and suitcases are littering the floor. My stuff is standing next to my bed, including my sword – the Cossack sabre – the old fur hat from Pokhlebin and the gloves from Zalewski. Both will be very useful on the journey ahead. Katja, the Red nurse, has packed my toes into plenty of cotton wool. Again I am a little afraid about the journey. The cold is really worrying me. But I have survived worse than that. The hospital here is a shithole and I am glad to get away.

Sunday, 24 January 1943, on the train to Brest

We are rolling! Yes! In contrast to all the rumours of the past weeks we are now going to Germany! We are sitting in leave train 844 from Stalino to Brest-Litovsk and I have a whole bench to myself. I can stretch my legs out and I have placed my briefcase on my lap where it forms a sturdy surface to write on. That way I am able to write a few lines about my recent adventures.

Yesterday we had to wait for a long time before anything happened. There was enough time to eat lunch, which consisted of bean soup with meat, also known as 'radio soup', as it will make itself heard in two hours, or 'special announcement soup': those who manage to find a piece of meat have to make a special announcement. At 13.00 we were shifted into the draughty hallway where I called for the head physician. The poor man is in a very bad state because he is slowly turning blind. His face is getting fatter and fatter from doing absolutely nothing and is now slowly growing over his eyes. Once we arrived I sent him to fetch the paymaster to talk about the bad provisions. When the paymaster had turned up, a debate was held right in the middle of the hallway, surrounded by grinning Landsers. That had a good effect; he disappeared with his tail between the legs and promised to sort out some extra rations for the journey.

A coach took us from the hospital to Stalino into a soldiers' home, where he arrived after four hours. It had taken us four hours to travel 12 kilometres across the icy, snow-covered roads. In the previous years the Russians have built lots of enormous multistorey buildings. I don't see them in the negative light in which they are described in the Göbbels press. I see them as warning signs of a major threat. The dangers formed by the emergent Soviet bourgeois. One day, the Russians will have all the things that we have. But their workers will live better and in more modern surroundings than the workers in the fascist and libertarian states. And what will happen then? Anyway – I really need to stop thinking that way. But we in the West need to keep our eyes open and the Russian bear has awoken from centuries of hibernation. We need to listen! By talking to the Russians I have learned a lot. There is a new Soviet intelligentsia. A class surging to the top from the lowest level of society. And it does so at breakneck speed and on a wide front. It won't be long until it doesn't require a teacher any more.

But anyway. I have distracted myself again. In the soldiers' home, where we lay on straw sacks until 19.00, I met several old comrades from the division. Riflemen of 114 and K6. Some of them remembered me well and our eyes started to glow when we talked about past and recent battles. One of them had ridden on my tank at Muratowo and another remembered how I had finished off that 52-ton tank. Krakow lay next to me and listened to us talking. And then the subject changed to our most recent losses and I found myself shocked! Kelletat has fallen, Jung has fallen, Hauptmann Jonas, Graf Plettenberg – too many to list them all, but among them were Stöcker, Zollenkopf's Adjutant and Feige, the Admiral's son, recently serving in 16.Pz-Div. – all of them have fallen. Oberleutnant Schneider has lost an arm and Wissenmann has fallen. I wanted to cry, but I couldn't do it. Should we win, then this victory has come at a high price. Again the best within our ranks have fallen. They also told me that comrade Scheibert has won the Knight's Cross. I am sure he deserved it.

We quickly got tired and slept for a little while until a man brought the news that a coach was waiting outside to take us to the station. At 21.00 we sat in the train. Together with the other officers, I am now sitting in an old, third-class, express wagon which offers enough room for us and the huge piles of luggage. The benches are short, but I can stretch my legs across the aisle in the middle of the wagon. This is not too difficult with my plaster cast and I rest the left leg on one of Krakow's crutches. Still more comfortable than in the turret of a Skoda tank.

From Stalino the journey took us to Yasinovataya, from where we continued on the German-made main railway line via Konstantinovka to Slavyansk. At the moment we are rolling towards Losovaya and it will probably be dark when we arrive there.

In Slavyansk we have drawn rations and were given a bowl of special announcement noodle soup each. If things don't get worse the journey will be quite bearable. Here in the cabin, which makes up half of the total space in the wagon, we also have a potbelly stove and during our last stop some comrades have stolen some coal for it. When the wind is coming from the wrong direction – as it is now – the thing smokes quite infernally. But who cares – as the old saying goes: many have frozen to death, but no one has ever died from stench. Earlier today, when temperatures had risen slightly outside, the steam heating kicked in. Now, however, it has switched itself off again. We are going north.

Monday, 25 January 1943, Poltava region

Slept well the previous night. It was almost too warm under the large pile of blankets. Bright sunshine outside – clear blue sky. But it is cold! The snow crunches under the feet of the women and prisoners of war who are shovelling snow on the station platform. Leutnant Krakow has just prepared himself a wonderful meal using a big onion. We used to do the same, but being 'old veterans of Russia', we had quickly given up on using this ingredient when even the Russians started airing their rooms to get rid of the terrible smell brought on by the consumption of onion. Everyone is winding up Krakow now, telling him that he will soon stink like a Jew. The train is making slow progress. At the moment we are stationary again – for what reason, no one knows. At the front there are two locomotives and another one is at the back of the train. That only arrived last night after we got stuck on a hill.

The Doctor, Krakow and Flamme are playing skat. Some officers from another wagon have come over to watch them play. There is a Hauptmann and commander of an armoured train unit here as well. At Tschernyschkow he was in command of two trains. I have taken photographs of one of them. His trains had then been attached to Gruppe Stahel and now he was delighted to hear that Stahel, Oberst and Kampfgruppe leader in a Luftwaffe field unit, had been decorated with the Oakleaves to the Knight's Cross. I had read that in a newspaper while I was still in hospital – the same newspaper, of 3 or 4 January, which had the Wehrmachtsbericht mentioning our 6. Panzer-Division in it. This, by the way, is only due to the merits of Major Bäke and the engagement where the thirty-seven Russian tanks were annihilated. I will surely learn more about everything that happened there once I am back with the Ersatz-Abteilung. I have to admit that it hit me quite severely to learn about the number of officers killed in SR114 and K6. By now nearly all the old brothers in arms of the first campaign in Russia have either fallen or been wounded so badly that they are not fit for duty any more. In our army the relation of men at the front to men behind the lines is supposed to be 1:8. So eight men serve in supporting roles to keep one fighting man in the trenches. We are told that in the Russian army, where the pool of available manpower is much larger than ours anyway, that ratio is 1:4. The Reds don't require such a massive overhead organisation. The Russians have enormous human resources and we allow our shirkers to serve behind the lines.

09.00: We are still not in Poltava. We are currently rolling through the first proper forest I have seen in ages. This makes me rather happy because it is a clear sign that we are moving further north and closer towards Germany.

10.00: We are standing in Poltava station. Lots of people are walking past our window. All of them have some duty here on the station. A proper mix of people and races: Italians, Turkmens, Uzbeks, Ukrainians, Slovaks, Romanians – all of them brothers in arms. We have just had our photo taken with the kind assistance of an Italian comrade. He was an Alpini, Italian mountain infantry, and I have to say that their kit isn't any worse than ours. There are lots of different uniforms to see here, including those of the OT, the Reichsbahn and of the Red Army, rows of prisoners of war who are waiting to be transported into camps. It can't be much more colourful in the camps of the English and the Americans. Only that the English have millions of Indians which they can force into their service. We should raise our own auxiliary formations from Russian volunteers. With those we could then defend the coasts of France and thus release several German divisions for service here in the East. And in France they could not defect to Belov's partisans either. I would really like to command such a Ukrainian or Russian contingent – they'd certainly be of more use than a German furlough battalion. There are lots of Ukrainian militia on the station. All young, strong and healthy lads. Why use them here on station duty? That's a job for our old daddies of the Landeschützen. Why should they serve in France committing adultery with the French ladies? And what about all our divisions guarding the Channel coast, like 302, 304 and 306? They would be good for service in Russia!

Again I can't fail to notice that the Russian women are employed on hard physical labour duties. The railway employs entire working columns consisting of only females, heaving sacks of coal, shovelling snow and sawing wood. They are wrapped in thick quilted jackets, wear fur caps and head shawls and around their arms cuff bands which read 'Deutsche Reichsbahn'. We have a whole lot of Red Cross nurses here on our train. They are far better equipped now than they were at the beginning of the war in Russia. Now they all have thick felt boots, fur caps and vests, quilted jackets and ski trousers. Our hen house here originates mainly from southern Germany.

Tuesday, 26 January 1943, near Kiev

We are standing in a goods yard and a few police officers have got on board. We – and the Hauptmann in particular – are now taking the piss out of them. With their fat arses they are sitting here telling us that they are on the way 'to the front'. The 'front' of these fatties, however, will be about 30 kilometres behind the actual front – in the best possible case. I am getting sick of these people.

The tantalising smell of toasted bread is wafting through the train. That's a thing which has become very popular here in the East, where bread is usually either mouldy or frozen. Because of that the Landsers have started toasting the bread on oven plates and the like – until the slices are dark brown and crispy. Any mouldy taste has dissipated after that treatment, and that it also thaws – well, that doesn't need to be pointed out.

There is a lot of traffic here on the station. We are drawing supplies and that is why we have to wait for such a long time. On the track next to ours there is a train full of comrades of SS 'Das Reich'. They are already disembarking here in the area of Kiev. There are also some hospital trains in the station; they can move much more quickly than we do as they can prepare the food themselves and only need to halt for a locomotive change. I wish I could travel on one of them. Would get me home much quicker.

Leutnant Krakow has turned out to be a hysterical and quarrelsome man. Not a person I could be around for longer periods of time. His entire lack of self-control is really getting on my nerves. The Doctor, however, is a well-educated and calm character, just like Leutnant Flamme who, even though he is only 20 years old and sometimes a little phlegmatic, turns out to be great company. Our 'caretaker', an OT man from Hanover, is a complete idiot. Totally useless. Again he has failed to find us any food. Alternatively he fails to find the coffee kitchen or – if he finds it – allows some Landser to snatch the last coffee away. He is a painter by trade and I am sure he could even make our old man lose his patience.

A train of the SS loaded with a cargo of VW-Schwimmwagen is rolling through at the moment. We have seen a lot of those in France during exercises. How long will it take until there is nothing left of these vehicles?

433

Things are lost quickly here in the East. I am wondering why we are making such slow progress. We have been on the rails for three days now and only just reached Kiev. By now we should have been in Brest! God knows when we'll arrive in Germany.

Wednesday, 27 January 1943, Ukrainian border

The train is now racing towards the old Russian border with great speed. Dense forest on both sides of the line. Our eyes are tired from looking outside into the white, snow-covered landscape. Now the sun has disappeared below the horizon and now it is clear that we are approaching the west. It is 16.00 but still not entirely dark. The three other gentlemen are playing cards. The train is going so fast that it is hard to write. We halt on what was once Polish territory and one can see the difference between eastern and central Europe here. Suddenly the houses have straight walls and are built of stone. The fields are looking good and placed in a logical manner. Even the forests are looking more tamed than those on the eastern side.

28 January 1943, medical collection point, Brest-Litovsk

Arrived at Brest station at 5 p.m. and after we had handed over our luggage, we and all our things were sent for delousing. The officers were deloused in a delousing train in the station. The delousing of the men was finished far more quickly as they didn't have as many special requests as the officers. I was part of the second group which, stark naked, was waiting in one of the wagons. With us sat an Oberst of the pioneers and the old Hauptmann Dressler. It reminded me of the advice we used to give to the recruits to just imagine their Oberst being stark naked if they were too nervous when facing such a high-ranking officer. That is what I had to think about while we were sitting there, naked and without any sign of rank. I then had the idea of remove my plaster cast with the excuse that I had discovered lice beneath it. That was a lot of work and while I managed to remove the plaster around the thigh and calf, that around my foot was too thick and sturdy. I then soaked the plaster under the shower and I was pleased as punch when I noticed that I could walk without it. Even better than the Doctor and Leutnant Krakow, who don't even have such a dressing.

29 January 1943, medical collection point, Brest

It is a wonderful morning; the sun is shining, I have slept well and had breakfast, and while I sit in the clean communal room of the collection point and write, we are all listening to the radio which is standing on a shelf on the wall. It feels like we have peace. This morning I shaved off my beard.

Saturday, 6 February 1943, Osnabrück-Haste

After a long journey I have now arrived in the reserve hospital in Haste, the former St Angela hospital. In Brest I couldn't write any more. We were examined by a doctor and then our entire group was brought to the station, where there was a train waiting for us. It was always a hell of a lot of work to load up all the officers' luggage. I could easily carry all my things myself because I only had my sabre, a few blankets, my dispatch case and my black briefcase. Krakow, the Doctor and Flamme always require some additional men to carry their things and help loading. And in Brest that needed to be done twice. The hospital is housed in the former Polish army barracks, and that has got its own railway connection and it was from there that a train brought us back to the main station in Brest, where luggage had to be loaded onto the other train.

From Brest we travelled in a second-class wagon to Frankfurt. As usual, I rested my legs on Krakow's crutches which made for comfortable sitting. The train was heated nicely. Our train was supposed to carry only wounded personnel from the Eastern Front, but in Brest a Major of the local field post service climbed on board. We tried our best to kick him out again. The medic Unteroffizier, supported by murmured approval of the officers on board, applied all kinds of polite and impolite measures to steer him out of the door. But then the train guard intervened and allowed the Major, who has some kind of important passport, to stay on board. We tried to ignore the old officer with his billiard-ball-shaped head.

In Frankfurt/Oder we arrived on the morning of 30 January, just at the time when the civilian workers came into the city and suddenly found ourselves, with our straw shoes, fur caps, overcoats and luggage, surrounded by a mass of workers. They stared at us like we were the apes in Hagenbeck Zoo. A man shouted 'the poor soldiers!' We would have liked nothing better than to punch them all in the face.

In the medical collection point, which was housed in an old grammar school, I didn't get into the same room as Krakow and the Doctor. I had been standing outside to guard the luggage and when I came in, the first floor was already full. I didn't want to stay in the Mark Brandenburg and after 'spying' around a little I learned that there was a train leaving for Cologne in the evening. With a few gifted cigarettes I secured a place on the reservation list. After lunch I went into town accompanied by the Oberst of the pioneers. The goal was to ring home and to do a little shopping. I urgently needed a stick now, because in Germany I could not use my sabre as a walking stick any more. In a café we listened to a speech by Hermann Göring on the radio. I had very mixed feelings about the whole Stalingrad business. We then obtained a couple of walking sticks, made our telephone calls and then limped back to the grammar school from where, after a massive dinner with lots of German beer, I was transported to the station again.

When the train reached Vlotho on the Weser, I talked to the Stabsarzt, asking him to register me as unfit for transport when we reached Bielefield. He understood why that was necessary and gave me a referral for Bielefeld hospital. A medic was to help me out of the train, where he was to call the hospital for me, announcing my imminent arrival. Yet the train only halted at the platform for a couple of minutes, then the whistle sounded and it pulled out again so quickly that the medic only just managed to jump back on board. He didn't have the time to call the hospital – I was lucky!

I went to the local command, where I received a train ticket to Paderborn and – after a nice journey – arrived at Paderborn station on 31 January, from where I made a call and soon a car pulled up which took me into town where

I had dinner with a few Leutnants of the regiment. After such a long time it was very interesting to be in the old city of Paderborn again, a visit which revived many old memories. On Monday I reported to Saalbach and spent the rest of the morning with Funk, who is now Saalbach's Adjutant. Chubby Lothar Herberts, who had also just been discharged from hospital, joined us, as did old Wilhelm Lope. After lunch, where we were joined by a Herr Lange from Osnabrück, we went into Funk's room, where we four emptied two bottles of Steinhäger and another two of Italian vermouth. I later went out to fetch my coat, Funk had gone back into Saalbach's office, while Lope and Herberts continued boozing. We had all agreed to go out together in the evening to have dinner and a few more drinks in Horn. Funk came to meet me and together we went back to Lope's office, where we found him, stinking drunk and gasping for air, lying in a large pool of vomit. Fatso Herberts was nowhere to be seen. He was probably lying unconscious in some gutter. We decided not to go out after all and I went to bed early. At 5 a.m. I took the train to Osnabrück. I was picked up from the station by Ernst, who at first didn't recognise me with my fur cap and the thick overcoat. He had brought a car with him which brought us home in no time – in the evening we had canned peaches!

Now I am in a reserve hospital in Haste in an officer's room together with a few warriors of the Heimat Front. Food is excellent. I have now learned that taking the plaster cast off wasn't a good idea as I am now suffering from periostitis, which means I have to stay in bed. Today Sister Vitalis, a nun from Paderborn but acting like a butcher's wife, squeezed out an ulcer which had formed next to the wound. The bloody pus spurting from it soiled the entire bed, and when she tried to empty the ulcer further she accidentally rammed one of her fingers into the open wound. The pain was so bad that I nearly fainted. But at least I got rid of that blighter of an ulcer and received a new Rivanol dressing – that will surely get rid of the inflammation. The radio is playing and I am waiting for visitors who do not arrive. Better catch some sleep.

19.00
Had dinner and visitors did arrive after all. Ernst brought me a tracksuit and a parcel from Anneliese from Naples. Without visitors it would have

been a rather boring evening. Outside in the common room the radio is playing 'reports from the front' made by the propaganda companies. Who listens to this nonsense? These reports are unrealistic, boring and good for nothing, at least for a frontline soldier.

Sunday, 7 February 1943, Haste hospital

Sundays are always the most boring days of the week. In addition I have a mighty headache. The doctor saw me earlier and told me that it could well take two months until I am back on my feet. It's hard not to despair. If it wasn't for the excellent food and care we are getting here, I would already have deserted back to the replacement unit. There at least the comrades would offer me entertainment and I would get all the news of the regiment.

Today at 15.30 Ruth gave birth to our son! He shall be named Wilhelm. He weighs 3,500 grams, measures 54 centimetres, blond hair, blue eyes – he is entirely healthy.

Thursday, 11 February 1943, St Angela, Haste

So, I am now a proud father! Last Tuesday I visited Ruth and had a first look at our son. He is a feisty little lad! Sadly I didn't feel too well after having received the Eubasin shot against the inflammation. Dr Uthmöller took me with him in his car and also brought me back to hospital afterwards. By now I am fine again, better than I have been for days. Since the plaster has come off my leg has become a lot thinner. And due to the inflamed wound it is very hard to stand up. It will be a long time before the leg is back to what it once looked like.

Monday, 15 February 1943, Haste

One year ago today Ruth and I were in Hamburg at a public talk about eternal peace after the Nine Years War. That was on a Sunday and afterwards we went to a concert in the Conventgarten. And now we are a small family and our boy is sleeping in his basket. In the meantime I have been fighting in Russia again and now I am in hospital with a shot-up leg. Yesterday, Mother and Father came from Hamburg to visit me. I am feeling quite good. The hole in my leg has shrunk a little and the pus is pushing little bone splinters out of the wound. I have been getting massages for a few days now and hot-air baths beneath a red-light box. I still think that exercise would be more useful to build my leg up again than these artificial measures. What really ails me is a constant headache. I don't know when I will be able to get rid of this side-effect of war. Because that is what it seems to be. I have seen Stabsarzt Dr Dörfflein, the ear, nose and throat specialist, and he told me that this is a common side-effect of combat stress, physical weakness due to the wound and also of the numerous concussions of my brain.

Friday, 19 February 1943

The Stabsarzt and I have been in town to see a film at the cinema. We watched *Wen die Götter lieben*, a film about Mozart. When we walked to the Capitol, I met a few old friends from my time in the Hitler Youth, all of whom are now in the army. Many of our age group have fallen and after the war they will leave a huge gap in our ranks. Many have been severely wounded, have become cripples, and I can only hope that fate will grant us victory so that we'll be able to take proper care of these comrades. I have to admit that the news that Rostov and Kharkov have been evacuated doesn't furnish me with lots of hope that this is actually going to happen. But now, after listening to the latest speech of Jupp Göbbels, one at least sees that something is being done and that in the coming spring we will give the Russkis a proper beating. But that is still a long way off. I have seen and done enough at Stalingrad – we have to stand fast, survive and do everything to turn this critical situation around.

Later I went to the KMT, the former Alsberg department store. Has been completely bombed out and now there are inmates of a concentration camp cleaning up the debris. Looking at their faces, they are Slavs – Russians or Poles, maybe also some Czechs. The Russians have the same numb facial expressions as the Russian prisoners of war at the front. The houses everywhere have been much damaged by bombing and there are large numbers of foreign workers in chocolate-brown uniforms – Dutch and Flemish workers serving in labour battalions and tasked to rebuild and repair the damage. All of them are strong young men in their prime – the same age group which here in Germany has been sent to fight at the front.

There was also a large group of female Ukrainian labourers. With their simple clothing and the typical headscarves they formed a stark contrast to the more elegant local women. But they work well and hard, and there are never any complaints about them. In general the Russian women are used to hard work, much harder than the women here could ever imagine. The Russian women wear a patch on their sleeves, similar to the 'P' of the Poles. It is a purple square with the letters 'OST' stitched onto it. They are also known as 'Ostarbeiterinnen' and in many cases the NSV has supplied them with clothing which makes them look quite presentable.

Göbbels recently gave a public speech in the Berlin Sportpalast in which he asked the German people to continue to stand behind the Führer and to bear the increased burden resulting from total war. We soldiers now know that the coming summer will see the continuation of German blows against the Russians and that even those who have so far been deferred from military service will be drafted in. We see dozens of these people in hospital every day when they come in to be examined for some small ailment. Between now and the coming summer we can make useful soldiers out of them and that should also be enough time to produce enough weapons and equipment to launch a new offensive. During this winter the Eastern Front has again swallowed a great number of divisions and we will not be able to get over the loss of the entire 6th Army anytime soon. The comrades who were lost in Stalingrad were, in the majority, of best Westphalian and Rhenish blood. In the coming summer one man will have to fight for two to be able to avenge them.

Monday, 1 March 1943, Haste reserve hospital

Having spent the weekend at home with my wife and child, I now know that I have become too used to being at war. The peace and quiet at home isn't good for me, so this morning, as quickly as I could, I fled back into my hospital room. Here in the army, surrounded by my comrades, is my real home. Here I am not only tolerated, but I have an actual raison d'être: I can breathe freely again. I am free to do what I want and also manage to regain some kind of inner calm. I would like to know how many others feel as if they have lost their place at home after so many years of service or if I am just a misfit.

Yesterday I had a phone call with Herbert in Hamburg. His Luftwaffe school has been evacuated from the Kerch peninsula back into the Reich, where it has been disbanded. Herbert will be transferred to the flying personnel or some Luftwaffe infantry unit in Russia. For the moment his unit is in Fürstenwalde. So Herbert's first stint in Russia didn't last very long. Who knows if he is even getting back there now – in the Luftwaffe anything is possible.

If my headache doesn't get better anytime soon, I will ask to be sent to a spa. I am sick of this old woman's ailment! And that they prescribed me a pair of reading glasses makes it even worse! Even though I have to admit that they do help a little. If I then consider my emerging baldness, I can't deny that I am on the best route to turning into an old man. The result of six years of service and war! I can put some weight on my leg again and I hardly notice the wound any more. I have trained hard not to show any sign of limping and to stop dragging the injured leg after me when climbing stairs. The wound is still weeping a little, but looking at the fact that the bone was broken and that only two months have passed since then, it is looking quite good.

Tuesday, 2 March 1943, Haste hospital

While I am writing this the sirens are wailing! Air-raid warning! I won't bother going into the cellar until I can hear that the Flak battery here behind the hospital is opening up. In recent days these alarms were mostly caused by individual aircraft and stragglers and these are not worth running around for. Even though there are beds for everyone down there in the cellar, there are nicer places to be. And when one rolls over to get some sleep they sound the all-clear and we can climb up to the second floor again. No – not with me. I'd rather sit through the alarm in my comfy bed. Yesterday the Tommies were over Potsdam and Magdeburg and on their way back they flew over Osnabrück. The Flak started firing everywhere, so Stabsarzt Henschen and I went down into the cellar. While we were sitting there a group of nurses came down the stairs, who had been woken by the alarm. Nurse Friedel had been so terrified by the reports of the 8.8-cm battery on the Sonnenhügel that she had just quickly thrown on a red silk kimono, under which she wore more or less nothing. Due to that she didn't want to come down the final flight of stairs into the brightly illuminated cellar. Someone supplied her with a blanket which she wrapped around herself before she finally came down. Nurse Marianne had swapped her shoes, wearing her left shoe on the right foot. Everyone laughed when she stumbled through the narrow corridor – the sound of the Flak battery was so loud and terrifying that many of the women were completely terrified.

There was a Serbian General with us in the cellar – he had fallen sick in the camp here in Eversburg and is being treated here, as are a large number of Frenchmen who are working here in the city and as such are being decently treated.

Tuesday, 9 March 1943

Today I had surgery on my leg. Dr Uthmöller has scraped the hardened pus off the broken bone and now I am lying in my little bed with a splint on my leg, again dependent on the assistance of the people around me. With that the infernal torture with shit pans and pee bottles is starting once more. My arse is hurting from lying in bed while outside there is glorious, sunny weather. I have been in town every day these past weeks; the wound had closed up, leaving only a small hole to drain it and I could walk very well. But the bone was still infected and below the wound a large abscess had formed. This was drained today and they have also scraped the rest of the wound clean, taking out several old trouser scraps which have been in there since the day I was wounded.

This morning I got a morphine injection, which made me feel very dizzy. Then Soller, the masseur, arrived and shaved the leg around the wound. At

9 a.m. I was lying in the operating room, where they strapped me to a metal frame and injected something into my arm which made me fall asleep. When I woke up at 12.30 p.m. Nurse Irene was sitting next to me, holding my hand, and told me that I had been screaming and crying in my sleep for over an hour.

Nurse Irmgard Schneider told me that in my morphine-soaked state I had told her not to be so terrified when she hears the 'Achtung!' announcing the imminent arrival of the Stabsarzt in Hall 3, which is separated from the massage room by a thin wooden wall. But to tell the truth she is terrified and always tries to make everything look and sound as busy as possible. When the Stabsarzt is near we support her in every possible way. I repeatedly slap my hand on my naked thigh to make it sound like a massage is ongoing, while a comrade runs the motor of the electric shaving apparatus, repeatedly changing the cutting length by pulling and pushing a lever which makes the shaver howl like the siren of a dive bomber. In addition we always make sure that irradiation lamps are placed next to the beds – every effort is made to appear more busy than we actually are! Nurse Irmgard is the daughter of the very well-known and popular Osnabrück surgeon Dr Schneider and we do everything in our power to assist her.

I am now lying here waiting for the air-raid alarm.

14 March 1943

I have received mail from Leutnant Krakow who is in hospital in Bad Polzin, his hometown. He is feeling quite well there and has two more comrades to play skat with. In the bed next to me there is an army apothecary who had his appendix removed. He is getting a lot of female visitors. When Ernst came to visit later, he and the apothecary argued with me about the German population who now, during total war, allegedly don't want to be part of it any more, because the English keep dropping bombs night after night. Many people in certain circles who hold no sympathy for 'Nazis' now try to stir up unrest in the population and it is they who are the problem, not the English bombs.

Thursday, 8 April 1943, St Angela, Haste

I haven't written for several weeks, but a lot has happened in that time. Today, three weeks ago, I received the news that I had been awarded the German Cross in Gold. On Wednesday they took another X-ray of my leg, which resulted in what I hope will be the last surgical work they do on it! This operation didn't do me well at all. I couldn't eat for a week and had to puke whenever I tried to eat something and when they changed my bandage one evening I suffered a complete mental breakdown.

5

Fragments, December 1943

Loose leaves, December 1943

But now I am sitting here in Nish as an instructor for the Bulgarians, teaching them our experiences in this combat school. The school consists of three infantry companies, fully equipped with weapons, one pioneer and one signal company, a battery of light field howitzers and our tank-assault gun training command. This is led by Hauptmann Heimke, of the Grossdeutschland Regiment, who has just arrived from the Reich. As the name suggests, the training command consists of one platoon with five Panzer IVs with a long 7.5-cm gun and a platoon of five Stug III assault guns, equally armed with long 7.5-cms. I am in command of the tank platoon, while Oberleutnant Baldauf has the assault guns. Baldauf is a Swabian and from the Sturmartillerie-Lehr-Regiment, a great comrade, and we have already established brotherhood over drink. His nickname is Balbo and he is the most charismatic joker.

The school, which is subordinated to the military attaché in Sofia, is commanded by Oberst Dr Zimmermann, also a Swabian and an infantryman by trade. Then there is an Oberleutnant von Gilsa, artillery and tactics instructor. The infantry instructor is Knight's Cross holder Hauptmann Sigfried Weber, whose brother is a U-boat commander and also wears the Knight's Cross. Weber is a fresh and sympathetic man who also lives in the 'Panzerburg', into which I will also move once my predecessor Oberleutnant von Schell has moved out. Schell has lost his patience with some stupid Bulgarian Hauptmann, insulted and screamed at him for being too clumsy to serve in a tank. This led to a complaint and the OKH has sent him back to the replacement unit.

16 December 1943

The evening in the theatre of Nish now lies behind me and tonight I have to attend an officers' evening which the Bulgarians host in their casino. The evening in the theatre, which was hosted by our combat school, wasn't very impressive – we have organised better with my old company. The only thing of note was the building itself and I have to admit that I didn't expect to see buildings of this kind in Nish. It even had a traversable stage! The soldiers' home is, just like the theatre and other public buildings, a flat-roofed construction. Not popular in Germany, but certainly of great popularity in the east and south-east. And who would have thought that there would be a room with hot and cold running water, central heating and a clean, modern furnishing in this nest of 40,000 people right in the middle of partisan territory. Yes, in Berlin I had a proper writing desk and a radio in the room, but I have quickly taken a liking to the place here, and the Gypsy band playing in the communal room in the evening makes me forget that there is no radio.

I usually have my dinner in the school's casino in the Hotel Grand Orient where in the evening one can buy two slices of cake and a big cup of coffee for 55 Pfennigs. Later one can […]

[page missing]

About the Bulgarian evening I can say that I at least had the chance to eat my fill there, and that they served an exceptionally nice Bulgarian red wine and later an even better Serbian, slightly sparkling, white wine. I sat next to the translator Atew, a chemical engineer by trade, who had once studied in Germany, in Aachen to be precise. On the other side sat a Bulgarian Oberst who didn't know any German words except for 'Prost!' The food was exceptionally nice too. First we had an oily white bean salad with smoked ham, followed by a meatloaf with lots of paprika, pickled cabbage and potato. As a dessert the Bulgarians served bread and cheese. Between each course we were served a large shot of slivovitz. Later the Bulgarians sang several very sad but also very beautiful folk songs in their language and it is a shame that we Germans did not reply in kind to sing some of ours for the Bulgarians. The night came to an abrupt end when the air-raid siren sounded and we all had to rush out to the bunker. All in all, however, a most successful and enjoyable evening.

21 December 1943

Today we conducted a live firing exercise on the range, on which the Bulgarians racked up a surprisingly good score. A small incident occurred in the morning when we found that the firing range was full of sheep. We approached the old shepherd, who wore a huge fur hat, a sheepskin jacket and breeches with leather gaiters, and tried to make him understand that he needed to get the sheep off the range. We tried to speak to him in Serbian, Bulgarian and Russian – a few men even tried to speak Polish to him. All our Bulgarian translators talked to the man in their language. That went on for at least fifteen minutes, after which the shepherd started to grin and smile at us before saying: 'Schafe weg, ich laufen! Schnell, schnell!' – in German! And then he started running as fast as his old legs could carry him, down the range with his huge furry dog, shouting at his sheep, 'Schnell, schnell Schafe!' while one of the Bulgarian translators turned to me and said: 'Oh, it seems that he speaks German too.' Later that day I asked one of the Bulgarian officers what influence Bulgaria had on the Balkans and if the Serbs would stick to the Bulgarians, fight for Tito's gangs or if they felt like Serbs. To get an answer to that question we pulled up next to an old man who was standing on the roadside and our translator asked him that question. His reply surprised us: 'I feel like a German,' he said. 'I am a German citizen, because the Germans are now masters here' – the people here on the Balkan are an odd bunch.

We were three men in an Opel Blitz lorry loaded with barrels and sacks of grain and a couple of Serbian workers. The road was so bad that we could not go very fast and when we turned around a corner into another street, half a dozen or so Serbs jumped on the lorry to hitch a ride. The Feldwebel said that they could drive with us; most of them would be working in German offices anyway and they all spoke at least some German. But then we passed a large group of very dubious-looking characters standing alongside the road who bowed down deeply and lifted their hats when they saw us. We all agreed that these looked like they had a guilty conscience, and so it would be best to string them all up. Just to make sure. Partisan scum.